Study Guide

Kelly Bouas Henry
Missouri Western State College

Essentials of
Psychology
Second Edition

Douglas A. Bernstein
University of South Florida/University of Surrey

Peggy W. Nash
Broward Community College

HOUGHTON MIFFLIN COMPANY   BOSTON   NEW YORK

Editor-in-Chief: Kathi Prancan
Senior Sponsoring Editor: Kerry Baruth
Senior Development Editor: Jane Knetzger
Editorial Assistant: Rachel Levison
Senior Manufacturing Coordinator: Priscilla J. Bailey
Marketing Manager: Ros Kane

The author acknowledges Bridget Schoppert and Amanda Allman for their contributions to previous versions, and Michele Fitzpatrick-Somody and Claire Hunter for their editorial assistance.

Printed in the U.S.A.

ISBN: 0-618-12298-2

23456789-POO-05 04 03 02 01

CONTENTS

Preface   iv

Developing Your Critical Thinking Skills   vi

Developing Your Writing Skills   vii

Studying Linkages   viii

Reading a Textbook   ix

Chapter   **1**   Introduction to the Science of Psychology   1

Chapter   **2**   Biology and Behavior   18

Chapter   **3**   Sensation and Perception   33

Chapter   **4**   Consciousness   51

Chapter   **5**   Learning   65

Chapter   **6**   Memory   82

Chapter   **7**   Thought, Language, and Intelligence   99

Chapter   **8**   Motivation and Emotion   115

Chapter   **9**   Human Development   130

Chapter   **10**   Health, Stress, and Coping   145

Chapter   **11**   Personality   157

Chapter   **12**   Psychological Disorders   171

Chapter   **13**   Treatment of Psychological Disorders   187

Chapter   **14**   Social Psychology   202

Appendix   Statistics in Psychological Research   219

PREFACE

TO THE STUDENT

This *Study Guide* was designed to help you master the material in *Essentials of Psychology*, by Douglas A. Bernstein and Peggy W. Nash. The Study Guide supplements the textbook but does not replace it. If used properly, the Guide should help you not merely to memorize but to take command of the key facts, concepts, and issues discussed in the text.

Each Study Guide chapter corresponds to a text chapter and is divided into eight sections: Learning Objectives, Key Terms, Concepts and Exercises, Critical Thinking, Personal Learning Activities, What Should I Write About, The Internet, and Multiple-Choice Questions.

1. *Learning Objectives* The Learning Objectives will strengthen your command of textbook material by focusing your attention on its specific goals: to be able to describe, compare, and explain the important information in each chapter. To help you master these learning objectives, I have identified the textbook pages to which each objective corresponds.

2. *Key Terms* Terms that are underlined in the Chapter Outlines are also defined in the Key Terms section. I have tried to help you fix these terms in your memory: For many of them, I provide an illustrative example. For others, I present an idea to help you remember the key term. You will also find a number in parentheses at the end of each definition to identify the page on which the term is first defined and explained in the *textbook*.

   NOTE: I urge you to create your own examples of key terms as part of your study program. If you do so successfully, you will have taken a giant step toward mastering the material.

3. *Concepts and Exercises* This section will help you achieve selected learning objectives. The exercises apply key psychological concepts to situations from everyday life. You are asked to identify the concepts being applied. At the end of the exercises, I provide the correct answer to each exercise, along with an explanation of why the answer is correct.

4. *Critical Thinking* This section will help you sharpen your critical thinking skills by asking you to answer the five critical thinking questions presented in your text in relation to a particular situation or scenario. The five questions and their answers are stated in the answer section.

5. *Personal Learning Activities* Active involvement is an excellent way to improve your understanding of and memory for the psychological issues, principles, and concepts described in *Essentials of Psychology*. I have included personal learning activities to help you practice using the new information contained in each chapter.

6. *What Should I Write About?* Writing about a topic is a great way to become actively involved with the material in this text. I have included a section that is geared to help you select topics for term papers, as well as to help you develop and organize that topic.

7. *The Internet* This section reminds you that you have many additional resources for mastering each chapter available on the internet.

8. *Multiple-Choice Questions* Once you have carefully worked through the previous sections, you will be ready to test your comprehension of the material covered. Every *Study Guide* chapter contains two multiple-choice quizzes, each consisting of fifteen questions. At the end of the chapter, the correct answers are given, along with an explanation of *why* each is correct and why the alternatives are incorrect.

If multiple-choice exams are part of your course, the multiple-choice quizzes in the *Study Guide* will provide a valuable way to prepare for them. Begin by taking Quiz 1. Next, check your answers against the answer key and fill in the number of items you answered correctly. For any items you miss, turn to the text pages listed next to the answers and reread the relevant sections. Write down, in your own words, information that will help you to better understand the material. Also, review the appropriate Key Terms. Then reread the questions you missed on Quiz 1 to be sure you understand why the correct answer is correct and why the others are not.

Then take Quiz 2 and score it, noting the explanations of right and wrong answers. Finally, restudy the textbook and *Study Guide* materials as necessary. By following this procedure, you will build incrementally toward mastery of the contents of the text.

Finally, turn to the table at the end of the *Study Guide* chapter and circle the item numbers that you answered correctly the first time through Quizzes 1 and 2. (Quiz 2 is shaded to help you distinguish between your first and second tries at mastering the material.) The table will provide you with valuable information to further guide your studying. Look for a pattern in your results. Are you answering most of the definitional items correctly, but not the comprehension or application questions? Is there a topic that you mastered and another for which no items are circled? Write in the number of items you answered correctly on the first and second quizzes. Did you improve?

In the shortened example below, the student circled the item numbers of questions that she or he correctly answered. The resulting pattern indicates that the student did well on definitional items, but not as well on application items. The table also shows that the student correctly answered more of the questions on current approaches (in the lower half of the table) than on historical schools (in the top half of the table). In addition

to recognizing the need to review the historical approaches, the student should note that out of twenty-two items, he or she answered only eleven correctly. Perhaps the student should take additional notes on the chapter, write examples of the key terms, and consult the course instructor before the first graded quiz or exam.

As you can see, I have designed each chapter of this *Guide* as a sequenced program of study, and each section builds on the one before it. However, if you believe that a different sequencing of sections will work better for you, feel free to give it a try.

Here's to your success!

TOPIC	TYPE OF QUESTION		
	DEFINITION	COMPREHENSION	APPLICATION
History			
Structuralism		(2)	(1)
		1	(3)
Gestalt			
		(4)	(2)
Psychoanalysis	3		
Functionalism		4	
Behaviorism			
			5
Approaches			
Eclectic		5	
Biological	7		
Ethology			
	10		
Evolutionary		8	
Psychodynamic		9	
		9	(6)
Behavioral		6	(10)
Cognitive	11		
		11	7
Humanistic		12	
			8, 12

TOTAL CORRECT BY QUIZ:

QUIZ 1:	
QUIZ 2:	

Developing Your Critical Thinking Skills

If you were to memorize every fact in the textbook, you might still miss its essentials. Much as sports announcers often say that the statistics of a game don't begin to indicate the contribution of a certain player, so, too, the facts conveyed by a college textbook often represent only a small part of its message. Thus, even if you forget many pieces of information within a year or two, you may retain something far more valuable from your introductory course in psychology.

What is there beyond the facts? Psychology and other disciplines have certain methods for defining, uncovering, and interpreting facts; they have certain ways of thinking. More generally, psychology and other fields of study rely on the ability to think critically—to evaluate claims, ideas, and evidence. Learning these ways of thinking enriches your ability to understand the world long after you may have forgotten specific pieces of information.

At its simplest, thinking critically means evaluating information rather than merely accepting it because it is endorsed by some authority or because it flatters your prejudices. In 1986, for example, a U.S. government commission declared that pornography is dangerous; it linked pornography and crime. You might be inclined to accept this conclusion because of the authority behind the commission or because you find pornography repugnant. But if you think critically, neither reason will be sufficient. At a minimum, you will ask why the commission came to that conclusion. What was their evidence? Even beyond asking for the reasons behind a conclusion, however, critical thinking requires the ability to evaluate those reasons. (The reasons for the commission's conclusions regarding pornography can be faulted on several grounds; they are evaluated in Chapter 14 of the text.) Is the argument logical? What is the source of the evidence that backs up the argument? If it's an experiment, were the experimental methods sound? Learning how to ask and answer questions like these is a first step in becoming skillful at critical thinking.

Throughout the text, the authors' discussions provide examples of critical thinking, illustrating how to examine the assumptions underlying an assertion, to evaluate evidence for an assertion, and to draw reasonable conclusions. In addition, each chapter of the textbook includes a section, labeled "Thinking Critically," that is devoted to critical thinking about one specific topic or assertion. In each case, the section examines the issue by considering five questions:

1. What am I being asked to believe or accept?
2. What evidence is available to support the assertion?
3. Are there alternative ways of interpreting the evidence?
4. What additional evidence would help to evaluate the alternatives?
5. What conclusions are most reasonable?

These questions represent steps that you can apply in thinking about most assertions, as the textbook explains. You can think critically without using these specific steps, but they constitute one useful model for critical thinking. Take time to consider the "Thinking Critically" sections, not only for their content, but also as a model of a way of thinking.

For further practice at critical thinking, do the Critical Thinking exercises in each chapter of the *Study Guide*. These will help you understand the importance of the five critical thinking questions and how to apply them. When you come across an issue of particular interest in your reading of the text, try applying these five steps to the discussion. No textbook can examine every issue in depth; if some of the steps are not fully explored in the text, try doing further research to follow these steps yourself. Or take a very specific assertion implicit in the discussion and explore it further by applying the five steps to that assertion. Most of all, as you read, remember to think critically. Throughout the text, the authors have tried to stimulate your own thinking. Just as they examine the flaws in existing research and acknowledge the many psychological questions that remain unanswered, so too should you probe what the authors have written and ask your own questions about it.

Applying the authors' model of critical thinking during the course should bring you at least four benefits. First, it should reinforce the habit of thinking critically. Are you going to buy brand X based on the endorsement of Candice Bergen or Michael Jordan? Will you take melatonin because others claim it is good for you? We hope this course will help you strengthen the habit of questioning claims and evaluating arguments for yourself. Second, the practice gained by applying the text's model of critical thinking should sharpen your critical-thinking skills. These skills can help you in every phase of life—whether you are weighing a politician's promises or the advantages of taking a new job, or searching for a new car or a way to reorganize a department. Third, going through this sequence of steps should lead you to a better understanding of the material and to wiser conclusions. Finally, thinking critically is likely to improve your memory of the material. As discussed in Chapter 6 of the textbook, organizing and thinking about information makes that information easier to remember.

Developing Your Writing Skills

Part of most students' college careers will involve writing term papers. Although these types of assignments can initially be very intimidating, they almost always are valuable learning experiences for students who give the assignment the time and attention it deserves. And for any one who is tempted to believe that writing term papers is an arcane exercise—think again. Many top employers cite writing skills as a "must-have" in a potential employee. The same skills that make you a good term paper writer will make you attractive to an employer, so developing those skills is an important goal to adopt during your college years.

Because developing your writing skills is so important to your future career options, I have included a section in each chapter of this study guide entitled "What Should I Write About?" to assist you in this process. The title of the section suggests that it will focus on how to decide on a term paper topic—and that is true. But as you progress through the textbook and study guide, you will see that this section's focus grows to address general problems that students tend to encounter as they develop and organize the topic they have selected.

Selecting an appropriate term paper topic is the initial hurdle to overcome in writing a term paper. Students tend to encounter several pitfalls as they choose an initial topic, and the sections on writing in the earlier chapters of this study guide will address those problems. Those sections will provide helpful tips on how to choose a topic that is neither too broad, nor too narrow, and how to look for clues that a topic will be interesting to you. If you are going to invest the time in writing a term paper, you want to be sure that the topic is interesting enough to keep you motivated. Once you have identified the topic, though, there are other hurdles to overcome.

Developing the term paper topic is the next hurdle. The writing sections embedded in the chapters toward the middle of this study guide will focus on how to develop your term paper topic. These sections will include hints on how to do research that will yield valuable information that will elaborate on your topic. In addition, I share strategies that have been successful for other writers in developing their topics. Although you wouldn't want to use all of the strategies in a single paper, you might try a sampling of these strategies and determine which one works best for you. This section should give you an idea of how to proceed so that you don't get the awful "writer's block" after you first identify your topic. Once you have developed the topic though, it is time to think about how to organize the information into a coherent whole.

The writing sections in the chapters toward the end of this study guide focus on organizing information. Several strategies are suggested—pro/con papers, papers with different views of the same issue presented, analysis of different views, and so on. Again, it would probably not be in your best interest to use all of these strategies in a single paper. The result would be likely to be more disorganized than if you had use no particular strategy. However, it probably is worth your while to try several of these strategies, and then decide which one works best for the topic you have selected.

As you try the various writing strategies suggested throughout the "What Should I Write About?" sections, you will hopefully begin to identify what strategies work best for you. That is a big step towards honing your writing skills. But you also need to pay attention to where you work best, and at what time of day you do your best work. Writing is a challenging process for even the best of writers. Don't assume that you will be able to produce great work no matter what the working conditions are. You need to actively identify and seek out the times and conditions that you know you are likely to be able to concentrate and think clearly about an issue. If you skip this step, no matter what strategy you use, you will probably not be performing at your peak.

Finally, don't forget that writing is like any skill—it gets better with practice. Practice means taking time to work on improving your skills. It means identifying areas where you know you are weak, and seeking out ways to improve in those arenas. It means doing something over and over and trying to improve each time that you repeat the act. Writing a term paper doesn't mean you will sit down and hammer out a perfect draft the first time. Good writers are more likely to sit down and hammer out *something,* and then focus on improving that something into something *great.* It can be discouraging at first, but if you practice your writing, seek feedback on it, and work to incorporate that feedback to improve each draft of a paper, you will find that you become a better and better writer. In fact, you'll probably find that the next time you have to write a term paper, that your first draft on it is light years ahead of the first draft you wrote on the previous paper. At that point you have an opportunity to reach even higher.

Continuously improving your writing skills is time-consuming and effortful. But it is worth it. It is worth it both in terms of the marketability this skill will afford you upon graduation, and in terms of personal development. Being able to articulate your thoughts, and the thoughts you have discovered through research, on an issue through writing will provide you with self-confidence. I hope that using the strategies suggesting in this Study Guide will prove helpful to you in this endeavor.

Studying Linkages

A first glance at your textbook might suggest that introductory psychology resembles a cafeteria, consisting of a series of unrelated topics. Here is a little chemistry of the brain, over there a little biology of reproductive systems, and for dessert, a description of social pressures. But unlike a cafeteria, the diversity of topics in the textbook reflects not an attempt to satisfy every taste, but an effort to analyze essential parts of a complex whole. The diversity is necessary because all of these topics are pieces of the puzzle of psychology. If you wanted to understand why a friend became addicted to alcohol, for example, you would want to explore not only the person's history but also his relationships and the effects of chemicals on his brain.

Obviously you cannot study all of these topics at once; you would examine them one at a time. So, too, the textbook focuses on one aspect of psychology at a time. Eventually, however, it helps to put the pieces together. Much as parts of a jigsaw puzzle may take on new meaning when you see where they fit, so too the pieces of psychology take on new dimensions once you see how they are related. For example, the chemical messengers used in the brain (introduced in Chapter 2) are interesting in their own right; but your knowledge about them takes on new significance when you consider how these chemicals can be affected by drugs (discussed in Chapter 4) and by certain treatments for psychological disorders (discussed in Chapter 13).

To help you see how the pieces of psychology fit together, the authors of *Essentials of Psychology* have paid special attention to the ties among the aspects of human psychology, among the different areas of psychological research, and among the chapters of the textbook. These ties are all forms of what the authors call *linkages*, and the text highlights them in several ways. First, cross-references and discussions throughout the text point out how topics in one chapter are related to discussions that appear in other chapters. Second, at the end of each chapter, a Linkages diagram presents questions that illustrate a link between the current chapter and the topic of other chapters in the text. These questions are then repeated in the margin next to where they are explored. Finally, a Linkages section discusses in some depth one specific question from the Linkages diagram.

You could read the text profitably without paying special attention to the Linkage elements, but they can help you gain a clearer view of psychology as a whole, a deeper understanding of specific issues, and a framework on which you can build your knowledge of psychology. And when you organize your knowledge and relate one piece of information to another, you improve your ability to remember the information. The Linkages diagrams in particular can be used in many ways as tools for learning and remembering information. Here are some suggestions.

Before reading the chapter, read the questions in the Linkages diagram. They will give you a feeling for the topic of the chapter and for the broader significance of specific issues. In each diagram, some of the questions are discussed in the current chapter and some in other chapters. Can you answer any of the questions? Do any of them concern a topic you have already read about in the text? If so, what do you remember about it? You might go to the page number given after the question, look for the question in the margin on that page, and scan or read the discussion. This will refresh your memory for concepts or facts related to the material to be discussed in the current chapter.

After reading the chapter, you can use the diagram to check your memory and understanding of the chapter. Try writing answers to those questions in the diagram that were discussed in the chapter. Check your answers against the text discussions. (Again, the page numbers in the diagram indicate where the discussion occurs.)

The diagrams can also help you go beyond the textbook in gaining and organizing knowledge of psychology. Suppose you are studying for a final exam and want to check your understanding of the topic of learning. You might go first to the Linkages diagram in the Learning chapter and check whether you can answer the questions; then you might flip to the Linkages diagrams in other chapters, find questions tied to Learning, and try to answer those questions. Also, keep in mind that the diagrams in the text provide only a sampling of linkages; there are many others. Finding additional linkages on your own can further your understanding of psychological issues and improve your memory of the material in the text. Finally, the questions in the Linkages diagrams or linkages that you find yourself may provide interesting topics for term papers.

Reading a Textbook

Effective learners engage in a very deep level of processing. They are active learners, thinking of each new fact in relation to other material. As a result, they learn to see similarities and differences among facts and ideas, and they create a context in which many new facts can be organized effectively.

Based on what is known about memory, we suggest two specific guidelines for reading a textbook. First, make sure that you understand what you are reading before moving on. Second, use the *PQ4R method*, which is one of the most successful strategies for remembering textbook material (Anderson, 1990; Chastain & Thurber, 1989; Thomas & Robinson, 1972). PQ4R stands for the five activities that should be followed when you read a chapter: survey, question, read, recite, and review. These activities are designed to increase the depth to which you process the information you read.

1. **Preview** One of the best ways to begin a new chapter is by *not* reading it. Instead, take a few minutes to skim the chapter. Look at the section headings and any boldface or italicized terms. Obtain a general idea of what material will be discussed, how it is organized, and how its topics relate to one another and to what you already know. Some people find it useful to preview the entire chapter once and then survey each major section in a little more detail before reading it.

2. **Question** Before reading each section, stop and ask yourself what content will be covered and what information should be extracted from it.

3. **Read** Read the text, but think about the material as you read. Are the questions you raised earlier being answered? Do you see the connections between the topics?

4. **Reflect** As you read your text, think of examples of concepts that might apply to your own life. Create visual images that reflect the concept, and ask yourself how each concept might be related to other concepts within that chapter and in other chapters you have already read.

5. **Recite** At the end of each section, stop and recite the major points. Resist the temptation to be passive by mumbling something like, "Oh, I remember that." Put the ideas into your own words.

6. **Review** Finally, at the end of the chapter, review all the material. You should see connections not only within a section but also among the sections. The objective is to see how the author has organized the material. Once you grasp the organization, the individual facts will be far easier to remember.

At the end, take a break. Relax. Approach each chapter fresh. Following these procedures will not only allow you to learn and remember the material better but also save you considerable time.

Chapter 1

Introduction to the Science of Psychology

LEARNING OBJECTIVES

1. Define psychology. (p. 3)

2. Define empiricism. (p. 4)

3. Discuss the history of psychology. Compare the goals and beliefs of structuralism, Gestalt psychology, psychoanalysis, functionalism, and behaviorism. Describe introspection and the functional analysis of behavior. (pp. 5–7)

4. Compare and contrast the basic assumptions of the six approaches to psychology: biological, evolutionary, psychodynamic, behavioral, cognitive, and humanistic. Define eclectic. (pp. 8–10)

5. Name the psychological subfields. Give examples of the questions and issues associated with each subfield. (pp. 10–13)

6. Explain why the field of psychology is unified, despite its many areas of specialization. Describe the linkages between psychology and other fields. (pp. 13-14)

7. Explain why psychologists have become increasingly interested in the influence of culture on behavior and mental processes. Define and give examples of sociocultural variables. Compare and contrast individualist and collectivist cultures. (pp. 14–17)

8. Define critical thinking. Be able to assess claims by using the five-step process presented in the text. (pp. 17–19)

9. Name the four main goals of scientific research in psychology. (p. 20)

10. Explain how the reliability and validity of evidence are checked. (p. 20)

11. Describe the evolution of a theory. (p. 20)

12. Describe the three basic research methods used to describe and predict a phenomenon and give examples of each. Explain the advantages and disadvantages of each method. (pp. 20–23)

13. Describe the experimental research method and give an example of it. Define variables. (p. 23)

14. Explain why an experiment allows investigation of causation. (p. 23)

15. Define and explain the role of independent and dependent variables and of experimental and control groups in an experiment. (p. 23)

16. Define hypothesis and operational definition. (pp. 23–24)

17. Define confounding variables. Discuss the problems presented by confounding variables in the interpretation of experimental results. Define random variables, placebo effect, and experimenter bias. (p. 25)

18. Define random assignment and double-blind design. Explain the purpose of each in an experiment. (pp. 25-26)

19. Define quasi-experiments. Explain why they are used as experimental designs. (p. 26)

20. Define sampling, random sample, and biased sample. Discuss the importance of sampling in data collection. (pp. 26–27)

21. Summarize the use of descriptive and inferential statistics in evaluating research results. (p. 28)

22. Define correlation. Describe how the absolute value and sign of a correlation coefficient are interpreted. (p. 28)

23. Explain why correlations do not imply causation. Describe the role of alternative hypotheses in the interpretation of a correlation. (pp. 28-29)

24. Define statistically significant. Describe the role of statistical significance in thinking critically about scientific research. (p. 29)

25. Describe the ethical guidelines that psychologists must follow. (pp. 29–30)

26. Define behavioral genetics. (p. 30)

27. Explain how family, twin, and adoption studies help to establish the relative roles of genetics and environmental variables. (pp. 30-32)

KEY TERMS

I. THE WORLD OF PSYCHOLOGY: AN OVERVIEW

1. **Psychology** is the science of behavior and mental processes. (p. 3)

> *Example:* Behavior is any action an organism performs, including those you can and cannot see (for example, jogging, laughing, heart rate, and blood pressure). Mental processes are activities involved in thinking (for example, remembering, dreaming, and forming opinions).

2. **Empiricism** is the position that facts should come from observation rather than conjecture. (p. 4)

> *Example:* Instead of speculating about why a group may follow the advice of a poor leader, psychologists will interview group members or design an experiment to answer the question.

3. **Consciousness** is the mental experience that arises from sensory and perceptual systems. (p. 5)

> *Example:* When you eat an apple, you experience it through your senses: you see its redness, taste its sweetness, and so on. You integrate sensations into a perception that you are eating an apple; that is, you are conscious of the apple and its taste.

II. APPROACHES TO THE SCIENCE OF PSYCHOLOGY

4. The **biological approach** assumes that biological factors—such as genetics, brain activity, or hormonal activity—are the most important factors determining behavior and mental processes. (p. 9)

> *Example:* People who are chronically depressed may have abnormal levels of certain chemicals important to mood.

5. The **evolutionary approach** assumes that human and animal behavior is the result of evolution through natural selection. (p. 9)

> *Example:* Psychologists study the adaptive value of behavior (running away from threats), the anatomical and biological systems that make the behavior possible (muscular construction of limbs), and the environmental conditions that encourage or discourage it (a culture may not approve of people running away).

6. The **psychodynamic approach** assumes that our behavior results from our struggle to fulfill instinctive desires and wishes despite society's rules. (p. 9)

> *Example:* Freud might have said that surgeons express aggressive instincts in a manner that is approved of by society (performing surgery in an operating room rather than stabbing a stranger in a dark alley).

7. The **behavioral approach** assumes that the rewards and punishments that each person experiences determine most behaviors and thoughts. (p. 9)

> *Example:* Doctors become surgeons because they are rewarded by their salaries, by the respect their positions receive, or by the satisfaction they receive from healing.

8. The **cognitive approach** assumes that mental processes guide behavior. The brain takes in information; processes it through perception, memory, thought, judgment, and decision-making; and generates integrated behavior patterns. (p. 9)

> *Example:* A psychologist taking the cognitive approach might try to understand a devastating plane crash by studying the decisions and judgment calls the pilots had to make just before and as the plane was going down.

> *REMEMBER:* Cognition means "thinking." The cognitive approach assumes thoughts guide behavior.

9. The **humanistic approach** assumes that people control their behavior. This approach is thus unlike other models, which assume that biology, instincts, or the presence of rewards and punishments in the environment control behavior. The humanistic approach also assumes that people have an inborn tendency to grow toward their unique potential. (p. 10)

> *Example:* The innate tendency to grow toward one's unique potential is analogous to the development of a flower that will bloom if it receives adequate light, water, and nourishment. People, too, will achieve their potential if their environments provide the correct psychological and physical nourishment.

10. **Cognitive psychologists** study sensation, perception, learning, memory, judgment, decision making, and phenomena related to these basic mental and behavioral processes. (p. 11)

> *Example:* Is the memory of how to tie shoes developed, stored, and retrieved in the same ways as the memory of a friend's telephone number?

11. **Biological psychologists** study the biological factors that underlie behavior and mental processes. (p. 11)

Example: Eating certain foods changes the chemical interactions within and between nerve cells in your brain, thereby possibly inducing drowsiness.

12. **Personality psychologists** study what makes one person different from others and look at the relationships among personality characteristics, behavior, and mental processes. (p. 11)

Example: Why are some people consistently optimistic and others pessimistic?

13. **Developmental psychologists** study the causes and effects of changes in behavior and mental processes over the life span. (p. 11)

Example: How do people develop morals, social skills, and intellectual abilities?

14. **Quantitative psychologists** develop statistics to evaluate data and improve the validity of tests. (p. 11)

Example: Researchers may consult a quantitative psychologist about how to analyze the results of a study.

15. **Clinical and counseling psychologists** study abnormal behavior and mental processes, what causes them, and how to treat them. Clinical psychologists also evaluate how well and why a treatment works. (p. 11)

Example: Is schizophrenia hereditary? What therapy produces the best results with schizophrenic patients?

16. **Community psychologists** attempt to prevent psychological disorders and to treat people in their own communities. (p. 11)

Example: Some community psychologists examine the problems students have in making the transition from high school to college and design programs to lessen these problems.

17. **Educational psychologists** study learning and teaching methods. (p. 11)

Example: Educational psychologists found that when students take notes in their own words, they recall the information better.

18. **School psychologists** study how to diagnose learning disabilities, specialize in IQ testing, and set up programs based on the findings of their tests and evaluations. (p. 11)

Example: School psychologists identify students' academic strengths and problems and tailor programs to meet students' needs.

19. **Social psychologists** study how people influence one another and the interactions between people in groups. **Industrial-organizational psychologists** study social influences on job performance. (p. 11)

Example: How is behavior influenced by the type of group or situation a person is in? In a crowd, an anonymous person may be boisterous; however, when recognized as an individual (for example, in a classroom), the same person may be quiet and obedient.

III. HUMAN DIVERSITY AND PSYCHOLOGY

20. **Sociocultural variables** are factors that differ across cultures to shape people's experiences and how they interpret them. (p. 15)

Example: In some cultures, social class is considered changeable by pursing education and a career; in other cultures, social class is viewed as a binding, inherited characteristic.

21. A **culture** is the accumulation of values, rules of behavior, forms of expression, religious beliefs, occupational choice, and so on, for a group of people who share a common language and environment. (p. 15)

Example: In some cultures, religious practices require a lot of loud singing and open expression of emotion and experience. In other cultures, religious practice is more formal and staid.

IV. THINKING CRITICALLY ABOUT PSYCHOLOGY

22. **Critical thinking** is the process of evaluating propositions or hypotheses and making judgments about them on the basis of well-supported evidence. (p. 18)

Example: Consider the five steps of critical thinking. (a) What am I being asked to believe or accept? What is the hypothesis? (b) What evidence is available to support the claim? Is it reliable and valid? (c) Are there alternative ways of interpreting the evidence? (d) What additional evidence would help to evaluate the alternatives? (e) What conclusions are most reasonable based on the evidence and the number of alternative explanations?

REMEMBER: If you find this concept difficult to understand, consider what it means to think uncritically. (What thought processes might have been omitted? What thought processes have led to incorrect conclusions?) Then go back and review the five sets of questions in the example above.

V. RESEARCH DESIGNS IN PSYCHOLOGY

23. **Reliability** is the degree to which results are repeatable or consistent. (p. 20)

Example: Several studies show that students who complete sample test items score higher on tests than students who do not complete sample items.

24. **Validity** is the degree to which results accurately describe a phenomenon. (p. 20)

Example: When participants score higher on a test of aggression and friends also rate them as higher in aggression, this is evidence of the test's validity.

25. A **theory** is a cohesive cluster of explanations of behavior and mental processes. Theories are not definitive; they are constantly amended as researchers collect and analyze new data. (p. 20)

Example: Finding that people under stress often overeat or drink more alcohol led to the theory that behaviors that appear self-destructive may be stress alleviators.

26. **Naturalistic observation**, a method of gathering descriptive information, involves watching behaviors of interest, without interfering, as they occur in their natural environments. (p. 20)

Example: A researcher interested in how much time children of different ages play alone could observe children at a playground.

REMEMBER: A researcher *observes* a phenomenon in its *natural* environment.

27. **Case studies** are used to collect descriptive data through the intensive examination of a phenomenon in a particular individual, group, or situation. Case studies are particularly useful for studying rare or complex phenomena. (p. 21)

Example: Biological psychologists cannot alter a person's brain in the laboratory for the purposes of study; therefore, they are interested in people who have suffered brain injuries in accidents. Researchers examine these patients intensively over long periods of time.

28. **Surveys** are questionnaires or special interviews administered to a large group. Surveys are designed to obtain descriptions of people's attitudes, beliefs, opinions, or behavioral intentions. (p. 22)

Example: Social psychologists interested in learning what teenagers from families of varying income levels think of marriage can administer a questionnaire to a sample of teenagers.

29. **Variables** are specific factors or characteristics that can vary. Researchers examine and describe relationships between variables. (p. 23)

Example: Moods, decision-making processes, emotions, eating behaviors, chemical activity in the brain, heart rate, and types of clothing worn are just some of the many variables of possible interest to psychologists.

30. An **experiment** allows a researcher to control the data-collection process. A random sample of subjects is selected and divided into a control group and an experimental group. Both groups are identical in every way except the administration of the independent variable to the experimental group. The dependent variable is then measured in both groups. Any difference in the dependent variable between the two groups is caused by the independent variable. Experiments show causation. (p. 23)

REMEMBER: An experiment is a trial or test of a hypothesis.

31. **Independent variables** are manipulated or controlled by the researcher in an experiment. They are administered to the experimental group. (p. 23)

Example: An experiment is conducted to test the effects of alcohol on reflex speed. Two groups of subjects are randomly selected. One group, the experimental group, is given alcohol (alcohol is the independent variable), and the other group, the control group, is given a nonalcoholic beverage.

32. **Dependent variables** are the behaviors or mental processes affected by the independent variable. They are observed and measured before and after the administration of the independent variable. (p. 23)

Example: In the experiment examining the effects of alcohol on reflex speed, the dependent variable is reflex speed.

REMEMBER: The measure or value of the dependent variable depends on the independent variable.

33. The **experimental group** receives the independent variable in an experiment. (p. 23)

Example: In the experiment examining the effects of alcohol on reflex speed, the group who receives alcohol (the independent variable) is the experimental group.

34. The **control group** provides a baseline for comparison to the experimental group and does not receive the independent variable. This group is identical to the experimental group in every way *except* that these subjects *do not* receive the independent variable. (p. 23)

Example: In the experiment examining the effects of alcohol on reflex speed, the group who received the nonalcoholic beverage is the control group.

REMEMBER: The control group provides the control in an experiment. Comparing the measure of the dependent variable in both the control and experimental groups indicates whether the independent variable is causing the changes in the dependent variable or whether these changes occurred by chance.

35. A **hypothesis** is an assertion or prediction stated as a testable proposition, usually in the form of an if-then statement. (p. 23)

Example: If rats have access to toys, *then* they can practice behaviors similar to those used in running a maze and perform better than rats raised without access to toys.

36. An **operational definition** is a statement of the specific methods used to measure a variable. (p. 24)

Example: If we are conducting a study regarding the effects of caffeine on anxiety, we would have to decide exactly *how* we plan to measure anxiety. Our operational definition of anxiety might be changes in blood pressure or the subjects' answers to an anxiety questionnaire—whatever logically fits our research hypothesis.

37. **Confounding variables** are factors affecting the dependent variable in an experiment instead of or along with the independent variable. Examples of confounding variables include random variables, experimenter bias, and the placebo effect. (p. 25)

38. **Random variables** are uncontrollable factors that could affect the dependent variable in an experiment instead of or along with the independent variable. (p. 25)

Example: An experimenter wishes to test the effects of a teaching technique on test performance. The subjects are assigned randomly to the control and experimental groups. The researcher doesn't know it, but most of the students in the experimental group are much brighter than the control group students.

The data may suggest that the students who received the teaching technique scored higher than those who didn't. In this case, however, intelligence is a random variable that, instead of the independent variable, could be responsible for the results.

39. **Random assignment** is a process of assigning participants to experimental conditions such that each participant is equally likely to be assigned to the control or experimental group. Random assignment is useful because it tends to spread the effects of uncontrolled variables randomly across the control and experimental groups. (p. 25)

Example: An experimenter might have participants draw numbers out of a hat to determine the experimental condition of which they will be a part—even numbers for the control group and odd numbers for the experimental group.

40. A **placebo** is a physical or psychological treatment that contains no active ingredient but produces an effect on the dependent variable because the person receiving it believes it will. (p. 25)

Example: In an experiment on the effects of alcohol, a researcher may find that people who have been given a nonalcoholic beverage behave as though they're drunk only because they *believe* they have been given an alcoholic drink.

41. **Experimenter bias** occurs when a researcher inadvertently encourages subjects to respond in a way that supports her hypothesis. (p. 25)

Example: An experimenter hypothesizes that an expert will be able to persuade a group of people that decision A is better than decision B. After the expert has spoken to the subjects, the researcher asks them which decision they prefer. She can ask in several ways. Asking, Now, don't you think A is better than B? will bias her data more than if she asks, Which do you think is better, decision A or decision B?

42. In a **double-blind design** neither the experimenter nor the subjects know who has received the independent variable. (p. 25)

Example: The experiment studying the effects of alcohol on reflex speed (described in relation to Key Term 31) is repeated using a double-blind design. Neither the subjects nor the experimenter knows who has received alcohol and who hasn't. Thus subjects are prevented from changing their behavior simply because they think they have been given alcohol. At the same time, the experimenter is prevented from biasing observations of the subjects' behavior or mental processes.

43. **Quasi-experiments** are conducted when an experiment with adequate controls would be unethical or impossible. Because these designs are not completely controlled, the results are usually not as generalizable as true experimental results and must be tested repeatedly. (p. 26)

Example: You wish to test the hypothesis that alcohol has an adverse effect on fetal development. As an ethical psychologist you cannot instruct your subjects (pregnant women) to drink alcohol. You can, however, compare the development of children whose mothers drank alcohol during pregnancy to the development of children whose mothers did not.

44. **Sampling** is a procedure used to choose subjects for research. Ideally, the subjects chosen should be representative of the population being studied. (p. 26)

Example: If you are studying the behavior of gifted children, your sample should be drawn exclusively from this group.

45. **Random samples** are groups of subjects selected from the population of interest. A sample is random if every person in the population has an equal chance of being selected. If a sample is not random, it is said to be biased. (p. 26)

Example: A social psychologist is interested in studying the influence of parents on the career choice of first-year college students in the United States. If the sample is to be random, every first year student must have an equal chance of being selected as a subject. The researcher thus draws the sample from lists of first-year college students in schools all over the United States, not just from the schools in one state.

46. A sample is **biased** if everyone in the population of interest does not have an equal chance of being selected to participate in a study. (p. 26)

Example: If a researcher decides to survey "college students" and then only surveys students who live in on-campus dormitories, then his or her sample will be biased because college students who live off campus were not equally likely to be selected as those students living on-campus.

REMEMBER: Experimental results obtained from a biased sample may not be generalizable to the population of interest. The results are biased by characteristics of the subjects, not by the independent variable.

VI. STATISTICAL ANALYSIS OF RESEARCH RESULTS

47. **Data** are the numerical representations of research results. (p. 27)

Example: A quiz score of 9 correct out of 10 possible is a piece of data that represents your knowledge of information tested on that quiz.

48. A **correlation** is an indication of the relationship between two variables (x and y). The correlation coefficient (r), a number between −1.00 and +1.00, is a mathematical representation of the strength and direction of a correlation. The higher the absolute value of r is, the stronger the relationship is. A perfect correlation, whether positive or negative (where r equals + or −1.00), describes a perfect relationship; knowing the value of x allows the certain prediction of y. A positive correlation (where r varies from 0 to +1.00) describes two variables that change in the same direction: as x increases, so does y (and vice versa). A negative correlation (where r varies from −1.00 to 0) describes an inverse relationship: as x increases, y decreases (and vice versa). (pp. 28-29)

Example: In a small English town, the seasonal appearance of a large number of storks is positively correlated with the number of human births; as x (the number of storks) increases, y (the number of births) increases. If correlations indicated causation, we could say that the storks cause babies to appear. But correlations *do not* imply causation, and storks do not bring babies.

REMEMBER: Correlations do not indicate causation.

49. If a statistic is **statistically significant**, it is an indication that the group differences or correlation is larger than would occur by chance. (p. 29)

Example: If the difference between two group means is statistically significant, a researcher would conclude that the difference most likely exists in the population of interest. If the difference is not statistically significant, a researcher would conclude that the difference occurred by chance—possibly because of an unrepresentative sample or the presence of confounding variables.

VII. ETHICAL GUIDELINES FOR PSYCHOLOGISTS

VIII. LINKAGES: PSYCHOLOGICAL RESEARCH AND BEHAVIORAL GENETICS

CONCEPTS AND EXERCISES

No. 1: Research in a High School

Completing these exercises should help you to achieve Learning Objective 4.

Imagine you are a psychologist conducting research on violence at a local high school.

Questions

Identify which approach would be most likely to focus on each of the following to understand the students' behavior.

1. Do negative consequences such as detentions and expulsions deter a person from acting in a violent way? _____

2. Are certain types of decision-making styles more common among the violent students than the nonviolent students? _____

3. Is violent behavior related to a student's inability to deny other impulses? _____

4. Are the hormones associated with stress reactions at higher levels among students involved in violence? _____

Approaches

Biological
Evolutionary
Psychodynamic
Behavioral
Cognitive
Humanistic

No. 2: Choose Your Method

Completing this exercise should help you to achieve Learning Objectives 12 and 13.

From the list below, choose the best research method for obtaining the answer to each of the following questions.

1. Does a lack of sleep cause changes in problem-solving ability? _____

2. Throughout history, very young children have occasionally been lost in the wild and found several years later. Recently another such child was discovered. Has growing up in the wild affected his cognitive development? _____

3. What is the average five-year-old's attention span at a playground? _____

4. How do people residing near nuclear reactors feel about the nuclear arms race? Are their opinions different from those of people living far from nuclear facilities? _____

   A. surveys
   B. experiments
   C. naturalistic observation
   D. case study

CRITICAL THINKING

Completing this exercise should help you to achieve Learning Objective 8.

Sam, a rookie police officer, has been assigned to Martina, an experienced detective who is going to show him the ropes. Martina smiled when Sam proudly told her that he had two college degrees and graduated with honors. "Sam," she said, "a college degree shows that you have learned many facts, but hopefully college has also helped you to think critically about those facts. The most important thing you need to do in this job is ask yourself five questions. If you know the answers, or at least how to go about finding the answers, you will solve most of your cases." Sam, doubting that a detective's entire method of crime solving could be distilled down to five questions, decided to humor Martina and play along. "O.K., what are they, these five questions I have to ask myself?"

Help Martina by listing the five critical thinking questions as they might be used in a criminal investigation.

1. _____

2. _____

3. _____

4. _____

5. _____

PERSONAL LEARNING ACTIVITIES

1. In a recent newspaper or magazine find a report describing a psychological study. Does it give details of empirical research or does it primarily focus on opinions, assumptions, and unsupported generalizations? (Learning Objective 2)

2. Listen to a radio or television talk show and attend to the comments made about people's behaviors. Try to classify the statements under the approach they are most like. For example, do people say that hormones or feelings of which they are unaware caused someone's behavior? (Learning Objective 4)

3. Finish the sentence "I am" twenty different times, using a different ending each time. Once you are finished, label each statement as being more individualist (I) or collectivist (C) in nature. For example, an individualist statement might be "I am smart" because that statement does not refer to any kind of relationship with a collective, or group. "I am Jewish" would be a more collectivist statement because it does refer to a group membership. After you have labeled your own 20 statements, ask friends from different parts of the world, or country, to go through the same exercise. Do certain parts of the country or world seem to be more likely to have a higher percentage of individualist statements than others? (Learning Objective 7)

4. Take a survey and try asking the same questions in different ways. See if you can affect the results. (Learning Objective 12)

5. Develop a rating scale for room neatness. How will you operationally define the various levels of neatness? Next visit the homes of several friends and rate them using your neatness scale. Do you see a link between neatness level and personality? (Learning Objectives 12 and 16)

WHAT SHOULD I WRITE ABOUT?

Choosing a term paper topic is the first and most important step in writing a successful term paper. Typically, an instructor assigning a term paper will give you some guidance as to what topic the paper should cover. This guidance may be quite broad (as in "any topic of interest to you in psychology") or quite narrow ("the impact of structuralism on later developments in psychology"). Once your instructor gives you the broad or narrow topic you are to write on, you have several decisions to make.

First and foremost, you must decide how to frame the assigned topic in a way that will make the assignment of interest to you, while staying true to the topic area. This may involve narrowing the topic somewhat if the assignment was broad, or focusing it in a way that you find intriguing, if the assignment is narrower. For example, if you are to write on any topic of interest to you in Chapter 1 of your psychology textbook, you might narrow that down to a smaller topic, such as "the differences between individualist and collectivist cultures", if that topic interests you. If the assigned topic is not terribly interesting to you, think about how it relates to other things that are of interest to you. If you find culture not terribly interesting, you might peer deeper into what culture means in choosing your topic. Perhaps geographical and language differences aren't your thing, but you might choose to focus on cultural differences in religious values. Here are some strategies to help guide you to a topic that you find interesting when you write term papers:

1. Was there anything in the assigned reading on which your paper will build that you found inherently interesting? You will know this by paying attention to when you find your mind wandering during the reading and when the reading seems to fly by because you are so engrossed.

2. If nothing jumps out at you right away, try to relate the topic to something you do find exciting. For example, you might find the assigned topic of "research methods in psychology" somewhat dull, but if you can relate to something you do enjoy, for example, philosophy, you could write a term paper on "philosophy of science."

3. Ask yourself how this topic relates to other disciplines. Think of all the different courses you might be required to take in college—sociology, world religions, philosophy, geography, calculus, and so on. If you try to relate your assigned topic to another discipline, you might find a topic that will really be interesting to study.

Once you have picked a topic you care about, you can go on to additional questions, such as "who is your audience?" and "how narrow or broad should my topic be?". These questions will be the focus of this section in later chapters.

THE INTERNET

The Psychabilities web site that accompanies this text offers many resources relevant to this chapter. They include NetLab exercises, Thinking Critically and Evaluating Research exercises, ACE chapter quizzes, recommended web links, and articles on current events, books, and movies. Go to http://college.hmco.com, select Psychology, and then this textbook.

MULTIPLE-CHOICE QUESTIONS

SAMPLE QUIZ 1

1. Psychology is the study of
    a. the development of cultures, religions, and societies.
    b. behaviors and mental processes.
    c. earth, nations, plant life, and animals.
    d. how people relate to each other.

2. A psychologist who thinks current behavior is caused by unconscious conflicts was most likely trained in
   a. behaviorism.
   b. functionalism.
   c. gestalt psychology.
   d. psychoanalysis.

3. Sometimes Janessa treats her clients with drugs, but at other times she tries to change the patterns of rewards and punishments the person receives. Janessa's approach can best be described as
   a. behavioral.
   b. biological.
   c. eclectic.
   d. humanistic.

4. Dr. Atilano says that behavior is caused by activity in the nervous system, genetic inheritance, and hormones. Dr. Atilano takes a _____ approach to psychological phenomena.
   a. biological
   b. psychodynamic
   c. behavioral
   d. cognitive

5. An instructor tells you that the evolutionary approach best characterizes her viewpoint. Which of the following statements is she most likely to agree with?
   a. Each person learns what behaviors are best.
   b. Over generations, maladaptive behaviors will become less and less common in a species.
   c. People do what makes them feel good.
   d. We inherit only adaptive behaviors.

6. Maria watches people to discover what unwritten rules for behavior they are following. Maria sees that people tend not to sit next to another person on the bus unless empty seats are limited. Maria's interests are most like psychologists in the _____ subfield.
   a. clinical
   b. developmental
   c. personality
   d. social

7. Michelle studies how sociable, conscientious, and anxious children are at age 8. She intends to see if she can predict differences in the number of years of school they have completed by age 25. Michelle is most likely a _____ psychologist.

   a. community
   b. humanistic
   c. personality
   d. social

8. A quantitative psychologist would be most interested in which of the following questions?
   a. What mathematical methods can measure, describe, and predict intelligence?
   b. What type of management style would generate the highest productivity?
   c. What mental steps are involved in perception and decision-making?
   d. How do social skills evolve from the preschool years through old age?

9. Methods for collecting descriptive data include
   a. naturalistic observations.
   b. experiments.
   c. descriptive statistics.
   d. correlations.

10. After being struck by lightning, Nicole often runs down the street singing while wearing her underwear on the outside of her clothes. Nicole cannot concentrate on her work for more than 10 minutes, nor can she understand the comics she used to enjoy so much. To understand Nicole's condition, a researcher should use a(n)
    a. case study.
    b. experiment.
    c. naturalistic observation.
    d. survey.

11. Which of the following hypotheses should be tested with a quasi-experiment?
    a. Thinking of examples of concepts while studying improves students' performance on tests.
    b. An unpleasant odor presented for one hour will cause a mild negative emotional reaction.
    c. The loss of a job in a two-income family has a negative impact on marital communications.
    d. All of the above

12. Susan wants to study the effects of peer pressure on study habits in first-year students at her university. She needs to obtain a random sample. How should she choose the subjects for her experiment?
    a. Select one dormitory and ask all of the first-year students residing there to participate in the experiment.
    b. Randomly select names from the introductory psychology course roster.
    c. Randomly select names from the dormitory phone book.
    d. Randomly select names from a list of all first-year students at the university.

13. Monica claims that the more you study for a test, the worse you will do. What type of correlation does Monica believe describes the relationship between hours spent studying and score on the test?

a. $r = +1.5$
b. $r = -1.5$
c. $r = +.50$
d. $r = -.70$

14. Because experimenters follow the ethical guidelines for psychologists, participants in psychological research can expect to be
    a. informed about the study before they agree to participate.
    b. offered counseling.
    c. psychoanalyzed.
    d. sent home without knowing they were deceived.

15. The question that puzzles Marianne is why some psychological problems seem to run in families. Marianne would like to discover whether it is nature or nurture that more strongly influences certain behaviors; therefore, she has an interest in
    a. behavioral genetics.
    b. genetic engineering.
    c. "pop" psychology.
    d. replicability.

Total Correct (See answer key) _____

SAMPLE QUIZ 2

Use this quiz to reassess your learning after taking Quiz 1 and reviewing the chapter.

1. After speculating that a noisy environment reduces helping behavior, a psychologist using empiricism will most likely
   a. describe to talk-show viewers how noise affects us.
   b. design research to test the idea.
   c. try to reduce noise in the environment.
   d. try to help someone in a noisy environment.

2. Ming's research involves presenting participants with objects and asking them to report the sensations that they are experiencing. Ming is most likely a
   a. functionalist.
   b. structuralist.
   c. behaviorist.
   d. humanist.

3. Roberto studies what people enjoy about listening to classical music. Roberto claims that it would be useless to isolate and listen to only a rhythm, a violin part, or any other single aspect of music, because it is the perception of the complete piece that is important. Roberto's emphasis on not dividing music into parts is most similar to
   a. structuralism.

b. behaviorism.
c. gestalt psychology.
d. psychoanalysis.

4. Hassan believes his clients are basically good; therefore, he wants to see things from their point of view. Because Hassan also says that if he can understand a client's feelings and perceptions he will be better able to help them achieve their potential, Hassan is most likely a(n) _____ psychologist.
   a. developmental
   b. evolutionary
   c. humanistic
   d. social

5. A psychologist who wants to prevent disorders by ensuring children have proper nutrition and educational opportunities is most likely a(n) _____ psychologist.
   a. biological
   b. clinical
   c. community
   d. educational

6. Kwasi wants to know which study techniques are most efficient for which types of tests; therefore, he should consult a(n) _____ psychologist.
   a. behavioral
   b. clinical
   c. educational
   d. school

7. Cultures in which personal goals are more important than group goals are termed
   a. multicultural.
   b. individualist.
   c. collectivist.
   d. subcultural.

8. On a television program many people give testimony that they have never felt better than they have since they began using the Run-O-Sizer treadmill. Each person who is interviewed shows "before" and "after" photos depicting incredible weight loss and increased muscle tone. According to the critical thinking steps in your text, what should you do?
   a. Look for alternative ways of interpreting the evidence that the Run-O-Sizer works.
   b. Draw your conclusion about the worth of the Run-O-Sizer based on the strong testimonials.
   c. Decide whether to order the treadmill based on the price.
   d. Order only if they offer a money-back guarantee.

9. The Food and Drug Administration (FDA) has tested fluoxetine, a drug thought to decrease depression without causing weight gain. The experiment consisted of a random sample of depressed patients split into two groups. The experimental group received the drug; the control group received no treatment. The results were clear: those patients receiving fluoxetine experienced a decrease in depression without weight gain; those in the control group reported no change in depression or weight. Based on these results, should the FDA allow marketing of fluoxetine?
   a. No, the results may have been due to the placebo effect.
   b. No, the study should be repeated using a case study.
   c. Yes, the experimental design is appropriate and the results are clear.
   d. No, the results may have been due to incorrect sampling.

10. In the experiment done by the FDA on fluoxetine, which variable needs an operational definition?
   a. The independent variable
   b. Fluoxetine
   c. Depression
   d. The placebo

11. In the experiment done by the FDA on fluoxetine, the drug was the
   a. independent variable.
   b. dependent variable.
   c. operational measure.
   d. random variable.

12. Questionnaires or special interviews designed to obtain descriptions of people's attitudes, beliefs, opinions, and behavioral intentions are known as
   a. experiments.
   b. surveys.
   c. case studies.
   d. naturalistic observations.

13. Cleta had 20 participants show up to her experiment. She wants to assign the participants to the experimental and control groups, so for each participant she flips a fair coin. If the coin comes up heads, the participant goes into the experimental group. If the coin comes up tails, the participant goes into the control group. Cleta is using
   a. random assignment.
   b. random sampling.
   c. biased sampling.
   d. a double-blind design.

14. You are studying the effects of alcohol consumption on decision-making time. Your hypothesis states that as alcohol consumption increases, decision-making time will also increase. If your data describe a _____ correlation, your hypothesis will be supported.
   a. negative
   b. curvilinear
   c. positive
   d. statistically significant negative

15. A psychologist is planning to examine the contributions of heredity and environment to intelligence. Of the methods listed below, the psychologist is most likely to use a(n)
   a. adoption study.
   b. experiment.
   c. factor analysis.
   d. naturalistic observation.

Total Correct (See answer key) _____

ANSWERS TO CONCEPTS AND EXERCISES

No. 1: Research in a High School

1. The <u>behavioral</u> approach focuses on the consequences of behavior as an explanation for current behavior. (p. 9)

2. Psychologists with the <u>cognitive</u> approach would be most interested in knowing about beliefs, decision-making strategies, and perceptions. (p. 9)

3. The <u>psychodynamic</u> approach claims that people spend much of their energy trying to control their negative natural impulses. (p. 9)

4. A researcher with a <u>biological</u> approach would link behavior to hormone levels and other physiological differences such as brain activity, blood pressure, and muscle tension. (p. 9)

No. 2: Choose Your Method

1. *B* Experiments indicate causation. The question here is whether sleep loss *causes* changes in problem-solving ability. None of the other methods listed shows causation. (p. 23)

2. *D* This is a rare phenomenon, examination of which requires that a great deal of information be gathered about one person (the child). Researchers would conduct a case study in such circumstances. (p. 21)

3. *C* Naturalistic observation would provide the data necessary to answer this question. The researcher would *observe* the attention span of five-year-old children at the playground, rather than asking them about it. (p. 20)

4.   *A*   Surveys are used to find out people's opinions. (p. 22)

ANSWERS TO CRITICAL THINKING

Martina lists the five critical thinking questions for Sam. Each of her questions is followed by its parallel question from the text.

What do I think happened?
What is my hypothesis?

Why do I believe my hypothesis?
What evidence is available to support my hypothesis?

Is there a solution to the crime that explains all the evidence?
Are there alternative ways of interpreting the evidence?

What more do we need to prove I'm right?
What additional evidence would help to evaluate the alternatives?

Can I be certain that I'm right?
What conclusions are reasonable based on the evidence?

Throughout the remaining chapters, Sam and Martina have to solve a variety of cases. As you work through each case, sharpen your own critical thinking skills. Remember, critical thinking can be applied to every aspect of your life, not just to your psychology studies and exams.

ANSWERS TO MULTIPLE-CHOICE QUESTIONS

Circle the question numbers you answered correctly.

Sample Quiz 1

1. *b* is the answer. Psychologists research the actions and thoughts of organisms. Psychologists also try to help people who have difficulty coping. (p. 3)
    a. An anthropologist would probably study the development of societies.
    c. The focus of psychology is narrower; geography is the study of the earth and its many inhabitants.
    d. Psychology is much more than the study of human interaction; psychologists may study development, learning, memory, psychological disorders, and much more.

2. *d* is the answer. Psychoanalysis is a treatment strategy that assumes that people are influenced by conflicts of which they are unaware. (p. 6)
    a. Behaviorists emphasize that people learn from the consequences of their behavior. The behavioral approach does not recognize the unconscious as an influence on people's behavior.
    b. Functionalism wanted to understand how consciousness works, but did not study the unconscious.
    c. Gestalt psychology viewed consciousness as an experience that could not be divided into its parts; Gestalt psychologists did not concern themselves with the unconscious.

3. *c* is the answer. Many psychologists choose what they consider to be the best features of several approaches and use whatever feature or combination of features will be most helpful to a client. (p. 8)
    a. A person with a behavioral approach would try to change the pattern of rewards and punishments, but would not use drug therapy.
    b. The biological approach would view drug treatment as a reasonable way to alter the chemical or hormonal imbalances that caused the problematic behavior, but would not agree with altering the reward and punishment patterns.
    d. A humanistic psychologist would be interested in a person's unique perceptions; therefore, a humanistic psychologist would not prescribe drugs or change the consequences of a client's behavior.

4. *a* is the answer. Biological psychologists assume that nervous-system activity, hormones, and genetic inheritance cause behavior. (p. 9)
    b. The psychodynamic approach assumes that behavior results from our struggle to fulfill instinctive desires despite society's restrictions.
    c. The behavioral approach assumes that behavior is caused by people's past experiences of rewards and punishments.
    d. The cognitive approach assumes that behavior is caused by the thoughts involved with that behavior.

5. *b* is the answer. The evolutionary approach looks for evidence that organisms improve over generations. Those behaviors that were not helpful would be replaced by behaviors that were. (p. 9)
    a. The behavioral approach would agree that people learn what is adaptive for them, but the evolutionary approach would go on to say that organisms that cannot adjust to their environment do not survive.

c. A Freudian might take the view that people do what feels good, especially if a person has not learned about the limits society places on behavior.

d. We do not inherit *only* adaptive behaviors.

6. *d* is the answer. Social psychologists are interested in how people influence each other's behavior. (p. 11)

a. Clinical psychologists study disorders and find ways to assist people in coping with disorders.

b. A developmental psychologist researches the changes that take place in people as they age.

c. Personality psychology documents individual differences, but does not study how people are affected by others.

7. *c* is the answer. A personality psychologist conducts research on long-lasting differences between people much like Michelle's study of the association between a personality description and later behavior. (p. 11)

a. Community psychologists work to prevent psychological disorders.

b. A person with a humanistic approach would focus on immediate experience and current perceptions instead of looking for a relationship between early judgments and later behavior.

d. Social psychologists look for general rules about how people interact.

8. *a* is the answer. Quantitative psychologists study and develop methods of measuring and analyzing behavior and mental processes such as intelligence. (p. 11)

b. Industrial-organizational psychologists study social behavior, such as a supervisor's style of communication at work.

c. Cognitive psychologists study perception, learning, memory, judgment, and decision making.

d. Developmental psychologists research how and why behavior and mental processes change over the life span.

9. *a* is the answer. Methods for collecting descriptive data include naturalistic observation, surveys, and case studies. (pp. 20–23)

b. Experiments are used to conduct controlled research.

c. Descriptive statistics are used to describe and summarize data once it has been collected. Statistics are not a method of data collection.

d. Correlations are mathematical representations of the relationship between two variables. Correlations are usually based on descriptive data but are not a descriptive method of data collection.

10. *a* is the answer. A person with a rare condition is best studied in depth through a case study. (p. 21)

b. An experiment could not be conducted to see if lightning causes unusual behavior; it would be wrong.

c. A researcher wouldn't use naturalistic observation to gain understanding of a person with an unusual problem, because unobtrusively watching a person doesn't provide information about family background, health history, current physical condition, and so on.

d. To survey a person who is having trouble regulating her behavior and concentrating would be difficult, if not impossible. In addition, a survey includes more than one or a few participants because its purpose is to discover something about a group of people.

11. *c* is the answer. A hypothesis about the effect of job loss should be tested with a quasi-experiment to avoid long-term negative effects to the subjects. Testing this with an experiment would require subjects to quit their jobs. Such an experiment would be considered highly unethical and therefore cannot be allowed to take place. (p. 26)

a. Trying to improve students' study methods is not unethical.

b. Experiencing an unpleasant odor for a short time would not be harmful, and the negative emotional reaction could be counteracted by the researchers once the experimental session is over.

d. All of the above are not true.

12. *d* is the answer. Following this procedure will ensure that every student in the population Susan wishes to study (first-year students at her university) will have an equal chance of being selected for participation in the experiment. (p. 26)

a. The use of one dorm will not give every first-year student an equal chance of being selected. Also, a particular dorm might house a certain kind of student. For example, the majority of students living in a dorm located next to the College of Agriculture might be agriculture majors who live there because of the convenient location. But Susan is interested in *all* first-year students, not just agriculture students.

b. Some first-year students may not take introductory psychology. Therefore, first-year students do not all have an equal chance of being selected for the study.

c. Some first-year students may not have a phone or a listed phone number.

13. *d* is the answer. Monica is claiming that as hours spent studying increases, the test score will decrease. Because the two variables of interest—hours spent studying and test score—are described as moving in opposite directions, the correlation must be negative. Because a negative correlation has to be between zero and −1, the only option that could possibly fit the relationship Monica is describing is -.70. (p. 28)
   a. A correlation cannot take on a value greater than +1.00.
   b. A correlation cannot take on a value less than −1.00.
   c. A positive correlation would indicate that the two variables of interest changed in the same direction—either hours spent studying and test score both increase or both decrease. Monica proposes that as one increases, the other decreases, which indicates a negative correlation.

14. *a* is the answer. The ethical guidelines followed by psychologists require that researchers describe the study well enough for potential participants to give their informed consent to be involved. (pp. 29–30)
   b. Participants should not expect a psychologist conducting research to give them counseling. Perhaps if it became clear that a participant was in distress the researcher could recommend that he or she see a clinical or counseling psychologist, but not all researchers are trained in counseling.
   c. Psychoanalysis would be the job of a psychodynamic therapist, not a researcher conducting a study.
   d. If an experiment requires that participants be misled, the researcher is required to disclose fully the reasoning behind the study after it is completed.

15. *a* is the answer. Behavioral genetics is the study of how genes (nature) and the environment (nurture) influence behavior. (p. 30)
   b. Genetic engineering and the field of behavior genetics are not the same thing. A genetic engineer, while interested in the role of genes in behavior, would use the results of genetics research to alter the gene set.
   c. "Pop" psychology is short for popular psychology, which offers answers that are easy rather than well-supported by research. A "pop" psychologist would be more likely to write an advice book than to conduct genetic research.
   d. Replicability means consistent results over many experiments. Replicating or repeating an outcome would most likely interest any scientist, but it does not describe the interest in problems that run in families.

Now turn to the quiz analysis table at the end of this chapter to find which areas you know well and which areas you need to work on. Circle the numbers in the table for items on Quiz 1 that you answered correctly.

ANSWERS TO MULTIPLE-CHOICE QUESTIONS

Circle the question numbers you answered correctly.

Sample Quiz 2

1. *b* is the answer. After speculating that a noisy environment reduces helping behavior, Matthews and Canon designed research that indicated that stimulus overload makes people less likely to help. (p. 4)
   a. Before empiricists describe a phenomenon, they study it.
   c. Trying to reduce noise in the environment before we know if it is the true cause of reduced helping behavior might be a waste of effort; therefore, empiricists see if their hunches are correct.
   d. Helping someone in a noisy environment, while it is a nice thing to do, does not show whether noise influences most people's helping behavior.

2. *b* is the answer. Structuralists used the method of introspection to determine the elements of or the structure of consciousness. (p. 6)
   a. Functionalists studied consciousness, but they used a more experimental approach rather than introspection.
   c. Behaviorists study behavior, not consciousness.
   d. Humanists are interested in people's natural tendency toward growth, not in identifying elements of sensation.

3. *c* is the answer. Gestalt psychologists criticized other approaches for splitting up experience into its components rather than studying consciousness as a whole experience. (p. 6)
   a. Structuralism tried to identify the elements of sensation through introspection. People using introspection would often divide their experience into parts such as quality, intensity, and clarity.
   b. A behaviorist studies behaviors and the rewards and punishments that follow.
   d. Psychoanalysis is a method for identifying hidden conflicts and memories that affect current behavior.

4. *c* is the answer. Humanistic psychologists are concerned with viewing things from their clients' perspective. (p. 10)
  a. Developmental psychologists study people across the life span.
  b. Psychologists with an evolutionary approach do not try to help clients improve. They believe that we inherit adaptive characteristics; therefore, they do not focus on a person's perceptions.
  d. Social psychologists research how people interact.

5. *c* is the answer. Community psychology not only provides counseling service in the community, but also works to reduce the number of risks that contribute to the appearance of disorders. (p. 11)
  a. Biological psychology investigates the influence of physiological factors on behavior, but does not seek to prevent disorders.
  b. Clinical psychologists are trained to help people once they have a disorder.
  d. Educational psychology focuses on learning and teaching strategies, but would not address the prevention of disorders through nutrition.

6. *c* is the answer. Educational psychologists research studying and teaching techniques. (p. 11)
  a. A psychologist with a behavioral approach would know about incentives, but could not advise Kwasi on specific study techniques.
  b. Clinical psychologists are concerned with psychological disorders, not study habits.
  d. School psychologists administer IQ tests, identify learning problems, and set up educational programs to assist students; however, they do not research general study strategies.

7. *b* is the answer. Individualist cultures emphasize and reward behavior that contributes to the success of the individual person even if it sometimes occurs at the group's expense. (p. 15)
  a. Multicultural refers to the existence of more than one culture within a given geographic boundary such as a country (Kenya) or a city (Los Angeles).
  c. Collectivist cultures emphasize and reward behaviors that contribute to the success of the group. Remember, collectivist cultures emphasize "collections" of people (groups) over the individual.
  d. Subcultures are part of a multicultural society.

8. *a* is the answer. To think critically about the product offered, we should ask ourselves if there are other ways of interpreting the evidence. For example, were the people giving their testimonials

because they were paid rather than because they used and benefited from the Run-O-Sizer? Are there other methods for achieving the same results? Could the photos have been altered to make the results look more dramatic? (pp. 18–19)
  b. Making your decision based on the testimonials would mean ignoring sources of information such as consumer magazines and fitness experts.
  c. The price is important to consider, but it says very little about the product's effectiveness or safety, or the likelihood you would use it.
  d. A guarantee might seem to make the purchase risk-free, but if the product is not worthwhile, you will have wasted time trying it and may still lose money. Therefore, a critical thinker will evaluate the claims made about the Run-O-Sizer before examining the guarantee.

9. *a* is the answer. The subjects in the experimental group may report less depression because they think fluoxetine has medicinal value. (pp. 25)
  b. Before the FDA approves a drug, a clear cause-effect relationship between the drug and the desired effect (decreased depression) must be demonstrated with very few side effects. Case studies are not used to detect cause-effect relationships; they describe a phenomenon of interest.
  c. The experimental design is incorrect. Both the experimental and the control groups should have been given pills. The experiment should be repeated using a double-blind design.
  d. Random samples are excellent for use in experiments and other types of research.

10. *c* is the answer. An operational definition, which will describe how depression is measured, can help the FDA determine whether patients experienced a change in level of depression. To understand why an operational definition is necessary, consider the following scenario. Joe, a subject in the experiment, is very, very depressed. After receiving the drug, he scores higher on the test. His test results show that he is still depressed, but not as depressed as he was prior to taking the drug. By using the test to operationally define depression, the FDA was able to measure a *change* in depression. If, however, the FDA had merely asked Joe how he felt, he might have responded that he was depressed both before and after taking the drug. (p. 24)
  a, b. The independent variable is fluoxetine. Measuring the amount of a drug administered to the subjects is easy. It doesn't require an operational definition.
  d. There was no placebo.

11. *a* is the answer. The treatment administered to the experimental group is always the independent variable. (p. 23)
    b. The dependent variable is depression.
    c. The operational definition of depression is a low score on a questionnaire.
    d. Because the sample used was purely random, the presence of random variables has been controlled.

12. *b* is the answer. Surveys are used to collect descriptive data on people's attitudes, beliefs, opinions, and behavioral intentions. (p. 22)
    a. Experiments are controlled methods of establishing a cause-effect relationship.
    c. Case studies are used to collect descriptive information from a particular individual, group, or situation. Case studies usually combine several forms of data collection—observations, interviews, tests, and analyses of written records. Case studies provide a close-up, in-depth view of subjects, whereas surveys paint a broad portrait.
    d. Naturalistic observation is used to collect behavioral information from the subjects' natural environment.

13. *a* is the answer. Cleta is assigning the participants to the experimental and control groups in such a way that each participant is equally likely to be assigned to either group. The process of assigning participants to experimental and control groups so that they are equally likely to be in either group is random assignment. (p. 25)
    b, c. Random and biased sampling refer to the processes used to select who will <u>participate</u> in your experiment, not to assign participants to groups.
    d. Tossing a fair coin is not biased, because each participant is *equally likely* to be in either group. A biased coin would mean that participants would be more likely to be assigned to one group rather than the other.

14. *c* is the answer. A positive correlation indicates that as one variable increases, the other variable increases. This type of relationship supports the data; as alcohol consumption increases, so does decision-making time. (pp. 28–29)
    a, d. A negative correlation indicates that as one variable increases, the other decreases. This relationship does not fit the data.
    b. There is no such thing as a curvilinear correlation. Curvilinear correlations do not exist.

15. *a* is the answer. The quasi-experimental studies used in such behavioral genetics research include adoption, family, and twin studies. (pp. 30–32)
    b. An experiment would be a controlled study in which, for example, subjects were assigned to families; therefore, it would not be ethical.
    c. Factor analysis is a correlational method used to identify variables, such as personality traits, that tend to occur together. Factor analysis would not help in determining what relative effect environment and genetics have on a variable.
    d. A psychologist using naturalistic observation would watch and record behaviors, but could make no conclusions about the impact of heredity or environment on something like intelligence.

Now turn to the quiz analysis table at the end of this chapter to find which areas you know well and which areas you need to work on. Circle the numbers in the table for items on Quiz 2 that you answered correctly.

For each question you answered correctly, circle its number. (Quiz 1 numbers are not shaded; Quiz 2 numbers are shaded.) Are there patterns in the types of questions or the topics you got wrong that could direct your further study? Did you improve from Quiz 1 to Quiz 2?

TOPIC	TYPE OF QUESTION		
	DEFINITION	COMPREHENSION	APPLICATION
Scope of Psychology	1		
History	2		
		1, 3	2
Approaches	4	3, 5	
			4
Subfields		8	6, 7
		5	6
Diversity			
	7		
Critical Thinking			
			8
Research Designs		9	10, 11, 12
	12		9, 10, 11
Statistical Analysis			13
			13, 14
Ethics			14
Behavioral Genetics		15	
	15		

TOTAL CORRECT BY QUIZ:

QUIZ 1:	
QUIZ 2:	

Chapter 2

Biology and Behavior

LEARNING OBJECTIVES

1. Define biological psychology. (p. 38)

2. Describe the nervous system. List the three main components of information processing that the nervous system performs. (pp. 38–39)

3. Compare and contrast neurons and glial cells with other body cells. (pp. 39–40)

4. Name and describe the features of neurons that allow them to communicate with one another. (p. 40)

5. Define and describe action potentials. Define myelin and discuss its effects. (p. 40)

6. Explain how refractory periods affect communication between neurons. (p. 40)

7. Define neurotransmitter and synapse and describe their roles in nervous system activity. (p. 41)

8. Describe the role of receptors in the communication process between neurons. Explain the role of postsynaptic potentials in the creation of an action potential in the postsynaptic cell. (p. 41)

9. Define neurotransmitter systems. Name the seven major neurotransmitters. Discuss the behaviors and mental processes associated with each of them. (pp. 42–44)

10. Describe the effects of nootropic drugs and the conclusions that are most reasonable about their use as "smart drugs." (pp. 45–46)

11. Name and describe the two major divisions of the nervous system. (p. 46)

12. Name the two components of the peripheral nervous system and describe their functions. (p. 46-47)

13. Name the two components of the autonomic nervous system and describe their functions. (pp. 46–47)

14. Describe nuclei and fiber tracts. (p. 47)

15. Describe the spinal cord and its functions. Define reflex. (p. 48)

16. Describe the methods used by scientists in their study of the brain. (p. 49, 50)

17. Name and define the three major subdivisions of the brain and describe their functions. Define brainstem. (pp. 49-53)

18. Name and define the structures in the hindbrain. Describe their functions. (pp. 49-51)

19. Name and define the structures in the midbrain. Describe their functions. (p. 51)

20. Name and define the structures in the forebrain. Describe their functions. (pp. 52-53)

21. Name the four lobes that make up the cortex and state their locations. (pp. 53–54)

22. Name the three functional divisions of the cortex and describe their functions. (pp. 54–57)

23. Define association cortex. Name the two areas of the association cortex involved in language production and comprehension, and describe the role of each. (p. 58)

24. Describe split brain studies and explain the function of the corpus callosum. (pp. 59–60)

25. Describe the lateralization of the cerebral hemispheres. (pp. 59–60)

26. Define synaptic plasticity. Explain why the brain has difficulty repairing itself after it has been damaged. Describe the methods used to help people recover from brain damage today. (pp. 60–61)

27. Describe the changes that occur in the nervous system throughout development. (pp. 61–62)

28. Define endocrine system, glands, and hormones. Compare and contrast the communication processes of the nervous and endocrine systems. (pp. 62–63)

29. Define the fight-or-flight syndrome. (p. 63)

KEY TERMS

1. **Biological psychology** is the study of the role of physical and chemical factors in behavior and mental processes. (p. 38)

Example: Changes in brain biochemicals are associated with depression.

REMEMBER: Biological psychology is the study of the <u>biological</u> factors that influence <u>psychological</u> phenomena.

I. CELLS OF THE NERVOUS SYSTEM

2. **Neurons** are the cells that make up the nervous system. Neurons can communicate with one another by receiving and sending signals. Three structures allow neurons to communicate: synapses, "excitable" (electrically polarized) membranes, and long thin fibers that extend outward from the cell called axons and dendrites. (See Figure 2.3 in your text.) (pp. 39–40)

REMEMBER: A neuron is similar to a computer in that information comes in, is processed, and is sent out.

3. **Glial cells** hold neurons in place and help to sustain them. (p. 39)

Example: A glial cell may secrete chemicals to stabilize a neuron's environment or to help repair a damaged neuron.

REMEMBER: Glial means "glue"; part of the glial cells' job is to "glue" neurons together.

4. **Axons** usually carry signals from the neuron cell body out to the synapse, where communication with other nerve cells takes place. Generally, each neuron has only one axon. (p. 40)

REMEMBER: <u>A</u>xons create <u>a</u>ction potentials. Most of the time, the action potential travels from the cell body to the end of the axon. (See Key Term 6.)

5. **Dendrites** are branches of the neuron that usually receive signals from the axons of other neurons and carry those signals to the neuron's cell body. Each neuron can have many dendrites. (p. 40)

REMEMBER: <u>D</u>endrites <u>d</u>etect signals from other neurons.

6. **Action potentials** are electrochemical signals that neurons use to communicate. When an action potential occurs, we say that the neuron has "fired". Action potentials are all-or-nothing activities; the cell either fires at full strength or does not fire at all. (p. 40)

REMEMBER: An action potential travels <u>a</u>way from the firing neuron's cell body on the <u>a</u>xon, and is <u>d</u>etected by the receiving neuron's <u>d</u>endrite.

7. A **refractory period** is a rest period between action potentials. Following one action potential, the neuron is not capable of sending another action potential for a brief period. The time during which the cell cannot fire is called the refractory period. (p. 40)

REMEMBER: A neuron <u>re</u>frains from firing an action potential during a <u>re</u>fractory period.

8. **Neurotransmitters** are chemicals that carry a signal from the neuron firing an action potential to the neuron receiving that signal. The neurons do not actually touch each other, so the neurotransmitters travel across a tiny gap to carry the signal from one neuron to the next (p. 41)

REMEMBER: *Neuro* refers to neuron. *Transmit* means to send something across space. Neurotransmitters *send* the signal or message *across* the space of the synapse.

9. A **synapse** is the very small gap between the cell sending a message (firing an action potential) and the cell receiving that message. Typically, the axon is the presynaptic cell and the dendrite is the postsynaptic cell. Neurotransmitters released from the presynaptic cell cross the synapse and fit snugly into the receptors on the postsynaptic cell. (p. 41)

REMEMBER: <u>Pre</u> means "before." The presynaptic cell comes before the synapse. <u>Post</u> means "after." The postsynaptic cell comes after the synapse. (See Figure 2.4 in your text.)

II. THE CHEMISTRY OF BEHAVIOR: NEUROTRANSMITTERS

III. THE PERIPHERAL NERVOUS SYSTEM: KEEPING IN TOUCH WITH THE WORLD

10. The **central nervous system (CNS)** is the major division of the nervous system that is encased in bone and includes the brain and spinal cord. Its primary function is to process the information provided by the sensory systems and to decide on appropriate courses of action for the motor system. (p. 46)

REMEMBER: The brain and spinal cord are *centrally* located. Your spinal cord is in the *center* of your torso; the brain is *centered* over your shoulders. Therefore, the brain and spinal cord make up the *central* nervous system. (See Figure 2.5 in your text.)

11. The **peripheral nervous system** is the major division of the nervous system that is not encased in bone. Its primary function is to relay sensory information to the

CNS and relay responses from the CNS to muscles, glands, and other body parts. It has two major subdivisions, the <u>somatic</u> and <u>autonomic</u> nervous systems. (p. 46)

> *REMEMBER: Peri* means "around." The peripheral nervous system is located *around* the center of your body. (See Figure 2.5 in your text.)

12. The **somatic nervous system**, which is part of the peripheral nervous system, transmits information from the senses to the CNS and carries signals from the CNS to the muscles that move the skeleton. (p. 46)

> *Example:* When you dance, the somatic nervous system transmits the sound of the music to your brain and carries the signals from your brain to the muscles that move your arms and legs.
>
> *REMEMBER: Soma* means "body." The somatic nervous system is involved with taking sensory information from the body parts, such as the ears, and sending signals back to the body, such as movement instructions to coordinate dance steps.

13. The **autonomic nervous system**, which is part of the peripheral nervous system, carries messages back and forth between the CNS and the organs and glands. The autonomic nervous system has two main divisions: the sympathetic and parasympathetic nervous systems. (p. 46)

> *Example:* While you dance, your peripheral nervous system may alter the expansion of your lungs so that you can inhale more oxygen.
>
> *REMEMBER:* The *autonomic* nervous system regulates the *automatic* functions of your body, such as breathing and blood pressure.

14. The **sympathetic nervous system**, which is part of the autonomic nervous system, prepares your body for action in the face of stress. (p. 47)

> *Example:* If you think you are being followed, your sympathetic nervous system may increase your heart rate, dilate your pupils, and cause other changes to ready your body to run away or fight.

15. The **parasympathetic nervous system**, which is part of the autonomic nervous system, calms you down once you are finished dealing with a stressor. The parasympathetic nervous system complements the work of the sympathetic nervous system. (p. 47)

> *Example:* If you see that you are not being followed by a stranger, but your best friend who is trying to catch up with you, the parasympathetic nervous system shuts down the changes initiated by the

sympathetic nervous system—slows your heart rate, contracts your pupils, and so on.

IV. THE CENTRAL NERVOUS SYSTEM: MAKING SENSE OF THE WORLD

16. **Nuclei** are collections of neuron cell bodies. (p. 47)

> *REMEMBER:* If you think of the CNS as a map of Boston, nuclei would represent "neighborhoods" on the map.

17. **Fiber tracts** (pathways or nerves) are collections of axons that travel together in bundles. (p. 47)

> *REMEMBER:* Again, if you think of the CNS as a map of Boston, fiber tracts would represent the large "superhighways" on the map.

18. The **spinal cord**, part of the central nervous system, receives signals from the somatic system in the periphery, such as vision, and relays them to the brain via fiber tracts within the spinal cord. The brain then relays signals to the muscles via fiber tracts in the spinal cord. (p. 48)

> *Example:* The sensory information from feeling the fur on a kitten travels through the spinal cord's fiber tracts on its way to the brain. When your brain makes the decision to pick up the kitten, it sends signals through the fiber tracts in the spinal cord on the way to the muscles in your hands and arms.

19. **Reflexes** are quick responses to incoming sensory information. The sensory information is processed in the spinal cord and the reflexive movement exits the nervous system and contacts the muscles. Reflexes are considered involuntary because the action occurs without instruction from the brain. (p. 48)

> *Example:* If you accidentally step on a pin embedded in your carpet, a withdrawal reflex occurs. The sensory neurons will take the information from your foot to the spinal cord, and the motor neurons will send the signal back to the foot to make it withdraw from the floor.

20. The **hindbrain**, a major subdivision of the brain, includes the medulla, reticular formation, and cerebellum. The hindbrain, an extension of the spinal cord, is housed in the skull and involved in controlling vital functions. (p. 49)

21. The **medulla** is located in the hindbrain. It helps to regulate blood pressure, heart rate, and breathing. (p. 49)

> *Example:* A person with damage to her medulla would most likely need artificial life support to

maintain breathing and perhaps would not survive the injury.

22. The **reticular formation** is not a well-defined area of brain tissue but a collection of nuclei and fibers that form a network of cells throughout the hindbrain and midbrain. The reticular formation is involved in arousal and attention. (p. 50)

Example: When you hear a loud noise while you are asleep, your reticular formation causes you to wake up.

REMEMBER: Reticular means "net-like." The cells of the reticular formation are not arranged in any distinct structure but, rather, thread throughout the hindbrain.

23. The **cerebellum** is located in the hindbrain. It controls fine motor coordination. (p. 51)

Example: Performing brain surgery requires delicate precision of movement so as to avoid damaging fragile tissue. A surgeon's cerebellum would be very active during an operation.

24. The **midbrain** is located between the hindbrain and the forebrain. Sensory information is integrated in the midbrain to produce the smooth initiation of movement. (p. 51)

Example: When you reach to pick up a cup of water, your midbrain helps you integrate the sensory information about where the cup is in space relative to your hand so that you can smoothly grasp the cup and raise it without knocking it over.

25. The **forebrain** is the most highly developed brain structure. It is responsible for the most complex aspects of behavior and mental processes such as memory, emotion, and decision making. The outer surface of the forebrain is the cerebral cortex. (p. 52)

Example: Many years ago a surgical procedure called lobotomy was used to treat several types of mental disorders. The surgery involved destroying large parts of the forebrain. Patients on whom this surgery was performed were often unable to perform complex cognitive tasks afterward.

26. The **thalamus** is located in the forebrain. This structure processes and relays sensory information on its way to higher centers of the brain. (p. 52)

Example: Jane has damage to her thalamus. She has normal processing of visual images with her eyes, but is unable to send that information on to be acted upon further by the brain. In fact, Jane reports being totally unable to see.

27. The **hypothalamus** is located in the forebrain. It regulates hunger, thirst, and sex drives, and is involved in emotion. (p. 52)

Example: Destroying certain parts of the hypothalamus causes an animal to cease eating and drinking. It will eventually die if not force-fed.

28. The **amygdala** is part of the forebrain. It plays an important role in combining the features of stimuli from two sensory modalities. (p. 52)

Example: When you eat ice cream, your amygdala is involved in your perception that the ice cream is both cold and sweet.

29. The **hippocampus** is also part of the forebrain. It is involved in learning and storing new pieces of information or new memories. (pp. 52–53)

Example: Going to class every day would be a waste of time if your hippocampus was damaged. Although you'd be able to understand everything the instructor said, you wouldn't be able to form a memory for the new information.

30. The **cerebral cortex** is on the surface of the forebrain and contains two cerebral hemispheres. It is divided into four lobes: frontal, parietal, occipital, and temporal. The cortex is also divided into three functional areas: the sensory cortex, the motor cortex, and the association cortex. (p. 53)

31. The **corpus callosum** connects the two cerebral hemispheres. Without the corpus callosum, the two sides of the cerebral cortex could not communicate regarding their respective activities. (p. 53)

REMEMBER: Corpus callosum begins with two c's. The corpus callosum connects the cerebral hemispheres.

32. The **sensory cortex**, located in the parietal, occipital, and temporal lobes, receives information from different senses, including touch, vision, and hearing. (p. 54)

Example: If you were to take a walk on the beach, your sensory cortex would be receiving various types of information in your lobes: occipital (the color of the water); parietal (the sandy feeling on your skin and the salt water on your face); and temporal (the sound of the surf).

33. The **motor cortex**, located in the frontal lobe, controls all voluntary movement. (p. 55)

Example: During that walk on the beach, your motor cortex would be sending information to your muscles to help you walk in the sand in a particular direction.

34. The **association cortex** exists in *all* lobes of the cortex. These regions of cortex receive information from more than one sense or combine sensory and motor information. These are the areas that perform such complex cognitive tasks as associating words with images and other abstract thinking. (p. 57)

> *REMEMBER:* Think of the *association* cortex as forming an *association* between many types of sensory and motor information.

35. **Synaptic plasticity** is the brain's ability to strengthen neural connections at synapses and to establish new synapses. (p. 60)

> *Example:* New synapses are formed in your brain when you learn new material.

V. THE ENDOCRINE SYSTEM: COORDINATING THE INTERNAL WORLD

36. The **endocrine system** is made up of cells that can communicate with one another. A wide variety of behaviors and mental processes are influenced by this system. Hormones, traveling via the bloodstream, affect coordinated systems of target tissues and organs by producing such responses as the <u>fight-or-flight syndrome</u>. (p. 62)

37. **Glands**, the cells that make up the endocrine system, secrete hormones. (p. 62)

> *Example:* The pituitary, adrenals, testes, ovaries, pancreas, and thyroid are all glands of the endocrine system.

38. **Hormones** are chemicals that, when released by the glands of the endocrine system, travel via the bloodstream and communicate with other cells, thus influencing behavior and mental processes. (p. 62)

> *Example:* A woman's menstrual cycle is governed by the timed release of several different hormones from the pituitary and ovary glands.

39. The **fight-or-flight syndrome**, caused by the release of hormones, is a coordinated set of responses to danger that prepares the organism for action. The heart beats faster, the liver releases glucose to be used as energy, and the organism is placed in a state of high arousal. In short, the organism is prepared to stay and *fight* or to *flee* very quickly. (p. 63)

Example: Any scary experience will induce the fight-or-flight syndrome. Hearing strange noises at night, giving your first speech in college, or almost being hit by a car can be very frightening. If you have been in any of these situations, you may recall how your heart suddenly thudded.

CONCEPTS AND EXERCISES

No. 1: The Organization of the Nervous System

Completing this exercise should help you achieve Learning Objectives 11, 12 and 13.

The organizational chart on page 23 is all mixed up. Correct the mistakes.

No. 2: The Functions of the Brain

Completing this exercise should help you achieve Learning Objectives 17, 18, 19, 20, 21, 22, and 23.

In the year 3000, parents can decide what kinds of special talents their children will have by requesting changes in the genetic coding for the children's brain structures. Below are instructions from several sets of parents. Pick the part of the brain (from the list below) that the doctor must manipulate. Answers may be used more than once or not at all.

1. Rob and Laura want their son to have the very fine hand dexterity necessary to become a world-class pianist. _____

2. Frank and Jean want their daughter to be a translator for the United Nations. This career will require her to understand the subtle inflections of many languages. _____

3. Stewart and Lori want their daughter to be a morning person. _____

    A. medulla
    B. left cerebral hemisphere
    C. hypothalamus
    D. cerebellum
    E. Wernicke's area

```
                            motor systems
                           /             \
                    somatic               sympathetic
                   /      \               /          \
            autonomic   parasympathetic  central nervous system   sensory system
                              \          /        \              /          \
                               \        /          \            /            \
            nervous system      spinal cord      brain    peripheral nervous system
```

CRITICAL THINKING

Sam and Martina are working on a murder case. The victim, a thirty-year-old male by the name of Jerry, was found dead in his office by his partner at 6:00 A.M. Jerry had multiple stab wounds. His girlfriend, Lisa, told Sam and Martina that she and Jerry had gone out to dinner. Jerry dropped her off at her apartment early, saying that he and his partner had to go back to the office and finish a presentation for the following day.

Lisa did have an alibi. She lived with her sister Susan in a high rise in the city. Susan said that she heard Lisa come in and go straight to bed at around 9:00 P.M.

The partner, Stephen, did not have an alibi. He said that Jerry was supposed to call and let him know whether the meeting was still on. If it was, then they were going to meet at 9:30 at the office. Stephen said he didn't receive a phone call and assumed the meeting and presentation were called off. He stayed home and read until 10:00 P.M. and then went to bed.

Meanwhile, back at the office . . . Sam, with youthful enthusiasm, called the pathologist before the doctor could possibly have been done with his report. Exasperated by Sam's impatience, the doctor told Sam what he knew so far. The cause of death was indeed the stabbing. Also, the man had a stomach full of undigested Chinese food.

Sam hung up the phone and grinned. "That's it," he said. "If the guy's stomach is still full, then he had to have been killed right after dinner. Let's say they get to the restaurant at 7:30. Let's say dinner takes an hour, they drive fifteen minutes to his office, and she kills him and takes a train home to the 'burbs."

Martina laughs to herself. She remembers that she made the same mistake that Sam was making today when she first started on the force. (They just didn't teach enough biology in school!) Martina knows that once the sympathetic nervous system is activated, as it is when an individual is really scared, the parasympathetic system ceases its activity.

Using the five critical thinking questions in your text, state Sam's original hypothesis and his evidence. Based on the clues in the story, what do you think Martina's alternative hypothesis is?

1. What is Sam's hypothesis?

2. What evidence does he have?

3. What is Martina's probable alternative hypothesis?

4. What is the evidence that supports her hypothesis? What else would you want to know if you were Martina?

5. What conclusion can be drawn?

PERSONAL LEARNING ACTIVITIES

1. To learn the structures of a neuron, come up with an activity to illustrate their functions. For example, you could line up with several friends and have them hold a wadded-up piece of paper in their left hands. Imagine that your right arm is a dendrite, your body is a cell body, and your left arm is an axon. Have everyone hold their arms out to their sides with the left hand holding the paper over the neighbor's cupped right hand. Have the person on the far right begin by dropping the piece of paper into the neighbor's hand. As soon as a paper ball is dropped in your hand, visualize a signal traveling across your right arm, across your body, and causing your left hand to release your paper. Explain what the ball of paper and right hand

represent. Can you think of a way to show the role of ions in an action potential or to show how neurotransmitters bind with receptors? (Learning Objectives 4, 7, and 8)

2. Write a letter to a friend explaining the nervous system branch or brain structure responsible for a behavior you exhibited during high school. For instance, you could explain that the sympathetic nervous system was responsible for your sweaty palms and racing heart during a first date. (Learning Objectives 12, 13, and 21)

3. Draw a conceptual map of the brain. Position the most primitive, vital functions at the bottom and the most advanced functions at the top. How could evolution have influenced brain development? (Learning Objectives 18, 19, and 20)

4. List the things you are good at doing. Does the list suggest that one cerebral hemisphere is dominant? (Learning Objective 25)

5. If it were possible to use brain scans to find out which areas of a person's brain were most active, should we use them in career assessment? (Learning Objectives 16, 18, 19, and 20)

WHAT SHOULD I WRITE ABOUT?

If you have found a topic that interests you, you are only partially through answering the question, "What should I write about?" The next step is to spend a few moments determining who your audience for the paper will be. Knowing at what level to "pitch" the paper is an important factor to be aware of before you start the writing process. If you aren't sure who you are writing for, you might end up trying to write a really high level paper that appears convoluted, instead of a clear paper at a moderate level that a peer could understand. For example, if you are supposed to write on a topic in biological psychology that is of interest to you, you need not feel that you have to write a complex analysis of the role of mitochondria in neural transmission. You may be better off writing a simple explanation that same topic. You have to know your audience.

As you write term papers, you may first assume that the audience is your instructor. After all, he or she will be the person grading the paper, right? Many students think they need to write at their instructor's level of knowledge. But at most colleges and universities, instructors have advanced degrees in the fields in which they are teaching. Attempting to write at a level beyond your knowledge typically ends up producing a convoluted paper. Picking a topic that is too complex for your knowledge base will not impress your instructor. Writing well on a topic that is within your reach is a

much better strategy. You would be much better off focusing on a topic like "How Seratonin Impacts Depression" than a topic for a more advanced audience.

Here are some strategies to help guide you to a topic that is appropriate for your audience when you write term papers:

1. Sometimes a good way to think about your audience is to ask yourself the following question: Could you explain this topic to your best friend and have them understand it? If you can't explain it well to a friend, chances that you explain it to your instructor's satisfaction are slim.

2. Are you sure the instructor is the only audience? Has the assignment included any special instructions as to who your audience is? For example, does your instructor tell you to go through a peer review process? If so, your instructor is telling you that your peers—as much as he or she—is your audience.

3. Don't focus entirely on picking a topic at your audience's level and forget to pick a topic that will interest them. If the audience is your instructor, think about what kind of topics he or she seemed really interested in during class. If the audience is your peers, then you can pay attention to the topics that really seem to get your peers involved in discussion in class. Chances are that if both your instructor and peers are interested in the topic,, you will probably enjoy writing about it as well.

Once you have found a topic you are interested in and that is appropriate for you audience, you need to focus on how narrow or broad that topic will be. We will focus on this in the following chapter.

THE INTERNET

The Psychabilities web site that accompanies this text offers many resources relevant to this chapter. They include NetLab exercises, Thinking Critically and Evaluating Research exercises, ACE chapter quizzes, recommended web links, and articles on current events, books, and movies. Go to http://college.hmco.com, select Psychology, and then this textbook.

MULTIPLE-CHOICE QUESTIONS

SAMPLE QUIZ 1

1. Eleni's neurons are not functioning well together. Each neuron seems to be able to send and receive action potentials, but the neurons are just not holding together as a "team." Which cells in Eleni's nervous system are responsible for the neuron's functioning well together?

a. axons
b. dendrites
c. mitochondria
d. glial cells

2. This is a story from the neuron kingdom. The king of the neurons wanted to be able to create action potentials at his will, so he decreed that certain fibers would be under his control. Which of the following should he command to create an action potential?
a. Neurotransmitters
b. Dendrites
c. Axons
d. Synapses

3. Myelin serves what purpose in the nervous system?
a. It accelerates an action potential's movement.
b. It is a chemical that travels across the synapse.
c. It causes an inhibitory postsynaptic potential.
d. It causes an excitatory postsynaptic potential.

4. Walt Disney has made a new version of the movie *Fantastic Voyage*. The main characters are stuck in an axon with a short _____. If they do not find their way back to the cell body quickly, they will soon be hit by another electrochemical pulse.
a. nucleus
b. synapse
c. refractory period
d. synapse

5. While you are spying on a neuron neighbor, you see an equal number of "fire" and "don't fire" postsynaptic potentials reach the cell body near the axon. You know this will
a. cause an action potential.
b. cause neurotransmitters to be released.
c. keep the neuron from sending a message.
d. keep the neuron from receiving a message.

6. Marcus enjoys a good aerobic workout six times a week. Most of the time he experiences a "runner's high" due to the release of
a. endorphins.
b. acetylcholine.
c. GABA.
d. glutamate.

7. When a nerve in his arm is stimulated, Larry watches in surprise as his fist clenches. Larry's _____ nervous system has been activated
a. autonomic
b. central
c. temporal
d. peripheral

8. After Bart hit her in the arm, Lisa felt a throbbing pain. "Mom," she cried, "Bart has activated the pain receptors in my _____ nervous system."
a. autonomic
b. acoustic
c. central
d. somatic

9. You are setting the table for a romantic dinner. While lighting the candles, you begin to daydream and the match burns your fingers. You quickly pull your hand away from the flame, dropping the match into a sink of water. What part of your nervous system was responsible for your decision to pull your hand away from the flame?
a. glial cells
b. peripheral nervous system
c. brain
d. spinal cord

10. Kwan Li's auto accident caused her to have difficulty with her piano playing. She could no longer play even pieces that she knew well. When the doctors tested her, she also had difficulty tracking with her eyes the movement of a finger held in front of her face and difficulty in tracing drawings with a pen. Damage to Kwan Li's _____ would most likely cause such motor skill difficulties.
a. cerebellum
b. diencephalon
c. parietal lobe
d. occipital lobe

11. After an illegal drug damaged an area of Judy's brain, she could not learn anything new. In fact, when her family moved, she continued to go to the old house and was very surprised to find another family was living there when "yesterday" she lived there. Which area of Judy's brain was most likely damaged?
a. all synapses
b. hippocampus
c. cerebellum
d. diencephalon

12. Leonard is moving his left arm. A positron emission tomography (PET) analysis of Leonard's brain would show the most increased activity in the
a. left motor cortex.
b. right motor cortex.
c. left somatosensory cortex.
d. right somatosensory cortex.

13. When her vision is blocked by a screen, Sue cannot name objects by using only the sense of touch with her left hand, but she can do so with her right hand. Sue can use the sense of touch to retrieve a

previously held object from among several choices using the left hand only or the right hand only. Which part of Sue's brain was most likely damaged?

a. hippocampus
b. midbrain
c. parietal lobe
d. corpus callosum

14. Anne Marie is about one month old. Which part of her brain shows the most activity?

a. Thalamus
b. Reticular formation
c. Cerebellum
d. Frontal cortex

15. Ted is trying to make a study sheet to help him learn the differences between neurotransmitters and hormones. Which of the following statements on his list is *not* correct?

a. Neurotransmitters travel via the bloodstream and hormones travel across synapses.
b. Both hormones and neurotransmitters stimulate only those cells and organs that have receptors for them.
c. Hormones and neurotransmitters regulate complex behaviors and mental processes.
d. All of the above are correct.

Total Correct (See answer key) _____

SAMPLE QUIZ 2

Use this quiz to reassess your learning after taking Quiz 1 and reviewing the chapter.

1. A basketball team without a coach is like a body of neurons without

a. axons.
b. mitochondria.
c. dendrites.
d. glial cells.

2. Andy Axon says, "Even with all of this (these) _____ wrapped around me, I can't seem to get my signals to the synapse fast enough for the boss."

a. myelin
b. receptors
c. neurotransmitters
d. vesicles

3. Pretend your class is demonstrating the roles of various structures of a neuron. If you are playing the role of an action potential, you should

a. go in through an open gate in the axon.
b. run from the cell body to the end of the axon.

c. begin running from the cell body, but start slowing down at the end of the dendrite.
d. float across the synapse and bind with a receptor.

4. Scientists have discovered a virus that binds to postsynaptic receptors and prevents the reception of neurotransmitter signals. On which parts of nerve cells would this virus most likely be found?

a. Nuclei
b. Axons
c. Cell bodies
d. Dendrites

5. The bartender says, "Here's a drink that's sure to build up your memory muscles. You'll never forget where your car keys are again!" According to the "Thinking Critically" section of your text, the bartender is offering a drink containing

a. glial cells, which improve memory in 75 percent of research participants.
b. glial cells, which improve memory in 25 percent of research participants.
c. nootropic drugs, which are about as effective as drinking a cup of coffee.
d. nootropic drugs, which are effective about 90 percent of the time in improving memory.

6. For a robotic arm, Josie has designed the mechanical equivalent of muscles, tendons, joints, and sensory input sites. When her friend sees the plans, she exclaims, "Don't you need to add something like our _____ nervous system? How will the robotic arm decide what to do?"

a. autonomic
b. central
c. temporal
d. peripheral

7. As Rhoda exits her apartment, she feels a blast of cold winter air hit her face. Rhoda's _____ nervous system is responsible for relaying that information from her skin to the brain.

a. somatic
b. sympathetic
c. parasympathetic
d. central

8. Jim stood next to his classic car with wax in hand, but jerked his hand away as soon as he touched it. "Wow," he exclaimed, "I'll have to wait 'til the car cools off before I start waxing, but I'm glad that my _____ created a reflex so I wouldn't get burned!"

a. brain
b. autonomic nervous system
c. spinal cord
d. brain and spinal cord

9. Tonya, enviously watching her figure skating rival during practice, admires Nancy's well-rehearsed movements. Tonya remarks to her friend that Nancy must have a finely developed
   a. cerebellum.
   b. hypothalamus.
   c. thalamus.
   d. hippocampus.

10. When a firecracker explodes and you quickly turn in the direction of the sound, the _____ helps you to make those movements smoothly.
    a. thyroid
    b. amygdala
    c. occipital lobe
    d. midbrain

11. Conchita can meet a person or read the same story over and over for months but will never recall either. Which part of Conchita's brain was most likely damaged?
    a. cerebellum
    b. hippocampus
    c. medulla
    d. striatum

12. Almyra has a tumor in one of her lobes which has caused her to be unable to move her left leg. Her _____ lobe on the _____ side of the brain is the one most likely affected.
    a. frontal; left
    b. frontal; right
    c. parietal; left
    d. parietal; right

13. Which of the following is *not* true? The corpus callosum
    a. connects the two cerebral hemispheres.
    b. contains many fibers.
    c. is enlarged in cases of severe epilepsy.
    d. allows the brain to function as a whole.

14. You have found an injured cat that cannot move the right side of its body very well. What kind of brain damage might explain the cat's condition?
    a. A severed corpus callosum
    b. Impaired functioning of the motor cortex in the left cerebral hemisphere
    c. A dysfunctional hypothalamus
    d. Impaired functioning of the somatosensory cortex in the right cerebral hemisphere

15. Which of the following is *not* a characteristic of our brains that would make complete recovery from brain damage difficult?
    a. Adult brains cannot generate new neurons.
    b. The brain, prior to damage, has millions of neural connections.
    c. Glial cells eliminate damaged neurons.
    d. Neurons cannot change their functions.

Total Correct (See answer key) _____

ANSWERS TO CONCEPTS AND EXERCISES

No. 1: The Organization of the Nervous System

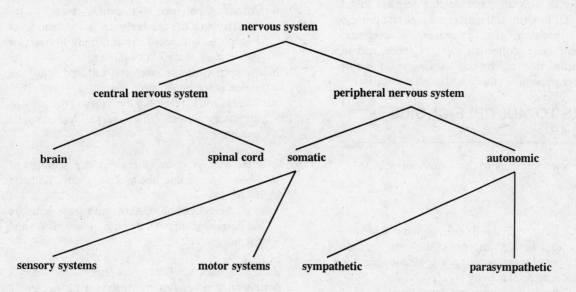

No. 2: The Functions of the Brain

1. *D* The cerebellum is involved in fine motor movement. (p. 51)

2. *E* The left cerebral hemisphere, specifically Wernicke's area, is responsible for understanding language. (p. 58)

3. *C* The suprachiasmatic nuclei in the hypothalamus regulate circadian rhythms. (p. 52)

ANSWERS TO CRITICAL THINKING

1. Sam's hypothesis is that Lisa killed Jerry.

2. The fact that Jerry's stomach is still full of Chinese food leads Sam to believe that the murder was committed right after dinner.

3. Martina knows that digestion (controlled by the parasympathetic nervous system) stops if the sympathetic nervous system is stimulated for any reason, such as onset of fear. She probably thinks that Stephen showed up at the office later that evening and killed Jerry.

4. If you were Martina, you would probably want to get the complete pathology report, which would include the time of death. Most likely, it was after 9:00 P.M. when Susan, Lisa's sister, heard Lisa come home and go to bed. (Martina might also want to check out Jerry and Stephen's relationship at the office.)

5. If the answer to Martina's continued investigation turns out the way she thinks it will, she will probably be able to conclude that Stephen killed Jerry. *NOTE:* Critical thinking is a constant process of hypothesizing, examining evidence, rehypothesizing, collecting more evidence, and so on. Martina may not be correct. Can you think of any other hypotheses that could explain this data?

ANSWERS TO MULTIPLE-CHOICE QUESTIONS

Circle the question numbers you answered correctly.

Sample Quiz 1

1. *d* is the answer. Glial cells are the glue that holds neurons together. Glial cells help the neurons function well together; they are responsible for coordinating neural activity. (p. 39)
   a, b. Although both axons and dendrites are needed for neurons to communicate, the information in this question indicates that both of these neural structures are functioning correctly, as the neurons can both send (axons) and receive (dendrites) action potentials.
   c. Mitochondria in neurons are responsible for generating energy for the cell. This question indicates no problem with energy, just in coordination between the neurons.

2. *c* is the answer. Action potentials occur in axons. (p. 40)
   a. Neurotransmitters are released after an action potential.
   b. Dendrites detect signals.
   d. The synapse is a gap, not a fiber. Neurotransmitters released after an action potential cross this gap.

3. *a* is the answer. (p. 40)
   b. A neurotransmitter travels across the synapse and fits into postsynaptic receptors.
   c, d. Myelin doesn't influence the nature of the postsynaptic potential.

4. *c* is the answer. An axon with a very short refractory period has very little time between action potentials. If the refractory period were longer, the characters in the axon would have more time to make an escape. (p. 40)
   a. Axons do not have a nucleus.
   b. The size of a synapse does not affect the rate of action potentials.
   d. The size of the synapse will not affect the length of time between action potentials.

5. *c* is the answer. An equal number of "fire" and "don't fire" signals will cancel each other out. (p. 41)
   a. An action potential will occur if enough "fire" signals reach the cell body. In this situation, not enough have reached the cell body to override the number of inhibitory signals.
   b. Neurotransmitters are not released until an action potential occurs.
   d. The neuron *is* receiving messages in the form of excitatory and inhibitory postsynaptic potentials.

6. *a* is the answer. Endorphins produce feelings of well-being, including those known as "runner's high." (p. 44)
   b, c, d. Acetylcholine, GABA, and glutamate are neurotransmitters related to movement and memory.

7. *d* is the answer. The motor nerves in Larry's peripheral nervous system caused his fist to clench. (p. 46)

a. The autonomic nervous system is responsible for automatic functions like digestion, heart rate, and breathing.
b. The central nervous system consists of the brain and spinal cords and its function is to weigh information and make decisions.
c. There is no temporal nervous system. You may have been thinking of the temporal lobes, which are responsible for hearing.

8. *d* is the answer. Lisa's somatic system relays information about touch, taste, and temperature to the brain. (p. 46)
a. The autonomic nervous system is responsible for automatic functions like digestion, heart rate, and breathing.
b. Acoustic is not a nervous system.
c. The central nervous system consists of the brain and spinal cords and its function is to weigh information and make decisions.

9. *d* is the answer. When you burn your hand on a flame, you initiate a reflexive response to get away from the heat. A reflex is processed entirely in the spinal cord—you need not wait for information to get to the brain to decide you are being burned. (p. 48)
a. Glial cells are responsible for turning glucose into energy, not processing reflexes.
b. The peripheral nervous system does not do any processing or decision-making.
c. The brain is responsible for processing and decision making, but not in reflexes, which happen involuntarily.

10. *a* is the answer. The cerebellum controls well-rehearsed movements like piano playing and assists the eyes in tracking a moving object. (p. 51)
b. The diencephalon is made up of the thalamus, which relays sensory information, and the hypothalamus, which regulates drives.
c. The parietal lobe receives information from the skin senses, but would not account for difficulty in memories of rehearsed movements or difficulty in tracking.
d. The occipital lobe receives information from the eyes, but would not account for difficulty in movement.

11. *b* is the answer. The hippocampus helps to form new memories. (p. 52)
a. If all synapses were damaged, no messages could be transmitted from neuron to neuron.
c. The cerebellum is the part of the hindbrain which controls movement.
d. The diencephalon is the part of the forebrain which contains the hypothalamus and thalamus. The hypothalamus and thalamus regulate

hunger, thirst, and sex drives and relay sensory information.

12. *b* is the answer. The right motor cortex controls movement on the left side of the body. (pp. 58 & 55)
a. The left motor cortex controls movement on the right side of the body.
c, d. The somatosensory cortex receives skin-related information such as pressure and temperature.

13. *d* is the answer. When the corpus callosum is cut, the two hemispheres are no longer joined. Without the corpus callosum, the information coming to the right side of Sue's brain (from her left hand) cannot reach the language centers on the left side of the brain. Sue can recognize the feel of the object because that task doesn't require help from the left hemisphere. (pp. 59-60)
a. The hippocampus is responsible for helping to store new memories. Sue could remember what the object was, as evidenced by her ability to choose it by touch.
b. The midbrain helps a person start moving. Sue doesn't have a problem with starting to move.
c. If Sue's parietal lobe were damaged, she would have trouble sensing touch, pressure, and temperature on her skin. Because she can choose the object, she must not have trouble with this lobe.

14. *a* is the answer. Newborns have relatively high neural activity in the thalamus. (p. 61)
b. The reticular formation is not overly active in newborns.
c. The cerebellum and forebrain motor areas are not very active in newborns, a fact that may explain their uncoordinated movement.
d. The frontal cortex begins to show increased activity at eight or nine months, when an infant's cognitive abilities start to appear.

15. *a* is the answer. Neurotransmitters travel across synapses, and hormones travel via the bloodstream; therefore, statement *a* is incorrect. (pp. 62–63)
b, c. Both are true.
d. *a* is incorrect.

Now turn to the quiz analysis table at the end of this chapter to find which areas you know well and which areas you need to work on. Circle the numbers in the table for items on Quiz 1 that you answered correctly.

ANSWERS TO MULTIPLE-CHOICE QUESTIONS

Circle the question numbers you answered correctly.

Sample Quiz 2

1. *d* is the answer. Glial cells are responsible for holding together—or coordinating—neurons, just as a coach coordinates the efforts of a team. (p. 39)
   a, c. Axons and dendrites are responsible for communication between neurons, but not for coordinating the activity or functioning of neurons.
   b. Mitochondria are responsible for generating energy in neurons, not coordinating activity between neurons.

2. *a* is the answer. Myelin speeds the action potential on its way. The neuron, despite the myelin wrapped around its axon, cannot seem to get action potentials down the length of the axon to the synapse fast enough for the boss. (p. 40)
   b. Axons have receptors, but they do not affect conduction speed.
   c. Neurotransmitters are stored in vesicles in the ends of axons, not wrapped around axons.
   d. An axon at rest is polarized. Vesicles are located at the very tip of the axon and do not influence the speed of an action potential.

3. *b* is the answer. The electrochemical pulse known as an action potential shoots from the cell body to the end of the axon. (p. 40)
   a. Certain substances do move into the axon through gates, but the action potential moves from the beginning to the end of the axon.
   c. The postsynaptic potential does dissipate as it reaches the cell body, but an action potential starts and finishes at the same rate.
   d. After an action potential has reached it, a neurotransmitter floats across a synapse to bind with a receptor.

4. *d* is the answer. Axons release neurotransmitters at synapses, and the most common arrangement is to have postsynaptic receptors on dendrites. (p. 41)
   a, c. Nuclei are neuron cell bodies in which processing and integration of neural signals occurs.
   b. Axons release neurotransmitters and generally do not have receptors.

5. *c* is the answer. Although nootropic drugs have shown some effectiveness, they mainly affect attention. (pp. 45-56)
   a, b. Glial cells are the glue that holds together neurons and directs their development.
   d. Nootropic drugs are not effective 90 percent of the time.

6. *b* is the answer. The central nervous system takes in data, processes it, and decides on actions. (p. 46)
   a, d. The peripheral nervous system and its subsystems, the autonomic and somatic systems, do not weigh information and make decisions as the central nervous system does.
   c. There is no temporal nervous system. You may have been thinking of the temporal lobes, which receive sound information from our ears.

7. *a* is the answer. The somatic nervous system receives sensory information and passes it on to the brain. (p. 46)
   b, c. The sympathetic and parasympathetic nervous systems are part of the autonomic nervous system which handles automatic functions like heart rate and pupil dilation.
   d. The central nervous system is made up of the brain and spinal cord, both of which are involved in our sensation of cold air. However, the question asked for the system which sent the information to the central nervous system.

8. *c* is the answer. Reflexes are created by the spinal cord without any help from the brain. (p. 47)
   a, d. The brain receives information about the pain and the reflexive action after the fact, but does not create the reflex.
   b. The autonomic nervous system handles automatic functions like digestion and heart rate, but not reflexes.

9. *a* is the answer. The cerebellum controls finely coordinated and well-rehearsed movements. (p. 51)
   b, c. The hypothalamus and thalamus regulate hunger, thirst, and sex drives and relay sensation information.
   d. The hippocampus helps to form new memories.

10. *d* is the answer. The midbrain helps with smooth initiation of movement, such as tracking an object with your eyes as you turn your head or turning toward a loud noise. (p. 51)
    a. The thyroid gland regulates metabolic rate.
    b. The amygdala links various areas of the brain and contributes to our emotional experience.
    c. The occipital lobe processes visual information.

11. *b* is the answer. Damage to the hippocampus causes the inability to form new memories. Conchita cannot form new memories for people or stories. (p. 52)
    a. The cerebellum controls movement, not memory.
    c. The medulla regulates vital functions like heart rate and breathing.
    d. The striatum controls movement, not memory.

12. *b* is the answer. The frontal lobe contains the motor cortex. The right side of the brain controls the left side of the body. (pp. 55)
   a. The left leg is controlled by the *right* frontal lobe.
   c, d. The parietal lobe receives sensory information from the skin.

13. *c* is the answer. The corpus callosum, a massive bundle of fibers, connects the two cerebral hemispheres. It has been surgically severed, not enlarged, in cases of severe epilepsy to decrease the spread of electrical seizures. (p. 59)
   a, b, d. All are true.

14. *b* is the answer. The motor cortex in the left hemisphere controls the movement of the body's right side. (p. 55)
   a. A severed corpus callosum will only prevent the right hemisphere from communicating with the left hemisphere.
   c. A damaged hypothalamus causes malfunction in eating, drinking, sex drives, and, possibly, emotional responses.

   d. The right somatosensory cortex receives sensory information from the body's left side. Thus, motor functioning will not be impaired.

15. *d* is the answer. Neurons *can* change their functions and make new connections with other neurons; therefore, this is not a characteristic that would make recovery from brain damage difficult. (pp. 60-61)
   a, b, c. It is true that adult brain cells cannot divide and generate new brain cells and that the brain has so many neural connections that exact replication following brain damage would be highly unlikely. Finally, glial cells do eliminate damaged brain cells before they have a chance to regenerate. Therefore, each of these *is* a characteristic making recovery from brain damage difficult.

Now turn to the quiz analysis table at the end of this chapter to find which areas you know well and which areas you need to work on. Circle the numbers in the table for items on Quiz 2 that you answered correctly.

For each question you answered correctly, circle its number. (Quiz 1 numbers are not shaded; Quiz 2 numbers are shaded.) Are there patterns in the types of questions or the topics you got wrong that could direct your further study? Did you improve from Quiz 1 to Quiz 2?

TOPIC	DEFINITION	COMPREHENSION	APPLICATION
			TYPE OF QUESTION
Cells			1
			1
Action potentials			2, 3, 4
			2, 3
Synapses and communication			5
			4
Chemistry			6
		5	
Peripheral nervous system			7, 8
			7
Central nervous system			
		6	
Spinal cord			9
			8
Brain			10, 11
		9	10, 11
Cerebral cortex			12
Lateralization and plasticity			13
	13	15	12, 14
Development		14	
Endocrine system	15		

TOTAL CORRECT BY QUIZ:

QUIZ 1:
QUIZ 2:

Chapter 3

Sensation and Perception

LEARNING OBJECTIVES

1. Define sense, sensation, and perception. Explain the difference between sensation and perception. (p. 70)

2. Define accessory structure, transduction, receptor, and coding. Define adaptation and give an example. (pp. 70–71)

3. Define psychophysics and absolute threshold. Explain the influence of internal noise and response criterion on performance. (pp. 71–72)

4. Define signal-detection theory. Explain how sensitivity response affect signals detection. (p. 72)

5. Describe Weber's law. Define just-noticeable difference (JND). (p. 72)

6. Define wavelength, frequency, and amplitude. Define visible light and explain how light intensity and light wavelength are related to what you sense. (pp. 73–74)

7. Define and describe the accessory structures of the eye, including the cornea, pupil, iris, and lens. Define retina and explain how accommodation affects the image on the retina. (p. 74)

8. Define photoreceptors, rods, and cones. Describe how these structures are involved in transduction and dark adaptation. Define fovea and explain why visual acuity is greatest in the fovea. (p. 75)

9. Describe the path that visual information follows on its way to the brain, including the roles of the optic nerve, optic chiasm, primary visual cortex, and feature detectors. Explain what creates the blind spot. (pp. 75-76)

10. Define hue, saturation, and brightness. (p. 77)

11. Describe the trichromatic and opponent-process theories of color vision. Discuss the phenomena each explains. Describe the physical problem that causes colorblindness. (pp. 77–79)

12. Define sound. Describe psychological characteristics of sound, including loudness, pitch, and timbre. Discuss the relationship between pitch, frequency, and wavelength as well as that between amplitude and loudness. (pp. 80–82)

13. Name and describe the accessory structures of the ear. Describe the roles of the cochlea, basilar membrane, hair cells, and auditory nerve in the process of auditory transduction. Name and describe the types of deafness. (pp. 82–83)

14. Describe how information is relayed to the primary auditory cortex. Explain how the cortex processes the messages received from the auditory nerve. Describe the process of coding auditory information. Discuss the relationship between place theory and volley theory. (pp. 83–84)

15. Describe the sense of smell (olfaction) and the sense of taste (gustation). Describe the relationship among taste, smell, and flavor. (p. 85)

16. Describe the transduction process in the olfactory system. Discuss the path that olfactory information follows to the brain. Define pheromones and discuss their impact on human behavior. Define papillae. (pp. 85–87)

17. Define somatic sense. Describe the transduction process in the skin senses, including touch, pain, and temperature. (pp. 87–88)

18. Describe the gate control theory of pain sensation. Define analgesia. Name the body's natural analgesics. (pp. 89-90)

19. Describe the evidence concerning acupuncture and the conclusions that are most reasonable. (pp. 90–91)

20. Define proprioceptive and kinesthesia. Name the source of kinesthetic information. Describe the types of information that the vestibular sense provides. Discuss the role of the vestibular sacs, otoliths, and semicircular canals in the sensation of vestibular information. (pp. 91–92)

21. Describe the two basic principles of perceptual organization: figure-ground and grouping. Define and give examples of proximity, similarity, continuity, closure, texture, simplicity, common fate, common region, and synchrony. (pp. 94–95)

22. Define and describe depth perception. Describe the stimulus cues that influence depth perception, include relative size, height in the visual field,

interposition, linear perspective, reduced clarity, light and shadow, and textural gradient. (pp. 95–97)

23. Describe the depth cues provided by the visual system, including accommodation, convergence, and binocular disparity. (p. 97)

24. Describe the cues used to perceive motion. Include a discussion of looming, the brain's ability to process movements of the eyes and head, and the illusion called stroboscopic motion. (pp. 97-98)

25. Define perceptual constancy. Give examples of size, shape, and brightness constancy. (pp. 98–99)

26. Describe the impact of culture and experience on perception. (pp. 100–101)

27. Compare and contrast bottom-up processing and top-down processing. Discuss how expectancy, motivation, and schemas can influence top-down processing. Describe how top-down and bottom-up processing work together. (pp. 101–104)

28. Describe an infant's perceptual abilities and the methods used to study them. (pp. 104–105)

29. Define attention. Give examples of overt and covert orienting. Explain parallel processing. Describe factors that affect the ability to direct or divide attention. Describe the research using reaction time and PETS. (pp. 106–108)

KEY TERMS

I. SENSING AND PERCEIVING THE WORLD

1. A **sense** is a system that translates information from outside the nervous system into neural activity, which provides the brain with information about the environment. (p. 70)

   Examples: Seeing, hearing, smell, touch, and taste

2. **Sensations** are messages from the senses that provide a link between the self and the world outside the brain. (p. 70)

   Example: Feeling a touch on your mouth is a sensation. Knowing that you have been kissed—instead of, say, scratched—and by whom is a perception.

3. **Perception** is the process by which we take raw sensations from the environment and interpret them, using our knowledge and understanding of the world, so that they become meaningful experiences. (p. 70)

Example: After being in school for years, you will recognize the sign +. You know what it is and what it is used for. However, at your first birthday, you would have been unable to understand this sign.

REMEMBER: Sensation is the message that is sent to the brain about an object's characteristics. Perception is the brain's interpretation of what is sensed. For example, your senses may tell your brain that there is a bright light filling the top half of your visual system and that the light energy has many different wavelengths. Your brain interprets these messages and perceives a sunset.

II. SENSORY SYSTEMS

4. **Accessory structures** modify sensory stimuli prior to transduction. (p. 70)

   Example: The lens in the eye bends light before it is picked up by photoreceptors in the retina and transduced into neural activity.

5. **Transduction** is the process whereby receptors translate stimulus energy into neural energy that the brain can interpret. (p. 70)

   Example: Photoreceptors in the eye pick up information about light and change it into neural energy, which tells the brain about what is in the visual field.

6. **Receptors** are specialized cells that detect certain types of energy (such as light or sound) and convert it into neural energy through transduction. (p. 70)

   REMEMBER: Just as a receptionist *receives* people, the receptors in the sensory systems *receive* information about the world.

7. **Adaptation** occurs when a constant stimulus is applied to the body. Initially, the receptors in the skin fire rapidly, but their activity decreases over time. (p. 71)

   Example: Try to feel your underwear. You probably had to concentrate to feel it against your skin, if you felt it at all. The reason is that the skin receptors in contact with your underwear may have fired rapidly when you got dressed this morning, but now have decreased their activity.

8. **Coding** is the conversion of an item's physical features into a specific pattern of neural activity, which represents those features in the brain. (p. 71)

   Example: Someone has just touched your cheek. How do the neurons communicate to the brain that your face has been caressed and not slapped? Coding must convey the intensity of the stimulus to your brain so that it can interpret the touch as a caress or a slap.

REMEMBER: Your brain interprets messages or sensations as if they were a type of Morse *code.*

9. **Absolute threshold** is the amount of stimulus energy necessary for a stimulus to be detected 50 percent of the time. (p. 71)

Example: When you listen to a stereo, you can choose different levels for volume. When you have the stereo volume set so low that you can only hear it 50% of the time, you are at the absolute threshold for sound.

10. **Internal noise** is the spontaneous, random firing of nerve cells. Sometimes, when internal noise is "loud" enough, we perceive a nonexistent stimulus. This can cause variation in the amount of stimulus energy necessary for an absolute threshold. (p. 72)

Example: The noise of the nervous system resembles that of static on a radio. It is meaningless, background activity that is internal to the nervous system.

11. The **response criterion** is a person's willingness or reluctance to respond to a stimulus. A bias in either direction is created by changes in expectancy and motivation. (p. 72)

Example: Dr. Charles, a cancer specialist, sees cancer patients who have been referred to him by other physicians. Therefore, when he looks at patients' x-rays for the first time, he expects to perceive cancerous shadows. Therefore, he is likely to perceive even faint shadows as cancer when, in reality, none may exist.

12. **Signal-detection theory** is a mathematical model that can help explain why a person does or doesn't detect a stimulus. This model attributes perception to stimulus sensitivity and response criterion. (p. 72)

13. **Sensitivity** is the ability to detect a stimulus. This capacity is influenced by internal neural noise, the intensity of the stimulus, and how well a person's nervous system is working. (p. 72)

Example: Mary Pat is hard of hearing and would be less sensitive to external auditory stimuli.

REMEMBER: In contrast to the response criterion (influenced by a person's motivation and expectancies), sensitivity reflects physical changes in the nervous system, sensory system, or stimulus.

14. **Weber's law** states that the amount of stimulus that you have to add before you just notice a difference or change in that stimulus depends on and is proportional to the original amount of the stimulus. (p. 72)

Example: Imagine that a book weighing ten pounds is in your knapsack. You notice a change in the weight of your knapsack after adding two pounds of books. According to Weber's law, if you started out with twenty pounds of books, you would need to add four pounds of books before you would notice a difference. The proportion of 2 to 10 is the same as the proportion of 4 to 20.

15. A **just-noticeable difference (JND)** is the smallest difference in stimulus energy that can be detected. (p. 72)

Example: During a power outage, your roommate lights twenty candles while you are in the basement coping with the fuse box. When you get back, you tell her that the room is still too dark and ask her to light another candle. She replies that she will have to light several more candles before you can "just notice the difference" in the light in the room.

16. **Wavelength** is the distance from one peak to the next in the wave. Wavelength is related to frequency; the longer the wavelength, the lower the frequency or pitch of the sound. (p. 73)

REMEMBER: Long Wavelength and Low Pitch: they both begin with L.

17. **Frequency** is the number of complete waves that pass a given point in space in one second. As the wave's frequency increases, so does the sound's pitch. (p. 73)

REMEMBER: Frequency means "how often." The frequency of a sound wave tells you how often a complete wave or cycle passes a given point in one second.

18. **Amplitude** is the height of the wave from baseline to peak. Loudness is determined by the amplitude of a sound wave. (p. 73)

REMEMBER: When you amplify something, you make it greater. The greater the amplitude of the sound wave, the greater the loudness of the sound.

III. SEEING

19. **Visible light** is electromagnetic radiation that has a wavelength of 400 to 750 nanometers. (p. 74)

20. **Light intensity** is a physical dimension of light waves that refers to how much energy the light contains; it determines the brightness of light. (p. 74)

REMEMBER: Just as a higher-amplitude sound wave is experienced as a louder sound, a higher light intensity is experienced as a brighter light.

21. **Light wavelength** is the main determinant of what color you perceive. (p. 74)

Example: A light wavelength of about 500 nanometers is perceived as green.

22. The **cornea** is the curved, transparent, protective layer on the outside of the eye. (p. 74)

REMEMBER: Like a plastic wrap covers a bowl, your cornea covers the opening to your eye, yet it allows light to pass through.

23. The **pupil** is an opening, located behind the cornea that looks like a black spot in the middle of your eye. Light passes through it to get to the retina at the back of the eye. (p. 74)

24. The **iris** is the colored part of the eye that controls the amount of light that passes into the eye by dilating or constricting the pupil. (p. 74)

25. The **lens** bends light rays, thereby helping to focus them on the retina at the back of the eye. (p. 74)

26. Transduction takes place in the **retina**, a network of several different types of cells. (p. 74)

REMEMBER: Transduction is the process of converting incoming energy (wavelengths of light) into neural activity.

27. **Accommodation** is the process whereby the muscles holding the lens in place either tighten or loosen to change the curvature of the lens, thereby focusing the visual image. The degree to which the muscles pull the lens is related to the distance of the object being viewed. (p. 74)

REMEMBER: Think of the muscles (when they change the curvature of the lens) as helping the eyes to <u>accommodate</u> to the distance of the object they are looking at.

28. The **photoreceptors** in the retina code light energy into neural energy. The photoreceptors of the eye are called <u>rods</u> and <u>cones</u>: rods code light and cones code color. (p. 75)

REMEMBER: <u>Photo</u> means "light," and <u>receptors</u> "receive." Photoreceptors receive light from the visual environment.

29. **Rods** are photoreceptors that are located in the retina. They are very sensitive to light but cannot distinguish color. (pp. 77–75)

Example: The program for Rakesh's school play had pages of different colors, but while in the dark Rakesh couldn't tell the difference.

30. **Cones** are photoreceptors located in the retina that can detect color. It is because cones are less sensitive to light that we have difficulty seeing color in the dark. (p. 75)

REMEMBER: Cones are photoreceptors that can detect color. The <u>C</u> in cones reminds us of <u>c</u>olor. Cones, as compared to rods, are less sensitive to light. Thus they need more light to be stimulated. When you are in the dark, the lack of light decreases cone stimulation, which, in turn, decreases your ability to see color.

31. **Dark adaptation** is the adjustment made by our eyes when the amount of light in our environment decreases. In the dark, rods synthesize more light-sensing chemicals, and people can begin to see more and more clearly. (p. 75)

Example: When Rakesh first sat in the darkened auditorium to watch the school play, he could not read the title on the program. After about a half hour he had no trouble seeing the title.

32. The **fovea** is located in the center of the retina. A very high concentration of cones in the fovea makes spatial discrimination or acuity (visual accuracy) greatest in the fovea. (p. 75)

REMEMBER: Use the following sentence to help you remember the definition of fovea: <u>FO</u>cusing <u>V</u>ery <u>E</u>asy in this <u>A</u>rea.

33. The axons of ganglion cells come together at one point in the back of the retina to make up the **optic nerve**. No photoreceptor cells are at the point where this nerve leaves the eye, creating a blind spot. (p. 76)

34. A **blind spot** is located at the exit point of the optic nerve from the retina. It is termed "blind" because it has no photoreceptors and is therefore insensitive to light. (p. 76)

35. **Feature detectors** are cells in the visual cortex. Visual cortical cells respond best to particular types of features. (p. 76)

Example: When Jenny looks at a red cube, one layer of feature detectors in the cortex may code which area of the visual field is red and what the background colors are. Another layer of cells may be firing in response to the horizontal and vertical orientations of the lines in the cube.

REMEMBER: Cortical cells detect features, so they are called <u>feature detectors</u>.

36. **Hue**, the essential "color" of an object, is determined by the dominant wavelength of light. (p. 877)

Example: Red and green are two different hues with two different wavelengths. (See also Key Term 22.)

REMEMBER: Black, white, and gray are not considered colors because they do not have their own dominant wavelengths.

37. **Saturation** is the purity of a color. If many waves of the same length are present, the color is more pure or saturated. (p. 77)

Example: The next time you go to a fast-food restaurant, compare the pictures of food on the wall with the actual food you buy. The colors or hues are the same. However, the pictures appear to be more vibrant. The reason is that the pictures are saturated with wavelengths of similar lengths, whereas the food reflects a broad variety of wavelengths.

38. The **brightness** of colors corresponds to the overall intensity of the wavelengths making up light. (p. 77)

39. The **trichromatic theory** states that because any color can be made by combining red, green, and blue light, there must be three types of visual elements, each of which is most sensitive to one of these three colors. Indeed, there are three types of cones that are most sensitive to red, green, and blue wavelengths. (pp. 77–79)

REMEMBER: <u>Tri</u> means "three" and <u>chromo</u> means "color." The trichromatic theory is concerned with the sensation of three colors.

40. The **opponent-process theory** states that visual elements sensitive to color are grouped into three pairs, and that each pair member opposes or inhibits the other. The pairs are red-green, blue-yellow, and black-white. Each element signals one color or the other, but not both. The members of each pairs inhibit each other, and when one member is no longer stimulated, the other (previously inhibited) member becomes activated. (p. 79)

Example: When you stare at a green, yellow, and black "American flag" you stimulate one member of each pair. After you stop staring at it, you see an afterimage of a red, white, and blue American flag because those members are no longer inhibited.

REMEMBER: The colors within each pair are <u>opponents</u>; they are competing.

IV. HEARING

41. **Sound** is a repetitive change in the pressure of a medium like air. This activity can be represented in wave form. (p. 80)

Example: When an object (such as a violin string) vibrates, molecules in the air move, causing temporary changes in air pressure that stimulate the ear.

42. The **loudness** of a sound is determined by the <u>amplitude</u> (See also Key Term 18) of sound waves and is measured in decibels. (p. 81)

Example: People using a sound system in an auditorium control the loudness of the sound coming from the speakers by adjusting the amplitude of the sound waves with their equipment.

43. **Pitch**—how high or low a sound is perceived to be—is determined by the <u>frequency</u> (See also Key Term 17) of sound waves. (p. 82)

Example: Spanky sang a note of the wrong pitch, so his friend told him to sing a slightly higher note. When the frequency of the sound waves coming from Spanky's mouth increased, his friend sensed a higher note.

44. **Timbre** is the quality of a sound that distinguishes it from other sounds. The mixture of frequencies and complex wave forms that make up a sound determine timbre. (p. 82)

Example: The next time you listen to music, try to identify the instruments that you hear. The sound of each instrument has a unique timbre. A note played on the piano has a much different sound than the same note played on the cello or the tuba.

45. The **pinna**, an accessory structure of the ear, collects sound waves and channels the sound down through the ear canal. It is the part of the ear that you can see. (p. 82)

REMEMBER: Make a visual image to help yourself remember the name of this structure. You have heard of the game "Pin a tail on the donkey." Simply change the name and the picture in your mind to "<u>Pin a ear</u> on the donkey."

46. The **eardrum**, or tympanic membrane, located at the bottom of the ear canal, vibrates when struck by sound waves. (p. 82)

REMEMBER: The eardrum is stretched tightly across the end of the ear canal, just like the skin stretched tightly across the head of a drum.

47. The **cochlea** is a spiral structure in the inner ear where transduction occurs. (p. 82)

REMEMBER: The cochlea is like a coiled hose; it contains fluid that moves when sound waves come in.

48. The **basilar membrane** is the floor of the cochlea. When vibrations come through the oval window and into the cochlea, the basilar membrane moves. As this membrane moves, it moves the hair cells that touch it. The hair cells, in turn, stimulate neural activity in the auditory nerve. (p. 82)

REMEMBER: The basilar membrane, which runs along the base of the cochlea, moves the hair cells to create a neural signal. Imagine placing your thumb over the bristles on a toothbrush. The bristles bend when you press on them, much like the hair cells are moved when the basilar membrane reacts to the sound wave going through the fluid. Your thumb represents the pressure from the basilar membrane, and each bristle represents a hair cell that will now translate the pressure into neural activity.

49. The **auditory nerve** is a bundle of axons that run from the inner ear to the brain. (p. 82)

REMEMBER: The auditory nerve receives signals from the hair cells and carries them to the thalamus. From the thalamus, the signals are relayed to the primary auditory cortex in the temporal lobe of the brain.

50. The **place theory** helps explain the coding of auditory stimuli. It states that a particular place on the basilar membrane responds most to a particular frequency of sound, determining the pitch of a sound. (p. 84)

REMEMBER: In your mind, create an image of the basilar membrane all curled up inside the cochlea. Along the length of the membrane, mentally write the names of musical notes. Each place on the membrane is associated with one note or pitch.

51. The **volley theory**, or frequency matching theory, helps explain the coding of auditory stimuli. It states that the firing rate of a neuron (how many times a neuron fires per second) matches the frequency of a sound wave (how many cycles or complete waves occur in a second). (p. 84)

REMEMBER: The frequency of the neuron's firing matches the frequency of the sound wave.

V. THE CHEMICAL SENSES: TASTE AND SMELL

52. Olfaction is our **sense of smell**. Receptors in the upper part of the nose detect chemicals in the air. (p. 85)

REMEMBER: Olere means "to smell" and facere means "to make." Olfaction literally means "to make a smell." If you prefer, you can use the following story to help you remember this word. My grandfather worked in a paper mill that was very old and produced an incredibly awful smell. Just remember that the OL' FACTory smells.

53. Gustation refers to our **sense of taste**. Receptors in the taste buds pick up chemical information from substances inside the mouth. (p. 85)

REMEMBER: The first letters of the words in the following sentence spell gustation: Gus's Uncle Sam Tasted All The Indian's ONions.

54. The **olfactory bulb** is a structure in the brain that receives information from nerves in the nose. Neural connections from the olfactory bulb travel to many parts of the brain, especially the amygdala. (p. 85)

Example: The axons that synapse in Tyrone's olfactory bulb signaled that a flowery odor was being experienced. The information went on to Tyrone's amygdala, where memories of a friend who wore the same flower-scented perfume were activated.

55. **Pheromones** are chemicals that animals release into the air. Other animals may experience behavioral and physiological changes as a result of smelling the pheromones. However, there is no evidence that people give off or can smell pheromones that act as sexual attractants. (p. 86)

Example: Female pigs immediately assume a mating stance after smelling a pheromone called "androsterone" in a boar's saliva.

56. **Papillae** are groups of taste buds. Each taste bud responds to all four categories: sweet, sour, bitter, and salty. However, each responds best to only one or two of them. (p. 87)

Example: The combination of signals from Maggie's papillae results in a salty and sweet taste, which Maggie perceives as caramel corn.

VI. SENSING YOUR BODY

57. The **somatic senses**, also known as the **somatosensory systems**, are distributed throughout the body instead of residing in a single structure. The senses include touch, temperature, pain, and kinesthesia. (p. 87)

> *REMEMBER:* <u>Soma</u> means "body." The somatosensory system senses what happens to the body in terms of touch, temperature, pain, and kinesthesia.

58. The **gate control theory** states that the nervous system has two methods of preventing pain information from reaching the brain. Other sensory information from the skin may take over the pathways the pain impulses would use to travel up the spinal cord to the brain. Alternatively, the brain can send signals down the spinal cord and prevent pain signals from ascending the spinal cord and entering the brain. (p. 89)

> *REMEMBER:* The nervous system can use the spinal cord as a gate that will allow only so much information to go through it in either direction. To better understand this concept, think of what happens when a movie lets out. There are so many people coming *out* the doors that nobody can get *into* the theater for a few minutes. Similarly, to prevent pain information from reaching its destination, the brain may send information *down* the spinal cord that blocks the pain signals from *ascending* the spinal cord or other skin senses may compete for the same pathway to the brain.

59. **Analgesia** is the absence of pain sensation in the presence of painful stimuli. (p. 89)

> *Example:* Aspirin is an analgesic drug. Our bodies make chemicals, called natural analgesics, which can reduce pain sensation. Endorphins are natural analgesics. Serotonin, a neurotransmitter, also plays a role in blocking pain sensation.

60. The **proprioceptive sensory system** provides us with the ability to know where we are in space and what each of our body parts is doing relative to all other body parts. Kinesthesia, which is part of the somatosensory system, and the vestibular system provide proprioceptive information to the brain. (p. 91)

61. **Kinesthesia** is the sense that tells you where your body parts are in relation to one another. (p. 91)

> *Example:* You must know where your head is in relation to your hands to be able to touch the tip of your finger to your nose while your eyes are shut.

62. The **vestibular sense** tells the brain about the position of the body in space and its general movements. The vestibular sacs and the semicircular canals in the inner ear provide vestibular information. (p. 92)

> *Example:* Doing something as simple as a handstand requires vestibular information. If your vestibular senses were not working, you would not know if you were upside-down or right-side-up.

VII. PERCEPTION

VIII. ORGANIZING THE PERCEPTUAL WORLD

63. Figure-ground is a principle of perceptual organization. The **figure** is that part of the visual or auditory field that has meaning and stands out from the rest of the stimulus. It is the part of a sensation that you tend to pay the most attention to. (p. 94)

64. The part of the visual or auditory field that is not the figure, is the **ground**. The ground tends to be the part of a sensation that you pay less attention to because it is not as meaningful as the other stimuli. (p. 94)

65. **Gestalt** literally means "whole figure." Gestalt psychologists believe that our perception of a whole object is more than just the sum of that object's various parts. (p. 94)

> *Example:* What do you see at the end of this sentence? •
>
> Now what do you see below this sentence?
>
> • • • • • • • • • • • • • • • • • •
>
> Like most people, you probably "saw" a dot at the end of the first sentence and a line below the second. A Gestalt psychologist would argue that there is nothing about a dot that tells you about the characteristics of the line. Therefore, perception of the line must be something more than just the sum of the properties of many dots.

66. **Depth perception** is the perception of distance and allows people to experience the world in three dimensions. (p. 95)

67. **Convergence** is a depth perception cue that is part of our visual system. The closer an object is, the more your eyes must turn inward to focus on it. Your brain uses information from the muscles that move your eyes inward to perceive depth. (p. 97)

> *Example:* Try to focus on the end of your nose. You will feel your eyes strain as they attempt to "find" your nose. Slowly shift your focus to an object across the room, and you will feel your muscles relax. Your eyes do not have to converge as much

when focusing across the room, which your brain processes as a distance cue.

68. **Binocular disparity** is the difference between the two retinal images and tells the brain about depth. The greater the difference is between the two images, the closer an object is. (p. 97)

Example: Hold your arm straight out in front of your face, and focus on the tip of one finger. To see the disparity in the two images that your eyes see, look at your finger first with one eye and then with the other. Now focus on an object at the far end of the room. Again, shut one eye and then the other. There should be a greater difference between the images your eyes saw when you focused on your finger than between those your eyes saw when you focused on the object far away from you.

69. **Looming** is a motion cue. Objects that enlarge quickly are perceived as moving toward the viewer instead of just growing in size. (p. 97)

Example: Ted is in a fight on the playground. He knows that the fist that is quickly getting bigger and bigger is moving toward his face. He doesn't perceive the fist as simply growing in size.

70. **Stroboscopic motion** is an illusion in which lights or images flashed in rapid succession are perceived as moving. Stroboscopic motion allows us to see movement in the still images of films and videos. (p. 98)

Example: When you watch a video of a baby's first steps, you are actually seeing 30 snapshots per second of that baby walking. Instead of perceiving 30 still pictures per second, though, you perceive seeing the baby move.

71. **Perceptual constancy** is the ability to perceive sameness even when the object on the retina changes. We have perceptual constancy for size, shape, and brightness. (p. 98)

Example: At a concert, you end up sitting very far from the stage. As you look at the members of the band, you perceive them as being adults rather than children, because of the constancy of their size.

IX. RECOGNIZING THE PERCEPTUAL WORLD

72. **Bottom-up processing** refers to aspects of recognition that depend primarily on the brain's reception of stimulus information regarding the basic features of that stimulus. (pp. 101-102)

Example: When presented with an image of the letter "A," feature detectors for "/ ," " – ," and "\" are

activated, and then the features are recombined to create the perception of "A."

73. **Top-down processing** refers to aspects of recognition that begin at the "top" (the brain), guided by higher-level cognitive processes and by psychological factors such as expectations and motivation. (pp. 101, 102–103)

Example: Jill's friend says that the cloud looks like a soda can with a straw sticking out of it. When Jill first looks at it, she sees a soda can and straw, although the cloud looks as much like a candle, cup, or piece of candy as it does a can.

74. **Schemas** are mental models of what we know, which are created based on experience. Schemas create perceptual sets, which affect our top-down processing. (p. 102)

Example: Claude's schema for nurse includes characteristics like "wears white" and "is a woman." When a man dressed in regular clothes called his name in the doctor's office, Claude didn't respond at first, because the man didn't fit his schema of a nurse.

X. ATTENTION

75. **Attention** is the process of directing psychological resources to enhance information processing. (p. 106)

Example: Sonia leans forward and listens intently to the speaker.

CONCEPTS AND EXERCISES

No. 1: Processes in Sensation

Completing this exercise should help you to achieve Learning Objectives 2, 8, 11, and 17.

Name the sensory process demonstrated in each of the following incidents.

1. Lori has just stepped into the shower with her watch on. She did not realize the watch was on her arm until it got wet. _____

2. In general, the faster a neuron fires, the more intense the stimulus is. _____

3. Jill is six years old. She awakens with a bad dream in the middle of the night. She decides to play with her crayons and coloring book. She becomes frustrated, however, because she cannot see the colors in the dim light. _____

No. 2: Perception on the Playground

Completing this exercise should help you to achieve Learning Objectives 21, 22, and 23.

Many childhood activities and games require the ability to perceive figure-ground, grouping, and depth. Match the grade-school activities listed below with the appropriate cues or principles of perception from the list that follows. Answers may be used once or not at all. Each problem may have more than one answer.

1. One hundred children are to participate in a spelling bee. Because the children sit down when they've made a mistake, the audience knows that only those children left standing are part of the group that has not misspelled a word. _____

2. As Alice runs to get in the line progressing back into the building, she sees a *line* of students instead of separate individuals. _____

3. Roy is playing softball. He knows that he has hit the ball very far because he can barely see it as it soars through the air. _____

4. Sally is calling to Penny and Ali, who are across the playground. She knows that Ali is closer because she is blocking part of Penny from Sally's view. _____

5. The fifth graders are performing a play in the gym. Mark, a fourth grader, wants to sit with his pals. As he looks for them among the sea of faces in the bleachers, the heads of people seem to be getting smaller and smaller, creating a difference in texture on his retina. _____

6. Children play a game called "Duck, Duck, Goose." Everyone stands in a circle. One or two people are chosen to leave the circle. They walk around the circle, touching each person as they go and saying "Duck." Eventually, they touch someone and say "Goose." The "goose" must chase the person all the way around the circle and try to catch him or her. Even though there are always two to four individuals missing from the circle, everyone still perceives a circle. _____

7. Consuela is staring at her sister's engagement ring. When she looks at it up close, she notices that the image of the ring looks different from one eye to the other. When she looks at it from a greater distance, she sees that the images from her two eyes are more similar. _____

  ° Similarity
  ° Reduced clarity
  ° Simplicity
  ° Proximity
  ° Textural gradient
  ° Linear perspective
  ° Binocular disparity
  ° Interposition
  ° Relative size

CRITICAL THINKING

Sam and Martina have been called to Marsh Landing, a resort-like residential neighborhood. Recently, several jewelry robberies have occurred in this area. The thief apparently knows his trade very well. He steals only the "good stuff." Mr. and Mrs. Fletcher, who live in Marsh Landing, reported a robbery last night—the seventh in the past two weeks.

Sam and Martina talk to the Fletchers about what happened. They gave Sam and Martina a list of the items that were stolen: a ring, a bracelet, several pairs of cuff links, and a brooch.

Martina continues to ask questions. "Did you see the thief, Mr. Fletcher?"

"Oh, yeah, he woke me up when he came into the room. I was too scared to say anything, though. I didn't know if he was dangerous. Besides, it took him all of five minutes to locate our jewelry box and take our things. He tiptoed out of the bedroom and I think he went out through the back door."

"Well, what did he look like?" Martina asked.

"He was about six feet tall, and he was wearing a pink T-shirt and olive-green khakis. I think he had black hair. I also noticed that he stood very straight; he had great posture."

"Is the jewelry insured, Mr. Fletcher?"

Mrs. Fletcher piped up, "Oh yes—my goodness, dear, that jewelry was quite expensive. We took out a special policy on it last year."

Sam turns to Martina and says, "This has to be the same guy. Only the *valuable* jewelry is gone. And, as in every other hit, nothing but jewelry has been taken."

Martina just shakes her head. Sam was jumping to conclusions again.

"Mr. Fletcher, do you have a night-light in your room? And if so, is it located near the jewelry box?"

"No, Martina, we don't," Mr. Fletcher replied.

Using the five critical thinking questions in your text, state Sam's original hypothesis and describe his evidence. Based on the clues in the story, what do you think Martina's alternative hypothesis is?

1. What is Sam's original hypothesis?

2. What evidence does he have?

3. What is Martina's probable alternative hypothesis?

4. What is the evidence that supports her hypothesis? What else would you want to know if you were Martina?

5. What conclusions can Martina draw?

PERSONAL LEARNING ACTIVITIES

1. Take a survey of the people you know to find out how many of them have corrected vision or other aids to sensation.

2. Try to approximate your absolute threshold for tastes. You could have someone prepare several glasses, some of which are plain water, the rest of which have varying amounts of salt or sugar in them. How much must be there before you notice it? Does the amount change if you try the experiment at another time of day? (Learning Objective 3)

3. Prepare additional analogies for how parts of sensory systems work. The action of the hair cells on the basilar membrane in hearing, for example, might be likened to the action of reeds that move when a wave washes over them in a river. (Learning Objectives 2, 7, 8, 9, 13, 16, and 17)

4. What errors in perception have you made? Did the illusions in Figures 3.23 and 3.24 fool you? Have you experienced a situation like the error in depth perception that follows? Large rock formations or mountains may appear to be near to the inexperienced viewer, because it is hard to compare them to the surroundings. Although they could be a day's journey away on foot, people new to the area can't see that a tree at the base is a tiny dot on their retina, and that, therefore, the mountain must be far away. (Learning Objective 22)

5. Experiment on the cues you use to maintain your balance. In a place with room to move, stand without touching anything, close your eyes, and then lift one foot. Lead a blindfolded friend around a building, being careful to indicate obstacles, steps, and turns. Have the friend report on the experience of moving without benefit of sight. (Learning Objective 20)

WHAT SHOULD I WRITE ABOUT?

Once you have determined who your audience is, you need to shape your topic. It is important to determine how narrow or broad your topic should be *before* you begin writing your term paper. Taking this step will help you to conduct research at the library more efficiently. For example, you may have decided that you are interested in writing about colorblindness after reading this chapter, and you may have decided to write this at a level that it pitched at your peers, but you haven't determined how to frame your topic. Colorblindness is a rather general topic. Do you plan to look at one type of colorblindness or both? Do you want to explain the biological mechanisms that produce colorblindness? Or

would you prefer to focus more on how colorblind individuals deal with this particular limitation?

On the other hand, you don't want to end up with a topic that is too narrow. Sometimes students become so focused on narrowing their topic that they pick something that will be very difficult to actually research. When you do a term paper, make sure your topic is focused enough that you know what you are looking for, but broad enough for you to find plenty of research. For example, if you decide you are going to write on stroboscopic motion in Japanese cinema, you may find that your topic is so narrow that you have trouble finding research to support your ideas. Stroboscopic motion in films is narrow enough to give you some guidance, but broad enough to provide you some room to investigate the phenomenon.

Here are some strategies for focusing your topic:

1. Ask yourself what kind of research your textbook describes about this topic. Were there only a few citations in that section? Was the section extremely brief? If so, you might want to consider broadening your topic. If the section was long and full of research citations, you might focus your topic a bit more.

2. How many questions are you able to generate about that topic? If you are able to generate a lot (more than ten questions), you may need to narrow your focus to one or two of those questions. If you can only think of one question, you may want to broaden your topic to include other questions.

3. Finally, do a quick literature search on PsychLit or another search engine. Are you having trouble finding key words that locate articles relevant to your proposed topic? If so, you might consider broadening your focus so that you can include more research in your term paper.

THE INTERNET

The Psychabilities web site that accompanies this text offers many resources relevant to this chapter. They include NetLab exercises, Thinking Critically and Evaluating Research exercises, ACE chapter quizzes, recommended web links, and articles on current events, books, and movies. Go to http://college.hmco.com, select Psychology, and then this textbook.

MULTIPLE-CHOICE QUESTIONS

SAMPLE QUIZ 1

1. An accessory structure
   a. is where transduction occurs.
   b. functions as a receptor.
   c. modifies incoming stimuli prior to transduction.

d.   changes stimulus energy into neural energy.

2.   Vicki is sailing toward shore. Her expectation of seeing shore soon will _____ her response criterion for perceiving land.
a.   increase
b.   decrease
c.   have no effect on
d.   delay

3.   Which of the following would *not* affect a person's sensitivity?
a.   The level of internal noise in the nervous system
b.   The person's motivation
c.   The condition of the person's sensory system
d.   The intensity of the stimulus

4.   It is too dim for Carly to see what she is reading; therefore, she should _____ by turning on a lamp.
a.   increase the light intensity
b.   increase the light wavelength
c.   decrease the light intensity
d.   decrease the light wavelength

5.   While Becky watched a basketball game on TV, Cindy asked her, "Is this OK for dinner?" Becky didn't look away from the game, and thought, based on her peripheral vision, that Cindy held up a TV dinner, so she said, "Sure." Only when Cindy served Becky a plate of brussel sprouts did Becky realize that her visual acuity wasn't very good because she was relying primarily on
a.   bipolar cells.
b.   cones.
c.   ganglion cells.
d.   rods.

6.   Ashanti cannot hear. All of the structures in his hearing system work, except for those that transduce the sound waves. Ashanti's _____ do not work; therefore, he has _____ deafness.
a.   hair cells; nerve
b.   hammer, anvil, and stirrup bones; conduction
c.   semicircular canals; conduction
d.   tympanic membranes; nerve

7.   If the place theory is true, which of the following would cause the *least* amount of auditory impairment?
a.   Sitting in front of the speakers at a rock concert
b.   Hearing a pure tone with a very high amplitude
c.   Working in a factory where there are many noisy machines
d.   Listening to Bach at full volume over your headphones

8.   The nerves that signal what is touching Gary's face are firing very, very rapidly. Which of the following most likely happened?
a.   He was just punched in the mouth.
b.   He was just kissed on the cheek.
c.   He just took a drink of water.
d.   A fly just landed on his nose.

9.   Marina hit her elbow on the doorway. According to the gate control theory, in order to reduce the amount of pain she is feeling, Marina should
a.   use the image of a closing gate to give herself the expectation that the pain will end.
b.   rub the sore area.
c.   think about anything other than the pain.
d.   do any of the above.

10.   Ally has lost her kinesthetic sense. Ally will most likely be unable to
a.   be sure her hand is raised without looking at it.
b.   detect the flavor of her ice cream cone.
c.   feel the warmth of the sun on her face.
d.   respond to pain.

11.   A Cyclops has only one eye. What depth cue based on the properties of her visual system would a Cyclops *not* have?
a.   Linear perspective
b.   Movement gradient
c.   Convergence
d.   Reduced clarity

12.   When Jean sees her cat from one angle, she has no difficulty identifying her, but from another angle Jean isn't even sure that what she's seeing is a cat. Jean is having difficulty with
a.   closure.
b.   interposition.
c.   proximity.
d.   shape constancy.

13.   Which of the following does not contribute to the creation of a perceptual set?
a.   Context
b.   Expectancy
c.   Past experience
d.   Sensitivity

14.   When Frieda first looked at an advertisement, she noticed only that it showed a glass of cola on a tray. After her friend Cal told her that he saw two cows kissing in the blur on the left ice cube, Frieda instantly noticed the cows. "You're right; I can see them," said Frieda, "but I think I see them mostly due to _____, since you made me expect them to be there."
a.   bottom-up processing
b.   top-down processing

c. common fate
d. similarity

15. Ron hears his mother call his name across the room. Upon hearing his name, Ron turns his head in the direction of his mother and asks what she wants. When Ron turns his head toward his mother, he is engaged in _____ of attention.
   a. the Stroop task
   b. covert orienting
   c. overt orienting
   d. a perceptual set

Total Correct (See answer key) _____

SAMPLE QUIZ 2

Use this quiz to reassess your learning after taking Quiz 1 and reviewing the chapter.

1. Kelly's contact lens scratches her cornea and causes her to experience discomfort in her eye until it heals. Which part of Kelly's visual sensory system has been impaired?
   a. An accessory structure.
   b. A receptor cell.
   c. A feature detector.
   d. Her primary visual cortex.

2. Shari studies the factors that will affect whether a cheese lab technologist will notice white curd specks in a loaf of yellow processed cheese. Specifically, Shari needs to know how to improve sensitivity and change response criterions; therefore, Shari should study
   a. signal detection theory.
   b. extrasensory perception.
   c. optical acuity theory.
   d. Weber's law.

3. Jake is a detective. He is usually very good at his job but has been making mistakes lately. Last night, he was on a stakeout and let Benny slip away. Which of the following explanations would point to inadequate sensitivity as the reason for Jake's mistake?
   a. Jake was sure that Benny was going to sleep that night instead of making a break for it.
   b. Jake fell asleep in the car at about 5:00 A.M.
   c. Jake knew that Benny's partner was across the street aiming a gun at Jake. If Jake had made a move, he would have been shot.
   d. Jake knows that he is going to retire soon; a few mistakes will not mar his record.

4. Rhoda, who is visiting her sister, just turned out the bathroom light and has to grope along the wall to feel her way back to the bedroom. After being in

bed again for about forty-five minutes, she realizes that she can see well. Why?
   a. Ganglion cells have been activated.
   b. Her rods have built up their light-sensing chemicals.
   c. The muscles that control her lenses have adapted to the dark.
   d. The dendrites in her optic nerve have finally resynthesized.

5. Evelyn tried on a pair of sunglasses with red lenses. After wearing them for a few minutes, Evelyn took them off and realized that everything she looked at now had a green tint. The theory that best explains the afterimage seen by Evelyn is the _____ theory.
   a. cones.
   b. bipolar cells.
   c. ganglion cells.
   d. rods.

6. The pitch of a dog whistle is so high that humans cannot hear it. What physical dimension of sound would describe such a high pitch?
   a. A waveform with a very high frequency
   b. A waveform with a very low frequency
   c. A waveform with a very high amplitude
   d. A waveform with a very low amplitude

7. When Adriana pushes forward on the backs of her pinnas near her scalp, she notices that she can no longer tell where a high-pitched sound is coming from. Adriana's action has directly affected her
   a. accessory structures.
   b. cochlea.
   c. timbre.
   d. transduction mechanisms.

8. Andre's papillae do not work. Which of the following statements is Andre most likely to make?
   a. "I miss the feeling of a hot shower on my skin."
   b. "Green and red both look gray to me."
   c. "I couldn't smell the toast burning."
   d. "Nothing tastes right any more."

9. Excellent proprioception would be required for which of the following careers?
   a. Chef
   b. Wine taster
   c. Acrobat
   d. Musician

10. When you arrive at a party, you are distressed to discover that people have already paired off. Although couples are just talking while sitting near to each other, you think that no one is available to talk to. The perceptual grouping principle most likely causing your perception of the party

attenders as several pairs of people rather than as individuals is
a. closure.
b. continuity.
c. figure-ground.
d. proximity.

11. A burglar will paint her face black and wear dark clothing in order to keep people from using which principle of perceptual organization or grouping?
a. Proximity
b. Figure-ground
c. Closure
d. Similarity

12. Which perceptual process is influenced most by expectations and motivation?
a. Bottom-up processing
b. Internal noise
c. Top-down processing
d. Sensitivity

13. When Lou looks at a lily, her brain matches its features (stem, petals, fragrance, and color) to the perceptual category "flower." Such feature analysis is characteristic of _____ processing.
a. bottom-up
b. ecological
c. illusory
d. top-down

14. John, a newlywed, is expecting his wife home from work in ten minutes. Suddenly, her footsteps are on the stairs. He jumps up and runs out the door, ready to scoop up his wife. To his embarrassment, he almost kisses the landlord. What type of processing caused John's close call?
a. Feature analysis
b. Bottom-up processing
c. Perceptual set
d. Auditory gradients

15. Although Alan appears to be listening as Rich talks about his new clothes, vacation plans, and exercise routine, Alan is thinking through his list of errands to run. Alan has
a. covertly shifted attention.
b. overtly shifted attention.
c. used parallel distributed processing.
d. used serial processing.

Total Correct (See answer key) _____

ANSWERS TO CONCEPTS AND EXERCISES

No. 1: Processes in Sensation

1. Your inability to feel a watch on your wrist is due to the adaptation process. When you put on your watch, the cells in the skin begin to fire rapidly and then decrease their activity back to a baseline rate. When Lori stepped into the shower, the cells that would detect the presence of her watch had long ago returned to a baseline firing rate. If you think about it, you will realize that the process of adaptation is very necessary. For just a moment, make yourself notice everything that is touching you. Without adaptation, all of the information would feel as though it were new—as if you had just put on all of your clothes, had just sat down, and had just put on your makeup and jewelry. Without adaptation, we would be overloaded with sensory information. (pp. 71)

2. A neuron's firing rate tells the brain how intense a stimulus is. This is the coding process. (p. 71)

3. Jill is experiencing dark adaptation. Her cone and rod cells have adapted so that she can see shapes and images. However, the rods, which work best in dim light, cannot pick up color information. That is why Jill cannot see the colors of her crayons. (p. 75)

No. 2: Perception on the Playground

1. *Similarity.* This is a grouping principle. Those children who are standing all have similar orientations. This will tell the audience which children belong to the group of disqualified people and which children are still in the spelling bee. (p. 94)

2. *Simplicity.* This is a grouping principle. We perceive the most simple pattern in an object. Seeing many individual students would be much more complicated than just seeing a line of people. Continuity would be an equally good answer. We perceive sensations that appear to create a continuous form (a line) as belonging together. (p. 95)

3. *Reduced clarity.* This is a depth cue. The clarity with which Roy can see the ball is reduced as it gets farther and farther away. Relative size, also a depth cue, would be an equally good answer. As the size of the ball gets smaller, Roy perceives it as being farther away. (p. 96)

4. *Interposition.* This is a depth cue. Objects that block the view of other objects are closer to us. Ali is blocking the view of Penny; therefore, Ali is closer to Sally. (p. 96)

5. *Textural gradient*. This is a depth cue. Mark knows that the objects that create a smaller image and different texture on his retina are farther away. (p. 97)

6. *Closure*. This is a grouping principle. Even though parts of the circle are missing, the children still perceive the group as a circle. Their perceptual abilities allow them to fill in the gaps. (p. 95)

7. *Binocular disparity*. This is a depth cue. Objects that are closer to us produce more disparate, or different, retinal images than objects viewed from far away. (p. 97)

ANSWERS TO CRITICAL THINKING

1. Sam hypothesizes that the same jewelry thief who has been in the neighborhood for the past several weeks is also the culprit in the Fletcher burglary.

2. The fact that the Fletchers live in Marsh Landing and that the thief took only the good jewelry supports Sam's hypothesis.

3. Martina believes that the Fletchers made the whole thing up so they could claim the insurance money.

4. Martina knows that because rods are more active in the dark, Mr. Fletcher wouldn't be able to tell what colors the thief was wearing (hence the night-light question). Martina should also find out if the Fletchers are having money troubles. Financial problems may have been their motive for faking the crime.

5. Martina probably can't conclude anything just yet, but she is well on her way to supporting her hypothesis. *NOTE:* Critical thinking is a constant process of hypothesizing, examining evidence, rehypothesizing, collecting more evidence, and so on. Martina may not be correct. Can you think of any other hypotheses that could explain the data?

ANSWERS TO MULTIPLE-CHOICE QUESTIONS

Circle the question numbers you answered correctly.

Sample Quiz 1

1. *c* is the answer. An accessory structure modifies the stimulus in some way prior to transduction. For example, the pinna of the ear collects sounds to be funneled into the ear canal. (p. 70)
   a. Transduction takes place in the receptors.
   b. Receptors are involved in transduction. Accessory structures modify a stimulus in some way prior to transduction.

   d. Transduction is the process of changing stimulus energy into neural energy. Transduction takes place at the receptors.

2. *b* is the answer. Vicki's expectations of seeing a light on shore soon will decrease her response criterion. This means she will need less stimulus (light) to perceive that she is seeing a shore light. (p. 72)
   a. Increasing Vicki's response criterion means that she will be less likely to perceive a stimulus.
   c. *b* is the answer.
   d. The response criterion is the willingness or reluctance to respond to a stimulus; therefore, it is not something that can be delayed.

3. *b* is the answer. Sensitivity is the ability to detect a stimulus. Motivation affects whether we do perceive a stimulus, but it does not affect our ability to perceive a stimulus. (p. 72)
   a. A very high level of internal noise may be mistaken for a very faint stimulus. This will alter sensitivity.
   c. The sensory system's physical health can affect its ability to perceive a stimulus. For example, a person with burned finger tips will be unable to detect slight pressure very well.
   d. The intensity of a stimulus will affect our ability to detect it. If the stimulus is below absolute threshold, it will be undetectable.

4. *a* is the answer. Light intensity determines brightness. Carly should increase intensity to increase brightness. (p. 74)
   b, d. Wavelength determines color.
   c. Decreasing light intensity would dim the light.

5. *d* is the answer. Rods are predominant in the periphery of the retina. If Becky uses peripheral vision, her acuity will be poorer. (p. 75)
   a, c. Bipolar and ganglion cells receive information from the rods and cones; the lack of information from the cones causes the poor vision.
   b. Cones are located primarily in the fovea, or center, of the retina and are responsible for its high visual acuity.

6. *a* is the answer. Hair cells are the transduction mechanisms for hearing; if they or the auditory nerve malfunction, nerve deafness results (p. 82)
   b. The hammer (malleus), anvil (incus), and stirrup (stapes) are accessory structures. If these middle-ear bones are fused, conduction deafness results.
   c. The semicircular canals are the parts of the inner ear used for the vestibular sense.

d. Tympanic membranes (eardrums) send vibrations to the bones of the middle ear; they do not transduce sound waves.

7. *b* is the answer. A very pure tone has only one frequency. According to the place theory, a specific frequency will cause a specific place on the basilar membrane to move. A damaging pure tone would therefore cause damage to only one location. (p. 84)

a, d. Both rock and orchestral music would be made up of many frequencies, thus causing damage all along the basilar membrane.

c. Machinery noise consists of many frequencies, thus causing damage all along the basilar membrane.

8. *a* is the answer. The intensity or heaviness of an object touching the skin is coded by the number of active neurons as well as by the speed with which they are firing. Many of Gary's neurons are firing rapidly, so the touch must be heavy. Getting punched in the mouth is the heaviest touch among the choices. (p. 88)

b, c, d. A kiss on the cheek, the feel of a glass against one's lips, and the feel of a fly on one's nose would cause only a few neurons to be active, and they would not fire very rapidly.

9. *b* is the answer. According to the gate control theory of pain, other sensations can compete with the pain sensations for the pathways to the brain. If Marina rubs her elbow, the rubbing may overpower some of the pain sensations and thereby reduce her pain. (p. 89)

a. An image of a closing gate might help Marina reduce her pain, but visualizations are not covered in the gate control theory. The gate control theory states that signals coming up the spinal cord or down from the brain may block the pain sensations.

c. Thinking about something else may reduce Marina's pain, but the gate control theory does not address this.

d. Only *b* is correct.

10. *a* is the answer. Kinesthesia gives us knowledge of the position of our body parts by sending information from our muscles and joints. (p. 91)

b. Gustation and olfaction would allow Ally to detect ice cream flavors.

c, d. The feeling of warmth on skin and responding to pain are part of the somatosensory systems, but are not kinesthetic senses.

11. *c* is the answer. The brain receives and processes information from the eye muscles about the amount of muscular activity. The eyes must converge, or

rotate inward, to project the image of an object on each retina. The closer the object is, the greater the convergence is, and thus the greater is the muscular activity reported to the brain. The brain of a Cyclops would receive no information about the convergence since a Cyclops has only one eye. (p. 97)

a. Linear perspective is a depth cue that can be seen with one eye.

b. A movement gradient is a depth cue that can be seen with one eye.

d. Reduced clarity is a depth cue that can be seen with one eye.

12. *d* is the answer. (pp. 95-96)

a, b. Both the grouping principle closure and the depth cue interposition would require that something was blocking Jean's view of the cat.

c. Proximity is a grouping principle that automatically organizes objects that are close together into a group.

13. *d* is the answer. A perceptual set is a readiness to perceive a stimulus in a certain way. Sensitivity is the ability to perceive an object *at all,* not an indication of *how* we perceive it. (pp. 72, 102)

a. Context can change the way we perceive an object. For example, the sound of "reed" means two different things depending on the context of the sentence. "The oboe contains a reed." "I like to read."

b. Our expectations, based on past experience and context, can create a perceptual set.

c. Our past experiences can create perceptual sets. A person who does not have children may take some time to realize that children's bloodcurdling screams may not always signify pain. Anyone who has been around children for any length of time knows that they sometimes scream while they play and that alarm is not always the necessary response.

14. *b* is the answer. Frieda's bottom-up processing sent on information about the features of the objects in the advertisement, but it was Cal's suggestion that caused her to see the cows. (pp. 102–103)

a. The expectation of what was in the picture influenced the perception. Frieda *did* use bottom-up processing, but it doesn't explain the difference between her two impressions.

c. Common fate is the grouping principle that uses similar movement to place objects into a group.

d. Similarity is the grouping principle that states that the more resemblance there is between items, the more likely they will be grouped.

15. *c* is the answer. When a person is paying attention to what he or she appears to be paying attention to,

the individual is engaged in overt orienting. (p. 106)

   a. The Stroop task is used to study the effects of divided attention on performance.

   b. Covert orienting occurs when an individual appears to be paying attention to one thing, and is actually attending to something else mentally.

   d. A perceptual set is a readiness to respond to a particular stimulus in a particular way.

Now turn to the quiz analysis table at the end of this chapter to find which areas you know well and which areas you need to work on. Circle the numbers in the table for items on Quiz 1 that you answered correctly.

ANSWERS TO MULTIPLE-CHOICE QUESTIONS

Circle the question numbers you answered correctly.

Sample Quiz 2

1.   *a* is the answer. The cornea is an accessory structure in the visual sensory system that bends the light along with the lens so that light will focus on the retina. (p. 74)

   b. Receptor cells in the visual sensory system are rods and cones. The cornea is not a receptor.

   c. A feature detector is a cell in the cortex that detects specific features of stimuli.

   d. The primary visual cortex is the part of the brain responsible for processing visual information once it has been transduced.

2.   *a* is the answer. Signal detection theory addresses the factors that influence whether we will perceive a stimulus. (p. 72)

   b. Extrasensory perception (ESP) is defined as the ability to perceive stimuli without the use of the five ordinary senses, but it does not address ordinary perception.

   c. Optical acuity theory is not a term.

   d. Weber's law addresses the perception of differences between stimuli, not stimulus detection itself.

3.   *b* is the answer. Changes in internal noise, stimulus intensity, or the workings of the sensory system alter sensitivity. If Jake is asleep, his visual sensory system is not working. Jake's eyes must be open before he can see Benny creep by the car. (p. 72)

   a. If Jake thought that Benny was in for the night, then his expectations of activity would decrease. This would increase the necessary response criterion but would not affect sensitivity.

   c. If Jake thought that Benny's partner was aiming a gun at him, then his motivation to grab Benny might have been lowered. Jake may think he is too close to retirement to take chances. This would affect Jake's motivation, not his sensitivity.

   d. If Jake is not concerned about his record, he may not be as attentive at work. This would lower his response criterion (he is probably a bit reluctant to hear Benny) and increase his absolute threshold (the amount of noise required before Jake hears Benny).

4.   *b* is the answer. The rods, which are photoreceptors in the retina, allow us to see well in the dark. When the lights are first turned out, the rods must become activated. This process takes between a half-hour and forty-five minutes. (p. 75)

   a. Ganglion cells receive information from both rods and cones, but it is the rods that are responsible for dark adaptation.

   c. The muscles of the lens do help us to focus on objects in the environment. However, the level of light in the environment does not affect the efficiency of these muscles.

   d. Dendrites are fibers that are permanent fixtures. They do not have to be resynthesized.

5.   *b* is the answer. The opponent-process theory explains afterimages. When one color in a pair has been inhibited, it will "overreact" and become activated when the other color is no longer stimulated. (p. 79)

   a. There is no such thing as a computational theory of color vision.

   c. Trichromatic theory cannot explain afterimages; it describes how three colors can be combined to create all colors.

   d. Volley theory is another term for the frequency-matching theory of hearing.

6.   *a* is the answer. A very high frequency will produce a very high-pitched sound. (p. 82)

   b. A very low frequency will produce a very low-pitched sound.

   c. A very high amplitude will produce a very loud sound.

   d. A very low amplitude will produce a very soft sound.

7.   *a* is the answer. The pinnas (outer ears) are accessory structures; they modify the sound waves entering the ears. (p. 82)

   b. The cochlea is in the inner ear and would not be directly affected by Adriana's action.

   c. Timbre is a quality of sound not related to the pinnas.

    d. The transduction mechanisms for hearing are in the cochlea and would not be directly affected by movement of the pinnas.

8. *d* is the answer. Papillae contain taste buds. (p. 87)
    a. Feeling a hot shower is the responsibility of the somatosensory system.
    b. If green and red appear the same, one type of iodopsin, the photopigment in cones, may be missing.
    c. Olfaction does not receive information from taste buds.

9. *c* is the answer. Proprioception, which includes kinesthesia and the vestibular sense, is the ability to know where the body parts are in space and in relation to each other. An acrobat would need excellent proprioception. (p. 91)
    a, b. A chef would need very discriminating taste buds, as would a wine taster.
    d. A musician would require an ability to discriminate sounds.

10. *d* is the answer. The people closer to each other are seen as groups. (p. 94)
    a. The grouping principle closure fills in gaps.
    b. Continuity groups seemingly unbroken forms.
    c. Figure-ground divides the perceptual scene into features that are emphasized and those that are not.

11. *b* is the answer. Burglars want to fade into the background. Painting their faces black and wearing dark clothing make it very difficult to see the burglars as separate from the background of the dark sky. (p. 94)
    a. Proximity is the tendency to perceive objects that are close together as part of a group.
    c. Closure is the ability to fill in the gaps when sensory stimulation is missing. The black paint and dark clothing do not cause a lack of stimuli but do affect our ability to distinguish background and foreground.
    d. Things that are similar are perceived as part of the same group. This question deals with just one burglar, not groups of burglars.

12. *c* is the answer. (p. 102)
    a. The contribution of our sensory systems to the process of perception is called bottom-up processing. For example, lateral inhibition causes us to see edges and contrasts quite clearly. Our expectations and motivation do not alter lateral inhibition.
    b. Internal noise is the spontaneous, random firing of neurons and is unaffected by expectations and motivation.
    d. Sensitivity is influenced by internal noise, stimulus intensity, and the health of the sensory systems, not expectations or motivation.

13. *a* is the answer. Feature analysis is part of bottom-up processing. It is usually followed by top-down processing, but that is not described in the item. (p. 102)
    b. There is no such thing as ecological processing; you may have been thinking of the ecological view of perception.
    c. Illusory processing is a made-up term.
    d. Top-down processing and bottom-up processing work together. Lou's top-down processing probably started as soon as the perceptual category "flower" was activated, but her inference that, for example, the flower was given to her by someone who likes her is not described in the question.

14. *c* is the answer. John has a perceptual set; he expects the footsteps on the stairs to be his wife's. (p. 102)
    a, b. Feature analysis is a type of bottom-up processing. If John had analyzed the features of the footsteps in order to determine if they were his wife's, he would not have almost kissed the landlord. John's expectations made him think that he heard his wife.
    d. There is no such thing as an auditory gradient.

15. *a* is the answer. Covert orienting is a shift of attention that isn't possible for the casual observer to see. (p. 106)
    b. An overt attention shift would be turning away from Rich to stare at a person approaching you.
    c, d. Parallel and serial processing are types of searches.

Now turn to the quiz analysis table at the end of this chapter to find which areas you know well and which areas you need to work on. Circle the numbers in the table for items on Quiz 2 that you answered correctly.

For each question you answered correctly, circle its number. (Quiz 1 numbers are not shaded; Quiz 2 numbers are shaded.) Are there patterns in the types of questions or the topics you got wrong that could direct your further study? Did you improve from Quiz 1 to Quiz 2?

TOPIC	TYPE OF QUESTION		
	DEFINITION	COMPREHENSION	APPLICATION
Sensory Systems	1, 3	2	
	1		2
Seeing			4, 5
		3	4, 5
Hearing		6	7
			6, 7
Chemical Senses			
			8
Sensing Your Body			8, 9, 10
			9
Organizing			11, 12
			10, 11
Recognizing		13	14
	12	13	14
Attention			15
			15

TOTAL CORRECT BY QUIZ:

QUIZ 1:
QUIZ 2:

Chapter 4

Consciousness

LEARNING OBJECTIVES

1. Define consciousness. (p. 116)

2. Define state of consciousness. Distinguish among the various levels of conscious activity: conscious, nonconscious, preconscious, and unconscious or subconscious. Give an example of each. (pp. 116–117)

3. Describe blindsight, priming, and the mere-exposure effect. (pp. 117–118)

4. Define subliminal perception. Discuss the debate about the effects of subliminal perception on behavior. Describe the research on subliminal messages in rock music. (pp. 118–121)

5. Define altered state of consciousness. (p. 121)

6. Compare and contrast slow-wave and REM sleep. Be sure to discuss how the two types of sleep differ in terms of physiological arousal and brain activity. (pp. 123-124)

7. Describe a night's sleep. Discuss the changes in sleep that occur over the course of the life span. (p. 124)

8. Discuss the symptoms of insomnia, narcolepsy, sleep apnea, sudden infant death syndrome (SIDS), sleepwalking, nightmares, night terrors, and REM behavior disorder. Specify the sleep stages in which sleepwalking, nightmares, night terrors, and REM behavior disorder occur. (pp. 124–125)

9. Define circadian rhythm and discuss the brain's role in regulating sleep patterns. Discuss jet lag and explain how to reduce the fatigue and disorientation that results from shifts in sleep patterns. (pp. 125–126)

10. Discuss the effects of sleep deprivation. Describe the manner in which the body compensates for lost REM and non-REM sleep. Discuss the hypotheses on the reasons for both types of sleep (pp. 126–127)

11. Define dreams and lucid dreaming. (pp. 127-128)

12. Discuss the various theories that explain why people dream, including wish fulfillment and activation-synthesis theory. (p. 128)

13. Define hypnosis and describe the process of becoming hypnotized. (p. 129)

14. Define hypnotic susceptibility, age regression, posthypnotic suggestions, and posthypnotic amnesia. Describe the changes people experience during hypnosis. (p. 129)

15. Compare and contrast the role, state, and dissociation theories of hypnosis. (p. 130)

16. Discuss the applications and limitations of hypnosis. (p. 131)

17. Define and describe the effects of meditation. List the common characteristics of meditation techniques. (pp. 131-132)

18. Define psychoactive drugs and psychopharmacology. Explain the function of the blood-brain barrier and discuss how agonist, antagonist and other types of drugs work. (pp. 132–133)

19. Define substance abuse. Distinguish between psychological dependence and physical dependence, or addiction. Define withdrawal syndrome and tolerance. (pp. 133–134)

20. Discuss the influence of expectations on drug effects. (p. 134)

21. Define depressant. Describe the effects of alcohol and barbiturates on the nervous system and behavior. (pp. 134–135)

22. Define stimulant. Describe the effects of amphetamines, cocaine, caffeine, nicotine, and MDMA on the nervous system and behavior. (pp. 135–136)

23. Define opiates. Describe the effects of opium, morphine, codeine, and heroin on the nervous system. (p. 137)

24. Define hallucinogens. Describe the effects of LSD and marijuana on the nervous system and behavior. (pp. 137–138)

KEY TERMS

1. **Consciousness** is the awareness of both external stimuli and your own mental activity. (p. 116)

> *Example:* At this moment, you are aware of the words printed on this page. You may also be aware of noises around you, such as a radio playing or a jet flying overhead.

I. THE SCOPE OF CONSCIOUSNESS

2. **State of consciousness** refers to the characteristics of consciousness at any particular moment. (p. 116)

3. The **conscious level** of consciousness holds the thoughts and mental processes that you are aware of from moment to moment. (p. 116)

> *Example:* You are conscious of the words you are reading at this moment.

4. The **nonconscious level** of activity includes physiological processes that you are not conscious of. Training in techniques such as biofeedback can make you conscious of them indirectly. (p. 116)

> *Example:* Your brain is sensing the amount of sugar in your blood, but you cannot consciously experience this activity, even if you try to attend to it.

5. The **preconscious level** of activity stores sensations, memories, inferences, and assumptions that are not at the conscious level but that can be easily brought into consciousness. (p. 117)

> *Example:* Before reading this sentence, you probably did not feel your socks or your underwear on your skin. But now that you are attending to them, you can feel these physical sensations. They were at the preconscious level but were easily brought into consciousness, in this case by a shift in attention.

6. The **unconscious level** of activity, according to Freud, holds sexual, aggressive, and other impulses as well as once-conscious but unacceptable thoughts and feelings that would cause anxiety if they became conscious again. (p. 117)

> *Example:* A wish to kill your sister is a thought that could cause you anxiety. According to Freud, this thought would be kept in the unconscious to prevent it from doing so.

7. The **subconscious level** of mental activity includes mental processes that are important but normally inaccessible. Unlike Freud's unconscious, subconscious material isn't necessarily negative. (p. 117)

> *Example:* In studies of priming, people could not remember having seen certain words on a study list; however, they could solve anagrams of those words faster than anagrams of words they had not seen previously. The influence of having studied the words was subconscious and inaccessible.

8. **Altered states of consciousness** occur when changes in the stream of consciousness are noticeably different from normal waking experience. (pp. 121)

II. SLEEPING AND DREAMING

9. **Slow-wave sleep** is a term for the first four stages of sleep, when breathing is slow, heartbeat is regular, and blood pressure is reduced. (p. 123)

> *REMEMBER:* These stages of sleep are called slow-wave sleep because your EEG shows slower and slower waves as you progress through the four stages of this type of sleep.

10. **REM (Rapid eye movement) sleep** is characterized by EEG and physiological measures (heart rate, respiration, blood pressure) that are similar to those that occur when the person is awake. During REM sleep, the eyes move rapidly back and forth, and muscle tone decreases to the point of near-paralysis. (p. 123)

> *REMEMBER:* This stage is called paradoxical because physiologically our bodies and brains are very active while our muscles are functionally paralyzed.

11. **Insomnia** is the inability to fall or stay asleep. People with insomnia report feeling tired during the day. (p. 124)

> *REMEMBER:* The Latin word <u>in</u> means "no," "not," or "without." <u>Somnus</u> means "sleep." Therefore, <u>insomnia</u> means "without sleep."

12. **Narcolepsy** is a disorder in which people fall directly into REM sleep from an active, waking state. They experience all the physiological changes that occur during REM sleep, including reduced muscle tone. (p. 124)

13. **Sleep apnea** is a disorder in which people stop breathing momentarily while sleeping, up to hundreds of times per night. Apnea episodes wake the sleepers, and thus people suffering from this disorder feel unrested in the morning and tired throughout the day. (p. 125)

14. In **sudden infant death syndrome (SIDS)**, a sleeping baby stops breathing but does not awaken and therefore suffocates. (p. 125)

15. **Sleepwalking**, which occurs during non-REM sleep and is most common during childhood, is walking while asleep. Awakening a sleepwalker is not dangerous. (p. 125)

16. **Nightmares** are frightening dreams that occur during REM sleep. (p. 125)

17. **Night terrors**, which occur during stage 4 sleep, are frightening non-REM dreams that bring on intense fear after waking. These fearful episodes may last for as long as half an hour. (p. 125)

18. **REM behavior disorder** is similar to sleepwalking, but it occurs during REM sleep. The normal paralysis that accompanies REM sleep is absent, thus allowing a person to act out dreams. This can be especially dangerous when the dreams are of a violent nature. (p. 125)

19. **Circadian rhythm** is a term for the physiological and behavioral patterns that repeat on a 24-hour cycle. These cycles are governed by an internal biological clock. (p. 125)

20. **Jet lag** is a disruption of the sleep-wake cycle. Physiologically, the body is ready to wake up or sleep at an inappropriate time of day for a particular time zone. Jet lag is common among travelers arriving in time zones very different from their own, especially when traveling from west to east. (p. 126)

21. **Dreams** are storylike sequences of images, sensations, and perceptions that occur during REM sleep. (p. 127)

22. **Lucid dreaming** is knowing during a dream that you are dreaming. (p. 128)

REMEMBER: The word <u>lucid</u> means "clear" or "readily understood." Lucid dreamers clearly know while still asleep that they are dreaming.

III. HYPNOSIS

23. **Hypnosis** is an altered state of consciousness brought on by special techniques and characterized by susceptibility to suggestions made by the hypnotist. (p. 129)

Example: Maria, who is hypnotized, believes that she can see a cat sitting on her lap because the hypnotist has suggested to her that a cat is there.

24. **Hypnotic susceptibility** is the degree to which people can become hypnotized and follow a hypnotist's suggestions. (p. 129)

25. The **state theory** of hypnosis maintains that hypnosis is a special altered state of consciousness. Supporters of the state theory believe that real, significant changes in basic mental processes take place during hypnosis. (p. 130)

26. The **role theory** of hypnosis states that people only play the "role" of being hypnotized, which includes complying with the hypnotist's directions. (p. 130)

27. **Dissociation theory** contends that hypnosis is a splitting of the central control of thought processes and behavior. The hypnotized person agrees to give some of the control to the hypnotist. (p. 130)

IV. PSYCHOACTIVE DRUGS

28. **Psychoactive drugs** bring about psychological changes by affecting the physiological functioning of the brain. (p. 132)

Example: LSD, a psychedelic, changes the perception of sensory information and drastically alters thought processes.

29. **Psychopharmacology** is the study of psychoactive drugs. (p. 132)

30. The **blood-brain barrier** is part of the structure of the blood vessels that supply the brain. Many chemicals cannot permeate the barrier, and thus do not have access to brain tissue. (p. 133)

31. **Agonists** are drugs that mimic the effects of a particular neurotransmitter by binding to its receptors. (p. 133)

Example: Agonists for endorphins stimulate endorphin receptors, resulting in the same mood-elevating response as an endorphin would cause.

32. **Antagonists** prevent neurotransmitters from having an effect by blocking receptors' ability to accept specific neurotransmitters. (p. 133)

Example: Naloxone, an endorphin antagonist, keeps endorphins from binding with receptors, thereby preventing a "high."

33. **Substance abuse** is the self-administration of drugs in ways that are disapproved of by one's culture. (p. 133)

34. **Psychological dependence** is the process whereby a person needs to continue taking a drug, despite its

adverse effects, in order to maintain a sense of well-being. (p. 133)

35. Physical dependence, or **addiction**, is the process whereby the body has a physical need for a drug. Addicts who discontinue drug use typically experience very unpleasant, and often dangerous, withdrawal symptoms. (p. 134)

 Example: Carol's addiction to a barbiturate became evident when, after attempting to quit using the drug, she experienced restlessness, violent outbursts, convulsions, and hallucinations.

36. A **withdrawal syndrome** is what occurs when a drug to which a person is physically addicted is removed. Symptoms vary from drug to drug, but usually include an intense craving for the drug and its effects. (p. 134)

37. **Tolerance**, a by-product of addiction, is the process whereby repeated use of an addictive substance results in the body's requiring ever-increasing amounts of the drug to achieve the same psychological and physical effects. (p. 134)

 Example: After using cocaine daily for several weeks, Jesse began to need more and more of the drug to achieve the same "high" as he had initially experienced.

38. **Depressants**, which include alcohol and barbiturates, reduce activity in the central nervous system. (p. 134)

 REMEMBER: Depressants usually make a person sedate or calm.

39. **Stimulants** increase central nervous system and behavioral activity. They include amphetamines, cocaine, nicotine, caffeine, and MDMA. Overdoses of cocaine, especially of crack cocaine, can be deadly. (p. 135)

40. **Opiates**, including opium, morphine, heroin, and codeine, produce sleep and pain relief. These substances are highly addictive, and overdoses can be fatal. (p. 137)

 REMEMBER: In Chapter 2 you learned that your brain produces a class of neurotransmitters called endorphins, which have effects similar to those of morphine.

41. **Hallucinogens** or psychedelics, such as LSD and marijuana, cause a loss of contact with reality and changes in thought, perception, and emotion. Because many of these changes are similar to symptoms of psychotic forms of mental illness, these drugs are sometimes referred to as psychotomimetics, meaning they mimic psychosis. (p. 137)

CONCEPTS AND EXERCISES

No. 1: Types of Consciousness

Completing this exercise should help you to achieve Learning Objective 2.

Several types of activities are described in the following list. Decide whether these activities are conscious, preconscious, nonconscious, or unconscious. Answers may be used more than once or not at all.

1. Belinda, enjoying the taste of her favorite food, thanks her mother for preparing it. _____

2. Carmen is putting an adhesive bandage on a cut. She cannot feel the neural activity in her brain that is directing her hand movements. _____

3. Leslie Anne has been in a car accident. She is so busy helping people that she does not feel the pain from her broken collarbone. _____

No. 2: Stages of Sleep at a Slumber Party

Completing this exercise should help you to achieve Learning Objectives 7 and 8.

Joanna's daughter is having a slumber party. The noise died down about one hour ago. Joanna decides to see if everyone is asleep. Match the listed stages of sleep or sleep disorders with the description of what Joanna finds when she checks on the girls. Answers may be used more than once or not at all.

1. LaVonne is perfectly still except for a few twitches of her face and hands. Joanna notices that the girl's eyes are moving rapidly back and forth even though they are closed. _____

2. Joanna spies Isabella in the corner of the room all curled up but clearly still awake. She tells Joanna that it is always hard for her to fall asleep no matter what the time. _____

3. Suddenly Brenda sits up in her sleeping bag. Staring straight ahead, she lets out a bloodcurdling scream. It takes Joanna half an hour to calm her. What has Brenda just experienced? _____

4. Joanna counts only six girls in the room. She knows that there should be seven. She makes a quick search of the house and finds Juliette stumbling around the living room, still asleep. _____

- Sleep apnea
- Insomnia
- Night terrors
- Nightmares

° REM sleep
° Stage 1 sleep
° Sleepwalking

CRITICAL THINKING

Sam and Martina have been put on a case involving a robbery at a house in the country. The thieves left no marks on any doors or windows. Sam assumes, given the rural location, that the owners didn't lock the house every night and so asks the husband what their habits are regarding the doors and windows. The owner, named Jack, says, "We used to live in the city where we locked our doors every night. When we moved out here, we just kept up the habit. I lock up every night while Leona is gettin' ready for bed. And, no, we haven't given a key to anyone else." Sam, however, is convinced that Jack must have given keys to someone else and then forgotten about it.

Meanwhile, Martina and Leona are chatting like long lost friends and eating pie in the kitchen. Leona is describing a hypnosis demonstration in which she has just participated. The hypnotist told her that for two weeks she would go outside and howl at the moon like a dog. She laughs and says, "For the first couple of nights, Jack came out just to see if I would do it, but now he sleeps right through the noise. I still don't believe it myself." Martina asks, "Who gets up first in the morning, you or Jack?" "Oh, I don't know; it varies, I guess," Leona replies.

Sam comes grumpily into the kitchen and motions Martina over to the door for a private consultation. "I'm sure these old folks just gave the wrong kind of neighbor a key. We should go question all the neighbors in the vicinity."

Martina shakes her head slowly and tells Sam to have some pie. She says that Jack and Leona didn't give a key to anyone and that even if they did, that person didn't rob the house.

Using the five critical thinking questions in your text, the clues in the story, and what you have learned in this chapter, answer the following:

1. What is Sam's hypothesis?

2. What evidence supports Sam's hypothesis?

3. What is Martina's alternative hypothesis?

4. What evidence supports Martina's hypothesis?

PERSONAL LEARNING ACTIVITIES

1. Examine your own behavior for habits that occur at the preconscious level of consciousness. For example, do you bite your nails or twist your hair without

realizing it until someone brings it to your attention? (Learning Objective 2)

2. Evaluate your amount of sleep. Do you sleep more or less on weekends? Can you tell a difference in your motivation level on days after you have had less sleep? (Learning Objective 9)

3. Keep a record of the number and type of instances in which you see hypnosis used in a television program (soap opera, sitcom, etc.). Which theory—role, state, or dissociation—does the show seem to portray as the hypnotized person's experience? Is one theory portrayed more often than another? Does the use of hypnosis on television fit with the more or less controversial applications discussed in your text? (Learning Objectives 15 and 16)

4. Study your use of any psychoactive drugs you ordinarily ingest. For instance, do you have a caffeinated drink in the morning and find that you feel drowsy without one? Are there times when you are more likely to need a pain reliever, an allergy medication, or a sleep aid? (Learning Objective 18)

5. While you watch a few of your favorite television programs, note any statements or actions that relate to drug use. Are there misperceptions about the effects of any drugs? Do people casually mention that they "have" to get a cup of coffee or an alcoholic drink? What types of messages relate to legal and illegal drug use? (Learning Objectives 18, 21–24)

WHAT SHOULD I WRITE ABOUT?

Sometimes it seems like the hardest part of writing a term paper is getting started. Picking a topic can be overwhelming the first few times you have to write such a paper. There may be many topics that interest you, making it difficult to narrow down your choices. In a chapter like *Consciousness*, it seems that every topic looks exciting. How can you decide whether you should write a paper on consciousness in general or on one of the states of consciousness?

If you pay attention to how your textbook is organized, you may find that question not so difficult to answer. First, your textbook is organized into major sections. In this particular chapter, you have sections on states of consciousness, sleeping and dreaming, hypnosis, and psychoactive drugs. Each of these sections might be taken as a suggestion that a topic that cuts across both of them is too broad. A term paper is a chance to explore research on a topic, and if you try to write a paper on consciousness in general, you may find yourself overwhelmed with the amount of research available. Particularly if you are a beginner at writing term papers, you should try to choose a topic that falls within on of the major sections of your text.

But the way your text is organized in sections is not the only way to learn how to select a paper topic. Another thing you should notice, as you decide on a topic, is the number of citations associated with the topic you are considering. Within each section, research is cited to support the statements your textbook authors are making. When you write a term paper, you will need to have plenty of citations to back up the statements that *you* are making. If you are considering a topic that has few cites associated with it, you might begin to wonder if there will be much research on that area. An example of such a topic in this chapter is the section on "Levels of Consciousness." Contrast that section to the section on "Mental Processing Without Awareness." The latter section has a lot more research cited within it, which gives you a good start on reading material from which to build your term paper. The former section has only a few, which means you might have more difficulty finding research associated with that topic. In this example, a paper on "Processing without Awareness" or "Priming" would probably be a better choice than a paper on "Levels of Consciousness."

Here are some questions to ask yourself as you try to choose a paper topic:

1. Is the topic you have been thinking about one that cuts across sections of your psychology text? If so, you may want to see if you can narrow it down to a topic that falls within a single section. As you become a better and better writer, it will be less risky to choose a topic that cross-cuts sections, but if you are a beginner, you might select a topic within a single section.

2. Which specific topics in the chapter have a lot of research cites associated with them? Examples in this chapter include priming, sleep disorders, and circadian rhythms. There are many other good topics in this chapter, but do pay attention to the number of cites associated with any topic you are considering.

THE INTERNET

The Psychabilities web site that accompanies this text offers many resources relevant to this chapter. They include NetLab exercises, Thinking Critically and Evaluating Research exercises, ACE chapter quizzes, recommended web links, and articles on current events, books, and movies. Go to http://college.hmco.com, select Psychology, and then this textbook.

MULTIPLE-CHOICE QUESTIONS

SAMPLE QUIZ 1

1. A faith healer claims to cure cancer by asking people to become aware of their livers and to control the liver's removal of impurities from the bloodstream. You know that this is impossible because the activities of the liver occur at the _____ level.
   a. preconscious
   b. nonconscious
   c. unconscious
   d. metaconscious

2. While riding to work on the bus, Sophia saw a garbage truck, which reminded her that she had not taken out her own garbage. The information that she had planned to take out her garbage before leaving for work existed at the _____ level before she saw the truck.
   a. unconscious
   b. subconscious
   c. nonconscious
   d. preconscious

3. You call up a potential date and get an answering machine message. In leaving your message, you mean to say "I'd like to see you," but instead say "I'd like to feel you." This Freudian slip is caused by id impulses originating in the
   a. preconscious.
   b. unconscious.
   c. subconscious.
   d. nonconscious.

4. During a psychology experiment, Duane looks through two viewing tubes so that each eye sees a different computer screen. A priming word was presented to one eye, though masked, so that Duane was not aware that he had been primed. The above experiment is *probably* trying to study
   a. the activation-synthesis theory.
   b. our ability to be aware of stimuli presented outside of our awareness.
   c. the mind-body problem—in other words, what the relationship is between the conscious mind and the physical brain.
   d. subliminal perception.

5. An EEG taken during REM sleep would most closely resemble which other stage of sleep?
   a. Stage 1
   b. Stage 2
   c. Stage 3
   d. Stage 4

6. Jane came home from class excited about a new love interest. While pacing around her apartment talking about how they met, she suddenly collapsed and entered REM sleep. Jane is most likely experiencing
   a. insomnia.
   b. sleep apnea.

    c. narcolepsy.

    d. REM behavior disorder.

7. Yesterday, James returned to the United States after spending a year studying in France. He is not sleeping well and complains of being tired. His friends say that he is irritable. James is most likely suffering from

    a. sleep apnea.

    b. a disruption of circadian rhythm.

    c. narcolepsy.

    d. REM rebound.

8. Barry has just served for four nights as a subject in a sleep study in which he was awakened each time he entered REM sleep. Now that the experiment is over, Barry will *most likely*

    a. be extremely irritable until his body has made up the lost REM sleep.

    b. sleep so deeply for several nights that dreaming will be minimal.

    c. experience an increase in sleep stages 1 through 4 for the next few nights.

    d. experience an increase in his REM sleep tonight.

9. REM sleep is most prevalent during

    a. infancy.

    b. puberty.

    c. young adulthood.

    d. old age.

10. Which of the following is *not* a current theory of why we dream?

    a. As we dream, our nerve connections are developing, checking, and expanding.

    b. We dream to satisfy unconscious urges.

    c. Dreaming allows us to solidify what we have learned the previous day.

    d. Dreaming reduces our level of mental activity, heart rate, and blood pressure.

11. Khalid's therapist suggests that they use hypnosis to help him to quit smoking. During hypnosis, the therapist tells Khalid that his next sight of a cigarette will make him feel nauseous. The therapist most likely is using _____ to help Khalid.

    a. age regression

    b. posthypnotic amnesia

    c. posthypnotic suggestion

    d. reduced planfulness

12. Eli's hypnotist suggested that Eli saw a big fluffy cat sitting in the chair next to him. Although no cat was present, Eli said that he could see its tail swishing back and forth. This is characteristic of which type of hypnotic behavior?

    a. Reduced planfulness

    b. Role-playing

    c. Reduced reality testing

    d. Redistributed attention

13. If Eli is pretending that he sees a cat seated next to him only because the situation provides him with a socially acceptable reason for seeing things that do not exist, this would support the _____ theory of hypnosis.

    a. dissociation

    b. lucid

    c. role

    d. state

14. An antagonist operates by

    a. altering the amount of neurotransmitter released by a neuron.

    b. fitting snugly into a neurotransmitter's receptor sites without acting upon the receptor.

    c. fitting snugly into a neurotransmitter's reception sites and acting on the receptor as a neurotransmitter would.

    d. blocking inactivation.

15. You see a person come into class and take what looks like an aspirin. By the end of class, this person reports seeing weird distortions of reality like "smelling colors." Later, the person panics because he thinks he is going crazy. The pill most likely contained

    a. LSD.

    b. barbiturates.

    c. cocaine.

    d. amphetamines.

Total Correct (See answer key) _____

SAMPLE QUIZ 2

Use this quiz to reassess your learning after taking Quiz 1 and reviewing the chapter.

1. Material that can be easily brought into consciousness is at the _____ level.

    a. nonconscious

    b. preconscious

    c. subconscious

    d. unconscious

2. Lorena dreamed that her friends kept giving her their books to carry. Soon Lorena was crushed under the huge stack of books she carried. In describing the dream, Lorena said, "I don't know why I had this dream; my friends are the pest. Oops, I mean the best." Lorena's Freudian psychoanalyst suggests that she can't consciously admit that she is angry with her friends. Lorena's therapist would most likely say that those negative

feelings are kept at the _____ level of consciousness.

a. nonconscious
b. preconscious
c. subconscious
d. unconscious

3. Which of the following is the best example of a process operating at the nonconscious level?
   a. Alice names all her teachers from kindergarten to the present.
   b. Brian accidentally calls his sister "creepy" instead of "sleepy" because he dislikes her, although he is not consciously aware of it.
   c. Chris now likes country music, but doesn't realize that it's due to hearing it at work.
   d. Derek uses biofeedback to help him control his blood pressure.

4. Which of the following statements about priming experiments is *not* true?
   a. People tend to respond faster or more accurately to previously seen stimuli.
   b. People tend to respond faster or more accurately to previously seen stimuli, even when they cannot consciously recall having seen those stimuli.
   c. Priming research demonstrates mental processing without awareness.
   d. Students who listened to tape recording of textbook chapters responded faster or more accurately on test questions covering the same material.

5. Your friend Jay suggests that to increase the sale of Chocomints at your next charity film festival you should insert the subliminal message "Eat Chocomints" in the film. According to the "Thinking Critically" section in the text, you should tell Jay that the "Eat Chocomints" message most likely would
   a. anger the audience.
   b. be more effective than a regular advertising campaign.
   c. have to appear more than once a minute to have an effect.
   d. not affect the audience.

6. Which stage of slow-wave sleep is the deepest?
   a. Stage 2.
   b. Stage 3.
   c. Stage 4.
   d. Stage REM.

7. Snookers the cat has decided that he wants a snack. However, his owner is taking a nap. Despite several minutes of tap-dancing on his owner's face, Snookers cannot wake her up. The cat's owner has most likely been asleep for
   a. no more than five minutes.
   b. no more than ten minutes.
   c. at least thirty minutes.
   d. This cannot be determined.

8. While dreaming she is climbing a rope, Sheandra jerks her arms and legs as though she is climbing, literally dragging the sheets and blankets off the bed. Sheandra has
   a. sleep apnea.
   b. sleepwalking.
   c. narcolepsy.
   d. REM behavior disorder.

9. Circadian rhythms are
   a. the natural beats of the body's cardiovascular system.
   b. the brain waves that occur during stage 4 sleep.
   c. regular physiological processes whose cycles repeat about every 24 hours.
   d. externally cued sleep-wake cycles.

10. Which of the following people would most likely have the greatest amount of REM sleep?
    a. A person who goes to bed and gets up at exactly the same time each day
    b. A ninety-year-old person on vacation
    c. A student who has been studying constantly for three days and three nights
    d. A person who has just recovered from hypersomnia

11. Melvin is having a terrible dream. He is being chased by a professional boxer, a psychotic killer, and an irate basketball coach. Realizing that this is only a dream, Melvin turns around and begins to beat the three of them unconscious with karate skills he never knew he had. This is an example of
    a. apneatic dreaming.
    b. lucid dreaming.
    c. narcolepsy.
    d. circadian exchange.

12. An example of a successful posthypnotic suggestion to Brendan is
    a. Brendan believes during hypnosis that he is unable to see.
    b. Brendan is instructed during hypnosis to cluck like a chicken whenever anyone says "Hi," and he does this when he is no longer hypnotized.
    c. Brendan cannot remember what happened while he was hypnotized.
    d. Brendan, while he is no longer hypnotized, is told that his pants are ripped, and he checks them.

13. Brendan believes during hypnosis that he cannot see. Later, Brendan tells you that he felt like he was sharing control over his actions with the hypnotist. It was as if he could not control his ability to see while he was hypnotized. Brendan's description of his experience agrees most with the _____ theory of hypnosis.
    a. dissociation
    b. lucid
    c. role
    d. state

14. A mantra is
    a. a person trained in meditation.
    b. the object or sound the meditator focuses on.
    c. the position a person assumes when meditating.
    d. a special form of meditation.

15. Mariah ingested a drug that binds directly to her GABA receptors to enhance neurotransmission at GABA synapses. This drug is *probably*
    a. cocaine.
    b. a psychedelic.
    c. an opiate.
    d. alcohol.

Total Correct (See answer key) _____

ANSWERS TO CONCEPTS AND EXERCISES

No. 1: Types of Consciousness

1. *Conscious.* Belinda is aware of the taste of the food in her mouth. (p. 116)

2. *Nonconscious.* Carmen is not and cannot become aware of the neural activity in her motor cortex. (p. 116)

3. *Preconscious.* Leslie Anne has her attention focused on the people who need her help. Once she attends to the pain in her collarbone, it will easily come into consciousness. (p. 117)

No. 2: Stages of Sleep at a Slumber Party

1. *REM sleep.* LaVonne is not moving because muscle tone decreases to near-paralysis during this stage. The eyes move rapidly back and forth. (p. 123)

2. *Insomnia.* This sleep disorder is characterized by an inability to fall asleep. (p. 124)

3. *Night terrors.* Night terrors are vivid and terrifying dreams that occur during stage 4 sleep. It often takes quite a while to calm people after they have a night terror experience. (p. 125)

4. *Sleepwalking.* Juliette is taking a tour of the house, but she is still asleep. This is sleepwalking. (p. 125)

ANSWERS TO CRITICAL THINKING

1. Sam's hypothesis is that someone used a key to get into the house.

2. The evidence in support of the hypothesis is that none of the doors or windows had marks on them typical of forcible entry. Sam also believes that Jack has just forgotten that he gave a key to someone.

3. Martina believes that Leona has probably gone out every night since her hypnosis escapade to "howl at the moon." She probably hasn't remembered to lock the doors when she comes back in because that has been Jack's responsibility for years. Therefore, any passing burglar could have just walked into the house.

4. The evidence supporting Martina's hypothesis is that if either Jack or Leona consistently got up first and left the house each morning, one of them would probably have noticed the unlocked door. However, if the first person up varied, then each probably assumed the other had unlocked the door on the way out of the house.

ANSWERS TO MULTIPLE-CHOICE QUESTIONS

Circle the question numbers you answered correctly.

Sample Quiz 1

1. *b* is the answer. The activity of the liver is nonconscious. Nonconscious processes are those physiological activities, such as blood pressure, that people cannot become directly aware of. (p. 116)
   a. Preconscious activities are those that are easily brought into consciousness.
   c. The unconscious level is where Freud believed unacceptable impulses reside.
   d. Metaconscious is not a term from your text.

2. *d* is the answer. Memories stored at the preconscious level, such as a childhood birthday party or where you left your keys, are easy to access. (p. 117)
   a. Negative memories and desires are kept out of consciousness at the unconscious level, according to Freud.

b. Memories at the subconscious level are difficult to access, similar to those at the unconscious level.

c. Nonconscious processes are those physiological activities, such as nervous system activation, that people cannot become directly aware of.

3. *b* is the answer. Unacceptable sexual and aggressive urges are pushed into the unconscious, according to Freud. (p. 117)

a. Preconscious activities are physical sensations and memories that are easily brought into consciousness.

c. The subconscious level is similar to the unconscious level, because both operate outside our awareness. However, subconscious is the term used by people who do not accept Freud's view that it stores mainly unacceptable impulses relating to sex and aggression.

d. Nonconscious processes are those physiological activities, such as brain activity level, that people cannot become directly aware of.

4. *b* is the answer. Priming research shows mental processing without awareness. (p. 118)

a. The activation-synthesis theory suggests that we dream due to meaningful activation of our cerebral cortex by REM sleep.

c. Priming research cannot determine the relationship between our mind and physical brain.

d. Subliminal perception requires that the original stimulus was too faint or presented too quickly for you even to perceive it. In addition, studies of subliminal perception are generally concerned with persuasion through subliminal messages. In priming studies, the original stimulus is noticed and considered by the participants, but then not remembered consciously as having been seen before—perhaps because too many were presented or because they are asked about them in a different context.

5. *a* is the answer. The EEG during REM sleep looks similar to that of stage 1; it appears as though the person is awake. (p. 123)

b, c, d.. The EEG appears to slow down in stages 2, 3, and 4. The waves would look slower on the EEG.

6. *c* is the answer. People who have narcolepsy often fall asleep in the middle of an active waking state. They immediately shift into active sleep. (p. 124)

a. Insomnia is the inability to fall asleep or stay asleep.

b. Sleep apnea occurs when people stop breathing while sleeping, often hundreds of times a night.

d. REM behavior disorder is a lack of the near-paralysis that usually happens during REM sleep. Having muscle tone/control allows people to act out dreams, with dangerous results.

7. *b* is the answer. James has disrupted his circadian rhythm by changing time zones. (p. 126)

a. Sleep apnea occurs when sleep is interrupted because the sleeper has stopped breathing.

c. Narcolepsy causes people to shift into active sleep in the middle of an active waking state.

d. REM rebound occurs when people have been deprived of REM sleep, which causes them to have much more than the usual amount of REM sleep on the first uninterrupted night's sleep.

8. *d* is the answer. Barry will probably double the percentage of time he spends in REM sleep during his first uninterrupted night's sleep, due to the REM rebound effect. (p. 127)

a. Barry might be irritable, but that isn't the primary effect of REM sleep deprivation.

b. Because Barry will increase the percentage of time he is in REM sleep, he may have more dreams than usual.

c. A higher percentage of time will be spent in REM sleep than usual, not slow-wave sleep.

9. *a* is the answer. An average infant sleeps 16 hours a day; about 8 hours of that is spent in REM. (p. 127)

b, c, d. As people get older, they spend less and less time asleep. Most of the loss is a decrease in REM sleep.

10. *d* is the answer. During dreaming, our mental activity, heart rate, and blood pressure are similar to those of a person who is awake. They are not decreased. (p. 123, 128)

a, b, c. These are all possible explanations of why people dream.

11. *c* is the answer. The therapist is giving a suggestion during hypnosis that will influence Khalid after he is no longer hypnotized. (p. 129)

a. In age regression, the person seemingly returns to childhood in thoughts or actions while hypnotized.

b. Posthypnotic amnesia is a person's inability to remember what happened while he or she was hypnotized.

d. A characteristic of people who are hypnotized is reduced planfulness. Khalid may tend not to initiate actions while hypnotized, but the therapist is trying to change his later behavior; therefore, this is not the best answer.

12. *c* is the answer. The ability to see things that are not there, or not to see things that are there, is the result of a reduction in reality testing. (p. 129)
   a. Hypnotized people do not initiate plans on their own. They usually prefer to wait until the hypnotist tells them what to do. This is not, however, the reason Eli saw the cat when it was not there.
   b. An example of role-playing would be acting like a cat or feeling as though you were someone else or a different age.
   d. When attention is redistributed, one of the senses may seem to fill perceptions. For example, the hypnotist's voice may seem to be the only stimulus. Redistributed attention would not explain why Eli saw a cat that did not exist.

13. *c* is the answer. Eli is acting in accordance with the social role of being a hypnosis subject; therefore, he is not in a different state. (p. 130)
   a. The dissociation theory states that people will experience changes in mental processes if enough control is relinquished to the hypnotist. (p. 178)
   b. This is not a theory of hypnosis. You may have been thinking of lucid dreaming.
   d. State theorists would argue that hypnosis causes an altered state of mental activity, not compliance with a social role.

14. *b* is the answer. An antagonist blocks other neurotransmitters or drugs from using the receptor. It "antagonizes" them! (p. 133)
   a. Drugs may change the amount of neurotransmitter available, but an antagonist doesn't have this function.
   c. This describes the actions of an agonist.
   d. Some drugs may block inactivation, but an antagonist doesn't operate that way.

15. *a* is the answer. LSD and other hallucinogens create distortions in perception and loss of identity. Unpleasant hallucinations and delusions can occur even during the first use of LSD. (p. 137)
   b. The main effect of barbiturates are sleepiness, loss of muscle coordination, and lowered attention.
   c. Cocaine is a stimulant that encourages self-confidence and well-being, but may also cause insomnia, paranoia, seizures, and strokes.
   d. Amphetamines, which are also stimulants, increase arousal and suppress appetite, but put a person at risk for anxiety, insomnia, and heart problems.

Now turn to the quiz analysis table at the end of this chapter to find which areas you know well and which areas you need to work on. Circle the numbers in the table for items on Quiz 1 that you answered correctly.

ANSWERS TO MULTIPLE-CHOICE QUESTIONS

Circle the question numbers you answered correctly.

Sample Quiz 2

1. *b* is the answer. Preconscious memories can be recalled easily. (p. 117)
   a. Nonconscious processes are those physiological activities that people cannot become directly aware of.
   c. Subconscious activity includes thought processes that cannot easily be brought into consciousness, such as priming and mere-exposure. This label is used by those who disagree with Freud's theory about the unconscious.
   d. Unconscious processes are also not easily brought into consciousness. Freud suggested that socially unacceptable urges are kept in the unconscious.

2. *d* is the answer. A Freudian would say that unacceptable thoughts and memories are kept in the unconscious to protect a person from anxiety. (p. 117)
   a. Nonconscious activities are those biological activities that Lorena cannot become directly aware of.
   b. The preconscious level of consciousness can be easily accessed. It includes memories that you are not aware of, but could be.
   c. The subconscious is similar to the unconscious, because neither is easily accessible, but Freudians did not use this term. In addition, the term subconscious is used for the level at which research-supported processes such as the mere-exposure effect and priming take place.

3. *d* is the answer. Nonconscious activity is not available to our conscious awareness. In biofeedback training, a machine would indicate Derek's blood pressure, but he could not feel it. (p. 116)
   a. Alice is using her conscious memories to name her teachers.
   b. Brian may have an unconscious dislike of his sister.
   c. Chris may be experiencing the mere-exposure effect, which occurs at the subconscious level of consciousness.

4. *d* is the answer. While people have been able to match up word pairs, figure out rules used in a seemingly random presentation, and tend to like previously seen material better, it would be making too great a leap to assume that priming would be a good study technique. (pp. 117–118)
    a, b, c. All these are true.

5. *d* is the answer. Subliminal perception does not control our behavior. (pp. 119–120)
    a. No evidence suggests that subliminals will anger people.
    b. Regular advertising campaigns that are consciously perceived are more influential than something subliminal.
    c. Presenting subliminal images more than once a minute will still not cause people to buy Chocomints.

6. *c* is the answer. Stage 4 is the deepest stage of slow-wave sleep (p. 123)
    a, b. Stages 2 and 3 are not the deepest stages of slow-wave sleep.
    d. REM sleep is not a stage of slow-wave sleep.

7. *c* is the answer. During stage 4, a very deep sleep that occurs about thirty minutes after falling asleep, it is difficult to rouse someone. (p. 123)
    a. After five minutes the sleeper would be in stage 1 or just entering stage 2 (not deep sleep).
    b. After ten minutes the sleeper would be in stage 2 or 3 (not deep sleep).
    d. It can be determined. Snooker's owner is in a very deep sleep, and the timing of the first episode of stage 4 sleep can be determined from sleep-cycle research.

8. *d* is the answer. REM behavior disorder is a lack of the near-paralysis that usually happens during REM sleep. Without the near-paralysis, Sheandra is able to act out her dreams. (p. 125)
    a. Sleep apnea occurs when people stop breathing while sleeping, often hundreds of times a night.
    b. Sleepwalking occurs during non-REM sleep, when it is less likely the person is dreaming—and the person also gets out of bed!
    c. People who have narcolepsy often fall asleep in the middle of an active waking state. They immediately shift into active sleep.

9. *c* is the answer. Circadian rhythms are the cycles of behavior and physiological activity that repeat about once every 24 hours. (p. 125)
    a. The cardiovascular system is only one part of our physiological activity.
    b. Brain waves most characteristic of stage 4 sleep are very slow waves.
    d. External cues play a role in circadian rhythms, but the cycles are there even in total darkness.

10. *c* is the answer. When people go without REM sleep, they have more REM periods than usual when they finally do sleep. (p. 127)
    a. People who go to sleep and get up at the same time every day will not have their REM periods interrupted. Therefore, their REM periods will not increase in number or length.
    b. The older people get, the less time they spend asleep. Most of the decrease is in REM sleep.
    d. People with hypersomnia have plenty of time to go through REM sleep. Upon recovery, they have no REM deficiency to correct.

11. *b* is the answer. Lucid dreaming occurs when the dreamer is aware that it is a dream even while it is happening. (p. 128)
    a. Apneatic dreaming is a made-up term.
    c. Narcolepsy causes people to fall into active sleep in the middle of an active waking state.
    d. You may have been thinking of circadian rhythm, but the 24-hour activity cycle doesn't explain a dream in which someone responds in a certain way only because he knows he is dreaming.

12. *b* is the answer. Posthypnotic suggestions are given during hypnosis, but are followed after hypnosis. (p. 129)
    a. Brendan may believe he is unable to see during hypnosis due to reduced reality testing. This is not posthypnotic because it occurs during hypnosis.
    c. Not remembering what occurred while under hypnosis is posthypnotic amnesia.
    d. This sounds like a joke that could work on anyone—hypnotized or not.

13. *a* is the answer. The dissociation theory states that people will experience changes in mental processes if enough control is relinquished to the hypnotist. (p. 130)
    b. This is not a theory of hypnosis. You may have been thinking of lucid dreaming.
    c. The role theory of hypnosis says that people are complying with a social role, and are not in a different state.
    d. State theorists would argue that hypnosis causes an altered state of mental activity, but they do not include releasing control to the therapist and a dissociation of abilities (like sight) from central control.

14. *b* is the answer. (p. 131)
    a. There is no special name for a person well versed in meditation.
    c. Many different types of positions have been used to meditate. Their only common characteristic is that they are comfortable.

d. Several different techniques of meditation exist, but none of them is called a mantra.

15. *d* is the answer. Depressants such as alcohol increase the activity of the neurotransmitter GABA. (p. 134)
   a. Cocaine is a stimulant that acts on dopamine receptors.
   b. A psychedelic or hallucinogen is more likely to act on serotonin systems.
   c. Opiates act on glutamate and endorphin receptors.

Now turn to the quiz analysis table at the end of this chapter to find which areas you know well and which areas you need to work on. Circle the numbers in the table for items on Quiz 2 that you answered correctly.

For each question you answered correctly, circle its number. (Quiz 1 numbers are not shaded; Quiz 2 numbers are shaded.) Are there patterns in the types of questions or the topics you got wrong that could direct your further study? Did you improve from Quiz 1 to Quiz 2?

TOPIC	TYPE OF QUESTION		
	DEFINITION	COMPREHENSION	APPLICATION
Scope of Consciousness			
Levels			1, 2, 3
	1		2, 3
Research			4
		4	
Subliminal perception			
			5
Sleep and Dreams			
Sleep stages		5	
		6	7
Disorders			6
			8
Reasons for sleep		9	7, 8
			9, 10
Dreams		10	
			11
Hypnosis			
Experiencing			11, 12
			12
Theory			13
			13
Meditation			
	14		
Psychoactive Drugs			
Psychopharmacology	14		
Classes of drugs			15
		15	

TOTAL CORRECT BY QUIZ:

QUIZ 1:
QUIZ 2:

Chapter 5

Learning

LEARNING OBJECTIVES

1. Define learning. (p. 146)

2. Define classical conditioning, unconditioned stimulus, unconditioned response, conditioned stimulus, and conditioned response. Give an example that illustrates the process of classical conditioning and label the parts of your example using these terms. (pp. 147–148)

3. Describe the processes of extinction, reconditioning, and spontaneous recovery. Give an example of each. Explain Figure 5.3 in your text. (pp. 148–149)

4. Define and give examples of stimulus generalization and stimulus discrimination. Describe the adaptive balance between these two phenomena. (p. 149)

5. Describe the role that timing, predictability, and signal strength play in conditioned response development. (pp. 149-150)

6. Discuss how attention influences the process of classical conditioning. Define and give an example of second-order conditioning. (p. 150)

7. Explain and give examples of biopreparedness. Explain why conditioned taste aversion is a special case of classical conditioning. (p. 151)

8. Describe the role of classical conditioning in the development and treatment of phobias, and in the diagnosis and treatment of Alzheimer's disease. (pp. 151–152)

9. Define habituation and give an example. Describe opponent-process theory and explain how it applies to drug addiction. (pp. 152–153)

10. Define the law of effect. (p. 154)

11. Describe instrumental or operant conditioning and explain how it differs from classical conditioning. (p. 154)

12. Define operants and reinforcers. (p. 154)

13. Define positive reinforcers and negative reinforcers and give examples of each. (p. 154)

14. Define escape conditioning and avoidance conditioning. Give an example of each that highlights their similarities and differences. (pp. 154–155)

15. Define discriminative stimuli. Explain and give an example of stimulus control. Explain how stimulus discrimination and stimulus generalization can work together. (pp. 155-157)

16. Define shaping. Explain when it is used in operant conditioning. (p. 157)

17. Discuss the differences between primary and secondary reinforcers. (pp. 157–158)

18. Explain the difference between continuous and partial reinforcement schedules. Compare and contrast fixed-ratio, variable-ratio, fixed-interval, and variable-interval schedules. Be sure to describe how these schedules affect response patterns and discuss the partial reinforcement extinction effect. (pp. 158–160)

19. Define punishment and describe its role in operant conditioning. Explain how punishment differs from negative reinforcement. Discuss the disadvantages of and guidelines for using punishment. (pp. 160–162)

20. Discuss how operant conditioning can be used to treat problematic behavior. (pp. 162–163)

21. Define learned helplessness and give an example of it. Describe the experiments used to study learned helplessness and the results. (pp. 163–165)

22. Define and give an example of latent learning and a cognitive map. (pp. 165–166)

23. Define insight. Discuss how insight differs from classical and operant conditioning. (pp. 166–167)

24. Define observational learning and vicarious conditioning. Discuss their similarities and differences. (pp. 167–169)

25. Describe the research on the effects of television violence. State what conclusions are most reasonable based on the evidence available. (pp. 169–171)

26. Describe the potential causes of cultural differences in scholastic achievement. (p. 171)

27. Define active learning and give an example. (p. 172)

28. Describe the roles of practice and feedback in skill learning. (p. 172)

KEY TERMS

1. **Learning** is the modification of preexisting behavior and understanding through experience. People learn primarily by identifying relationships between events and noting the regularity in the surrounding world. (p. 146)

I. CLASSICAL CONDITIONING: LEARNING SIGNALS AND ASSOCIATIONS

2. **Classical conditioning** is a procedure in which a neutral stimulus is paired with a stimulus that elicits a reflex or other response until the neutral stimulus alone elicits a similar response. Organisms learn the relationships and associations between stimuli. (p. 147)

Example: Cat owners who feed their cats canned food and use an electric can opener know that just the sound of the opener will cause the cat to come running into the kitchen and salivate. The sound of the opener (an originally neutral stimulus) is paired with food (a stimulus that elicits a reflexive response such as salivation or other behavioral responses such as running into the kitchen) until the sound alone elicits the response. This occurs because the sound of the electric opener predicts the presence of food.

REMEMBER: Throughout the chapter, the word response is used. It is equivalent to a behavior or mental process. If you become confused by the use of this word, simply substitute the words mental process or behavior, and the sentence's meaning should become clear.

3. An **unconditioned stimulus (UCS)**, in classical conditioning, is the stimulus that elicits a response without conditioning or learning having to take place. (p. 147)

Example: In the cat example in Key Term 2, food is the unconditioned stimulus; it naturally causes the cat to salivate.

REMEMBER: Unconditioned means "unlearned." Cats do not have to learn about food every time in order to respond to food.

4. An **unconditioned response (UCR)**, in classical conditioning, is the automatic or reflexive response to the unconditioned stimulus. (p. 147)

Example: In the cat example in Key Term 2, salivation is an unconditioned response. This behavior or response is reflexive or unlearned and occurs in the presence of the unconditioned stimulus (food).

5. A **conditioned stimulus (CS)**, in classical conditioning, is the stimulus that, only *after* repeated pairings with the unconditioned stimulus, causes a conditioned response that is similar to the unconditioned response. (p. 148)

Example: In the cat example in Key Term 2, the sound of the can opener is the conditioned stimulus because it initially elicited no response from the cat (as a neutral stimulus). Only when the sound of the opener was paired with the presentation of food did the sound predict the presence of food (UCS) and cause the cat to run to the kitchen and salivate.

REMEMBER: Conditioned means "learned." The conditioned stimulus is originally neutral; the organism must learn that it predicts the presence of the UCS.

6. A **conditioned response (CR)**, in classical conditioning, is the learned response elicited by the conditioned stimulus. (p. 148)

Example: In the cat example in Key Term 2, the cat's response of running to the kitchen and salivating when it hears the can opener is the conditioned response.

7. **Extinction**, in classical conditioning, occurs when the conditioned stimulus, after being presented without the unconditioned stimulus, loses its predictive value. Eventually, the conditioned stimulus no longer elicits the conditioned response. In operant conditioning, a response is extinguished when it is no longer reinforced. (p. 148)

Example: The story "The Boy Who Cried Wolf" is an example of extinction in classical conditioning. Shepherds learned that hearing someone cry "Wolf!" (CS) meant that a wolf (UCS) had appeared, and consequently they would run (CR) for help. When one little boy repeatedly cried "Wolf!" for no reason, the other shepherds stopped responding (CR) to his cry (CS) because it no longer predicted the presence of a wolf (UCS).

REMEMBER: To become extinct means to "no longer exist." In the above example, the CR (running) no longer exists when the cry of "Wolf" (CS) is heard.

8. **Reconditioning**, in classical conditioning, refers to the repairing of the CS and the UCS after extinction has

taken place. During reconditioning, an organism learns more quickly than it did the first time that the CS predicts the UCS. (p. 148)

> *REMEMBER:* Conditioning involves the association of two stimuli such that one (CS) begins to predict the occurrence of the other (UCS). Reconditioning is simply repeating this process.

9. **Spontaneous recovery** is the reappearance of the conditioned response when the CS is presented after extinction in the absence of reconditioning. (p. 148)

> *Example:* Pavlov's dogs were conditioned to salivate (CR) in response to the sound of a bell. After extinction (hearing the bell without receiving food), the dogs no longer responded. If, after a long time following extinction, the dogs heard the sound of the bell again, they would most likely salivate. The conditioned response would have spontaneously "recovered."

> *REMEMBER:* Spontaneously means "suddenly" or "without planning." In spontaneous recovery, the CR occurs suddenly or immediately after only *one* presentation of the CS (bell).

10. **Stimulus generalization**, in classical conditioning, occurs when an organism displays a conditioned response to a stimulus that is similar, but not identical, to the conditioned stimulus. In operant conditioning, several different but similar stimuli can inform an organism that, if a particular response is made, a reinforcer or punishment will be presented. (p. 149)

> *Example:* Nguyen was very curious as a child. He had never seen a spider (CS) before the time he picked up a big reddish-brown one to investigate it closely. Eventually, the spider bit him (UCS), causing him to become ill (UCR) for several days. Nguyen is now an adult and avoids (CR) all spiders, not just reddish-brown ones. He is reacting to stimuli that are similar, but not necessarily identical, to the original conditioned stimulus (reddish-brown spiders).

11. **Stimulus discrimination** occurs when an organism learns that stimuli similar, but not identical, to the conditioned stimuli do not predict the occurrence of the unconditioned stimulus. (See Key Term 22 for more information about discrimination in operant conditioning.) (p. 149)

> *Example:* Raoul the dog receives an injection (UCS) at the veterinarian's every four months. Raoul usually loves to ride in the car. However, whenever his owner drives Raoul to the veterinarian's (CS), Raoul whimpers (CR) for most of the ride. Raoul has learned to discriminate between the route to the veterinarian's and the route to other places.

12. **Second-order conditioning** occurs when a new neutral stimulus is associated with a conditioned stimulus and itself comes to produce the CR in the absence of the CS. (p. 150)

> *Example:* If Pavlov had turned on the light in the room before ringing the bell (CS) and the dogs eventually began to salivate (CR) as soon as he turned on the light, second-order conditioning would have occurred.

> *REMEMBER:* Second-order conditioning means that there is a second conditioned stimulus.

13. **Habituation** occurs when we learn not to respond to a repeated stimulus. A new stimulus often grabs our attention and earns a response; after a while, though, the new stimulus is not new and we no longer respond to it. (p. 153)

> *Example:* Shelley just received a large diamond engagement ring from her boyfriend. The first two weeks of wearing it, Shelley notices how it feels on her hand and looks at it often. After a while, though, Shelley becomes habituated to the feel and look of the ring and no longer notices it as much or as often.

II. INSTRUMENTAL AND OPERANT CONDITIONING: LEARNING THE CONSEQUENCES OF BEHAVIOR

14. The **law of effect** holds that if a response made in the presence of a particular stimulus is followed by a reward, that same response is more likely to occur the next time the stimulus is encountered. Responses that are not rewarded are less and less likely to be performed again. (p. 154)

> *REMEMBER:* The law of effect means the law of being effective. If an organism learns that a behavior produces a desired effect, such as good grades or money, the organism will repeat the behavior. If the behavior is ineffective (it doesn't produce anything, or it produces bad effects, such as a scolding), it will not be repeated.

15. Instrumental conditioning or **operant conditioning**, is a procedure during which an organism learns that certain responses are instrumental in producing desired effects in the environment. (p. 154)

> *Example:* Most students have learned that studying (response) results in receiving good grades (desirable effects).

16. An **operant** is a behavior that, in operant conditioning, brings about a consequence in an organism's environment. (p. 154)

REMEMBER: Operant responses are behaviors that operate on the world in some way.

17. A **reinforcer** is anything that increases the likelihood that a behavior will be repeated. Reinforcers can be positive or negative. (p. 154)

18. **Positive reinforcers**, in operant conditioning, are rewards. If presented following a behavior, they increase the likelihood of that behavior's future occurrence. (p. 154)

Example: If Rover gets a bone (a positive reinforcer) every time he rolls over, he will probably roll over frequently.

REMEMBER: A reinforcer always encourages the repetition of the behavior that it follows. A pleasant stimulus (+) is added (+) to the environment. You can remember this by thinking that a positive number times a positive number yields a positive number.

19. **Negative reinforcers**, in operant conditioning, are unpleasant stimuli that, if removed following a behavior or response, will increase the likelihood of that behavior's future occurrence. (p. 154)

Example: Hunger pains are unpleasant stimuli. Eating causes them to go away. People learn the habit of eating when they experience hunger pains because the pains disappear (negative reinforcers).

REMEMBER: A reinforcer always encourages the repetition of the behavior that it follows. In negative reinforcement a negative stimulus (–) is subtracted from (–) the environment. You can remember this by thinking that a negative number times a negative number always yields a positive number.

20. **Escape conditioning** occurs when an organism learns that a particular response will terminate an aversive stimulus. (p. 154)

Example: Lydia has recently set up a computer at home and now does most of her work there. Her cat, Spooky, has begun to sit next to the terminal and cry until Lydia gets up to feed him. Lydia has learned that her response of feeding the cat will remove the distracting sound of his cries.

REMEMBER: Escape and avoidance conditioning are sometimes confused. In order for escape conditioning to occur, the organism must first be in trouble.

21. **Avoidance conditioning** occurs when an organism responds to a signal in a way that prevents exposure to an aversive stimulus. (p. 155)

Example: Leslie has learned that by accepting most men's invitations for dates she avoids the awkwardness of explaining that she is not interested in them.

REMEMBER: Escape and avoidance conditioning can be confused. In avoidance conditioning, the organism avoids ever getting into trouble. In escape conditioning, the organism learns how to get out of trouble.

22. **Discriminative stimuli**, in operant conditioning, are signals to an organism that, should a particular response be made, reinforcement is available. Such a response is said to be under stimulus control because the response is usually made when only the discriminative stimulus is present. (p. 155)

Example: Alicia knows that her business partner is in a good mood if she is smiling, is not wearing her suit jacket, and has opened the blinds. These discriminative stimuli inform Alicia that she can approach her partner with a new idea (Alicia's particular response) and expect her partner to be supportive (reinforcement). Alicia's behavior is under stimulus control because Alicia will not approach her partner unless the discriminative stimuli are present.

23. **Shaping** is an operant conditioning process in which successive approximations of a behavior are reinforced until the entire desired behavior pattern appears.
(p. 157)

Example: Trainers at Sea World want to teach a whale to jump through a hoop. Since wild whales do not normally perform this behavior, the trainers must shape it. They might begin by rewarding the whale for jumping out of the water. Then they reward the whale for jumping toward a hoop and eventually for touching it. Each of these behaviors is a successive approximation of jumping through a hoop. Eventually, the entire behavior pattern will be learned and rewarded.

REMEMBER: To <u>shape</u> means to "mold into something." In shaping, the behavior must be gradually molded.

24. **Primary reinforcers** are inherent rewards. Thus, learning that the reinforcement is positive is not necessary. (p. 157)

Example: Food and water are primary reinforcers if you are hungry.

25. **Secondary reinforcers** are those rewards that have acquired meaning by their association with primary reinforcers. (p. 157)

Example: Before people used money in exchange for goods, they worked to produce or exchange life's basic necessities, such as food. Money, because it allows people to buy food and has therefore become associated with food, is a secondary reinforcer.

26. The **partial reinforcement extinction effect** occurs when a partial reinforcement schedule has been used in the operant conditioning process. The more difficult it is for the organism to predict the occurrence of reinforcement (meaning the behavior isn't rewarded every time), the harder the response is to extinguish. (p. 160)

REMEMBER: To extinguish an operant behavior, reinforcement is no longer given following a response. On a partial reinforcement schedule, an organism will have to perform a response more than once or wait for a period of time before realizing that responses are no longer being rewarded. An animal on a continuous reinforcement schedule can know after only one response that reinforcement has been withdrawn.

27. **Punishment** is the presentation of an aversive stimulus, which decreases the frequency of the immediately preceding response. (p. 160)

Example: For people who want to break their nail-biting habit, there is a fingernail polish with a bad taste. When people wearing this polish bite their nails, they are punished with an aversive stimulus (the taste of the polish). This is done to decrease the behavior (nail biting) immediately preceding the taste.
REMEMBER: Punishment has several side effects.

III. COGNITIVE PROCESSES IN LEARNING

28. **Learned helplessness** occurs when an organism believes that behaviors are not related to consequences. (p. 163)

Example: Children may develop learned helplessness if they find that no matter how much or how little they try to learn, failing grades always result. At that point they may no longer feel that it is worth trying to achieve at school.
REMEMBER: Organisms learn to be helpless.

29. **Latent learning** is learning that is not demonstrated at the time that it occurs. (p. 166)

Example: You discover that you enjoy your psychology class. However, you do not demonstrate the knowledge that you learned during the first lecture until the first test several weeks later.
REMEMBER: Latent means "not visible." What you have learned is not visible until a later time.

30. **Cognitive maps** are mental representations of the environment. (p. 166)

Example: When he was at college, Dale lost his sight in a car accident. When he got out of the hospital, he still knew how to get around the campus because he had a mental representation (or cognitive map) of the campus.

31. **Insight** is the sudden grasp of new relationships that are necessary to solve a problem and that were not learned in the past. (p. 166)

32. **Observational learning** occurs when people learn by watching others' responses. Learning takes place even if others' responses are not rewarded. (p. 172)

Example: Suppose you found a being from another planet on your doorstep. Charlie the alien is intelligent and looks just like a human being. That night, Charlie watches you brush your teeth. Then he picks up the toothbrush and imitates your behavior. This is not because he knows you get great checkups at the dentist. He is merely learning a behavior by watching you do it.

33. **Vicarious conditioning** occurs when an organism learns the relationship between a response and its consequences (either reinforcement or punishment) by watching others. (p. 167)

Example: Tara is the youngest of six children. By watching her brothers and sisters, she learns which behaviors her parents reward and which behaviors they punish.

CONCEPTS AND EXERCISES

No. 1: Learning in Advertising

Completing this exercise should help you to achieve Learning Objectives 2, 3, 11, 13, 18, and 19..

Advertising is all around you: television, magazines, radio, billboards, pencils, the backs of cabs, matchbooks, just about anywhere you look. The people who create these ads often use learning principles to persuade you to buy their products. In the following exercise, you are the ads' creator. It is your job to tell your boss the learning principle behind each of the following ad descriptions. Choose from the list at the end of the exercise. Answers may be used more than once or not at all.

1. *Television spot, thirty seconds.* Scene: The counter at a Brand X dry cleaner. An anxious-looking woman enters carrying a yellow dress with chocolate stains on it.

   Customer: I need to have this dress cleaned by noon.

   Counter clerk: Don't worry; it'll be ready at noon.

   Customer: I hope so. I really have to have the dress by noon.

   Counter clerk: We'll have it by noon. No problem.

   (Shift of scene: customer is at home, smiling as she talks on the phone.)

   Customer: Hi. I dropped a dress off there earlier—to be ready at noon. Can I pick it up now?

   (Pause. Customer's smile abruptly turns to a frown.)

   Narrator: Why take chances? Speedy Dry Clean guarantees that your clothes will always be ready on time.

   a. This is an example of _____ conditioning..

   b. The dress failing to be ready illustrates the use of _____ for the behavioral response of using a dry-cleaning service other than Speedy.

   c. The service guarantee that states, "Your clothes will always be ready on time" is an example of a _____ reinforcement schedule.

   d. How many times do you think Speedy Dry Clean can break the service guarantee before its customers will go to another dry cleaner? _____

2. *Television spot, thirty seconds.* Scene: Mother checking on sleeping child. Mother speaks very quietly.

   Mother: Jennifer went to the doctor today to get the stitches taken out of her knee. Before we went to the Stone Clinic, just mentioning the word *doctor* made her cry for fear of getting a shot. But the doctors and nurses at the Stone Clinic understand a child's needs; they're gentle, soothing, kind, and thoughtful. That makes Jennifer happy. I know that the Stone Clinic staff are experts in their fields, and as a mother (mother looks lovingly at Jennifer), that makes me very happy. (Mother leans over, smoothes Jennifer's hair, kisses her on the forehead, and tiptoes out of room.)

   a. This is an example of _____ conditioning.

   b. The doctors are a(n) _____.

   c. Jennifer's old fear of doctors is a(n) _____.

   d. What conditioning process caused Jennifer to lose her fear of doctors? _____

   ° Operant
   ° Positive reinforcement
   ° Negative reinforcement
   ° Punishment
   ° Classical
   ° Conditioned stimulus
   ° Conditioned response
   ° Unconditioned stimulus
   ° Unconditioned response
   ° Extinction
   ° Continuous
   ° Fixed interval
   ° Once
   ° Ten times
   ° One hundred times

No. 2: Teaching an Alien

Completing this exercise should help you to achieve Learning Objectives 4, 7, 11, 13, 15, 17, 19, 22, and 24.

To discover the prevalence of learning in our everyday lives, read the following story of Sam and Gufla, an alien. You will find many of the basic learning principles embedded in the plot. Afterward, answer the questions using the list of terms at the end of the exercise. Answers may be used more than once.

One day while playing in the park, Sam met someone he thought was a boy his own age. Thinking the boy was human, Sam began a conversation. Even though the stranger spoke perfect English, Sam soon realized that he was from another planet and had landed here by accident. Eight-year-old Sam was more curious than afraid and invited the alien home for dinner.

The trip home was eventful. Sam, worried about being late, decided to take a shortcut that one of his pals had told him about earlier. As the two boys entered a backyard, a snarling German shepherd charged them. Sam quickly figured out that the dog's chain could not reach to the fence. He and the alien, whom he had named Gufla, ran along the fence until they were out of the yard. After slowing down and catching his breath, Sam realized that he would have to tell Gufla a few things about the family and how to behave so that

Sam's mother would not suspect anything. Most important, Sam knew that he could not share his discovery with his sister, who would tell his mother. Gufla asked Sam what eating felt like. How would he recognize food? Sam replied that anything that smelled good was edible. Gufla promptly picked a rose from a garden they were passing and ate it. Sam laughed, but Gufla was holding his stomach because the rose, which had fertilizer on it, made him feel ill. Gufla vowed never to go near a rose again.

Sam told Gufla that anytime Sam nodded his head, Gufla could eat whatever his fork was touching. Anytime Sam shook his head, Gufla was not to eat whatever his fork was touching. Sam tried to explain that food, not napkins or salt and pepper shakers, tastes good, which is a pleasant feeling. By the time they reached Sam's driveway, Sam realized that there was not enough time to teach Gufla all the behaviors he would need to know, so Sam told Gufla to imitate Sam's behavior whenever he felt confused. Sam said that since it was Friday night, his mother might let them stay up and watch the late-night horror movie, a special treat, if all went well.

1. Sam's mother had probably successfully used _____ to decrease his tardiness.

2. Sam was using a _____ _____ to follow a shortcut home. This was also a case of _____ _____ since Sam had never taken this shortcut before, even though he had known about it before that day.

3. Sam decided not to tell his sister about his find. This illustrates a _____ _____. Sam did not want his sister to tell his mother about Gufla.

4. Gufla became ill after eating the rose, probably because it had fertilizer on it. This is an example of learning a _____.

5. Gufla knew that the direction in which Sam moved his head would be a _____ _____ because this would let Gufla know if what he put in his mouth (the behavior) would taste good or bad. Good food in this case is a _____ _____.

6. Gufla will watch and imitate what Sam does even though he won't really understand why he is doing it or if it will bring him any sort of pleasure. This is an example of _____.

7. Sam and Gufla may be allowed to watch a late-night movie if they behave well at dinner. This illustrates the use of a _____.

- Primary
- Secondary
- Avoidance conditioning
- Escape conditioning
- Punishment
- Positive reinforcer
- Taste aversion
- Discriminative stimulus
- Observational learning
- Cognitive map
- Latent learning

CRITICAL THINKING

Sam and Martina have just dropped a teenager, Rose, off at juvenile hall. She has been in trouble on and off for the past two years. They are discussing the causes of her delinquency.

Sam fumes, "Do you realize that's the fifteenth time she's been hauled down there in the past two years?"

Martina mumbles, "Hmmm."

Sam continues, "And do you realize that every time she does something, it's the same old thing? She waits till her dad comes back from a business trip, she tells him what she has done, they have a huge fight, and he brings her to us."

Martina mumbles again, "Hmmm."

Sam finally decries, "She's just a bad apple. She probably has an antisocial personality disorder."

Martina finally says, "Nope, I think Rose is a good kid at heart. Based on the pattern you describe, I think she has just learned to be bad."

Using the five critical thinking questions in your text, the clues in the story, and what you have learned in this chapter, answer the following:

1. What is Sam's hypothesis?

2. What is the evidence in support of Sam's hypothesis?

3. What is Martina's alternative hypothesis?

4. What is the evidence in support of Martina's hypothesis?

PERSONAL LEARNING ACTIVITIES

1. Based on the text's description of classical conditioning, write down an example of an unconditioned stimulus. What natural (unconditioned) response does it cause? Below your example of an unconditioned stimulus and response, write how you could pair the unconditioned stimulus with a neutral stimulus to eventually classically condition yourself. If your unconditioned stimulus, for instance, was a loud noise, perhaps you could have someone flash a

light just before making a loud noise until you respond to the light with the same jump you did to the loud noise. (Learning Objective 2)

2. Recall a time when someone tried to punish you. What emotional and behavioral reactions did you have? Did it, in fact, behave as a punishment and decrease your behavior or was it somehow reinforcing? (Learning Objectives 13 and 19)

3. Try to reinforce someone's behavior and watch for the effects. Perhaps a friend does a favor for you or a salesclerk is particularly helpful. You could show your appreciation immediately and see if the person is more likely to behave in the same manner again. (Learning Objective 13)

4. Have someone use observational learning to master a skill that you have. For instance, if you make a delicious casserole or know how to skate backwards, you could attempt to pass on those talents. What problems did you encounter? Was there a particular demonstration or explanation that made things clearer for your volunteer? Based on your first lesson, how much practice do you think will be required before the person masters the skill? What type of feedback was most helpful to the person? (Learning Objectives 24 and 28)

5. Use active learning when working with a classmate to understand material. For example, if you are studying with a psychology classmate, you could work on this chapter by comparing answers to Personal Learning Activity 1, which is an active learning exercise. (Learning Objective 27)

WHAT SHOULD I WRITE ABOUT?

As you look over your textbook for clues on topics to write about, don't feel bound to write about something your textbook author wrote about. Feel free to expand on their work, and to go beyond it. As you look at the topics covered in your textbook, let your imagination run to related topics that might be of interest to you. For example, your textbook tells you a little bit in this chapter about how Pavlov "discovered" classical conditioning. You might find a paper on the history of Pavlov's career a fun topic to research—one that is related to the topics covered in your text, but not a complete re-run.. In fact, exploring the history behind the subject matter in general can be a good strategy for choosing a term paper topic. Understanding where the subject matter comes from will give you a lot of insight into the subject itself. Other interesting histories worth exploring in this chapter include B.F. Skinner's career and the circumstances that led to Kohler's study of insight learning with chimpanzees.

If history doesn't appeal to you, don't feel stuck yet. Try thinking through other ways to view a topic covered in your text. For example, in this chapter, the text covers classrooms across the cultures. You might then choose to write a term paper on cultural differences in learning styles. Do people from different cultures learn differently? You could explore that question in a term paper.

You could turn a topic covered in your text on its head and see what you find, too. For example, your textbook covers the relationship between viewing television violence and later violent actions on the part of the viewer, and concludes that there is some compelling evidence for this relation. But can observational learning lead to peaceful, prosocial behaviors as well? This would make another fruitful topic for a term paper. It is clearly related to the chapter you just read, but not completely redundant with the information already covered in your textbook.

Here are some questions to ask yourself as you choose your next term paper topic:

1. Is there any topic you encountered in your text that peaked your curiosity about the history that led to that conclusion? If so, you could write a term paper that is a biography of that researcher's life, or of the part of that researcher's life that led up to that discovery.

2. What topics that were covered in your text made you think about different, but related, questions? Take the topics that most interested you as you read through the chapter, and then try to view that topic from a different angle. What questions come to mind as you do so?

THE INTERNET

The Psychabilities web site that accompanies this text offers many resources relevant to this chapter. They include NetLab exercises, Thinking Critically and Evaluating Research exercises, ACE chapter quizzes, recommended web links, and articles on current events, books, and movies. Go to http://college.hmco.com, select Psychology, and then this textbook.

MULTIPLE-CHOICE QUESTIONS

SAMPLE QUIZ 1

1. Branella, a scientist, has found that people will flinch whenever they hear a very loud sound. In her lab, she flashes a red light every time that she presents a loud sound to a subject. After a while, the subject will flinch after seeing the red light

flash, even if no loud sound occurs. In this learning, Branella used the loud sound as a(n)
a. conditioned stimulus.
b. unconditioned response.
c. conditioned response.
d. unconditioned stimulus.

2. Whenever Char smelled vanilla, it meant her dad had baked chocolate chip cookies. At first Char's mouth watered as she ate the cookies, but soon her mouth watered as soon as she smelled the vanilla. The neutral stimulus in this example is _____; the conditioned response is _____.
a. a cookie; eating a cookie
b. a cookie; smelling vanilla
c. the vanilla smell; baking cookies
d. the vanilla smell; salivating

3. A conditioned response will be learned *more* rapidly if the
a. UCS is strong.
b. UCS precedes the CS.
c. CS sometimes predicts the UCS.
d. CS is not as noticeable as the CR.

4. The main principle of Thorndike's law of effect is that
a. a rewarded behavioral response is more likely to be repeated than one receiving no reward.
b. the frequency and intensity of a stimulus determine its behavioral effects.
c. the likelihood of a repeated behavior is determined by the magnitude of its rewards.
d. humans learn to understand the world by monitoring the effects of their own behavioral responses.

5. In operant conditioning, negative reinforcers are
a. pleasant stimuli presented following a response.
b. unpleasant stimuli that are removed following a response.
c. methods of decreasing a response.
d. rewards considered basic to survival, such as food and drink.

6. Sometimes Amy hits her sister, Zoe, in the arm until Zoe says "I give," and then Amy stops. Because Amy stops hurting Zoe when she says "I give," Zoe says it whenever she is being hit. In this example of _____, the operant is _____.
a. negative reinforcement; Zoe saying "I give"
b. positive reinforcement; Amy stops hitting Zoe
c. punishment; Zoe saying "I give"
d. punishment; Amy stops hitting Zoe

7. Linda is always in a hurry and has come up with a way to prevent a particularly long traffic light from slowing her down on her way to work. If the light is yellow when Linda is two blocks away from the light's intersection, she detours down an alley and prevents herself from having to sit and wait at the long red light. Linda is demonstrating
a. escape conditioning.
b. stimulus discrimination.
c. avoidance conditioning.
d. stimulus generalization.

8. Suppose Chelsea wants to teach Socks, her cat, to attack Newt Gingrich. At first, if Socks hisses at Newt, she gets a kitty treat. Then, only if Socks tries to scratch Newt does she get a kitty treat. Then Socks gets a treat only if she bites Newt. Finally, Socks only gets a treat if she hurls herself into Newt's face, biting and scratching. This procedure illustrates
a. negative reinforcement.
b. classical conditioning.
c. vicarious conditioning.
d. shaping.

9. Mike is unsure of how to reward his son Greg for getting good grades. "Should I buy him a baseball glove? A Lava Lamp? Hmm, maybe a Pet Rock?" he thought. Mike's wife, Carol, suggested, "Why don't you give Greg some money? It's a nice _____ that he could use to get any of those things."
a. primary reinforcer
b. unconditioned stimulus
c. discriminative stimulus
d. secondary reinforcer

10. Larry's employer pays Larry $50 for every gold-plated backpack that he makes. This employer is using a _____ schedule of reinforcement.
a. fixed-ratio
b. fixed-interval
c. variable-ratio
d. variable-interval

11. Which reinforcement schedule produces the fastest extinction rate?
a. Fixed ratio
b. Fixed interval
c. Variable ratio
d. Variable interval

12. Julio and Carlos's mother asks them what they want for breakfast. Carlos replies, "I want some #$!@* corn flakes." His mother immediately yells, "Don't say that!" and repeats the question. Carlos replies, "Well okay, I'll have some #$!@* rice puffs." Carlos's mother becomes angry and

sends Carlos to his room. She then looks at Julio and says, "What do you want for breakfast?" Julio replies, "I don't know, but you can be sure I don't want any #$!@* cereal." Julio's response illustrates
a. the effectiveness of negative reinforcers.
b. stimulus discrimination.
c. the disadvantages of using punishment.
d. all of the above.

13. Eileen's boss always yells at her and criticizes her. To please her boss, Eileen has tried to change, but no matter what she does he continues to berate her. After a while, Eileen stops trying to please her boss. This is an example of
a. vicarious learning.
b. social learning.
c. classical conditioning.
d. learned helplessness.

14. Jerad watched a television show about parenting skills. A few months later, when Jerad was baby-sitting his nephew, he remembered and used the things he had watched on the show, even though he had not applied these skills before. Apparently, the lessons Jerad took from that TV show were examples of
a. insight learning.
b. latent learning.
c. stimulus generalization.
d. stimulus discrimination.

15. Professor Smythe asks questions of his class sporadically as he lectures. He requires all students in the class to write down their answers on cards and hold them up. Professor Blythe also asks questions, but students raise their hands only if the know the answer, and he only calls on one student per question. Who's students will do better on exams?
a. Professor Smythe's.
b. Professor Blythe's.
c. the students in each class should do equally well.
d. none of the students in either class will do well.

Total Correct (See answer key) _____

SAMPLE QUIZ 2

Use this quiz to reassess your learning after taking Quiz 1 and reviewing the chapter.

1. In classical conditioning, a neutral stimulus
a. is one that does not elicit a reflexive response.
b. is synonymous with an unconditioned stimulus.

c. causes an unconditioned response.
d. predicts the presence of an unconditioned response.

2. Letitia's first experience at the dentist was a traumatic one. During that first visit, the dentist used no anesthetic before drilling her teeth. Now, just sitting in the waiting room and hearing the whirring sound of the drill make Letitia nauseous. This is an example of what kind of conditioning?
a. Classical conditioning
b. Negative reinforcement
c. Instrumental conditioning
d. Positive reinforcement

3. When Antonio rode the Ferris wheel at the amusement park for the first time, he became very dizzy. Now when Antonio sees an advertisement for amusement parks, he feels nauseous. In this case, the unconditioned stimulus is
a. the Ferris wheel ride.
b. the feeling of dizziness.
c. nausea.
d. the sight of an amusement park.

4. In this case of Antonio's feelings about Ferris wheels, the conditioned response is
a. dizziness.
b. the Ferris wheel ride.
c. the sight of an amusement park.
d. nausea.

5. In the case of Antonio's feelings about Ferris wheels, the conditioned stimulus is
a. dizziness.
b. the Ferris wheel ride.
c. the sight of an amusement park.
d. nausea.

6. Stimulus generalization involves responding to stimuli that
a. had always occurred in the presence of the unconditioned stimulus.
b. produce a reflexive response.
c. are similar, but not identical, to the conditioned stimulus.
d. are similar to the unconditioned stimulus, but do not produce an unconditioned response.

7. On September 1, Jefferson High School's fire alarm sounded, and students ran from the building to escape the flames. For the next few weeks, the school experienced a rash of false alarms, and people began to ignore the sound. On December 15, a fire alarm sounded, and students ran from the building in panic. What phenomenon was responsible for the students' renewed fear?
a. Reconditioning
b. Spontaneous recovery

c. Stimulus control
d. Stimulus generalization

8. When Tamya was given chemotherapy, she developed a conditioned response to the food that she ate just prior to feeling nauseous. Tamya developed an aversion to the food rather than to the song she heard on the radio due to
   a. biopreparedness.
   b. generalization.
   c. simultaneous conditioning.
   d. signal strength.

9. Kent does not like to take drugs of any kind. When he goes to the dentist, he tries not to ask for any anesthesia. However, sometimes he cannot handle the pain of drilling, and so he lets the doctor give him a shot. This illustrates the use of
   a. a positive reinforcer.
   b. a negative reinforcer.
   c. punishment.
   d. all of the above.

10. In operant conditioning, discriminative stimuli
    a. automatically trigger a conditioned response.
    b. indicate the presence of reinforcement if a response is made.
    c. are successive approximations of a desired response.
    d. are similar, but not identical, to the conditioned stimulus.

11. Shaping is used when the conditioned response
    a. is physically difficult to perform.
    b. is to be decreased.
    c. has never been displayed before.
    d. is reflexive.

12. If you reinforce participants in your experiment after their first response and every ten minutes thereafter, you are using a _____ schedule of reinforcement.
    a. fixed interval
    b. fixed ratio
    c. variable interval
    d. variable ratio

13. Keleka's parents often deal with her misbehavior by not allowing her to watch her favorite TV program, *Speed Racer*. Marnie's parents deal with Marnie's misbehavior by spanking her. Keleka's parents are using _____ and Marnie's parents are using _____.
    a. punishment; negative reinforcement
    b. escape conditioning; avoidance conditioning
    c. negative reinforcement; punishment
    d. punishment; punishment

14. Advertisements for breath mints frequently involve a chance meeting of strangers who end up falling in love because they had great breath when they met. Advertisers are hoping that people who watch the commercial will learn by _____ that using breath mints will improve their love lives.
    a. vicarious conditioning
    b. observation
    c. classical conditioning
    d. stimulus control

15. Nancy arrived at a classroom for her one-day seminar teaching a spreadsheet computer program, but was shocked to find that it was a lecture hall of 200 or more seats and no computers were in sight. "I need to use a program in order to learn it," she exclaimed. Nancy would like the class to use _____ techniques.
    a. active learning
    b. latent learning
    c. cognitive mapping
    d. vicarious conditioning

Total Correct (See answer key) _____

ANSWERS TO CONCEPTS AND EXERCISES

No. 1: Learning in Advertising

1a. *Operant*. The customer is learning a relationship between a behavior (using a dry cleaner other than Speedy) and its consequence (clothes that aren't cleaned on time). (p. 154)

1b. *Punishment*. The fact that the dress is not ready will cause the customer problems and is therefore aversive. (p. 160)

1c. *Continuous*. Every time a behavior (going to Speedy Dry Clean versus any other dry cleaner) occurs, it is rewarded or reinforced (getting clothes back on time). (p. 158)

1d. *Once*. Behaviors learned on a continuous reinforcement schedule are very easy to extinguish. (pp. 158–159)

2a. *Classical*. Jennifer has learned that one stimulus (the doctor) predicts another (activities that cause pain). (p. 147)

2b. *Conditioned stimulus*. Jennifer was not always afraid of doctors; originally they were a neutral stimulus. When neutral stimuli begin to predict the presence of another stimulus, such as an injection, they become conditioned stimuli. (p. 148)

2c. *Conditioned response.* Since Jennifer had to learn to be afraid of doctors, this is a conditioned (or learned) response. (p. 148)

2d. *Extinction.* The association between the CS (doctors) and the UCS (activities that cause pain) has been eliminated or at least greatly diminished. The CR (fear of doctors) has also been eliminated. (p. 148)

No. 2: Teaching an Alien

1. *Punishment.* Sam has decreased his behavior of being late for dinner. Punishment decreases the occurrence of the behavior it follows. When Sam was late, he was probably punished. (p. 160)

2. *Cognitive map; latent learning.* Sam learned a shortcut by representing the information in his mind in the form of a map. We know that he learned the shortcut before he demonstrated his knowledge of it. (p. 166)

3. *Avoidance conditioning.* Sam learned to avoid having his sister inform his mother of his doings by simply not telling her what he did. (p. 155)

4. *Taste aversion.* Gufla learned that roses (CS) predict the presence of fertilizer (UCS). Fertilizer causes stomachaches (CR). Gufla will stay away from (CR) all roses (CS) in the future. (p. 151)

5. *Discriminative stimulus; primary positive reinforcer.* The direction in which Sam nodded his head would be a discriminative stimulus, or signal, that would let Gufla know when to make a response (eating whatever his fork touched) in order to receive the reinforcement of eating food. Food is a pleasant stimulus and basic to survival. Therefore, it is a primary positive reinforcer. (pp. 155–157)

6. *Observational learning.* Gufla will attend to what Sam is doing, retain the information, and reproduce it because Sam has told him to. Gufla is not performing each specific behavior to obtain a reward. (p. 167)

7. *Secondary positive reinforcer.* Watching a movie, although not basic to survival, is a pleasant stimulus. Therefore, this is an example of secondary positive reinforcement. (pp. 157-158)

ANSWERS TO CRITICAL THINKING

1. Sam hypothesizes that Rose has an antisocial personality.

2. Rose's history of being in trouble lends some support to his hypothesis.

3. Martina's probable hypothesis is that Rose has learned that she will be rewarded with her father's attention when she misbehaves. She probably has to go to extremes to get his attention since he is apparently so busy.

4. Martina will probably want to find out more about Rose's family situation.

ANSWERS TO MULTIPLE-CHOICE QUESTIONS

Circle the question numbers you answered correctly.

Sample Quiz 1

1. *d* is the answer. The loud sound elicits an unlearned reaction of flinching; therefore, it is the unconditioned (unlearned) stimulus. (p. 147)
   a. The red light is the conditioned (learned) response.
   b. Flinching in response to the loud sound is the unconditioned response.
   c. Conditioned responses are those that follow the conditioned stimulus. In this case, the red light also causes flinching, so the conditioned and unconditioned responses are the same behavior.

2. *d* is the answer. Originally the vanilla smell did not cause any response—it was the neutral stimulus—but after its association with the cookies (which *did* cause a response) it became the conditioned stimulus. Salivating was both the unconditioned and conditioned response. (p. 148)
   a. The cookie is the unconditioned stimulus that is experienced by eating it.
   b. The cookie is the unconditioned stimulus; smelling vanilla is an experience that accompanies the eating of the cookie. The vanilla smell is originally a neutral stimulus.
   c. The vanilla smell is the neutral stimulus, but the action of baking cookies has not been conditioned and is not in response to a learned stimulus.

3. *a* is the answer. If there is more of a UCS to get the attention of the learner, a response will be learned more quickly. If only a small amount of powdered food is placed on a dog's tongue after a bell is rung, the dog will be less likely to notice the food and make the association. (p. 150)
   b. If the UCS comes before the CS, the CS is not very predictive of when a UCS will happen. Learning is faster if the CS precedes the UCS by one-half to one second.
   c. Learning will be faster if the CS always predicts the UCS and only the UCS.

d. If the CS is not very noticeable, learning will be slower.

4. *a* is the answer. A behavior that is followed by pleasant events is more likely to be repeated. A behavior followed by unpleasant events is less likely to be repeated. (p. 154)

b, c. The effect of the strength of stimuli, operants, or reinforcers is not a main principle of Thorndike's law of effect.

d. Thorndike didn't say we needed to actively track the effects of our behavior; we just automatically have a tendency to repeat rewarded behaviors. In addition, humans are not the only beings influenced by instrumental conditioning.

5. *b* is the answer. In operant conditioning, reinforcers always produce a positive effect and work to increase a behavior. A negative reinforcer is a negative stimulus that is removed after the organism displays a desired response. (p. 154)

a. Positive reinforcers are pleasant stimuli that are presented after an organism displays a desired response.

c. Punishment and extinction are used to decrease the occurrence of a response. (You may be confusing punishment and negative reinforcers.) Remember, reinforcements (both positive and negative) increase the occurrence of a desired behavior.

d. Rewards that are basic to survival are primary reinforcements.

6. *a* is the answer. Zoe is being negatively reinforced for saying "I give." When she says it, Amy removes the unpleasant stimulus (hitting her arm). (p. 154)

b. Amy is not rewarded for stopping her hitting.

c. If Zoe were punished for saying "I give," she would be less likely to say it in the future.

d. If Amy were punished for stopping her hitting, she would be less likely to stop hitting in the future.

7. *c* is the answer. Linda keeps from encountering the long wait by turning down an alley; therefore, she *avoids* the situation. (p. 155)

a. Escape conditioning would apply only if Linda waited at the light and then did something to get out of waiting.

b. Stimulus discrimination refers to making a response in one situation rather than another, but the main issue in Linda's situation is how to avoid the long wait.

d. Stimulus generalization occurs when an animal or person responds to an event that is similar to one that indicated reinforcement in

the past. Linda isn't generalizing from other situations based on rewards.

8. *d* is the answer. In a shaping procedure, behaviors that are closer and closer to the desired behavior are rewarded. (p. 157)

a. Negative reinforcement would be taking away something unpleasant to encourage a behavior, but Chelsea is positively reinforcing Socks.

b. Classical conditioning is the learning of an association between a previously neutral stimulus and an automatic response. It doesn't involve rewards and punishments.

c. Vicarious conditioning occurs when someone learns from observing another person being rewarded or punished. If people see someone else punished for a behavior, they are less likely to behave in that manner.

9. *d* is the answer. Secondary reinforcers become rewards through their association with primary (unlearned) reinforcers. (p. 157)

a. A primary reinforcer generally satisfies basic physiological needs, such as the need for food and water.

b. Money is a learned reward, or secondary reinforcer. In classical conditioning, the unconditioned stimulus is one that causes an unlearned, reflexive response. While classical conditioning *may* be used to associate money with a primary reinforcer, money would then become a conditioned stimulus.

c. A discriminative stimulus is one that lets the person or animal know that reinforcement is available, but money *is* the reinforcer.

10. *a* is the answer. For each correct behavior (completed backpack), Larry receives a reward. This is a fixed ratio of one correct response to one reinforcement. (pp. 158-159)

b. Fixed interval schedules of reinforcement provide rewards for the first correct behavior after a specific length of time.

c. Variable ratio schedules of reinforcement provide rewards after an average number (varied) of correct responses.

d. Variable interval schedules of reinforcement provide rewards for the first correct behavior after a varied length of time.

11. *a* is the answer. A fixed-ratio schedule of reinforcement produces the fastest rate of extinction because the organism realizes very quickly that reinforcements have ceased to be presented and that after the appropriate number of responses has been made, the reinforcement should be there. A continuous schedule of

reinforcement, which is a type of fixed-ratio schedule, produces the fastest rate of extinction possible. (pp. 158-160)

b. Fixed intervals also produce a fast rate of extinction, but the organism must wait until the fixed interval elapses before it responds and finds no reinforcement.

c, d. Organisms on a variable schedule of reinforcement cannot predict when the reinforcement will appear. They therefore take longer to realize that the reinforcement is missing once the extinction process has begun.

12. c is the answer. Sometimes humans or animals do not understand what it is they are being punished for; this is one of the disadvantages of using punishment. Julio thought his mother was angry because Carlos wanted cereal, not because Carlos swore at her. (pp. 160–161)

a. Negative reinforcers are the removal of negative stimuli following a desired behavior. The boy's mother did not remove a negative stimuli; she added one by yelling and sending Carlos to his room.

b. Stimulus discrimination is found in classical conditioning scenarios. This is an example of operant conditioning.

d. c is the answer.

13. d is the answer. Eileen has learned that nothing she does will affect how much her boss criticizes her; therefore, she has "learned to be helpless" and stops trying to please him. (p. 163)

a. Vicarious learning is learning from watching others being reinforced or punished.

b. Social learning, or observational learning, is learning by watching others.

c. Classical conditioning doesn't involve rewards and punishments; it involves associations between reflexive responses and learned stimuli.

14. b is the answer. Jerad is demonstrating learning that wasn't evident at the time it first occurred. (p. 166)

a. Insight is a sudden realization of how to solve a problem.

c, d. In classical conditioning, stimulus generalization is responding to stimuli similar to the CS. Stimulus discrimination is *not* responding to stimuli similar to the CS.

15. a is the answer. Professor Smythe is using active learning to teach his students, which results in better learning and performance. (p. 172)

b. Professor Blythe is using a more passive learning process, which does not produce as much learning or as high performance.

c, d. Neither of these is true. Active learning produces better outcomes than passive learning.

Now turn to the quiz analysis table at the end of this chapter to find which areas you know well and which areas you need to work on. Circle the numbers in the table for items on Quiz 1 that you answered correctly.

ANSWERS TO MULTIPLE-CHOICE QUESTIONS

Circle the question numbers you answered correctly.

Sample Quiz 2

1. a is the answer. A neutral stimulus does not elicit a reflexive response. A neutral stimulus becomes a conditioned stimulus (CS) and elicits a conditioned response (CR) only after it is paired with an unconditioned stimulus (UCS). (pp. 147-148)

b. An unconditioned stimulus elicits a reflexive response or an unlearned response that happens automatically. Therefore, a neutral stimulus is not synonymous with an unconditioned stimulus.

c. A neutral stimulus does not elicit any response.

d. A neutral stimulus does not elicit any response. A neutral stimulus becomes a conditioned stimulus and elicits a conditioned response only when it is paired with an unconditioned stimulus.

2. a is the answer. The conditioned stimulus is the sound of the drill. The unconditioned stimulus is the use of the drill on the teeth. The unconditioned response is the pain that the drill causes. The conditioned response is nausea, which is elicited by the CS, the sound of the drill. (pp. 147-148)

b, d. Reinforcement, both positive and negative, is used in instrumental conditioning.

c. Instrumental conditioning involves learning an association between a behavior and its consequences. Letitia is learning an association between two stimuli: the sound of the drill and the feeling of the drill on her teeth.

3. a is the answer (see below).

4. *d* is the answer (see below).

5. *c* is the answer. Antonio's nausea in response to Ferris wheels is an example of classical conditioning. The conditioned stimulus is the sight of the amusement park. The unconditioned stimulus is the ride on the Ferris wheel. The unconditioned response is feeling dizzy. The conditioned response is feeling nauseous. (pp. 147-148)

6. *c* is the answer. An organism will generalize by responding to stimuli that are similar to the conditioned stimulus. (p. 149)
   a. Stimulus generalization is not dependent on whether the CS has occurred in the presence of the UCS. The generalized stimulus just has to be similar to the conditioned stimulus.
   b. In stimulus generalization, stimuli that are similar to the CS elicit a CR. This response is *always learned;* it is never reflexive.
   d. Generalization refers to responses made to stimuli that are similar to the CS, not to the UCS.

7. *b* is the answer. Spontaneous recovery is the recurrence of a conditioned response following extinction in the absence of reconditioning. (p. 148)
   a. Reconditioning is the re-pairing of the CS and the UCS after extinction. The fire alarm (CS) would have to be paired repeatedly with fire (UCS) again for reconditioning to occur.
   c. Operant conditioned responses are under stimulus control. This is an example of classical conditioning. The CS is the fire alarm, and the UCS is the fire.
   d. If stimulus generalization had occurred, the students would have run out of the building in response to an alarm (CS) that was similar, but not identical, to the original fire alarm. The students heard the same fire alarm in December and September.

8. *a* is the answer. Biopreparedness is a natural tendency to make certain associations, such as between food and nausea, rather than between a sound and nausea. (p. 151)
   b. Tamya did not generalize from one food to another; she associated the food with the nausea.
   c. In simultaneous conditioning, the CS and UCS arrive at the same time. Tamya didn't experience chemotherapy and food at the same time.
   d. High signal strength causes more rapid learning, but doesn't explain why she had a

conditioned response to the food rather than the song.

9. *b* is the answer. The negative reinforcer is the removal of drilling pain by the anesthetic. The behavior (asking for a drug to deaden the pain) will increase because the negative reinforcer has removed a potentially aversive stimulus (drilling pain). (p. 154)
   a. A positive reinforcer is a pleasant stimulus that is added to the environment following a desired response. In this example, an unpleasant stimulus, pain, is being removed; a pleasant one is not being added.
   c. If Kent was being punished, his behavior would be followed by an aversive stimulus or the removal of a pleasant one. Being relieved of pain is the removal of an unpleasant stimulus.
   d. *b* is the answer.

10. *b* is the answer. Discriminative stimuli allow the organism to discriminate between situations that will produce a consequence—a reinforcer or punishment—and those that will not. (p. 155)
   a. Discriminative stimuli let an organism know when to make a response; they do not cause a response. Conditioned stimuli elicit or cause a conditioned response. There are no conditioned stimuli in operant conditioning.
   c. Shaping involves rewarding successive approximations of a behavior (behaviors that come closer and closer to the desired response).
   d. Stimulus generalization in classical conditioning is when a conditioned response is made to a stimulus similar to the conditioned stimulus.

11. *c* is the answer. A behavior must occur before it can be reinforced. If an organism has never performed the desired behavior, behaviors that are successive approximations of the desired response are reinforced until the whole behavior appears. For an example of successive approximation, see the example of teaching your dog to "shake" in your text. (p. 157)
   a. Behaviors that are shaped are not always difficult to perform. For example, it is not physically difficult for a dog to roll over, but if the dog has never done so, its behavior must be shaped.
   b. Shaping is the creation of a new behavior, not the decreasing of an existing behavior.
   d. Shaping allows an organism to learn a new behavior. Reflexive behaviors are not new. Also, conditioned responses are learned, not reflexive.

12. *a* is the answer. In a fixed interval schedule, reinforcement is given after a set amount of time. (p. 159)
    b. In a fixed ratio schedule, reinforcement is given after a set number of desired behaviors.
    c. Variable interval schedules give reinforcement after an average amount of time has passed. If you were using variable interval you would give reinforcement after an average of ten minutes had passed.
    d. In variable ratio schedules of reinforcement, an experimenter would wait for an average number of desired behaviors before giving reinforcement.

13. *d* is the answer. Whether something positive is taken away or something negative is given, the person is experiencing punishment meant to decrease the probability of the behavior occurring again. (pp. 160-161)
    a, c. Negative reinforcement *increases* the likelihood of a behavior occurring again by taking away something negative.
    b. Neither girl is escaping or avoiding the negative consequences of her misbehavior.

14. *a* is the answer. By watching the commercials, people learn that use of breath mints is rewarded or reinforced by meeting an attractive stranger with whom they will live happily ever after. This is called vicarious conditioning. (p. 168)
    b. Observation learning does involve learning by watching the behavior of others. But the people being observed do not have to receive a reward or punishment in order for the person watching them to learn. Advertisements, as in this example, usually depict people being rewarded for buying and using the advertised products. Therefore, *a* is the better answer.
    c. This is an example of instrumental, not classical, conditioning.
    d. There is no stimulus mentioned in the question that lets a person know when to use breath mints. You may have thought that the presence of a stranger of the opposite sex was a discriminative stimulus, but this is not the case. The stranger is the reward or reinforcement in this example.

15. *a* is the answer. Active learning is learning by doing. When people consider how new information applies to them, when they practice using information in new situations, and when they answer questions about material they are studying, people remember more than if they only read, listen to a lecture, or try to memorize terms. (p. 172)
    b. Latent learning refers to learning that is not demonstrated at the time it occurs, but at a later time when the opportunity presents itself.
    c. Cognitive maps are mental representations of an environment.
    d. Vicarious conditioning occurs when people see others reinforced or punished for a behavior and learn that they should or shouldn't behave that way themselves.

Now turn to the quiz analysis table at the end of this chapter to find which areas you know well and which areas you need to work on. Circle the numbers in the table for items on Quiz 2 that you answered correctly.

For each question you answered correctly, circle its number. (Quiz 1 numbers are not shaded; Quiz 2 numbers are shaded.) Are there patterns in the types of questions or the topics you got wrong that could direct your further study? Did you improve from Quiz 1 to Quiz 2?

TOPIC	TYPE OF QUESTION		
	DEFINITION	**COMPREHENSION**	**APPLICATION**
Classical Conditioning			
Pavlov's discovery			1, 2
	1		2, 3, 4, 5
Responses, generalization, discrimination			
	6		7
Signaling and applications	3		
			8
Instrumental and Operant Conditioning			
Components	4, 5		6, 7
	10		9
Forming and strengthening behavior		11	8, 9, 10, 12
		11	12, 13
Cognitive processes in learning			13, 14
			14
Using research on learning			15
			15

TOTAL CORRECT BY QUIZ:

QUIZ 1:
QUIZ 2:

Chapter 6

Memory

LEARNING OBJECTIVES

1. Define encoding, storage, and retrieval and discuss the role of each in our ability to remember. Define and give examples of acoustic, visual, and semantic codes. Explain the difference between recall and recognition. (pp. 180–181)

2. Define and give examples of episodic, semantic, and procedural memories. (p. 181)

3. Define and give examples of explicit and implicit memories. (p. 181)

4. Define the levels-of-processing model of memory. Define maintenance and elaborative rehearsal and explain how these concepts relate to the levels-of-processing model. (p. 182)

5. Define transfer-appropriate processing model of memory. Discuss the emphasis placed on encoding and retrieval processes in this model. (p. 182)

6. Define the parallel distributed processing (PDP) model of memory. Describe the role of association networks in drawing inferences and making generalizations. (pp. 182–183)

7. Define the information-processing model of memory. Name the three stages of processing. (p. 183)

8. Define sensory memory and sensory registers. Discuss the capacity and duration of sensory memory. Explain the importance of selective attention in information processing. (pp. 184)

9. Define short-term memory (STM) and explain why it is sometimes referred to as working memory. Describe short-term memory encoding. (pp. 184–185)

10. Define immediate memory span and chunks. Discuss the role of long-term memory in the chunking process. (pp. 185–186)

11. Define the Brown-Peterson procedure. Describe the importance of rehearsal in maintaining information in short-term memory. (p. 186)

12. Define long-term memory (LTM) and discuss the relationship between semantic encoding and long-term memory. Describe the storage capacity of LTM. Discuss the studies illustrating the distortion of long-term memories. (pp. 187–188)

13. Describe the relationship between short-term and long-term memory. Define primacy and recency effects. (pp. 188–189)

14. Define retrieval cues and explain why their use can increase memory efficiency. Define the encoding specificity principle. (pp. 189–190)

15. Define context dependent and state dependent memories and give examples of each. Explain the mood congruency effect. (p. 190)

16. Describe the semantic network theory of memory and explain the principle of spreading activation. (pp. 190–192)

17. Define the tip-of-the-tongue phenomenon and explain how it relates to the semantic network theory of memory. (p. 192)

18. Define constructive memory and describe the studies examining the phenomenon. (pp. 192-194)

19. Describe how PDP memory models explain the formation of constructive memories. Explain how PDP networks can produce spontaneous generalizations, and how they explain the operation of schemas. (pp. 194–195)

20. Discuss the problems associated with eyewitness testimony in the courtroom. (pp. 195–197)

21. Define Ebbinghaus's method of savings. Explain his discoveries and indicate why they are important to memory research. (pp. 197–198)

22. Compare and contrast the decay and interference theories of forgetting. Define retroactive interference and proactive interference and give an example of each. (pp. 198–199)

23. Discuss the controversy surrounding repressed memories. Describe motivated forgetting and false memories. (pp. 199–202)

24. Describe the synaptic activity associated with forming new memories. Describe the role of the hippocampus in episodic and procedural memory formation. (p. 202)

25. Define <u>anterograde</u> and <u>retrograde amnesia</u> and discuss how these types of memory loss support a distinction between STM and LTM. (pp. 203–204)

26. Define <u>mnemonics</u> and explain why they improve memory. Give an example of the method of loci. (p. 205)

27. Explain why distributed practice is more effective than massed practice. Describe the PQ4R method of reading textbooks. Describe the best method of taking notes in a lecture. (pp. 205–206)

KEY TERMS

I. THE NATURE OF MEMORY

1. **Encoding** is the process of coding information so that it can be placed in sensory, short-term, or long-term memory. There are three types of codes: visual, acoustic, and semantic. (p. 180)

2. **Acoustic codes** are representations of the sounds we hear. (p. 180)

   Example: Think of your favorite song and hum it to yourself. The memory of how the melody sounds is an acoustic code in long-term memory.

3. **Visual codes** are representations of the images we see. (p. 180)

   Example: If you think of a Christmas tree or the car you would buy if you had enough money, you will most likely see images of these things in your mind. You do so because you have visual codes for them.

4. **Semantic codes** are representations of the meaning of experiences or factual information. (p. 180)

   Example: If you visit Israel, you may notice that the children can sing the top rock songs from the United States, but that they do not know what the words mean. This is because they are using an acoustic code to remember a song and sing it, but they do not have a semantic code for the meaning of the words.

5. **Storage** is the process of maintaining or keeping a memory. (p. 180)

   Example: Memories of your kindergarten class, your second-grade teacher, or the first home you lived in are old memories. They have been stored for quite some time.

6. **Retrieval** is the process of transferring memories from storage to consciousness. (p. 181)

   Example: Whenever you remember anything, you are retrieving that memory from storage. Some memories are retrieved so quickly that you are unaware of the process. Answer the following questions: How old are you? How many people have been president of the United States? Both questions require you to retrieve information, but the retrieval process is much easier for the first question than for the second.

7. **Episodic memory** is any memory of a specific event that happened while you were present. (p. 181)

   Example: The memory of your first pony ride, a surprise birthday party that you held for a friend, or your first day of college is an episodic memory.

   REMEMBER: Episodic memories are episodes that involved you.

8. **Semantic memory** contains factual knowledge. This memory differs from episodic memory in that its contents are not associated with a specific event. (p. 181)

   Example: Knowing that the freezing point is 32 degrees Fahrenheit, that red lights mean stop, and that the capital of the United States is Washington, D.C., are all examples of semantic memory. You probably cannot remember the specific time or episode during which you learned these facts.

9. **Procedural memory** holds "how-to" methods or processes that usually require some motor movement. (p. 181)

   Example: Knowing how to waltz, do a somersault, tie a tie, and drive a car are all procedural memories.

10. **Explicit memory** is the process of purposely trying to remember something. (p. 181)

    Example: While you are taking an exam, you are using explicit memory to retrieve information regarding the questions.

11. **Implicit memory** is the subconscious recall or influence of past experiences. (p. 181)

    Example: Although you don't understand why, you are nervous whenever you wait for a bus on a specific corner. Stored subconsciously is the memory of a frightening event from your childhood in which a stranger approached you at that corner, and you ran away.

12. The **levels-of-processing model** holds that differences in how well something is remembered reflect the depth with which incoming information is mentally processed. (p. 182)

REMEMBER: Maintenance rehearsal does not require much processing and is effective for encoding information into short-term memory. Elaborative rehearsal requires a great deal of processing and is effective for encoding into long-term memory.

13. **Maintenance rehearsal**, repeating information over and over, keeps information in short-term memory. (p. 182)

Example: Kan arrives in New York to visit his cousin Zhou, but loses Zhou's phone number. Kan calls directory assistance and the operator tells him the number. Kan repeats it over and over to himself while he inserts coins for the call.

REMEMBER: Maintenance rehearsal <u>maintains</u> information in short-term memory.

14. **Elaborative rehearsal** involves thinking about how new material is linked or related in some way to information already stored in long-term memory. It is an effective method of encoding information into long-term memory. (p. 182)

Example: Ursula is a world-class shopper. She has a mental image of all the major cities she has shopped in and images of the locations of all her favorite stores on each street. When Ursula wants to store information about a new store, she uses her mental image and places the new store on its street. She thinks about the new store in relationship to the stores surrounding it. Ursula is not just repeating the address of the new store, but is also relating it to the addresses of all the other stores that she knows.

REMEMBER: New information is <u>elaborated</u> with information already in long-term memory. The new address is elaborated by relating its location to all the old addresses of stores already in long-term memory.

15. The **transfer-appropriate processing model** suggests that memory retrieval will be improved if the encoding method matches the retrieval method. (p. 182)

Example: Samantha studied for an auto mechanics test by spending many weekends with her head under the hood of a car. However, much to her surprise, when it came time to take the test, the professor handed out a multiple-choice exam. Samantha, who felt that she had really learned the material, scored poorly. According to the transfer-appropriate processing model, Samantha did not do well because she encoded the material by applying what she had learned from the text, but the exam asked her only to retrieve specific facts. Samantha's encoding process wasn't appropriate for the retrieval process required by the exam.

REMEMBER: Think of this model as stating that the encoding process that <u>transfers</u> information into long-term memory must be <u>appropriate</u> (match) for the retrieval cues.

16. **Parallel distributed processing** (or **PDP**) **model** of memory suggests that the connections between units of knowledge are strengthened with experience. Tapping into any connection (via a memory process) provides us with access to all the other connections in the network. (p. 182)

Example: Zoë's knowledge that the term *neonate* means "newborn" is linked to her memory of seeing a premature infant taken to a neonatal unit. Both neonate and neonatal are connected to her memory that *neo* means "new." When Zoë thinks of neonate, an image of her nephew as a newborn is also readily accessible. This background made it easier for her to understand that a *neofreudian* is a person who developed a new version of Freud's theory.

17. The **information-processing model** of memory has three stages: sensory memory; short-term, or working, memory; and long-term memory. (p. 183)

Example: When you prepare for a psychology test, you may start by reading your notes. As you read your notes, the information you are taking in first must pass through your visual sensory memory before going to your short-term memory. In short-term memory, you are aware of the information you are studying. Finally, after elaborating on the information you are aware of in short-term memory, the information you study is stored in long-term memory for later retrieval at test time.

II. STORING NEW MEMORIES

18. **Sensory memory** holds sensory information for a fraction of a second in sensory registers. If the information is attended to and recognized, perception takes place, and the information can enter short-term memory. (p. 184)

Example: When children play with sparklers on the 4th of July in the United States, they often use the sparklers to "draw" circles in the air by rapidly rotating the sparkler so that a circle does appear visible for a brief moment. In fact, no circle actually exists, but the children's sensory memory holds each point of light as the sparkler rotates just long enough that a circle is perceived for a moment.

19. **Sensory registers** hold incoming sensory information until it is processed, recognized, and

remembered. There is a sensory register for each sense. (p. 184)

Example: When children playing with sparklers perceive that they are drawing circles, it is the visual sensory registry that is responsible for this perception.

20. **Selective attention** determines what information is held in sensory registers. Information that is not attended to decays and cannot be processed any further. (p. 184)

Example: Imagine going to New York's Times Square for New Year's Eve. The crowd is immense. Suddenly, you see someone waving a sparkler in front of you. Even though your eyes and ears are being hit with a variety of stimuli, your sensory registers will retain information about the person with the sparkler because you "selected" that particular stimulus to "attend" to.

21. **Short-term memory** (or **working memory**) receives information that was perceived in sensory memory. Information in short-term memory is conscious, but quite fragile, and will be lost within seconds if not further processed. (p. 184)

Example: If you look up a phone number and repeat it to yourself until you finish dialing, you will have kept it active in your short-term memory. However, it is likely that you will have forgotten it by the time you get off the phone, because you were using your working memory to process the new information coming in during the conversation.

22. An **immediate memory span** is the largest number of items or chunks of information that you can recall perfectly from short-term memory after one presentation of the stimuli. Most people have an immediate memory span of five to nine items. (p. 185)

Example: Use a telephone book to help you test your own immediate memory span. Read the first two names at the top of the page, look away, and then try to recall them. Then read the next three names, look away, and try to recall them. Continue this process, using a longer list each time, until you cannot repeat the entire list of names. The number of names that you can repeat perfectly is your immediate memory span.

23. **Chunks** are meaningful groupings of information that you place in short-term memory. The immediate memory span of short-term memory is probably between five and nine chunks of information. Each chunk contains bits of information grouped into a single unit. (p. 185)

Example: During her first night as a waitress, Bridget needed all five to nine chunks in short-term

memory to remember one order for one person. For example, a drink before dinner, a drink with dinner, a main dish, a type of salad dressing, a type of potato, and whether the customer wanted cream, sugar, or both with coffee made up five to nine chunks of information. After two years of waitressing, Bridget can easily hold in memory four to eight people's complete food and drink orders. Each person's order had become one chunk of information.

REMEMBER: Chunks can be anything—letters, numbers, words, names, or locations—just to list a few. The more information you can condense or group into one chunk, the more information you can hold in short-term memory.

24. The **Brown-Peterson procedure** is a research method that prevents rehearsal. A person is presented with a group of three letters they should try to remember and then counts backward by threes from an arbitrarily selected number until a signal is given. The counting prevents the person from rehearsing the information, and reduces the chances of remembering the three letters. (p. 186)

Example: You can see how the Brown-Peterson procedure affects your short-term memory by looking in the phone book at a number you do not already know. Look at the number, then look away and count backwards from 87 by threes until you hit 54. Can you remember the phone number now without looking? Most likely not, because the Brown-Peterson procedure prevented you from rehearsing the number.

25. **Long-term memory** is the stage of memory in which the capacity to store new information is believed to be unlimited. (p. 186)

Example: When you remember things for long periods of time, such as your 5th birthday party or multiplication tables, you are retrieving information from your long-term memory.

26. The **primacy effect** occurs when we remember words at the beginning of a list better than those in the middle of the list. (pp. 188-189)

Example: Sarah has just met a group of four people at her new school. However, she can only remember the name of the first person to whom she was introduced.

REMEMBER: Primacy means "being first." The primacy effect is the remembering of the first words in a list better than other words in the list.

27. The **recency effect** occurs when we remember the last few words on a list better than others on the list. The

list's final items are in short-term memory at the time of recall. (pp. 188-189)

Example: After hearing all her students' names once, Leslie tries to recite them one by one. She remembers the names of students in the first two rows (primacy effect) and the names of the students in the last two rows (recency effect), but she has difficulty recalling the names of students in the middle two rows.

REMEMBER: Recency means "that which occurred most recently." The last items of a list are presented most recently.

III. RETRIEVING MEMORIES

28. **Retrieval cues** help us recognize information in long-term memory. In other words, they help you "jog" your memory. (p. 189)

Example: On a multiple-choice exam, the answer appears somewhere in the question. Some of the words in the correct answer should jog your memory and allow you to answer the question correctly.

29. The **encoding specificity principle** maintains that if the way information is encoded and the way it is retrieved are similar, remembering the information will be easier. (p. 190)

Example: As Melanie's psychology instructor lectures, she often provides the class with vivid examples of each concept. Later, on quizzes and tests, many of the questions ask the students to identify examples of the same concepts discussed in lecture. The more similar the example on the quiz is to the example given in lecture, the easier it will be to identify the example correctly.

30. In **context-dependent** memory, the environment acts as a retrieval cue. This means that it is easier to remember information when you are in the location (context) where you originally learned that information. (p. 190)

Example: When taking his exam in his regular classroom, Leon's memory for lecture information is improved by glancing around at the chalkboard, peeling paint, and lecturer's desk. Although he doesn't realize it, he recalls the discussion of the opponent process color vision theory better because he is among familiar classmates and surroundings. Unfortunately, he does not remember as much of the information he studied in his room at home with the stereo blaring because there are fewer associated retrieval cues there than in the quiet classroom environment.

31. In **state-dependent** memory, your psychological or physiological state acts as a retrieval cue. When you are trying to remember, if you are in the same psychological state you were in at the time of learning, you will retrieve more material. (p. 190)

Example: In the evening when she studied psychology, Lydia had several cups of coffee to keep her alert. The next morning, she did not do well on the quiz. Later, when drinking coffee with some friends, she was in the same state as when she studied for the quiz, and, to her amazement, she remembered some of the material that had escaped her during the quiz.

32. **Spreading activation** describes the way in which information is retrieved from long-term memory according to semantic network theories. Whenever a question is asked, neural activation spreads from those concepts contained in the question down all paths related to them. (p. 191)

Example: When Jane thinks about pizza, this activates other concepts such as food, delivery, cost, etc.

IV. CONSTRUCTING MEMORIES

33. **Schemas** are summaries of knowledge about categories. We tend to automatically place people, objects, and events into classes. (pp. 194-195)

Example: If your schema for a classroom is a square room filled with desks, upon seeing people seated on pillows in a round room you might be likely to classify it as a lounge.

V. FORGETTING

34. The **method of savings** is a term introduced by Ebbinghaus to refer to the difference in the amount of time required to relearn material that has been forgotten and the amount of time it took to learn the material initially. (p. 197)

Example: If it took a participant twenty repetitions to learn a list of items, but only five repetitions to relearn the list a semester later, there would be a savings of 75 percent.

35. **Decay** is a mechanism whereby information not used in long-term memory gradually fades until lost completely. (p. 198)

Example: Marissa learned Spanish, but has not tried to speak it in years. When Marissa tries to say, "Hello, how was your day?" to her roommate, she cannot remember the vocabulary necessary.

36. **Interference** is a mechanism whereby the retrieval or storage of information in long-term memory is impaired by other learning (retroactive and proactive interference). (p. 198)

37. **Retroactive interference** occurs when information in memory is displaced by new information. (p. 198)

Example: You learned Latin in high school, but in college have been taking only Spanish courses. You now find it difficult to remember the Latin from high school because you remember the Spanish you have studied more recently.

REMEMBER: Retro means "back." New information goes back and interferes with old information.

38. **Proactive interference** occurs when old information in long-term memory interferes with the remembering of new information. (p. 198)

Example: If you have ever learned something incorrectly and then tried to correct it, you may have experienced proactive interference. Young children who take music lessons once a week experience this. They learn an incorrect note, and at their lesson the next week, their teacher points out the mistake. However, it is very difficult to play the correct note because the old memory of the wrong note interferes with the new memory of the correct note.

REMEMBER: Pro means "forward." Old information goes forward and interferes with new information.

39. **Anterograde amnesia** is a loss of memory for events that occur after a brain injury. Memory for experiences prior to the trauma remains intact. (p. 203)

Example: People with anterograde amnesia will not be able to remember the new people they meet, because they are unable to form new memories.

REMEMBER: Anterograde amnesia is a loss of memory for the future, or after some point in time.

40. **Retrograde amnesia** is a loss of memory of events prior to a brain injury. Memories encoded days or years before the injury or trauma can be lost. Usually most memories return. (p. 204)

Example: Characters on soap operas who experience head injuries will often wake up and not remember who they are of where they are from. They cannot retrieve memories from their past.

REMEMBER: Retro means "backward." The memory loss goes back in time.

41. **Mnemonics** are encoding methods that increase the efficiency of your memory. (p. 205)

Example: To remember the name "Hathaway," you might picture the person coming "half the way" to you.

CONCEPTS AND EXERCISES

No. 1: Memory Cues

Completing this exercise should help you to achieve Learning Objectives 1, 2, 10, 15, and 22.

There has been a robbery at a local bank. For questioning, the police have placed the witnesses in the locations they occupied during the robbery. Indicate what type of memory, code, or process is responsible for each statement. Draw your answers from the list following the exercise. Answers may be used more than once or not at all.

1. Police: We are questioning you here at the bank because we think it will improve your recall of the robbery. _____ What was the suspect wearing?

2. Teller 1: I know he had a coat on, but I don't remember the color. _____

3. Teller 2: I remember. It was green. _____

   Police (To teller 3): Where were you when the robbery took place?

4. Teller 3: I was standing in the manager's office when the man approached me and told me to unlock the door to the safe. _____

   Police: Did you have to look up the combination to the safe?

5. Teller 3: No, sir. The manager had just given me the new combination for the day ten seconds before the man approached me. I just grouped the numbers into a date so I'd remember them for the few minutes it would take me to walk from the office to the safe. Just as I'd finished thinking about the combination, the gunman was there ordering me to unlock the safe. _____

   Police: Did the man have any unusual speech characteristics?

6. Teller 2: Yes, he did. I remember hearing him slur his S's. _____

   Police (To teller 1): Please demonstrate the steps you follow in order to sound the alarm.

7. Teller 1: I have to step on this foot pedal like this. _____

   Police: Why did it take you so long to sound the alarm?

8. Teller 1: Well, sir, I've just started working at this bank. The alarm at my last job sounded at the push of a button. I guess I panicked a bit. I was looking for the button for a few seconds before I realized that here I have to push a foot pedal. _____

Police: Thank you, everyone. That will be all for now.

- ° Acoustic code
- ° Procedural memory
- ° Context dependence
- ° Chunking
- ° Semantic code
- ° Visual code
- ° Episodic memory
- ° Proactive interference
- ° Retroactive interference

No. 2: Learning How to Study

Completing this exercise should help you to achieve Learning Objectives 5, 26, and 27.

Below are descriptions of study methods that need improvement. Use the information you have learned in this chapter to fill in the blanks following the descriptions.

1. Rodney is taking a vocabulary improvement class. He is learning to recognize the roots of words and their meanings. He tries to memorize the material by repeating it to himself over and over again. Instead of doing this, he should probably try using _____.

2. Ginny is a college freshman. She is taking a course in biology, a subject she never had in high school. When she takes notes, she desperately tries to write down every word the instructor says. Instead, she should _____ the information.

3. Carin hates to read. She wants to get it over with quickly, so she reads large amounts of material at a time. Then she complains that she can never remember what she has just read. She should try using the _____ method.

CRITICAL THINKING

Sam is very frustrated. He had to release a suspect that he was sure was guilty, because the only witness couldn't remember what happened.

Sam had found the witness next to the scene of the crime about fifteen minutes after it happened. The witness was an old man who lived on the corner at the scene of the crime. He spent most of his time drinking and was in pretty bad shape. Sam pulled the witness in

and let him sleep in the jail, figuring that if the witness got a good, warm, and safe night's sleep, a hot meal, and a chance to sober up, he would be willing to talk. However, Sam's efforts were to no avail. The witness just couldn't remember what he had seen. In fact, all he wanted to do was get back to his corner so that he could get a drink.

Sam, crestfallen, tells Martina that he failed and had to let the witness go.

Martina says, "All may not be lost. Grab your coat and let's go."

"Where are we going?" asks Sam.

Martina replies. "First we are going to the liquor store, and then back to the scene of the crime."

Using the five critical thinking questions in your text, the clues in the story, and what you have just learned about memory, answer the following:

1. What is Sam's hypothesis?

2. What is the evidence in support of Sam's hypothesis?

3. What is Martina's alternative hypothesis?

4. What evidence must Martina gather to support her hypothesis?

5. What conclusions can Martina draw if the evidence she needs to collect supports her hypothesis?

PERSONAL LEARNING ACTIVITIES

1. Describe your earliest memories of several family members and see how well they match your relatives' recollections of the same events. (Learning Objectives 2 and 18)

2. Do an experiment to see the effects of maintenance versus elaborative rehearsal. One way to do this would be to read a list of about twenty words or names and repeat them to yourself several times. Then write down the time of day, your full name, address, and phone number (to clear the words from your short-term memory). Without looking at the list, write as many as you can. Next, study a list of twenty words or names by associating an image with each, clear your short-term memory, and then write as many as you can. Was there a difference? Does the size of any difference depend upon what type of information you are trying to learn? (Learning Objective 4)

3. Do you think your memory has improved with increasing age? Why or why not? What factors do you think most influence whether you will recall a phone number, an appointment, someone's name, or lecture information? (Learning Objectives 8, 11, and 12)

4. To understand how context-dependent memory works, try two very different locations for learning and remembering. After learning new information, test yourself on it in the same location in which you learned it—a classroom, or wherever you do your homework. After learning some other new material, go to an equally quiet but different place—the shower, your car, or even your closet—and test yourself. Notice the difference in how much you remember in the original location as compared to the different location. (Learning Objective 15)

5. Survey several students at your college to determine the effect of study style on grades. Make sure you asked each individual which type of practice they use as they study—distributed or massed practice. Then ask their GPA (Probably these people should be folks you are comfortable asking these questions!). Do the students who use massed practice have a higher average GPA? (Learning Objective 27)

WHAT SHOULD I WRITE ABOUT?

Over the last few chapters, we've discussed several strategies that you might be able to use as you develop your term paper topics. Here we introduce still another strategy for selecting a topic—examining the link between a process and an outcome. Although many undergraduates who are in the first year or so of their higher education are unfamiliar with this distinction, it is a useful one of which to be aware.

An outcome needs little explanation—it is the end result that one is interested in studying. The question that almost all researchers (and individuals writing term papers) encounter as they write is, "What makes certain outcomes happen, and suppresses others?" The answer to this question almost always has something to do with a *process*. For example, your textbook talks about the outcome known as "constructed memories." The question "How do constructed memories come about?" leads us to the issue of memory processes. How is it that memory works so that we can experience a memory as real and vivid, and yet be completely wrong? The study of how something works is the study of a process.

Many term paper writers focus mainly on picking an outcome of interest when they choose a term paper topic. But focusing only on the outcome makes it hard to develop the topic further. After all, there is only so much about any one *outcome* to describe. The study of what drives that outcome is typically a much more interesting path of analysis. Once you have identified an outcome you are interested in writing about, you should spend some time considering the processes that are linked to that outcome. For example, your textbook examines several perspectives on memory processes—information processing, parallel distributed processing, levels of processing model, and so on. Each one of these perspectives on memory processes might be able to illuminate how constructed memories are formed. They will almost certainly have different perspectives on this issue, which will allow you to analyze the various explanations of the outcome (constructed memories) as you write your paper.

Once you have identified an outcome of interest, try asking these questions to get you thinking about various process issues:

1. How do the different theories or models of which I am aware relate to the outcome I want to study?

2. Do the different theories or models provide different descriptions of the process that leads to the outcome?

3. Which theory or model has the more credible research to support it? (*Hint:* You can use the five "Thinking Critically" steps to determine the answer to this type of question).

THE INTERNET

The Psychabilities web site that accompanies this text offers many resources relevant to this chapter. They include NetLab exercises, Thinking Critically and Evaluating Research exercises, ACE chapter quizzes, recommended web links, and articles on current events, books, and movies. Go to http://college.hmco.com, select Psychology, and then this textbook.

MULTIPLE-CHOICE QUESTIONS

SAMPLE QUIZ 1

1. Steven heard his instructor say, "Remember to read the short stories by Christie, Cheever, Porter, and Sayers for next week." Because Steven isn't familiar with the names, he remembers them as "Krissy, Cleever, Porter, and Savers." Steven most likely used _____ encoding.
   a. acoustic
   b. episodic
   c. semantic
   d. visual

2. William is talking with his children. "You should have been there the first time that I saw your mother," he remembers. "I can still see her standing by the door asking me for directions to the freeway." William is drawing from his _____ memory.
   a. episodic
   b. semantic
   c. avoidance
   d. sensory

3. Nathan doesn't consciously think about an incident from his childhood when a red-haired neighbor gave him candy and comforted him after he skinned his knee. Due to the subconscious influence of that memory, however, Nathan tends to react positively to any red-haired people he meets; therefore, he is being influenced by his _____ memory.
   a. episodic
   b. explicit
   c. implicit
   d. procedural

4. Information first enters the sensory register where
   a. it passes directly to long-term memory.
   b. information may be attended to, analyzed, and encoded.
   c. it will all be transferred to short-term memory.
   d. the information from the sensory register disappears in approximately twenty seconds.

5. Homer Simpson is trying to remember the different functions of the control panel at the nuclear power plant where he works. He remembers the functions of the different buttons by thinking about the types of donuts that the buttons most resemble. For example, he is supposed to press a red button to shut off the reactors when they are about to have a meltdown. He remembers this because the red button reminds him of cherry donuts, which he only eats during hot weather. The type of processing that Homer is using is _____ rehearsal.
   a. levels-of-processing
   b. elaborative
   c. maintenance
   d. transfer-appropriate

6. While discussing memory, Dr. Johnson says, "Each unit of knowledge is ultimately connected to every other unit." Dr. Masters replies, "You charlatan! When the encoding process matches up with what is ultimately retrieved, memory is optimal." Dr. Johnson supports a(n) _____ model and Dr. Masters supports a(n) _____ model.
   a. levels-of-processing; information processing
   b. transfer-appropriate processing; levels-of-processing
   c. parallel distributed processing; transfer-appropriate processing
   d. information-processing; parallel distributed processing

7. Which of the following sentences would require the most chunks in short-term memory if you only knew how to speak English?
   a. John has many friends.
   b. *Ich liebe dich.*

c. *Je ne sais pas.*
d. –.–.–..–..–..– (Morse code)

8. In order to chunk efficiently, you will need to
   a. use your long-term memory.
   b. group many items into one chunk.
   c. transfer information quickly from short-term to long-term memory.
   d. all of the above.

9. Vinnie is exasperated. He has gone to the library to look up a book for class. Even though he checked his class notes before he left, he cannot remember the name of the book. What could account for his memory lapse?
   a. Inefficient storage in sensory memory
   b. Information not getting transferred to long-term memory
   c. Problems with selective attention
   d. None of the above

10. Since her brain injury last month, Margaret has not been able to form new memories. She has apparently retained very little of the events that have occurred after her brain injury. She suffers from
    a. anterograde amnesia.
    b. retrograde amnesia.
    c. positive transfer.
    d. negative transfer.

11. Alberta is a night owl. She loves to stay up late and study. However, she has so many classes this semester that she is forced to take her calculus class and study calculus in the morning when she is sluggish and a bit sleepy. Alberta's calculus teacher has given the class a take-home test. Alberta should take the test
    a. in the evening.
    b. in the afternoon.
    c. in the morning.
    d. whenever she feels like it.

12. To answer a question such as, "How many legs do spiders have?" a person will most likely use _____ memory.
    a. episodic
    b. semantic
    c. sensory
    d. short-term

13. An officer shows Sarah a box of office supplies believed to have been stolen from her store and then puts them at the back of the room. When Sarah is asked whether the staplers appear to be those stolen from her store, she thinks for a minute about the staplers she recalls seeing in the box and says they are like the ones stolen. To Sarah's

surprise, the officer then shows her that there are no staplers in the box! Sarah must have used _____ memories to answer the question.
a. constructive
b. elaborative
c. generalized
d. implicit

14. Last week, Sigrid had to memorize a poem to recite in front of the class. When she rehearsed at home, her mom told her that she had memorized an incorrect word and told her what to say instead. However, Sigrid had memorized the incorrect version so well that she had difficulty learning the correct word. This is an example of
a. retroactive interference.
b. proactive interference.
c. anterograde amnesia.
d. decay.

15. Kristi has memorized a list of names by imagining each person in a specific spot in her dorm room. One person is in the closet, another is under the bed, one is hanging upside down from the ceiling, and so on. She is using
a. context dependence.
b. distributed practice.
c. the encoding specificity principle.
d. the method of loci.

Total Correct (See answer key) _____

SAMPLE QUIZ 2

Use this quiz to reassess your learning after taking Quiz 1 and reviewing the chapter.

1. Al saw a movie called "Fight of the Kodiak" and immediately thought, "Kodiak is a bear, so this is going to have good scenery." Unfortunately, because Al only _____ encoded the name of the movie as "about a bear," he couldn't remember the actual name when someone asked him later what movie he saw.
a. acoustically
b. procedurally
c. semantically
d. visually

2. Gerianna is playing in her senior piano recital. Later, when her friends ask her how she can remember such long and complex pieces, Gerianna explains that these tasks involve _____ memory, and words cannot aptly describe it.
a. procedural
b. semantic
c. episodic
d. acoustic

3. As Kaliina completes a personal history questionnaire, she recalls her birthdate, names of schools she's attended, and relatives' names. Suddenly, she feels hot, flushed, and embarrassed, but doesn't know why. Kaliina's mom realizes that Kaliina subconsciously remembers the time she filled out a similar form and then fainted. When Kaliina tries to remember her personal information, she is using _____ memory; when she feels embarrassed, she is using _____ memory.
a. episodic; semantic
b. semantic; episodic
c. implicit; explicit
d. explicit; implicit

4. Which of the following is *most* important when trying to memorize information?
a. Thinking about new information in relation to existing knowledge
b. The length of exposure to this information
c. Shifting from medium to high stimulus intensity
d. Using a systematic scanning pattern

5. As Laura reads her psychology textbook, the image of each word is stored long enough to be processed and understood. Laura's _____ memory holds the images just long enough to allow stimulus identification to begin.
a. long-term
b. semantic
c. sensory
d. short-term

6. Warren is trying to remember the following list: table, rock, phone, apple. When recalling the list from his short-term memory, he makes a mistake and recalls the wrong word when trying to remember the word *rock*. Which of the following will *most likely* be the word that Warren recalls instead of *rock*?
a. Clock
b. Stone
c. Hair
d. Round

7. If you lost the ability to retrieve any information from long-term memory, you would not be able to
a. chunk information.
b. recognize information in sensory memory.
c. use the method of loci.
d. all of the above

8. Ramona's mother has given her a grocery list, and she is off to the store. As she enters the parking lot, she realizes that she forgot to bring the list with her. However, she can recall the first ten items on

the list and decides to buy just those. Her recollection of the first ten items on the list is an example of
a. the recency effect.
b. the primacy effect.
c. interference.
d. retroactive amnesia.

9. Ted showed his third-graders pictures of famous presidents. To quiz them, he gave them clues about what these people looked like. For example, "He wore a big black hat, enjoyed reading by the fireplace, was very, very tall, and had a black beard." These clues will function as
a. retrieval cues.
b. primacy cues.
c. contextual codes.
d. acoustic codes.

10. By having your review session for an exam in the same room in which the exam will be given, you are *most* *likely* to benefit from _____ memory.
a. flashbulb
b. semantic
c. state-dependent
d. context-dependent

11. Andy studied for his psychology exam. He then studied for his history exam. After studying for the history exam, Andy found that he had forgotten most of the psychology material he had studied previously. The *best* explanation for Andy's forgetting is
a. retroactive interference.
b. proactive interference.
c. internal inhibition.
d. semantic inhibition.

12. When Kris sees his son without clothes on after having his bath, Kris suddenly feels extremely worried. In a discussion of the incident during therapy, Kris recalls for the first time that he was sexually molested by a relative. Kris's therapist might describe this recollection as a(n) _____ memory.
a. elaborative
b. procedural
c. repressed
d. state-dependent

13. The memory that Kris has recovered should, according to the "Thinking Critically" section in your text, be
a. considered a constructed memory.
b. immediately accepted as an accurate memory.
c. examined through the use of other evidence.
d. recorded as a case of retroactive amnesia.

14. Jen has hippocampus damage; therefore, she has memory problems. Which of the following will she most likely be unable to do?
a. Learn how to solve a puzzle
b. Remember the names of new people she met ten minutes ago.
c. Remember a childhood birthday party
d. Remember how to ride a bike

15. Jacques was so involved in his social life his first semester that he almost flunked out. At the beginning of second semester, he asked his friends for their advice. Which friend should he *not* listen to?
a. Friend 1: "Read the material a second time."
b. Friend 2: "Create an outline for your lecture notes. You need to mentally organize the material somehow."
c. Friend 3: "Ask yourself questions about the material as you read, and then look for the answers in the text."
d. Friend 4: "Try to relate the material to information you already know."

Total Correct (See answer key) _____

ANSWERS TO CONCEPTS AND EXERCISES

No. 1: Memory Cues

1. *Context dependence.* The context, in this case the bank, acts as a retrieval cue and helps the witnesses remember as much as possible about the robbery. (p. 190)

2. *Semantic code.* Teller 1 remembers that the robber had a coat on but does not have a visual code containing the color of the coat. (p. 180)

3. *Visual code.* Teller 2 does have a visual code of the robber, which includes the color of the robber's coat. (p. 180)

4. *Episodic memory.* Teller 3 is remembering an event (or episode) in which he was a participant. (p. 181)

5. *Chunking.* Teller 3 has used chunking to remember the combination to the safe. He has grouped the numbers into one meaningful unit of information: a date. (p. 185)

6. *Acoustic code.* Teller 2 has an acoustic code for the sound of the robber's voice. (p. 180)

7. *Procedural memory.* Teller 1 has a procedural memory for how to sound the alarm. (p. 181)

8. *Proactive interference.* The old information, how to sound the alarm in the bank that Teller 1 used to work at, is interfering with her ability to remember how to sound the alarm at her present job. (p. 198)

No. 2: Learning How to Study

1. *Elaborative rehearsal.* Classical mnemonics are good tools for memorizing long lists of words, as Rodney has to do. Maintenance rehearsal is a good method for keeping information in short-term memory. However, it will not help Rodney place the information in long-term memory. (p. 182)

2. *Summarize.* Ginny should think about the lecture when she hears it in order to build a framework or overall organization for the material. She should write down only summaries of basic ideas. (p. 206)

3. *PQ4R method.* The PQ4R method is a series of six steps that will increase the amount of information Carin remembers from her reading assignments. (p. 206)

ANSWERS TO CRITICAL THINKING

1. Sam's hypothesis is that the witness simply cannot remember what happened.

2. The fact that after a hot meal, a good night's sleep, and the opportunity to sober up the witness can't remember supports Sam's hypothesis.

3. Martina remembers the concepts of context and state dependence. She hypothesizes that if the witness goes back to the corner where he lives (same context) and has a drink (same state), he will be better able to remember.

4. Martina needs to carry out her hypothesis—that is, question the witness on his corner, after he has had a drink, and see if he can remember.

5. Martina can't really draw any conclusions even if the man does remember. He could lie just to ensure that he is allowed to drink. Therefore, Martina can only follow up the clues that the old man provides and hope that his memory is accurate and that he is telling the truth. (*NOTE:* Critical thinking is a constant process of hypothesizing, examining evidence, rehypothesizing, and collecting more evidence. Can you think of any other hypotheses to explain the situation?)

ANSWERS TO MULTIPLE-CHOICE QUESTIONS

Circle the question numbers you answered correctly.

Sample Quiz 1

1. *a* is the answer. When acoustic codes are used the errors likely to be made are errors in remembering the sound of the words. (p. 180)
   b. Episodic memories are those of events you witnessed, but episodic is not a type of coding.
   c. Semantic encoding represents the meaning of the information. If Steven had used a semantic code, he might have remembered something about the meaning of the names (assuming he was familiar with them, which he wasn't) such as the titles of the stories or the homelands of the authors.
   d. A visual code would require a visual stimulus, but the instructor just said the names.

2. *a* is the answer. Episodic memories are personal recollections or memories of events in which you were involved. (p. 181)
   b. Semantic memories are memories of facts or meanings.
   c. Avoidance is not a type of memory.
   d. Sensory memory only holds information for a split second, so William could not draw a memory many years old from it.

3. *c* is the answer. Implicit memories are not purposefully recalled but do influence behavior. (p. 181)
   a. Episodic memories are memories of events, but Nathan has not recalled the childhood event; therefore, it is not what is influencing him.
   b. Explicit memories are those we purposely try to remember. Nathan has not tried to remember the childhood incident, nor has he remembered it.
   d. Procedural memories are skill memories. Nathan is not recalling a skill like bike riding; he is being influenced by a subconscious childhood memory.

4. *b* is the answer. Information must be attended to, analyzed, and encoded from sensory memory or it will not be moved to short-term and then to long-term memory. (p. 184)
   a. Information in sensory memory passes first to short-term memory.
   c. Not all sensory memories are transferred to short-term memory.
   d. Information in sensory memory lasts only a fraction of a second.

5. *b* is the answer. Homer is using elaborative rehearsal by associating the information about the

button functions with his knowledge of donuts. (p. 182)

a. Levels of processing is not a type of rehearsal. According to the level of processing model Homer is using a higher level of processing, which will be more successful in helping him to remember, but he is using elaborative rehearsal, not levels of processing rehearsal.

c. Maintenance rehearsal is OK for short-term memory, but doesn't work as well for long-term memory. It is better to elaborate on new information in order to remember it.

d. Transfer-appropriate is not a type of rehearsal. The transfer-appropriate processing models states that memory is better when encoding and retrieval are the same type of strategy.

6. c is the answer. Dr. Johnson believes all information is connected, which agrees with the parallel distributed processing model. Dr. Masters believes that the match between encoding and retrieval strategies is important, which agrees with the transfer-appropriate processing model. (p. 182)

a. Levels of processing relates to the degree of work a person does to encode information. Information processing relates to the transfer between sensory, short-term, and long-term memory.

b. Dr. Masters, not Dr. Johnson, believes that the match between encoding and retrieval strategies is important, which agrees with the transfer-appropriate processing model. Information processing relates to the transfer among sensory, short-term, and long-term memory.

d. Information processing relates to the transfer among sensory, short-term, and long-term memory. Dr. Johnson, not Dr. Masters, believes all information is connected, which agrees with the parallel distributed processing model.

7. d is the answer. Morse code uses a different "alphabet" than English does. A person who does not know Morse code would not have any information in long-term memory that would help put more than one symbol into one chunk. Therefore, the Morse code statement (which translates as the one-word sentence "No") would require the greatest number of chunks in short-term memory. (pp. 185–186)

a. The entire sentence could be one chunk for a native English speaker.

b, c. Both French and German use the same alphabet as English. Therefore, each word would be a chunk because information stored in long-term memory would help recognize the letters as words. However, each dot or dash of a Morse code letter would be one unit of new

information, causing that statement to require a greater number of chunks.

8. d is the answer. In order to chunk information efficiently, you must be able to use long-term memory to recognize the new information in short-term memory and create chunks, put as many items as possible into one chunk, and be able to transfer information quickly from short-term to long-term memory. (pp. 185-186)

9. b is the answer. When Vinnie remembered what it was he needed, he put that information into short-term memory. He then probably became distracted before the memory was transferred into long-term memory. (p. 186)

a, c. If Vinnie checked his class notes before he left for the library, information had probably already been processed and transferred from sensory to short-term memory. Selective attention determines what is held in the sensory registers for further processing.

d. b is the answer.

10. a is the answer. Anterograde amnesia is the inability to form new memories, or in other words, memory loss for everything that happens after a brain injury. (p. 203)

b. Retrograde amnesia is the loss of memory for events before a brain injury.

c, d. Positive and negative transfer are not terms used in the text.

11. c is the answer. Taking the test in the morning lets Alberta's state of mind act as a retrieval cue (utilizes state-dependent memory). (p. 190)

a, b, d. At any other time of the day, Alberta would not be in the same psychological state as she was when she learned the material.

12. b is the answer. Semantic memory contains general knowledge that isn't linked to a particular event. (p. 181)

a. Episodic memory would not answer a question about facts that are not related to a personally experienced event.

c. A person uses sensory memory to hear or read a question, but in order to answer the question the person must draw upon information in the semantic memory.

d. Short-term memory lasts only 20 seconds; therefore, it would be unlikely to contain the answer to a question of general knowledge.

13. a is the answer. Constructive memories can be very vivid. Sarah probably thought that staplers would be likely to be in the box of office supplies and

accidentally created a memory of their image. (p. 192-195)

b. There is no such thing as elaborative memories. Elaborative rehearsal is the term for linking new information to old information. Sarah was probably not rehearsing the information about what was in the box.

c. Generalized memories is not a term. You may have been thinking of semantic memories, but Sarah was not using her semantic memory to create the memory of a stapler.

d. Implicit memories are actual memories that we have not tried to retrieve but that affect us anyway. Since there were no staplers in the box, Sarah couldn't have an implicit memory of them.

14. b is the answer. Proactive interference occurs when the process of remembering new information is disrupted by the presence of old information. The old, incorrect version of the poem that Sigrid had memorized kept getting in the way of her learning the correct word. (p. 198)

a. For retroactive interference to be the correct answer, learning the new word in the poem should have interfered with Sigrid's ability to remember the old, incorrect version of the poem. Retroactive interference refers to new information disrupting the recall of old information.

c. Anterograde amnesia is the inability to form new memories after hippocampal damage. Sigrid's hippocampus was intact.

d. Decay is the gradual disappearance of a memory. Sigrid would have had to learn the new word and then forget it for this to be the right answer.

15. d is the answer. Kristi is using the method of loci to mentally place people in various spots in her dorm room. When she needs to remember these people, she will mentally look for them in her dorm room. (p. 205)

a. Kristi is using imagery, not her current environment (context), to recall information.

b. Distributed practice is taking a break between study sessions instead of "cramming." Kristi is not described as taking study breaks.

c. The encoding specificity principle refers to the similarity between information when it is learned and when it is retrieved. This is not a mnemonic.

Now turn to the quiz analysis table at the end of this chapter to find which areas you know well and which areas you need to work on. Circle the numbers in the table for items on Quiz 1 that you answered correctly.

ANSWERS TO MULTIPLE-CHOICE QUESTIONS

Circle the question numbers you answered correctly.

Sample Quiz 2

1. c is the answer. Semantic encoding is a meaning code, which makes it less likely that exact words (such as in a title) will be recalled, although the topic may be recalled. (p. 180)

a. Acoustic codes represent what something sounds like. If Al had acoustically encoded the movie title, he might have remembered the exact words, or words that sounded similar.

b. Procedural memory is the knowledge of how to do something; it is not a code.

d. Visual codes are images. Al coded the meaning of the title, not an image of it.

2. a is the answer. Gerianna's piano playing requires a skill memory, otherwise known as procedural memory. (p. 181)

b. Gerianna's semantic memory contains factual information and her summary of the meaning of events.

c. Gerianna's episodic memory contains memories of events at which she was present.

d. Acoustic is a type of coding commonly used in short-term memory.

3. d is the answer. Trying to recall personal information is using explicit memory; accidentally being influenced by a subconscious memory is an effect of implicit memory. (p. 181)

a, b. Kaliina is not remembering an episode from her life nor general knowledge.

c. Implicit memories unintentionally influence us; they are not the intentional recall of personal information. (See d.)

4. a is the answer. Elaborative rehearsal, which requires thinking of how new information fits with old, is the best of the choices given for memorizing information. (p. 182)

b. How long a person studies information is not the most important factor in whether the information will be remembered. If the person uses maintenance rehearsal, he or she may remember much less information than if the same amount of time were spent using elaborative rehearsal.

c. Increasing stimulus intensity, for example, by turning on more lights or increasing the print size of the material to be memorized will not have a significant effect on memorization.

d. Using a systematic scanning pattern is common when reading, especially in speed reading, but this answer choice indicates only that written material is being read or visual material is being viewed systematically. While reading or viewing something over and over (maintenance rehearsal) may seem to work, it is not as efficient or as effective as elaborative rehearsal.

5. *c* is the answer. Sensory memory lasts about a second, then the information is transferred to short-term memory or lost. (p. 184)
   a. Long-term memory can last for years; it is not a sensory register.
   b. Semantic memory is part of long-term memory. A network links information.
   d. Short-term memory is involved in reading, but it is not a sensory register.

6. *a* is the answer. The encoding of information in short-term memory is mostly acoustic; therefore, confusing "rock" with a word that rhymes is most likely. (p. 185)
   b. Remembering "stone" would indicate semantic encoding had taken place.
   c, d. "Hair" and "round" are least likely to be confused with "rock."

7. *d* is the answer. In order to chunk, you must use the information in long-term memory to help you group items into one chunk in short-term memory. The ability to recognize something in sensory memory involves retrieving a similar pattern of information or material from long-term memory. In order to use the method of loci, you must retrieve knowledge about a specific location or loci stored in long-term memory. (pp. 185-186, 205)

8. *b* is the answer. Remembering the beginning of a list but forgetting the middle constitutes the primacy effect. (pp. 188-189)
   a. If the question said that Ramona could remember the end of the list, recency effect would have been the correct response.
   c. If Ramona's memory of something she learned just prior to or after reading the grocery list prevented her from remembering all the items, this would have been the correct answer.
   d. There is no such thing as retroactive amnesia. (You may have been thinking of retrograde amnesia.)

9. *a* is the answer. Ted has listed features that should help his students recognize the correct information stored in long-term memory: the name *Abraham Lincoln.* (p. 189)
   b. Primacy cue is not a term. You may have been thinking of primacy effect.

c, d. When Ted's students hear his question, the clues will enter sensory memory as acoustic codes and then, after further processing, will enter short-term memory. However, the students will use the clues in short-term memory, not the acoustic codes, as retrieval cues to help them pull information out of long-term memory. There is no such thing as contextual coding. You may have been thinking of context dependence.

10. *d* is the answer. Context-dependent memories are affected by the environment in which they are learned and recalled. If the two environments are the same or very similar, recall will be improved. If they are different, recall will be harmed. (p. 190)
    a. Although not discussed in your text, flashbulb memories are those in which an image is captured and recalled, much like taking a picture with a camera.
    b. Semantic memory relates to the meaning of information, but it doesn't explain why being in the same environment during study and testing would help your exam performance.
    c. State-dependent memories are affected by the physical or psychological state of the person who is learning and recalling information. If the person is in the same mood or at the same level of arousal, memory will be improved.

11. *a* is the answer. Retroactive interference occurs when newly learned information goes back (retro) to interfere with previously learned information. Andy's newly learned history information is interfering with the previously learned psychology information. (p. 198)
    b. Proactive interference occurs when previously learned information interferes with learning new information.
    c, d. Internal and semantic inhibition are made-up terms.

12. *c* is the answer. A repressed memory is described as one that cannot be easily accessed. (pp. 199–202)
    a. Elaborative memory is not a term. You may have been thinking of elaborative rehearsal.
    b. Procedural memories are memories of skills, like piano playing. They are not traumatic memories.
    d. State-dependence of memory occurs when information is more easily retrieved when the person is in the same state as he was when the information was encoded.

13. *c* is the answer. Some apparently repressed memories may be accurate, but some may be

inaccurate. Therefore, corroborating evidence should be sought in each case. (pp. 199–202)

a. To assume that a recovered memory was constructed would not be wise, given that some recovered memories have been substantiated by other evidence.

b. To assume that a recovered memory is accurate would not be wise, given that some recovered memories have been shown to be false.

d. There is no such thing as retroactive amnesia. Retrograde amnesia would be the result of a brain injury. The person would most likely lose memory for more than one event prior to the injury.

14. *b* is the answer. Hippocampal damage usually results in anterograde amnesia, which is the inability to form new memories. Procedural memory formation and recall appears to be unaffected, however. (pp. 203–204)

a, d. Both of these are procedural memories. She could learn to solve a puzzle or could remember how to ride her bike.

c. Recall of a childhood event would be unaffected by anterograde amnesia.

15. *a* is the answer. Just rereading the material is not an effective way to learn information from a text. (pp. 205–207)

b, c, d. These are all good study habits to adopt.

Now turn to the quiz analysis table at the end of this chapter to find which areas you know well and which areas you need to work on. Circle the numbers in the table for items on Quiz 2 that you answered correctly.

For each question you answered correctly, circle its number. (Quiz 1 numbers are not shaded; Quiz 2 numbers are shaded.) Are there patterns in the types of questions or the topics you got wrong that could direct your further study? Did you improve from Quiz 1 to Quiz 2?

TOPIC	TYPE OF QUESTION		
	DEFINITION	COMPREHENSION	APPLICATION
Nature of Memory			
Processes			1
			1
Types			2
			2
Explicit and implicit			3
			3
Models		6	5
	4		
Acquiring Memories			
Sensory	4		
		5	
Short-term		8	7
			6
Long-term			9
			7
Distinguishing			10
			8
Retrieving Memories			
Cues and encoding			
			9
Dependence			11
	10		
Semantic memory			12
Constructing			13
Forgetting			14
			11
Repression			
		13	12
Biological bases			
			14
Memory improvement			15
			15

TOTAL CORRECT BY QUIZ:

QUIZ 1:
QUIZ 2:

Chapter 7

Thought, Language, and Intelligence

LEARNING OBJECTIVES

1. Describe the core functions that form a circle of thought. (p. 214)

2. Define information-processing system and thinking. Explain the sequence of events that occurs in the circle of thought in terms of an information-processing model. (p. 215)

3. Define cognitive maps and discuss their formation and use. Describe the manipulation of mental images. (p. 216)

4. Define concepts, formal and natural concepts, and prototype. Give examples of each. (pp. 216–217)

5. Define schema, scripts, propositions, and mental models and describe their role in the thinking process. (pp. 217–218)

6. Define deductive or formal reasoning, algorithms, and logic. Discuss the causes of errors in logical reasoning. Describe cultural differences in formal reasoning. (p. 219)

7. Define inductive or informal reasoning, and heuristics. Describe and give examples of the anchoring, representativeness, and availability heuristics. (pp. 220–221)

8. Describe the problem-solving strategies: decomposition, working backward, analogies, and incubation. (pp. 221–222)

9. Describe the use of comparative case studies to document the techniques used by successful problem solvers. (pp. 222–223)

10. Explain why multiple hypotheses, mental sets, functional fixedness, confirmation bias, and lack of attention to negative evidence can hinder problem solving. Give examples of each. (pp. 223–226)

11. Define artificial intelligence. Discuss the limitations of symbolic reasoning and the movement towards neural network approaches in artificial intelligence systems. (pp. 227–228)

12. Define creativity. Discuss the cognitive and personality traits necessary for creative thinking. Define divergent and convergent thinking. (pp. 227-228)

13. Define utility and expected value, and explain the role of each in the decision-making process. (p. 228)

14. Explain how our decision making abilities are influenced by biases and flaws in our perceptions of utilities, losses, and probabilities. Be sure to discuss loss aversion and the gambler's fallacy. (pp. 229–230)

15. Outline the typical discussion patterns found in groups trying to make a decision. Define group polarization and discuss the mechanisms that appear to underlie the phenomenon. Discuss the factors that influence the effectiveness of group decision making. (pp. 231-232)

16. List the components of language. Define grammar. (p. 232)

17. Describe language development in children. Define babblings and telegraphic speech. (pp. 232-233)

18. Discuss the roles of conditioning, imitation, and biology in language development. (p. 234-236)

19. Describe the impact of a bilingual environment on the development of language abilities. (p. 236)

20. Define intelligence. (p. 236)

21. Discuss the history of intelligence test construction. Explain the scoring methods used in the Binet and Stanford-Binet intelligence tests. (pp. 236–237)

22. Discuss the use and abuse of intelligence testing in the United Sates in the early 1900s. (p. 238)

23. Describe Weschler's intelligence test. Explain why it is different from tests that were used previously. Define verbal and performance scales. (pp. 238-239)

24. Explain how intelligence quotients or (IQ scores) are calculated today. (p. 239)

25. Define test. Describe the advantages of tests over other evaluation methods. Define and describe the usefulness of norms. (p. 240)

26. Define <u>reliability</u> and <u>validity</u>. Describe how correlation coefficients are used to evaluate the reliability and validity of tests. (p. 240)

27. Discuss the research evaluating the reliability and validity of IQ tests. (pp. 240-241)

28. Discuss the twin and adoption studies that illustrate the relative influence of genetic and environmental factors on IQ scores. (pp. 241-242)

29. Explain why a group intelligence score tells you nothing about the individuals in the group. Discuss the variables that affect group intelligence scores. (pp. 242-244)

30. Discuss the evidence for and against the argument that IQ tests are culturally biased. Be sure to mention the results of culture-fair intelligence tests. (pp. 244-246)

31. Explain Gardner's theory of multiple intelligences. List the eight types of intelligences he proposed. (pp. 246-247)

32. Describe the triarchic theory of intelligence. Give examples of analytic, creative, and practical intelligence. (pp. 247-248)

33. Describe the relationship between giftedness and success in our society. Define mental retardation and <u>familial retardation</u>. (pp. 248, 250)

KEY TERMS

I. BASIC FUNCTIONS OF THOUGHT

1. An **information-processing system** receives information, represents information through symbols, and manipulates those symbols. (p. 215)

REMEMBER: Psychologists consider people similar to information-processing systems in the way they take in information, pass it through several stages, and finally act on it.

2. **Thinking** can be described as part of an information-processing system in which mental representations are manipulated in order to form new information. (p. 215)

Example: As you learn new material, you think about the information you are reading, which involves trying to relate it to experiences you already have. This kind of elaboration of the material is manipulation of a mental representation.

II. MENTAL REPRESENTATIONS: THE INGREDIENTS OF THOUGHT

3. **Cognitive maps** are mental representations of familiar parts of your world. (p. 216)

Example: Lashon's friend asks, "How do you get to the mall from here?" To answer the question, Lashon pictures the roads and crossroads between their location and the mall and is able to describe the route for his friend to travel.

4. **Images** are visual pictures represented in thought. Cognitive maps are one example. (p. 216)

Example: When you think about what your mom looks like, you get a "picture" in your head. That picture is an image.

5. **Concepts** are basic units of thought or categories with common properties. Artificial and natural concepts are examples. (p. 216)

Example: The concept of "book" includes properties such as a paper or hard cover around pages with writing on them.

6. **Formal concepts** are concepts that are clearly defined by a set of rules or properties. Each member of the concept meets all the rules or has all the defining properties, and no nonmember does. (p. 217)

Example: A square is an artificial concept. All members of the concept are shapes with four equal sides and four right-angle corners. No other shapes share these properties.

7. **Natural concepts** are defined by a *general* set of features, not all of which must be present for an object to be considered a member of the concept. (p. 217)

Example: The concept of vegetable is a natural concept. There are no rules or lists of features that describe every single vegetable. Many vegetables are difficult to recognize as such because this concept is so "fuzzy." Tomatoes are not vegetables, but most people think they are. Rhubarb is a vegetable, but most people think it is not.

8. A **prototype** is the best, or most typical, example of a natural concept. (p. 217)

Example: Try this trick on your friends. Have them sit down with a pencil and paper. Tell them to write down all the numbers that you will say and the answers to three questions that you will ask. Recite about fifteen numbers of at least three digits each, and then ask your friends to write down the name of a tool, a color, and a flower. About 60 to 80 percent of them will write down "hammer," "red," and "rose" because these are common prototypes of the concepts tool, color, and flower. Prototypes come to mind most easily when people try to think of a concept.

9. **Schemas** are generalizations about categories of objects, events, and people. (p. 217)

Example: Dana's schema for books is that they are a bound stack of paper with stories or other information written on each page. When her fifth-grade teacher suggests that each student read a book on the computer, Dana is confused until she sees that the same information could be presented on a computer screen. Dana has now revised her schema for books to include those presented through electronic media.

10. **Scripts** are mental representations of familiar sequences, usually involving activity. (p. 217)

Example: As a college student, you have a script of how events should transpire in the classroom: students enter the classroom, sit in seats facing the professor, and take out their notebooks. The professor lectures while students take notes, until the bell rings and they all leave.

11. **Propositions** are the smallest units of knowledge that can stand as separate assertions. Propositions are relationships between concepts or between a concept and a property of the concept. Propositions can be true or false. (pp. 217-218)

Example: <u>Carla (concept) likes to buy flowers (concept)</u> is a proposition that shows a relationship between two concepts. <u>Dogs bark</u> is a proposition that shows a relationship between a concept (dog) and a property of that concept (bark).

12. **Mental models** are clusters of propositions that represent people's understanding of how things work. (p. 218)

Example: There is a toy that is a board with different types of latches, fasteners, and buttons on it. As children play with it, they form a mental model of how these things work. Then, when they see a button, or perhaps a doorbell, they will have an understanding of how it works.

III. THINKING STRATEGIES

13. **Formal or logical reasoning** is the collection of mental procedures that yield valid conclusions. An example is the use of an algorithm. (p. 219)

Example: When you solve a set of algebraic equations correctly, you have probably used formal reasoning to do so.

14. **Algorithms** are systematic procedures that always produce solutions to problems. In an algorithm, a specific sequence of thought or set of rules is followed to solve the problem. Algorithms can be very time-consuming. (p. 219)

Example: To solve the math problem 3,999,999 * 1,111,111 using an algorithm, you would multiply the numbers out:

$$\begin{array}{r} 3,999,999 \\ * \ 1,111,111 \\ \hline 4,444,442,888,889 \end{array}$$

This computation takes a long time. You could, however, use a heuristic to solve the problem: round the numbers to 4,000,000 ∞ 1,000,000, multiply 4 * 1, and add the appropriate number of zeros (000,000,000,000). Although simpler and faster, this heuristic approach yields a less accurate solution than that produced by the algorithmic approach.

15. Rules of **logic** produce correct conclusions based on propositions. If the propositions or assumptions are correct, and the rules of logic are followed, the conclusion will be valid. (p. 219)

Example: In the following case, the propositions are correct but the conclusion is not valid, because the rules of logic were not followed. All cats are mammals, and all people are mammals. Therefore, all cats are people.

16. **Informal reasoning** involves inducing a conclusion based on a set of facts or examples. (p. 220)

Example: You take a psychology class and find your teacher to be an interesting instructor. You take a second psychology class and find that instructor also to be interesting. The third psychology class you take has still another interesting teacher. You decide that psychology teachers are interesting people. You have induced this conclusion based on your observations of your three psychology teachers.

17. **Heuristics** are mental shortcuts or rules of thumb used to solve problems. (p. 220)

Example: You are trying to think of a four-letter word for "labor" to fill in a crossword puzzle. Instead of thinking of all possible four-letter combinations (an algorithmic approach), you think first of synonyms for labor—job, work, chore—and choose the one with four letters.

18. The **anchoring heuristic** is a biased method of estimating an event's probability by adjusting a preliminary estimate in light of new information rather than by starting again from scratch. Thus, the preliminary value biases the final estimate. (p. 220)

Example: Jean is getting ready to move to the city. Her parents lived there ten years ago and were familiar with the area that she wants to move into now. Ten years ago, it was an exceedingly dangerous neighborhood. Since that time, however, many changes have taken place, and the area now has one of the lowest crime rates in the city. Jean's parents think that the crime rate may have improved a little, but, despite the lower crime rate, they just cannot believe that the area is all that safe.

19. The **representativeness heuristic** involves judging that an example belongs to a certain class of items by first focusing on the similarities between the example and the class and then determining whether the particular example has essential features of the class. However, many times people do not consider the frequency of occurrence of the class (the base-rate frequency), focusing instead on what is representative or typical of the available evidence. (p. 220)

Example: After examining a patient, Dr. White recognizes symptoms characteristic of a disease that has a base-rate frequency of 1 in 22 million people. Instead of looking for a more frequently occurring explanation of the symptoms, the doctor decides that the patient has this very rare disease. She makes this decision based on the similarity of this set of symptoms (example) to those of the rare disease (a larger class of events or items).

20. The **availability heuristic** involves judging the probability of an event by how easily examples of the event come to mind. This leads to biased judgments when the probability of the mentally available events does not equal the actual probability of their occurrence. (p. 220)

Example: A friend of yours has just moved to New York City. You cannot understand why he has moved there since the crime rate is so high. You hear from a mutual acquaintance that your friend is in the hospital. You assume that he was probably mugged because this is the most available information in your mind about New York City.

IV. PROBLEM SOLVING

21. **Mental sets** occur when knowing the solution to an old problem interferes with recognizing a solution to a new problem. (p. 224)

Example: The last time his CD player door wouldn't open, Del tapped the front of it and it popped open. This time when it won't open, Del does the same thing—not noticing that the power isn't even on!

22. **Functional fixedness** occurs when a person fails to use a familiar object in a novel way in order to solve a problem. (p. 225)

Example: Lisa is very creative in her use of the objects in her environment. One day she dropped a fork down the drain of the kitchen sink. She took a small refrigerator magnet and tied it to a chopstick. She then put the chopstick down the drain, let the fork attach itself to the magnet, and carefully pulled the fork out of the drain. *If* Lisa had viewed the magnet as being capable only of holding material against the refrigerator, and the chopstick as being useful only for eating Chinese food, she would have experienced functional fixedness.

23. The **confirmation bias** is the tendency to look only for evidence that supports your hypothesis rather than evidence that might refute it. (p. 225)

Example: When Sue gets in her car is won't start. She thinks it is the battery. She fails to notice that the overhead light is on in her car, indicating that the problem could not possibly be the battery.

24. **Artificial intelligence (AI)** is the study of how to make computers "think" like humans. (p. 226)

Example: Lydia plays chess against a computer that has been programmed with rules, strategies, and outcome probabilities.

25. **Creativity** involves producing original, and useful, solutions to challenging problems or situations. (p. 227)

Example: When Jessica figures out how to keep her car running using the bottom of a Coke can as a radiator cap, she has hit upon a creative solution.

26. **Divergent thinking** is the ability to think along many different paths to generate multiple solutions to a problem. (p. 227)

Example: When Jules is asked to generate as many possible uses for a pencil as he can think of, he is engaged in divergent thinking.

27. **Convergent thinking** involves the use of logic and knowledge to narrow down the number of possible solutions to a problem. (p. 228)

Example: When you work on a multiple-choice test, you have to narrow down to the correct answer from four possible solutions. As you do this, you are engaged in convergent thinking.

V. DECISION MAKING

28. The **utility** of an attribute is its subjective, personal value. (p. 229)

Example: Andrew prefers large classes because he likes the stimulation of hearing many opposing viewpoints. In choosing courses, Andrew decides whether the positive utility of the preferred class size is greater than the negative utility of the inconvenient meeting time.

29. **Expected value** is the likely benefit a person will gain if he or she makes a particular decision several times. (p. 229)

Example: Jennifer doesn't have enough money for this month's rent. She knows that going on a shopping spree would be a wonderful stress-reliever in the short run, but the increase in her amount of debt would outweigh the enjoyment in the long run.

30. **Group polarization** is the tendency of groups to make extreme decisions. (p. 231)

Example: After Wayne suggested a protest march and was strongly criticized, the people in the majority decided that not only would they *not* protest, but they wouldn't even write a letter to the newspaper stating their view.

VI. LANGUAGE

31. **Language** is comprised of two elements: symbols, such as words, and grammar. (p. 232)

Example: The German and English languages use the same symbols (Roman characters), but each has a different set of rules for combining those symbols. The Russian language has different symbols (Cyrillic characters) as well as different rules of grammar.

32. **Grammar** is the set of rules for combining symbols, or words, into sentences in a language. (p. 232)

Example: It is more grammatically correct to say, "He poured milk into the glass" than to say "Milk he into the glass poured."

33. **Babblings** are the first sounds infants make that resemble speech. Babbling begins at about four months of age. (p. 232)

Example: While Patrick plays, he says, "ba-ba-ba."

34. **Telegraphic** speech describes the nature of the early sentences formed by eighteen- to twenty-four-month-old children. Sentences are often only two words long and communicate the message with simple words. (p. 233)

Example: Rick says, "Give ball" when he wants someone to give him a ball.

VII. TESTING INTELLIGENCE

35. **Intelligence**, according to Sternberg's working definition, is the combination of three characteristics: the possession of knowledge, the ability to use information processing to reason about the world, and the ability to employ that reasoning adaptively in different environments. Note, however, that psychologists do not agree on an exact definition of intelligence. (p. 236)

36. The **Stanford-Binet** test was a revised version of Binet's original test of mental abilities. Each set of age-graded questions could be answered correctly by a substantial majority of the children in that age group. Children were above average if they could correctly answer questions above their age grade. The score received, called mental age, was divided by chronological age and then multiplied by 100, resulting in an IQ. (p. 237)

Example: Mark's IQ has been tested. Although he is only twelve, he answered questions designed for children up to fourteen years of age. The following steps are used to determine his IQ.
  a. Mark's mental age is fourteen.
  b. Mark's chronological age is twelve.
  c. 14/12 = 1.16
  d. 1.16 ∞ 100 = 116.
  e. Mark's IQ is 116.

37. **IQ tests** are any tests designed to measure intelligence on an objective, standardized scale. (p. 237)

38. A **verbal scale** in the Wechsler tests measures verbal skills. (p. 239)

Example: These tests include remembering a series of digits, solving arithmetic problems, defining vocabulary words, and understanding and answering questions.

39. A **performance scale** in the Wechsler tests measures spatial ability and the ability to manipulate materials. (p. 239)

Example: One of the tasks on the performance scale is putting blocks together to match a given design.

Another task requires a person to look at a picture and decide what is missing.

40. **Intelligence quotient** (or **IQ score**) reflects relative standing on a test within a population of the same age group. IQ values reflect how far each score deviates from the age-group average. (p. 239)

Example: Thirty-year-old Davida and fifteen-year-old Christina each received IQ scores of 116. We know from their scores that they scored higher than 84% of their same-aged peers.

VIII. EVALUATING IQ TESTS

41. **Tests** are systematic procedures for observing behavior in a standard situation. Behavior is described with the help of a numerical scale or a category system. (p. 240)

Example: To give a test in a standard situation, the directions, setting, and scoring methods used are the same regardless of the people involved. An example of a numerical scale would be the calculation of an IQ.

42. **Norms** are descriptions of the frequency of particular scores. Norms provide information about how a certain person's test score compares to the population upon which the norms are based. (p. 240)

43. A **reliable** test is one whose results will be consistent or stable over repeated test occasions. (p. 240)

Example: Each time Connie takes an intelligence test, she scores at the mean for her age group.

44. A **valid** test is one that measures exactly what it is designed to measure. (p. 240)

Example: Defining a list of words is a valid test of vocabulary but may not be a valid test of intelligence.

IX. DIVERSITY IN MENTAL ABILITIES

45. **Familial retardation** is mild retardation. It is called familial because most people in this group come from families of lower socioeconomic status; and, they are more likely to have a relative who is also retarded than those suffering from a genetic defect.. Familial retardation results from a complex interaction between heredity and environment. (p. 250)

CONCEPTS AND EXERCISES

No. 1: Approaches to Problem Solving

Completing this exercise should help you to achieve Learning Objectives 3, 6, 7, 8, and 10.

Below are several problems. Read the description of each problem, and answer the questions following it.

1. Viola's parents have just moved to a suburb of Chicago. She is home for a visit for the first time since they moved. To her embarrassment, she is always getting lost. The streets seem to be arranged in a triangular pattern instead of a square one.

   ° What is Viola trying to develop?

2. Trixy and her brother Peter are home by themselves, and the lights have all gone off. Both children are terrified of the dark. Trixy remembers that her dad once told her about a fuse box. She hypothesizes that this is the problem. But Trixy and her brother do not want to enter the dark basement.

   ° How can they decide whether going to the basement is necessary?

   ° What have they avoided if they do this?

   ° What kind of evidence about their hypothesis are they ignoring?

3. Al is lost somewhere in Paris. He wants to get to a museum that a friend told him to visit, but he has no idea where he is. He stops someone on the street and asks for directions. The Parisian says that she can give Al either a tricky shortcut or a very long set of directions that will be easy to follow. Al decides to take the long way since it will guarantee his arrival at the museum, even though it will take a bit longer.

   ° What two choices did the Parisian offer Al?

   ° Which one did Al choose?

4. Carlotta, a color analyst at a paper mill, is upset because something is wrong with the paper's color as it comes off the machine. She and the people who work with her have thought about all the previous color problems they have encountered, but they cannot find a solution. Carlotta decides to bring in a person who has just started to work in the paper room and ask him what he thinks.

   ° What might be preventing Carlotta from solving the problem?

No. 2: The Testing Business

Completing this exercise should help you to achieve Learning Objectives 25, 26, and 30.

Sean Dorgan has recently begun a testing service. Following are some descriptions of his activities. Fill in the blank with the correct term by either choosing from the list at the end of the exercise or recalling the appropriate information from your reading. Answers can be used more than once.

1. Dorgan has just received information on a new test on the market. He has ordered a sample copy of the test and plans to give it to the same group of people twice. Dorgan is checking for _____.

2. Dorgan has just received a new achievement test. He knows that it has already been successfully tested for reliability. Since the test is reliable, does Dorgan have to test it for validity? _____

3. Dorgan wants to attract newcomers from foreign countries as clients. To do this, he will have to develop _____ tests.

4. Dorgan has just issued a memo to all his employees saying that all tests are to be administered in exactly the same way, given in the same room, and scored in exactly the same way. Dorgan wants to ensure that all of his tests are _____.

5. Dorgan has just received a new test of mathematical ability. He is confused because there are no math problems on the test. What kind of validity is he worried about? _____

   ° Standardized
   ° Culture-fair
   ° Reliability
   ° Content validity
   ° Construct validity

CRITICAL THINKING

Sam and Martina are just arriving at the scene of what promises to be a media event. Sylvia Star, a famous ninety-eight-year-old gossip columnist, has been found dead in her bed. Sylvia has a long list of enemies, and Sam, eager for action, immediately decides that she has been murdered. While Martina stands calmly in the bedroom doorway surveying the room, Sam scurries around looking for evidence of foul play.

In his search, Sam finds a glass of water on the bedstand. Smugly, he turns toward Martina and beckons her closer. "When I was in the academy," Sam said, "I read about this real rare drug case. The drug dissolves in water and can't be traced in the water or the body. I bet one of the people the old bird was writing about dumped some in this glass or paid off the maid to do it. No Sylvia, no bad press. Everybody knew she was an elderly woman with a heart problem. The murderer probably figured it would look like a heart attack. We should check her notes

for her next column and find out who was here today! And we should check out the maid!"

Martina, looking slightly bemused, takes a drink from the glass of water and says, "I couldn't disagree with you more on this one!"

Using the five critical thinking questions in your text, the clues in the story, and what you have just learned in this chapter, answer the following.

1. What is Sam's hypothesis?

2. What evidence supports Sam's hypothesis?

3. What is Martina's alternative hypothesis?

4. What evidence supports Martina's hypothesis?

PERSONAL LEARNING ACTIVITIES

1. Make a list of the defining characteristics of a natural concept, choose a prototype, and then identify things that fit or don't fit your definition. For the natural concept "home," perhaps you might list "has walls, floors, a roof, doors, and an address." What is the prototypical home? Now find examples of homes that have fewer and fewer of the features you have listed and decide whether they still have enough characteristics to earn the "home" label. Are residence halls, apartments, small houses, motel rooms, an underpass, and a cardboard box homes? How did you decide? (Learning Objective 4)

2. Experiment with the problem-solving strategies—decomposition, working backward, analogies, and incubation—to see if they can help you. For instance, you might try decomposition with a research paper assignment or try to think of an analogy to help you remember a biological process. (Learning Objective 8)

3. Watch a young relative or observe children in a day care center to see what early language use is like. Are the children at an age when babbling is most common, or are they forming words and/or sentences? If you hear errors, what sort are they? (Learning Objective 17)

4. List behaviors and abilities you consider to be intelligent. Now write your own definition of intelligence. What problems did you encounter in writing your definition? (Learning Objective 20)

5. Read the list and definition you wrote for Personal Learning Activity 4 and identify the approach you took to intelligence. Was your theory more similar to the triarchic theory or multiple intelligences theory? (Learning Objectives 31 and 32)

WHAT SHOULD I WRITE ABOUT?

As you develop your term paper topic, it is often useful to make sure you can connect your topic to interesting examples or case studies. If you can do that, it is helpful to build your term paper topic around analyzing that case study or example. Just like reading a textbook devoid of examples or interesting studies is dull, writing a term paper without these elements is also a struggle.

As you read through the chapter on *Thought, Language, and Intelligence*, look for the studies and examples that particularly peak your interest. If the cultural differences in the use of formal and informal reasoning peaked your curiosity, you might write a term paper analyzing those differences. It would be fun to highlight each difference with an example you found as you conducted your research.

Another potentially interesting topic in the current chapter might be language acquisition. We learn much through studies of both normal and abnormal circumstances. You could try to find examples of studies of "normal" language acquisition, such as how babies learn to babble and then speak telegraphically. Then you could contrast that to studies of "abnormal" language acquisition, such as how children who are deprived of learning language during their early years develop their communication skills. Based on this comparison, you could develop a "story" about how humans learn language, and the limitations on our ability to do so.

Sometimes it is even more interesting to generate your own example, rather than to find existing examples in your research. If you were writing a term paper on intelligence testing, you might decide to do your own primary research, rather than limiting yourself to existing research. For example, you might find examples of two types of intelligence tests for children, and then give the tests to a willing younger sibling or friend. You could then write about the differences in the tests, the results of the test, and how the child felt as he or she took the two tests.

Here are some questions to guide you as you try to identify examples of interesting term paper topics:

1. Were there any interesting examples in your textbook that you would like to follow up on? Do any of your text's examples strike you as non-prototypical examples that should be compared to more prototypical examples of a phenomenon?

2. Are there any concepts in the text that did not have many examples associated with it? Finding additional examples in the literature can clarify that concept, as well as give you a term paper topic to work on.

3. Are there any topics on which you could do your own primary research? If so, you could conduct your own project, supplementing your own work with published literature. You should contrast your own findings to the findings you read about.

THE INTERNET

The Psychabilities web site that accompanies this text offers many resources relevant to this chapter. They include NetLab exercises, Thinking Critically and Evaluating Research exercises, ACE chapter quizzes, recommended web links, and articles on current events, books, and movies. Go to http://college.hmco.com, select Psychology, and then this textbook.

MULTIPLE-CHOICE QUESTIONS

SAMPLE QUIZ 1

1. Which of the following statements is *most* accurate?
   a. The human brain is constructed much like a computer.
   b. We solve problems in the same way computers do.
   c. The brain and computer are both information-processing systems.
   d. Computers must always use heuristics to solve problems.

2. Try to figure out the name of the natural concept to which the following four items belong, and then choose the prototypical example of that concept.
   a. A fist
   b. A brick
   c. A gun
   d. Sharp fingernails

3. No matter which McDonald's franchise you visit, you will probably wait in a line of people, look at a menu on the wall, say something like "I'd like a Quarter Pounder with cheese," and be answered with "Would you like some fries with that?" This is an example of a
   a. stereotype.
   b. script.
   c. proposition.
   d. disjunctive artificial construct.

4. Jody believes that a college student who begins studying kinesiology during fall 1999 has only a 33 percent chance of receiving a degree by December 2003. Later, Jody hears that a kinesiology student has about a 90 percent chance of graduating by December 2003. Jody now believes that the actual probability is about 50 percent. She has been affected by a(n)
   a. algorithm.

b. anchoring heuristic.

c. representativeness heuristic.

d. availability heuristic.

5. "An action potential fires 'all or none' like a gun," says Jamila. Jamila is using _____ to help her understand the concept of threshold.

a. an analogy

b. decomposition

c. negative evidence

d. a script

6. Luna can't figure out her calculus problem. She decides to forget about the problem for a while at dinner. When she returns to her room, she realizes how to solve the problem. Luna used _____ to solve the problem.

a. deep structures

b. expert systems

c. incubation

d. prototypes

7. Beth is an advocate of her choir's decision to reprimand Tommy, one of the members. Even she is a little surprised, however, with the final decision to kick Tommy out. It seems extreme to her. The phenomenon that produced this decision is the process of

a. group polarization.

b. telegraphic speech.

c. artificial concepts.

d. representative utility.

8. Little Marcie is twenty-one months old and has already developed a fondness for Barney the dinosaur. She watches Barney on television and prefers looking at her Barney book over any other. Given normal development, Marcie is *most likely* to ask her mom to read her the Barney book by saying,

a. "Barney!"

b. "Barney book!"

c. "Mommy read Barney!"

d. "Mommy, read the Barney book!"

9. It is very difficult to acquire the ability to speak a second language if you don't start learning it as a child. It is difficult to learn a second language as an adult because we

a. can no longer speak telegraphically.

b. are past our critical period for language acquisition.

c. have lost our LAD.

d. are too old to be conditioned.

10. Terman would calculate an intelligence quotient by dividing

a. mental age by chronological age.

b. chronological age by mental age.

c. mental age by chronological age and multiplying the result by 100.

d. chronological age by mental age and multiplying the result by 100.

11. Wechsler's test of intelligence differs from the original Stanford-Binet test in that

a. Wechsler's test has two subscales: verbal and performance.

b. Wechsler's test is more culturally biased.

c. Wechsler's test requires greater familiarity with the English language.

d. Wechsler's test is a group test.

12. Which of the following is true with respect to reliability and validity?

a. A reliable test is always valid.

b. A valid test must have a substantial level of reliability.

c. There is no relationship between reliability and validity.

d. Reliability and validity are the products of standardization procedures.

13. Which of the following is true about how the interaction between heredity and environment affects intelligence?

a. A favorable environment can improve a child's performance, even if the inherited influences on that child's IQ are negative.

b. Inherited characteristics are fixed, but environmentally determined features are changeable.

c. The environment has very little impact on a person's intelligence.

d. Inherited characteristics have very little impact on a person's intelligence.

14. Devon is a ten-year-old from an inner-city culture. He is taking an IQ test that requires him to match patterns. Devon most probably

a. has mental retardation.

b. is taking a culture-fair test.

c. is taking a culture-free test.

d. is taking a mathematical achievement test.

15. Shlomo and Jaime are both twelve years old. They have been given identical boxes and are told to open them. Shlomo finds the latch and pushes it up, down, and then sideways. Even though he cannot get the latch to open, he persists in his efforts. Jaime realizes that the latch is not going to open the box, so he looks at it from many different angles, trying to find another way to open it. Shlomo is thinking _____, and Jaime is thinking _____.

a. convergently; divergently

b. divergently; convergently
c. convergently; convergently
d. divergently; divergently

Total Correct (See answer key) _____

SAMPLE QUIZ 2

Use this quiz to reassess your learning after taking Quiz 1 and reviewing the chapter.

1. Which of the following is *not* true of information-processing systems? Information-processing systems
   a. manipulate representations.
   b. rely on long-term memory only.
   c. receive information.
   d. represent information with symbols.

2. Natural and artificial concepts differ in that
   a. artificial concepts provide a way to classify objects, whereas natural concepts do not.
   b. natural concepts provide a way to classify objects, whereas artificial concepts do not.
   c. artificial concepts are fuzzy and sometimes difficult to define, whereas natural concepts are rigidly defined.
   d. natural concepts are fuzzy and sometimes difficult to define, whereas artificial concepts are rigidly defined.

3. The representativeness heuristic causes us to
   a. ignore overall probabilities.
   b. give improper weight to contradictory evidence when making a decision.
   c. focus on solutions that are easily brought to mind.
   d. consider only those hypotheses with which we are the most familiar.

4. Appendicitis is diagnosed as abdominal pain *and* a fever *and* an elevated white blood cell count. Katrina is sure that she has appendicitis, even though her only symptom is extreme abdominal pain. Katrina is
   a. suffering from a mental set.
   b. engaging in formal reasoning.
   c. ignoring negative evidence.
   d. dumb.

5. Mike and Cal are marketing executives working as a team for a Fortune 500 company. They have been given an extremely difficult project: they are to design a new consumer product. Mike wants to review all the market research on consumer needs, identify what the product must do to solve those needs, and then see if his company can build it. Cal wants go to the library and look up case histories of other companies noted for developing brilliant new products. Mike wants to use a(n) _____ process to solve the problem, and Cal is trying to use a(n) _____ to solve the problem.
   a. analogy; decomposition
   b. working backward; analogy
   c. analogy; visual representation
   d. incubation; visual representation

6. Winnie, a teacher, has been told that the test scores of one of her new students, Nelson, suggest that he is very bright. The principal has asked her to keep an eye on Nelson and let him know what she thinks of Nelson's intelligence. All through the first six weeks of the semester, she finds examples that seem to show that Nelson is indeed very bright. However, during the seventh week, she finds out that the records have been mixed up. Nelson's actual test scores show him as being strictly average. What explains Winnie's observations?
   a. Confirmation bias
   b. Functional fixedness
   c. Mental set
   d. Decomposition

7. Emmeline works as a lab technician in a neurobiological laboratory. She has just received an announcement that must be posted in the lab immediately. Because she cannot find any thumbtacks, she uses the ends of hypodermic needles to attach the announcement to the bulletin board. What pitfall in problem solving has Emmeline just avoided?
   a. Functional fixedness
   b. Confirmation bias
   c. Ignoring of negative evidence
   d. Faulty hypothesis testing

8. In Tarzan movies, a husband, his wife, and their baby are shipwrecked. The baby survives and is raised by apes until a doctor finds him twenty years later. The doctor takes the wild man out of the jungle, teaches him to speak French and English, and introduces him to society. Although the wild man's accents are not perfect, he manages to live in England for some time before choosing to go back to the jungle. Why are these movies unrealistic?
   a. A language acquisition device needs to be learned.
   b. A critical period may exist for language acquisition.
   c. The wild man should have been able to learn proper French and English accents.
   d. All of the above

9. Melissa learned two languages as she grew up: Chinese and English. Melissa is most likely to be
   a. confused by the two languages.

b. much smarter than other people in all ways.

c. more cognitively flexible and creative than others who speak only one language.

d. much less creative than others who speak only one language.

10. Kanitra routinely administers IQ tests to her class. She was puzzled by the score of one of her new students. This student, according to the test, had poor linguistic and spatial abilities. Yet, he could perform complex mathematical operations in his head with speed and accuracy, and he could play songs on the piano by ear. This student is a good example of

a. divergent thinking.

b. Spearman's g factor.

c. Sternberg's triarchic theory of intelligence.

d. Gardner's theory of multiple intelligences.

11. The original mental abilities test created by Binet was designed to

a. assess intelligence in children.

b. determine which children would benefit from special education.

c. determine which immigrants should be allowed into the country.

d. determine the intelligence of army recruits.

12. Which of the following would you *not* find on the performance scale of an intelligence test?

a. Block design

b. Maze solving

c. Picture completion

d. Mathematical word problems

13. Consuela is giving a test that she has devised to the same group of people twice. She is testing for

a. reliability.

b. validity.

c. norms.

d. none of the above.

14. Joel theorizes that knowledge of introductory psychology material is positively related to general vocabulary size. Joel uses his students' combined midterm and final exam scores (called "exam total") as his measure of introductory psychology knowledge. To find out if the exams have validity, Joel should compare the

a. exam total to students' scores on quizzes also taken during Joel's classes.

b. exam total to students' scores on a vocabulary test.

c. odd items on the combined exam to the even items on the combined exam.

d. midterm scores to the final exam scores.

15. If scientists ever capture an alien, they will want to check its creativity. Which of the following would be the best way to do that?

a. See how fast it learns to speak English.

b. Administer a verbal scale of the Wechsler.

c. Administer a performance scale of the Wechsler.

d. Administer a test of divergent thinking.

Total Correct (See answer key) _____

ANSWERS TO CONCEPTS AND EXERCISES

No. 1: Approaches to Problem Solving

1. Viola is trying to develop a cognitive map but she is trying to put them into a north-south-east-west square. (p. 216)

2. Trixy has hypothesized that the fuse box is the cause of the sudden loss of lights in her house. In order to avoid confirmation bias, she and Peter could look out the window to see if other houses are without lights. If that is the case, then the problem is not the fuse box but, rather, a major power failure in the neighborhood. When the problem is a blown fuse, only part of the house is dark. This is the symptom that Trixy and Peter are overlooking. They are ignoring negative evidence. (p. 225)

3. The Parisian offered Al a choice between a heuristic (the shortcut) and an algorithm (the sure but longer way to get to the museum). Al chose the algorithm. (pp. 219–220)

4. Carlotta has realized that being an expert has caused her to have a mental set. Therefore, she is bringing in someone who doesn't have old answers that will get in the way of thinking of new answers. (p. 224)

No. 2: The Testing Business

1. *Reliability.* (p. 240)

2. *Yes.* A test may be reliable but invalid because it does not test the correct abilities. (p. 240)

3. *Culture-fair.* In this way, unfamiliarity with the English language or Western culture will not bias the results. (pp. 244–246)

4. *Standardized.* (p. 240)

5. *Content validity.* He is worried about whether the questions on the test are related to the skills, or content, that the test is supposed to assess. (p. 240)

ANSWERS TO CRITICAL THINKING

1. Sam hypothesizes that Sylvia Star was murdered by a rare drug.

2. The evidence includes the following facts: Sylvia had lots of enemies, old and current; a drug could have been slipped into her drink; Sam knows a crime like that has been committed before; and there could be a connection between Sylvia's visitors that day and her current writing subjects.

3. Martina hypothesizes that the woman died of old age.

4. The probability of a death resulting from natural causes is the evidence Martina uses to support her hypothesis.

ANSWERS TO MULTIPLE-CHOICE QUESTIONS

Circle the question numbers you answered correctly.

Sample Quiz 1

1. *c* is the answer. Information-processing systems get information, code it, and manipulate it. Brains and computers both may be classified as information-processing systems. (pp. 215, 226)
   a, b, d. The brain differs from the computer because the brain uses heuristics and other educated guesses. Computers are better at tasks using algorithms rather than heuristics.

2. *c* is the answer. The concept is weapons, and a gun is the best example of a weapon. (p. 216)
   a, b, d. A fist, brick, or sharp fingernails all could be used as weapons, but that is not the prototypical use for these items.

3. *b* is the answer. Scripts are a type of schema that applies to the general sequence of events in a situation. The script for fast food restaurants generally includes ordering at a counter, paying, and taking the food somewhere to eat. (p. 217)
   a. Stereotypes are based on the representativeness heuristic, but don't apply as well to the sequence of events as a script does.
   c. Propositions are brief statements of fact, belief, or theory, such as, "Dogs are nice."
   d. You may have been thinking of artificial *concepts,* which are categories whose members all match clearly defined rules. Ordering at a fast food restaurant doesn't follow clearly defined rules; instead, it varies from person to person and business to business.

4. *b* is the answer. Jody has used the first (33%) figure as an anchor, and she doesn't drift far from it when she hears the 90% figure. Jody used the anchoring heuristic, which kept her second estimate close to her first. (p. 220)
   a. Algorithms are systematic procedures in which every possible solution is examined.
   c. The representativeness heuristic is used to make an educated guess about whether something has enough of certain key features to be considered part of a group. For example, you might notice a slip of paper in a bank and judge that it isn't money, because the back of it is plain white.
   d. If Jody were using the availability heuristic, she would have chosen the first estimate that came to mind—either 33% or 90%, depending on when she was asked. Jody would not have adjusted an estimate.

5. *a* is the answer. Jamila created an analogy for the problem of remembering how an action potential works. (p. 222)
   b. Decomposition is breaking apart a problem into subproblems and working on each.
   c. Ignoring negative evidence is an obstacle to problem solving.
   d. A script is a description of how you expect an event to go.

6. *c* is the answer. In incubation, the problem is set aside for awhile. (p. 222)
   a. Deep structure is the meaning of a sentence.
   b. Expert systems are computer programs that are capable of solving problems in a specific area.
   d. Prototypes are the most typical example of a natural concept.

7. *a* is the answer. Group polarization causes groups to make decisions that are more extreme than an individual would have made. (p. 231)
   b. A toddler using telegraphic speech communicates using two-word sentences.
   c. Artificial concepts are those which completely match a set of rules.
   d. You may have been thinking of the representativeness heuristic (something is a member of a category if it looks similar to other members of the category) or of utility (the positive or negative value of an option).

8. *b* is the answer. A 21-month-old generally is at a telegraphic speech stage. (p. 233)
   a. From 12 to 18 months of age a child is likely to use single words to communicate.
   c, d. Three and four-word sentences appears between 2 and 3 years of age.

9. *b* is the correct answer. Childhood is the critical period for learning language. If language is not learned during the early years, it is difficult to learn to speak the language fluently. (p. 234)

   a. Adults retain the ability to speak telegraphically, but more typically speak in complete sentences.

   c. A Language Acquisition Device, or LAD, is a biological aspect of humans that does not change.

   d. Adults can be conditioned.

10. *c* is the answer. The first intelligence quotient, developed by Terman, was calculated by dividing mental age by chronological age and multiplying the result by 100. (p. 237)

    a, b, d. None of these formulas is the way that Terman calculated the first intelligence quotient.

11. *a* is the answer. Wechsler's test contained two subscales: a verbal scale and a performance scale. (pp. 238-239)

    b. Wechsler developed the performance scale, which included items such as block design and spatial reasoning tasks, in order to avoid bias caused by lack of familiarity with the English language or Western culture.

    c. Performance scale items do not test language ability or cultural familiarity.

    d. Wechsler's test was designed for individual administration, not group testing.

12. *b* is the answer. If a test is valid, it must be reliable. If a test produces scores that vary from one test occasion to another, there is no way that the test would correlate highly enough with a criterion to establish validity. (p. 240)

    a. A test that is reliable is not necessarily valid.

    c. There is a relationship between reliability and validity, while a reliable test yields the same results repeatedly. A valid test must have a substantial level of reliability.

    d. If a test is valid, it measures what it is supposed to measure. This is not dependent on standardization procedures. Standardization does not guarantee validity.

13. *a* is the answer. The quality of the environment can cause children's IQ scores to increase. (pp. 241-242)

    b. The opposite is true: inherited characteristics are not necessarily fixed, and environmentally determined features are not necessarily changeable.

    c, d. Neither of these statements is true. Both genetics and the environment have a large impact on the development of intelligence.

14. *b* is the answer. Devon is taking a test that does not rely heavily on education and verbal abilities. This test is attempting to measure intelligence instead of the effect of cultural influences, such as an education. (pp. 244-246)

    a. Many normal children—not just those who are mentally retarded—take IQ tests.

    c. There is no such thing as a culture-free test.

    d. Devon is being asked to match patterns, not to do mathematical tasks. Additionally, an achievement test measures what has already been learned; Devon is taking an IQ test, which attempts to measure intelligence, not knowledge.

15. *a* is the answer. Shlomo is thinking convergently, but Jaime, by imagining all the possible ways to open the box, is thinking divergently. (pp. 227-228)

Now turn to the quiz analysis table at the end of this chapter to find which areas you know well and which areas you need to work on. Circle the numbers in the table for items on Quiz 1 that you answered correctly.

ANSWERS TO MULTIPLE-CHOICE QUESTIONS

Circle the question numbers you answered correctly.

Sample Quiz 2

1. *b* is the answer. Information-processing systems need sensory and short-term memory, in addition to long-term memory, to receive and process information. (p. 215)

   a, c, d. Information-processing systems manipulate representations, receive information, and represent information with symbols.

2. *d* is the answer. (p. 217)

   a, b. Both natural and formal (or artificial) concepts provide a way to classify objects.

   c. Artificial concepts have rigid definitions. If an object doesn't meet all the specifications, then it is not part of that particular artificial concept. Natural concepts are fuzzy. For example, an ostrich is a bird even though it doesn't meet all the criteria for "bird"—that is, it can't fly.

3. *a* is the answer. The representativeness heuristic leads us to look at an example and compare it to a larger class of items. We focus on the similar appearances of the example and the larger class of items, ignoring information on how often the larger class of items occurs (overall probability). (p. 220)

b. The anchoring heuristic causes us to give improper weight to contradictory evidence in making a decision.

c, d. The availability heuristic causes us to focus on the solutions that are most easily brought to mind and that are therefore most familiar. These are usually the hypotheses that have occurred most frequently in the past.

4. *c* is the answer. Negative evidence is a clue that isn't present and should be. Katrina doesn't have a fever, but she is ignoring that negative (absent) evidence. (pp. 225-226)

    a. A mental set is the tendency to use a previously-used strategy to solve a problem. The question does not state whether Katrina has encountered the same symptom set before and used this solution.

    b. Formal reasoning is the use of logic, algorithms, and strict guidelines for seeking solutions to problems. Katrina is ignoring some of the evidence, so she isn't looking at every possible answer to the question of what illness she has.

    d. An incorrect decision about the cause of one's pain doesn't necessarily indicate a lack of intelligence.

5. *b* is the answer. Mike wants to start with what the product has to do (an end point) and work backward to the solution of what the product will be. Cal wants to use an analogy: employing the same techniques that other companies employ in trying to solve the same kind of problem. (pp. 221-222)

    a. Cal, not Mike, wants to employ an analogy by looking at other companies' solutions to the same problem. Decomposition is breaking a problem into its subparts.

    c. Mike is trying to develop his own strategy, not use a strategy that has worked for anyone else facing a similar problem.

    d. Mike is not letting the problem incubate by laying it aside for awhile.

6. *a* is the answer. Winnie has a hypothesis that Nelson is very smart. She takes into consideration only the evidence that supports her hypothesis and ignores evidence that Nelson is only average. (pp. 225–226)

    b. Winnie is testing a hypothesis, not trying to find a solution involving the use of an object.

    c. A mental set means using the solutions to old problems to try to solve new ones. Winnie is not using old solutions to test her hypothesis about Nelson's intelligence.

    d. Decomposition is a way to simplify problem solving by breaking a problem into smaller

subproblems. Winnie is not engaged in this activity.

7. *a* is the answer. If Emmeline had thought of the hypodermics as being useful only for giving injections, she would have experienced functional fixedness. Instead, she used them for something other than their traditional function and solved her problem. (p. 225)

    b, d. Confirmation bias occurs because people always try to confirm, rather than refute, their hypotheses. Emmeline is not testing a hypothesis, so neither of these alternatives is correct.

    c. People ignore negative evidence when looking for explanations of some event. Emmeline is not looking for an explanation but, rather, for a way to solve a problem.

8. *b* is the answer. Many cases support the idea that a critical period exists for language development. The wild man was found when he was in his twenties and was past the critical period for language development. Therefore, he should not have been able to learn any language. (p. 234)

    a. The language acquisition device Chomsky proposed is innate.

    c. When people learn a second language after the age of twelve to fifteen, they usually cannot speak with a flawless accent.

    d. Only *b* is the answer.

9. *c* is the answer. Melissa is a balanced bilingual. Balanced bilinguals tend to show more cognitive flexibility and creativity than individuals who only speak one language. (p. 236)

    a, b, and d. None of these is true.

10. *d* is the answer. According to the multiple intelligences theory a person may be quite high in one type of ability and quite low in another. (pp. 246-247)

    a. Divergent thinking is the ability to generate many possible solutions to a problem.

    b. Spearman's g is the general intelligence factor. This would not explain how a person could perform well in one area and poorly in another.

    c. The triarchic theory suggests that there are three factors: information processing, learning from experience, and street smarts, but the student's high musical abilities and low linguistic abilities wouldn't be explained by this.

11. *b* is the answer. Binet's original test was designed to identify those children who would benefit from or need special instruction. (pp. 236–237)

a. Binet did not try to create an intelligence test. He only wanted to identify those children who would benefit from special instruction.

c, d. Psychologists in the United States revised Binet's test and used it to assess the intellectual capacity of immigrants and army recruits.

12. *d* is the answer. Although math skills in general do not require a great deal of language ability, mathematical word problems do. The test taker must be able to read, interpret, and set up the problem using language skills as well as mathematical reasoning in order to arrive at the solution. (pp. 238–239)

a, b, c. Block design, mazes, and picture completion are all problems that require no verbal skills.

13. *a* is the answer. A reliable test is one that gives stable and consistent answers. If a test is given twice and yields consistent results, it is considered reliable. (p. 240)

b. Giving the same test twice is a test of reliability, not validity. To check validity, you must make sure that the content of the questions relates to the skills or knowledge being tested or that the test scores are correlated with scores on other tests relating to the same constructs or criteria.

c. Norms are descriptions of the frequency of particular scores. In order to test for this, the same test would have to be given to a very large number of people, not the same people twice.

d. *a* is the answer.

14. *b* is the answer. Joel's theory about psychology knowledge is that it is related to vocabulary. To see if his theory about the construct is supported, Joel will have to compare psychology scores to vocabulary scores. (pp. 240-241)

a. If we assume that the psychology graduate school entrance exam is an accepted measure of psychology knowledge, then comparing it to the exam total score would be a test of criterion validity.

c. Comparing odd items to even items might measure split-half reliability, but wouldn't tell Joel anything about the construct.

d. Comparing midterm scores to final exam scores also wouldn't tell Joel whether his theory about vocabulary and psychology knowledge was supported. It might be a test of predictive validity, although midterms and final exams often cover different material.

15. *d* is the answer. Tests of divergent thinking measure creativity. (pp. 227-228)

a. The ability to learn a new language is not correlated with creativity.

b, c. IQ scores do not correlate highly with creativity.

Now turn to the quiz analysis table at the end of this chapter to find which areas you know well and which areas you need to work on. Circle the numbers in the table for items on Quiz 2 that you answered correctly.

For each question you answered correctly, circle its number. (Quiz 1 numbers are not shaded; Quiz 2 numbers are shaded.) Are there patterns in the types of questions or the topics you got wrong that could direct your further study? Did you improve from Quiz 1 to Quiz 2?

TOPIC	TYPE OF QUESTION		
	DEFINITION	COMPREHENSION	APPLICATION
Basic functions	1		
	1		
Mental representations			2, 3,
		2	
Thinking Strategies			4
		3	
Problem Solving			
Strategies			5, 6
			4, 5
Obstacles			
			6, 7
Decision making			7
Language			8, 9
			8, 9
Testing Intelligence		10, 11	
		11, 12	
Evaluating IQ Tests		13	12, 14
			13, 14
Diversity in Intelligence			15
			10, 15

TOTAL CORRECT BY QUIZ:

QUIZ 1:
QUIZ 2:

Chapter 8

Motivation and Emotion

LEARNING OBJECTIVES

1. Define motivation. Discuss the types of behaviors that motivation may help to explain. (pp. 257–258)

2. Define motive and describe the sources of motivation. (p. 258)

3. Define instinct. Discuss how instinct theory explains behavior. Explain the problems with this theory of motivation. (pp. 258–259)

4. Define homeostasis, need, drive, and drive reduction theory. Define primary and secondary drives and discuss their role in motivation. Describe the kinds of behavior that drive theory can and cannot explain. (pp. 259-260)

5. Define arousal. Discuss the relationship between arousal level and performance. Describe the arousal theory of motivation. (p. 260)

6. Describe how incentive theory accounts for human behavior. (p. 260)

7. Define hunger and satiety. Describe the role of stomach cues and the role of the brain in regulating hunger and eating. Be sure to list the nutrients and hormones that the brain monitors, and explain how the ventromedial nucleus and lateral hypothalamus might interact to maintain a set point. (pp. 261–263)

8. Discuss the factors that can override biological signals about satiety, including flavor and appetite. Explain how social rules and cultural traditions influence eating. (pp. 263–264)

9. Define obesity, anorexia nervosa, and bulimia nervosa. Describe behaviors and health problems associated with each of these eating disorders.

Discuss the potential causes of each disorder, and describe how it is treated. (pp. 264–266)

10. Describe the University of Chicago study of human sexual behavior and discuss its findings. Describe the sexual response cycle. Name the male and female sex hormones and explain their organizing and activating effects. (pp. 267–269)

11. Discuss the social and cultural influences on sexual motivation. Define heterosexual, homosexual, and bisexual orientation. Describe the evidence on the extent to which genes may determine sexual orientation. Define sexual dysfunction and give examples. (pp. 269–274)

12. Define need achievement. Describe the characteristics of people with strong achievement motivation and the factors that can affect its development. (pp. 274–276)

13. Describe the extrinsic and intrinsic factors that affect job satisfaction and dissatisfaction. Give an example of a job that has been designed for high levels of employee satisfaction and motivation. (pp. 276–277)

14. Define subjective well-being. Discuss the stability of subjective well-being and list the factors that appear to generate happiness. (pp. 277-278)

15. Describe Maslow's hierarchy of needs. Give examples of each kind of need. (p. 278)

16. Describe the four types of motivational conflicts, and explain the relationship between motivation and stress. (pp. 279–280)

17. Describe the defining characteristics of the subjective experience of emotion. Give examples of objective aspects of emotion. (pp. 280-281)

18. Describe the role of the brain in emotion and facial expressions. Describe how the parasympathetic and sympathetic systems are involved in emotional experience, including the fight-or-flight syndrome. (pp. 281–282)

19. Describe James's theory of emotion. Use the theory to explain an emotional experience. (pp. 284–285)

20. Discuss the research that evaluates James's theory. Describe the facial feedback hypothesis. Describe the various types of lie detector tests and discuss the assumptions on which they are based. (pp. 285–286)

21. Describe Schachter's modification of James's theory of emotion. Define attribution and give an example. (pp. 286–287)

22. Discuss the research that evaluates Schachter's theory. Define transferred excitation and give an example of its effects. (pp. 287-288)

23. Describe Cannon's theory of emotion. Discuss the updates to Cannon's theory. (pp. 288–289)

24. Compare and contrast James's, Schachter's, and Cannon's theories of emotion. (p. 289)

25. Discuss the role of facial movements in expressing human emotion. Describe Darwin's theory of innate basic facial expressions. Discuss the research that supports this theory. (pp. 289–291)

26. Describe the social and cultural factors involved in communicating emotion. Describe the role and sources of learning in human emotional expression. Define emotion culture and <u>social referencing</u>. (pp. 291–293)

KEY TERMS

I. CONCEPTS AND THEORIES OF MOTIVATION

1. **Motivation** is defined as those influences that account for the initiation, direction, intensity, and persistence of behavior. (pp. 257-258)

Example: What causes us to initiate the movements necessary to get up from the couch and get something to drink? What causes us to persist in our work, sometimes to the point of staying up all night? Why do some people exert intense effort and others no effort at all? These are the kinds of questions asked by people studying motivation.

2. A **motive** is a reason or purpose for behavior. One motive can often account for many behaviors. (p. 258)

Example: A woman drives a Jaguar, wears expensive sports clothes, and joins a country club. Her motive is to demonstrate that she belongs to a specific group of people who are quite wealthy.

3. **Instincts** are automatic, involuntary, and unlearned behavior patterns that are consistently displayed in the presence of specific stimuli. (p. 258)

Example: In some species of birds, baby birds instinctively respond to the striped beak of the adult birds by opening their mouths.

4. **Instinct theory** proposed that human behavior is caused by instincts. (p. 258)

Example: An instinct theorist would say that Nancy wants to have children because she has a reproductive instinct.

5. **Homeostasis** is the tendency of an organism to maintain its physiological systems at a stable, steady level, or equilibrium, by constantly adjusting to changes in internal or external stimuli. (p. 259)

Example: Suppose that you had to walk outside in bitterly cold weather. Your body would sense this change in an external stimulus (the cold) and would begin taking action to maintain your temperature. Shivering, an adjustment that generates body heat, would help keep your temperature from dropping.

6. **Drive reduction theory** states that biological needs, which are created by imbalances in homeostasis, produce drives. (p. 259)

Example: Oscar hasn't had anything to drink for hours. He has a need for fluids, which has caused a drive to find something to drink.

7. A **need** is a biological requirement for well-being. (p. 259)

Example: Because we cannot live without food and water, they are excellent examples of needs.

8. A **drive** is a psychological state of arousal that compels us to take action to restore our homeostatic balance. When balance is restored, the drive is reduced. (p. 259)

Example: When you have not eaten for a while, you experience a biological need to eat, which produces the psychological state of arousal known as the hunger drive. Hunger drives us to eat so as to restore balance to our systems.

9. **Primary drives** are drives that arise from biological needs. (p. 259)

Example: You have primary drives for obtaining food, water, and warmth. These are basic biological needs.

10. **Secondary drives** are learned through operant or classical conditioning. We learn drives that prompt us to obtain objects that are associated with the reduction of a primary drive. (p. 259)

Example: Joseph lives in Alaska. He has learned that it is necessary to pay his power bill on time (secondary drive) in order to stay warm (primary drive) during the winter.

11. **Arousal** is a general internal level of activation reflected in the state of several physiological systems. (p. 260)

Example: After the announcement about the pop quiz, Paola's heart rate, muscle tension, and brain activity increased.

12. **Arousal theory** states that people are motivated to behave in ways that maintain an optimal level of arousal. The level of arousal considered optimal varies from person to person. (p. 260)

Example: Jorge is sitting in his office after a twelve-hour day, unhappy and bored. His level of arousal is too low. He decides to take a vacation in a country he has never visited. Toward the end of his vacation, he begins to look forward to getting back to work. Now Jorge's level of arousal is too high. He wants to go back to a well-known environment where his arousal level will decrease.

13. **Incentive theory** states that human behavior is goal directed; we act to obtain positive stimuli and avoid negative stimuli. Positive stimuli or incentives vary from person to person and can change over time. (p. 260)

Example: When Joanna and David were first married, they saved money to buy a house (incentive). Now their mortgage is paid, and buying a house is no longer an incentive that guides their behavior. Instead, they save money to take vacations in Europe.

II. HUNGER AND EATING

14. **Hunger** is the state of wanting to eat. Stomach cues, signals carried by the blood, and hypothalamus activity indicate when we should eat. (p. 261)

15. **Satiety** is the state of no longer wanting to eat. It is triggered by the brain recognizing nutrients and hormones in the bloodstream. (p. 261)

Example: When James finishes eating a large pizza all by himself, he experiences a sense of satiety, meaning he no longer wants to eat.

16. **Obesity** is a condition of severe overweight and can contribute to diabetes, high blood pressure, and increased risk of heart attack. (p. 264)

17. **Anorexia nervosa** is an eating disorder characterized by an obsession with eating and self-starvation, sometimes to the point of death. Psychological factors associated with anorexia include a preoccupation with thinness and a distorted body image. (p. 265)

Example: Linda refuses to eat anything except one grapefruit per day. She exercises all the time, and is constantly thinking about ways to make herself thinner, even though she is already well underweight. Linda has anorexia nervosa.

18. **Bulimia nervosa** is an eating disorder in which a person consumes large quantities of food (binges) and then attempts to eliminate the food (purges) through vomiting or laxatives. (p. 266)

Example: Veronica comes home and eats a bag of Oreos, a bag of potato chips, and a container of ice cream in one sitting. She then proceeds to induce vomiting so that she will not gain weight from her binge. Veronica probably has bulimia nervosa.

III. SEXUAL BEHAVIOR

19. The **sexual response cycle** is the pattern of arousal before, during, and after sexual activity. (p. 268)

20. **Sex hormones** influence our motivation to participate in sex activity. (p. 269)

Example: Estrogens, progestins, and androgens are examples of sex hormones.

21. **Estrogens** and **progestins** are female hormones. They are found in males too, but females have more estrogen and progestin than they have male hormones. (p. 269)

22. **Androgens** are male hormones. Androgens are found in both males and females and play a role in sexual motivation. Testosterone is the principal androgen. (p. 269)

23. **Heterosexual** activity is sexual interaction with people of the opposite sex. (p. 270)

24. **Homosexual** activity is sexual interaction with people of the same sex. (p. 271)

25. **Bisexual** activity is sexual interaction with people of both sexes. (p. 271)

26. **Sexual dysfunctions** are conditions in which a person's ability or desire to have sex is diminished or gone. (p. 273)

Example: The most common sexual dysfunctions in men and women are, respectively, the erectile disorder and arousal disorder.

IV. ACHIEVEMENT MOTIVATION

27. **Need achievement** is reflected in the degree to which people establish specific goals, care about meeting those goals with competence, and experience feelings of satisfaction in doing so. People with a high need for

achievement prefer honest, even if harsh, criticism from a competent critic over unconstructive but pleasant comments. The development of this need is affected by parents, culture, and school experiences. (p. 274)

> *Example:* During grade school, Kelly chose to join an after-school math activity program that had regular tests in addition to projects. Kelly knew that she was good in math and wanted something new to challenge her.

28. **Subjective well-being** is a combination of judging one's own life as satisfying, frequently experiencing positive mood and emotion, and infrequently experiencing negative mood and emotion. (p. 277)

> *Example:* Jo Ann feels that her life is pretty good, she is generally happy, and hardly every gets really mad or sad. Jo Ann has high subjective well-being.

V. RELATIONS AND CONFLICTS AMONG MOTIVES

29. An **approach-approach conflict** occurs when you have to decide between two options, both of which are appealing to you. (p. 279)

> *Example:* Your parents offer to take you to Rome or Paris for vacation. You've never been to either city and would love to visit both, but you have to choose because you can't approach both options.

30. An **avoidance-avoidance conflict** occurs when you have to decide between two options, neither of which is appealing to you. (p. 279)

> *Example:* You were caught speeding excessively, and now you must either pay a $1,000 fine or spend 3 days in the county jail. You would prefer to avoid both options, but must choose one.

31. An **approach-avoidance conflict** occurs when you have to decide whether or not to engage in a single option that has both attractive and unattractive features. (p. 279)

> *Example:* Your best friend asks you to come over and help clean the bathrooms. You'd like to help out your friend and say "hi", but you don't feel like cleaning bathrooms.

32. A **multiple approach-avoidance conflict** occurs when you must decide between two or more options, all of which have both attractive and unattractive features. (p. 279)

> *Example:* You were accepted at the college you've always dreamed of attending, but were given no

scholarship or financial aid. You were also accepted at a college you really don't want to attend, but you received a full-ride financial aid and scholarship package. Deciding between these two colleges is a multiple approach-avoidance conflict.

V. THE NATURE OF EMOTION

33. An **emotion** is either a positive or a negative experience that is felt with some intensity as happening to the self, is generated in part by a cognitive appraisal of situations, and is accompanied by both learned and innate physical responses. (p. 281)

> *Example:* Imagine that your boss unjustly says your work is worthless. Rage wells up inside you because you have worked very hard. The involuntary experience of negative emotion just happens; you do not make it happen. Your cognitive appraisal of the situation is also important. You have determined that your boss is not kidding, but is very serious. When in a rage, you may feel your face flush and your heart rate increase (reflexive physical responses).

34. The **parasympathetic system**, a subdivision of the autonomic nervous system, is involved in activities relating to the growth and nourishment of the body. (p. 282)

> *Example:* Coleman is happily relaxing after a long day of classes. As he watches a comedy on TV, his heart rate slows, but digestion activity increases.

35. The **sympathetic system**, a subdivision of the autonomic nervous system, prepares the body for vigorous activity, such as the fight-or-flight syndrome. (p. 282)

> *Example:* When Miranda thinks she hears someone breaking into her apartment one night, her sympathetic system initiates the fight-or-flight syndrome, causing her mouth to feel dry, her pupils to dilate, her breathing to become rapid, and other changes associated with fear.

36. The **fight-or-flight syndrome** is a series of physiological changes in activity, controlled by the sympathetic nervous system, which prepares the body for combat (fight) or escape (flight) from threatening situations. (p. 282)

> *Example:* A fire alarm startles Coleman. In the fight-or-flight response activated by the sympathetic nervous system, his heart rate and breathing increase. Although he can't feel the difference as he walks to the stairway, his digestive activity has slowed and his blood sugar has increased.

VII. THEORIES OF EMOTION

37. **Attribution** is the process of identifying the cause of an event through cognitive appraisal. (p. 287)

   Example: Felicia was smiling as she studied. When she noticed it, she attributed it to her happiness about a trip she was planning for the weekend.

38. **Transferred excitation** occurs when arousal from one experience carries over to a different situation. People stay aroused longer than they think they do. If people have been aroused and then encounter a new situation, they may interpret their arousal as an emotional reaction to the new situation. (p. 287)

   Example: You have just run to class. Just outside the door of the classroom, one of the people working on your group project tells you that she could not finish her part of the paper that is due this period. Normally you would be angry, but your increased arousal from the run intensifies your emotion. You are not just angry; you are furious.

VIII. COMMUNICATING EMOTION

39. **Social referencing** occurs in ambiguous social situations. People use other's body language, including posture and facial expressions, to determine appropriate choices for their behavior. (pp. 292-293)

   Example: When Caryn reached for the candy dish, her mother frowned, so she stopped.

CONCEPTS AND EXERCISES

No. 1: Theories of Motivation

Completing this exercise should help you to achieve Learning Objectives 3, 4, 5, and 6.

Below is a list of several different behaviors. Which theory would best explain the motivation underlying each behavior?

1. Vivien has been working in a laboratory for six months. She has learned all the techniques necessary for the job and is now very bored. She wants to work for a different lab or apply to graduate school. _____

2. Diane spent the entire day working on the family farm. She and some friends went into town after work to have a cola. She realized several hours later that, although she was no longer thirsty, she was still drinking cola. _____

3. Karl and Sarah got married in the middle of the Great Depression when money for food and shelter was scarce. They have spent most of their lives working very hard and investing their money. Their children would like them to take some time off or retire and enjoy the fruits of their labor, but Karl and Sarah insist on working to make more money. _____

No. 2: Emotions at the Prom

Completing this exercise should help you to achieve Learning Objectives 19, 20, 21, 22, 23, and 24.

Following are some of the experiences of Franklin High students at their school dance. After each description, choose from the following list of options the phenomenon or theory of emotion that best matches the experience. Each answer may be used more than once or not at all.

1. Joya, after dancing a slow dance with Ted, walks back to where her friends are standing. She is smiling, a little breathless, and has a quickened heartbeat and shaky knees. Joya realizes that these responses indicate that she is happy. _____

2. Helen arrived at the dance twenty minutes late. She ran all the way from the parking lot to the school. She spent several minutes talking with her friends in the bathroom, brushing her hair, and putting on new lipstick. Just as she steps into the gym to survey the crowd, she trips and falls, ripping her dress. Absolutely furious, she yells at the boy who tries to help her up, "You idiot, look what you made me do!" What could explain her intense emotional reaction? _____

3. Cecelia is dancing with her boyfriend. She simultaneously realizes how much she loves him and notices how fast her heart is beating and that she has butterflies in her stomach. _____

   ° James's theory
   ° Schachter's theory
   ° Cannon's theory
   ° Transferred excitation

CRITICAL THINKING

Sam and Martina and another friend of theirs, Pete, are arguing about the reasons for a crime. A mobster named Joey killed Tony, a member of a rival family.

   Sam starts the conversation by saying, "Look, Martina, Joey has been part of the mob for years. He probably thought he had to knock Tony off before Tony killed him. The guy had a plain and simple goal—to live."

Martina returns, "I think he was just bored. There hasn't been a lot happening in the streets lately. I bet he just wanted a little fun. That's why he killed Tony."

Using the five critical thinking questions in the text, the clues in the story, and what you have learned about motivation, answer the following.

1. What is Sam's hypothesis?

2. What theory of motivation would support his hypothesis?

3. What is Martina's hypothesis?

4. What theory of motivation would support her hypothesis?

PERSONAL LEARNING ACTIVITIES

1. Why do you study psychology? List the reasons you study this subject. Try to identify whether your explanations fit with a particular theory of motivation. For example, if you wrote "curiosity," which theory would be best at explaining this motive? Which reasons would incentive theory explain? Is need for achievement a factor? (Learning Objectives 4, 5, 6, and 12)

2. Try to keep track of everything you ate in one day and where and when you ate it. Were you surprised by the results? What did you notice about where and when you were eating? Did you skip a meal or snack while doing something else? What influence did the flavor of the food or the presence of other people have on you? (Learning Objective 8)

3. If there were a drug which would make everyone crave only healthy foods, would you be in favor of it? Why or why not? (Learning Objective 8)

4. Think about the times that you experienced motivational conflicts—for example, when you had to decide whether to participate in an activity that had positive and negative aspects. Was it an approach-approach, approach-avoidance, avoidance-avoidance, or multiple approach-avoidance conflict? After you decided to participate (or not), did the positive or the negative features become more prominent? (Learning Objective 16)

5. Describe the way your family usually communicates emotions. For example, does your family approve of expressions of joy, anger, jealousy, love, guilt, and so on, or are some expressions discouraged? Do a broad smile, laughter, or screams of delight and jumping around more often express happiness? Some of these rules may stem from the emotion culture in which you live. Can you think of examples of differences between your family's emotion communication and the larger emotion culture in which you live? (Learning Objective 26)

WHAT SHOULD I WRITE ABOUT?

In this section of the last chapter, we discussed how using examples to generate a term paper topic could be helpful. At one point, it was even suggested that you should consider generating your own examples. Let's explore that idea a bit further now, focusing on how we could integrate what you learned in Chapter 1 about research methods in psychology with generating your own examples here.

A term paper topic can become an exciting inquiry if you choose to generate your own examples and research to support the position you end up taking in the paper. In the present chapter on *Motivation and Emotion*, there are plenty of concepts that relate to our every day lives. Doing an empirical study on one of those concepts can be a great way to jump start the writing process. After all, once you have done a study, your paper topic should be clear: you will describe the study and present the results. You can then finish by discussing how those results apply to every day life. So, how to you develop your own empirical study of a topic in *Motivation and Emotion*?

As always, you should start by choosing a topic that interests you. For example, many students find the topic of hunger and eating disorders fascinating. Almost everyone knows someone who claims to want to lose weight. If you know two such individuals, you might develop different weight loss plans for them and contrast how successful the results of the two plans were. This would be a "mini-experiment." A true experiment would have more than just one participant in each condition, but the logic behind the research strategies is similar.

Perhaps a field study is more to your liking. You could record your observations of how individuals you know have dealt with different motivational conflicts. Do approach-approach conflicts evoke a different thought process than avoidance-avoidance conflicts?

You could even conduct a survey. It would be interesting to design a survey to measure the emotional culture that different individuals have grown up in. Do you notice from your results that individuals from particular regions of the country tend to share similar emotional cultures, or does it seem to be more family-driven? The particular content of your survey, field study, or experiment is between you and your teacher. The point is that you could easily put to use the information on research methods to help generate a term paper topic that you could have fun writing about.

Here are some suggestions to consider as you develop your topic:

1. Make sure the study you design is viable given the resources you have. Don't choose to study the biological bases of hunger if you have no way to measure those processes. It would be much easier to study social influences on eating, because those are easier to see without expensive equipment.

2. Make sure the topic is something that you can ethically study given the method you intend to use. Developing a survey of sexual behavior may not be the best term paper topic, because typically people feel that these questions are very invasive. Studying the behavior of anorexics and offering a treatment method would also be an example of an unethical concept, because most undergraduate students are not qualified to offer such treatment. If you have any concerns about the ethics of your study, it is better to ask your instructor first.

THE INTERNET

The Psychabilities web site that accompanies this text offers many resources relevant to this chapter. They include NetLab exercises, Thinking Critically and Evaluating Research exercises, ACE chapter quizzes, recommended web links, and articles on current events, books, and movies. Go to http://college.hmco.com, select Psychology, and then this textbook.

MULTIPLE-CHOICE QUESTIONS

SAMPLE QUIZ 1

1. Nick carried a C average throughout his high school career until his last semester, when he achieved an "A" average. He had discovered that he would be ineligible to accept a football scholarship to the college of his choice without at least an "A" average in that semester. This example illustrates the role of motivation in
   a. discovering unity in diversity.
   b. relating cognitions to behavior.
   c. relating emotional experiences to behavior.
   d. explaining fluctuations in behavior over time.

2. Which of the following human behaviors would instinct theory have the *most* trouble explaining?
   a. Maternal behavior
   b. Aggressive behavior
   c. Thrill-seeking behavior
   d. Sexual behavior

3. Stewart desperately wants a job in the computer field. He has just finished an interview during which he was aggressive about his thoughts and ideas. An incentive theorist would say that Stewart
   a. has a strong aggressive instinct.
   b. thinks that being aggressive will land him the job.
   c. has a very high optimal level of arousal.
   d. is worried about having enough money to live on.

4. Dwayne enjoys spending quiet evenings at home, watching old movies. To best explain his motivation for this behavior using the arousal theory, we should say that Dwayne
   a. is rewarded by his enjoyment of the movies.
   b. has hectic, busy days and wants some peace and quiet in the evenings.
   c. has an emotional need fulfilled by watching the movies.
   d. has met his physiological needs and therefore can seek arousal.

5. Dr. Frankenberry just built a creature out of human body parts. The only problem is that the creature refuses to eat. Apparently, Dr. Frankenberry failed to hook up stimulating electrodes to the creature's
   a. ventromedial nucleus.
   b. paraventricular nucleus.
   c. lateral hypothalamus.
   d. thalamus.

6. Maxine has bulimia nervosa but not anorexia nervosa. Which of the following is most likely to describe her?
   a. Maxine has normal body weight.
   b. Maxine starves herself, causing severe physical damage and weight loss.
   c. Maxine is less willing to expend much effort to get food.
   d. Maxine's overeating has caused obesity, but she doesn't believe she has a problem.

7. William and Virginia are discussing the sexual response cycle. William says, "It really isn't fair that women can have orgasm after orgasm! We men have our orgasms and then have to wait around a while before we can have another one." Virginia says, "That is just the way things are—women don't have a _____ like men do!"
   a. plateau phase
   b. feedback loop
   c. refractory period
   d. resolution phase

8. Kate has a high need for achievement. Kate's parents most likely
   a. encouraged her to try new challenges and rewarded her successes.

b. always got involved with her work and even helped her finish assignments.

c. told her to quit torturing herself and give up when things got tough.

d. did not praise Kate very much because they did not want her to become satisfied and quit trying new things.

9. Magda claims that she will not be satisfied until she gets the respect she deserves for the job she does at work. According to Maslow's hierarchy of needs, Magda has

a. given up her biological needs because she probably was unable to fulfill them.

b. probably been poor all of her life.

c. had her lower needs fulfilled to an acceptable degree.

d. not had her lower needs fulfilled to an acceptable degree.

10. Marjorie asked Jerry to be her date at the sold out Nine Inch Nails concert. Jerry can't decide what to do. He really wants to see Nine Inch Nails, but he can't stand Marjorie. Jerry's situation is a good example of _____ conflicts.

a. approach-approach

b. avoidance-avoidance

c. approach-avoidance

d. multiple approach-avoidance

11. According to the textbook, which of the following would not be part of an emotional experience?

a. An increase in heart rate

b. Cognitive appraisal of a situation

c. Pupil dilation

d. All of the above are part of an emotional experience.

12. Kurt, who is about to take a lie detector test, has sneakily put a tack in his shoe. Kurt should jam the tack into his toe to show an increase in physiological response after

a. questions about his alibi.

b. control questions.

c. relevant questions.

d. questions about his age, education, and income.

13. Matt is very interested in a woman he met at the gym. When would be the best time for him to approach her to talk?

a. As she is warming up before her workout

b. During her workout

c. When she is toweling off right after her workout

d. In the parking lot after a shower

14. Gloria went to the doctor for her usual antiallergy shots. The nurse mistakenly gave her a shot of epinephrine, which caused a great deal of physiological arousal. As Gloria sailed out of the office, she decided that she was feeling shaky from drinking too much caffeinated coffee. Her lack of emotion despite physiological arousal can be explained by which theory of emotion?

a. Darwin's theory of emotion

b. James's theory of emotion

c. Schachter's theory of emotion

d. Cannon's theory of emotion

15. Jethro had never worn a tuxedo before. While trying on his tuxedo, Jethro used a short rope instead of a belt to hold his pants up. However, he saw that Jane, his upper-class socialite friend, grimaced when he did this; and, as a result, he replaced the rope with a leather belt. Jethro used _____ in deciding to use a belt.

a. social referencing

b. social facilitation

c. mood congruence

d. the mere exposure effect

Total Correct (See answer key) _____

SAMPLE QUIZ 2

Use this quiz to reassess your learning after taking Quiz 1 and reviewing the chapter.

1. Drew thinks that the concept of learning is vital to understanding motivation. Which of the following theories of motivation would he be least likely to agree with?

a. Opponent-process theory

b. Drive theory

c. Instinct theory

d. Incentive theory

2. Drive-reduction theory has the greatest difficulty explaining the behavior of

a. eating food when you are hungry.

b. earning money when you need to pay bills.

c. sleeping when you are very fatigued.

d. going to a horror movie for the thrill of it.

3. Jackson enjoys playing on the varsity basketball team. However, when his team is leading or losing by a lot, he becomes bored and loses interest in the game. He scores more points and is more interested in the games when the score is very close. Jackson's motivation is *best* explained by the _____ theory.

a. arousal

b. drive reduction

c. incentive

d. performance

4. People with a newly discovered syndrome feel compelled to eat when they encounter food. In fact, they may continue to eat although they can't physically handle more food. It is feared that if people with this syndrome were not monitored, they might literally eat themselves to death. What biological mechanism might account for this behavior?
   a. Damage to the lateral area of the hypothalamus
   b. Damage to fibers in the ventromedial nucleus
   c. Low glucose levels in the blood
   d. Aberrant elasticity of the stomach

5. Deidre is constantly worried about being fat. In addition, a few times a week, she will eat large quantities of food and then force herself to vomit. As a result, she also suffers from nutritional imbalances, intestinal damage, and dental problems. Deidre is *most likely* suffering from
   a. obesity.
   b. weight obsession.
   c. anorexia nervosa.
   d. bulimia nervosa.

6. Julie, who has a high need for achievement, is trying to decide where to work. Which job should she take?
   a. Company 1: high pay, little responsibility, great boss
   b. Company 2: low pay, lots of responsibility, mediocre boss
   c. Company 3: medium pay, lots of responsibility, chances for advancement, demanding boss
   d. Company 4: very high pay, easy work, not much chance for advancement, great boss

7. Jeannie, owner of a television and appliance store, wants to be sure that her employees feel satisfied with their jobs. She can best achieve this by
   a. letting employees decide what brands of products the store should sell.
   b. giving all employees a raise in their salary.
   c. decreasing the work load of the employees.
   d. allowing employees extra vacation time each year.

8. Paula is lonely. She chose a school that is far away from home, and all her friends are at different universities. She really misses being able to tell her best friend about her day. According to Maslow, Paula is not able to fulfill which need at this point in her life?
   a. Physiological
   b. Safety
   c. Belonging
   d. Esteem

9. Horatio is trying to decide what food to order at his favorite fast-food restaurant. The hamburger is tasty, but also high in fat (and thus is a poor nutritional choice). The grilled chicken is low in fat, tasty, and healthy, but it is very expensive. Horatio is experiencing a(n) _____ conflict.
   a. approach-approach
   b. avoidance-avoidance
   c. approach-avoidance
   d. multiple approach-avoidance

10. If a woman smiles when she thinks a joke is funny, but cannot force herself to smile, then there may be brain damage in the
    a. extrapyramidal motor system.
    b. basal ganglia or the thalamus.
    c. pyramidal motor system in the motor cortex.
    d. cerebellum.

11. You are driving down Main Street when a pedestrian runs in front of you. You swerve widely and only just miss him. After a few seconds, you notice that your heart is racing, your brow is wet with perspiration, your mouth is dry, and you are trembling. This reaction was activated by the _____ nervous system.
    a. central
    b. parasympathetic
    c. sympathetic
    d. somatic

12. Janet and Joan are experiencing identical patterns of physiological arousal: increased heart rate, sweaty palms, pupil dilation, and increased breathing rate. Janet feels happy, and Joan is very scared. Which theory of emotion can explain the differences in their emotions?
    a. James's theory of emotion
    b. Schachter's theory of emotion
    c. Darwin's theory of emotion
    d. Cannon's theory of emotion

13. Which theory requires the existence of unique physiological states for every emotion?
    a. James's theory
    b. Cannon's theory
    c. Schachter's theory
    d. Darwin's theory

14. Lori and Carol are discussing the places in town where they have met the best-looking men. Based on your knowledge of transferred excitation, which place do you think would be at the top of their list?
    a. A men's clothing store
    b. A laundromat
    c. A local dance bar
    d. A restaurant

15. Which of the following is the best example of facial feedback?

a. Jill notices that Lani grimaces as Jill steps into her apartment without wiping her feet, so Jill stops to wipe them.
b. Someone comments that you are looking especially wonderful.
c. You notice that you are smiling as you study and conclude you must be in a good mood.
d. You look for evidence that your roommate is lying by scanning your roommate's face carefully.

Total Correct (See answer key) ______

ANSWERS TO CONCEPTS AND EXERCISES

No. 1: Theories of Motivation

1. *Arousal theory*. Boredom put Vivian below her optimal level of arousal. Her attempts to reach her new goals will raise her arousal to its optimal level. (p. 260)
2. *Incentive theory*. Diane has been drinking cola for positive incentives—its taste and the way she feels—not because she is thirsty. (p. 260)
3. *Drive theory*. Karl and Sarah have learned a secondary drive of making money. They probably learned during the Depression that a lack of money prevented them from eating as much as they wanted. Therefore, they learned that making money, a secondary drive, was essential to reducing the primary drive of hunger. (p. 259)

No. 2: Emotions at the Prom

1. *James's theory*. This theory could explain Joya's emotional reaction since it is based solely on her physiological responses. She has decided that she is happy because she is experiencing all the physiological responses that occur with happiness. (p. 284)
2. *Transferred excitation*. Helen was probably still physiologically aroused from running into the school from the parking lot. She transferred this excitation to the anger she felt when she ripped her dress. This intensified her emotional reaction. (p. 287)
3. *Cannon's theory*. Cecelia is simultaneously experiencing the conscious emotion of being in love and a heightened physiological arousal. According to the Cannon theory, cognition and physiological reactions to emotion occur at the same time. (p. 288)

ANSWERS TO CRITICAL THINKING

1. Sam hypothesizes that Joey was motivated to kill Tony in order to avoid being killed himself.
2. The incentive theory of motivation would support this hypothesis.
3. Martina hypothesizes that since nothing was happening in the neighborhood, Joey killed Tony to increase his own level of arousal to an optimal level.
4. The arousal theory of motivation would support this hypothesis.

ANSWERS TO MULTIPLE-CHOICE QUESTIONS

Circle the question numbers you answered correctly.

Sample Quiz 1

1. *d* is the answer. Nick was motivated to change his behavior in order to get a college scholarship. (pp. 257-258)
   a. Nick's motivation did not uncover unity in diversity.
   b, c. Biology, emotion, and cognition affect motivation, but Nick's behavior shows how motivation affected his actions.
2. *c* is the answer. Instinct theory claims that behavior is motivated by unlearned responses to stimuli. Thrill-seeking behavior is least well explained by instinct theory. (p. 258)
   a, b, d. Instinct theorists have claimed that maternal, aggressive, and sexual behaviors are caused by instincts.
3. *b* is the answer. An incentive theorist would say that Stewart was behaving in a way that he thought would bring him closer to a goal or an incentive. (p. 260)
   a. An instinct theorist would say that Stewart has an aggressive instinct.
   c. An arousal theorist would say that Stewart has a very high level of optimal arousal.
   d. A drive theorist would say that Stewart wants the job so that he will have enough money to buy food.
4. *b* is the answer. Arousal theory states that people try to maintain an optimal level of arousal. According to arousal theory, Dwayne will seek relaxation when overaroused. (p. 260)
   a. This would fit with incentive theory.

c, d. These sound similar to Maslow's views; however, he did not directly address arousal in his hierarchy of needs.

5. *c* is the answer. The lateral hypothalamus serves as the "start eating" center; therefore, if Dr. Frankenberry didn't provide a way to stimulate it, the creature may not want to eat. (p. 262)
   a. The ventromedial nucleus is the "stop eating" center.
   b. The paraventricular nucleus plays a role in starting cravings for specific foods.
   d. The thalamus is a relay center for sensory information, but doesn't control hunger and eating.

6. *a* is the answer. Unlike anorexia nervosa, people with bulimia nervosa may be below, at, or above normal weight. (pp. 265-266)
   b. Maxine's bulimia nervosa causes her to eat large amounts of food and then purge it through vomiting or laxatives.
   c. Maxine may often expend great effort to get food for a binge.
   d. Although Maxine may be overweight, she most likely sees her eating behavior as a problem.

7. *c* is the answer. Men experience a refractory period during which they can't become aroused. (pp. 268-269)
   a, d. Both women and men have a plateau phase and a resolution phase.
   b. There is no feedback loop in the sexual response cycle.

8. *a* is the answer. Children whose parents encourage them to try new things and reward them for their successes develop a high need for achievement. (p. 275)
   b. Children with parents who interfered in their work would not develop a high need for achievement.
   c. Children with parents who let them give up would not develop a high need for achievement.
   d. A lack of praise would *not* encourage development of a high need for achievement.

9. *c* is the answer. According to Maslow, needs lower on the hierarchy must be fulfilled before higher needs become motivators. (p. 278)
   a, d. Needs lower on the hierarchy, such as physiological and safety needs, must be at least partially satisfied, according to Maslow.
   b. Having been poor all her life does not necessarily place Magda at a specific level of Maslow's hierarchy. If Magda had been poor, but had her biological, safety, belongingness, and esteem needs met, she could be seeking

self-actualization. According to the story, however, she wants the respect of coworkers; therefore, Magda has esteem as a motive.

10. *c* is the answer. Jerry is experiencing an approach-avoidance conflict, because the activity he is considering has both positive and negative characteristics. (p. 279)
    a. Approach-approach conflicts occur when people have to choose between two desirable alternatives. If Jerry was invited to the concert by someone he liked, but was also invited to go to New York for the weekend, which he also would like to do—and couldn't do both, then he would be experiencing an approach-approach conflict.
    b. Avoidance-avoidance conflicts occur when people have to choose between two undesirable alternatives.
    d. Multiple approach-avoidance conflicts occur when people have to choose between two or more alternatives, each of which have positive and negative aspects.

11. *d* is the answer. Physiological changes, cognitive appraisal, and interpretation of one's environment are all part of an emotional experience. (pp. 280-281)
    a, b, c. Each one of these is part of an emotional experience, so *d* is the best answer because it includes all of them.

12. *b* is the answer. Innocent people usually react more strongly to control questions such as, "Have you ever tried to hurt someone?" Therefore, Kurt should jam the tack in his toe after control questions, in order to produce physiological arousal. (p. 286)
    a. Questions about an alibi would not be good questions to seem upset about. Like questions that specifically refer to a crime, innocent people shouldn't react very strongly when asked about their whereabouts.
    c. Relevant questions are those that specifically refer to the crime. Guilty people react more strongly to relevant questions than to control questions.
    d. Reactions to relevant and control questions are compared in order to determine guilt or innocence. Questions about age, education, and income are neither control nor relevant questions.

13. *c* is the answer. People remain physiologically aroused longer than they think they do. The woman at the gym will feel calm by the time she is toweling off, even though she will still be somewhat aroused. If Matt approaches her at this

point, she will probably attribute any leftover arousal to him instead of to the exercise. (p. 287)

a. The woman at the gym will experience very little physiological arousal while she is warming up. If she does experience any arousal, she will attribute it to exercising, not to Matt.

b. Weightlifting and aerobics will cause physiological arousal. However, the woman will probably attribute her arousal to these activities instead of to Matt.

d. By the time the woman has showered and gone to the parking lot, she will no longer be aroused.

14. c is the answer. According to the Schachter theory, if we attribute arousal to a non-emotional cause (for example, caffeine), then the experience of emotion should be reduced. Gloria was not experiencing any emotion. She simply thought she had too much coffee that morning. (pp. 286–288)

a. Darwin did not propose a theory of how we experience emotion.

b. According to the James theory, Gloria should have interpreted her physiological arousal as resulting from an emotion.

d. According to the Cannon theory, Gloria should have cognitively experienced an emotion when she felt the physiological arousal. This cannot be the answer since Gloria felt the arousal but no emotion.

15. a is the answer. When people look at others' emotional expressions to see how they should act in an unfamiliar situation, they are using social referencing. (pp. 292-293)

b. Social facilitation, a term from the social psychology field, occurs when the presence of others improves a person's performance.

c. Mood congruence, a term from the memory field, is an example of state dependence of memory. A person in a positive mood recalls positive events more easily; a person in a negative mood recalls negative events more easily.

d. The mere exposure effect, a term from the consciousness area, is the tendency for people to like previously seen material better than new ones.

Now turn to the quiz analysis table at the end of this chapter to find which areas you know well and which areas you need to work on. Circle the numbers in the table for items on Quiz 1 that you answered correctly.

ANSWERS TO MULTIPLE-CHOICE QUESTIONS

Circle the question numbers you answered correctly.

Sample Quiz 2

1. c is the answer. Instincts are unlearned, automatic, innate responses to specific stimuli. (p. 258)

a. According to arousal theory, we behave in ways that maintain our optimal level of arousal. Some of the activities that increase or decrease the level of arousal are probably learned.

b. According to drive theory, we learn secondary drives.

d. According to incentive theory, we behave in ways that allow us to reach certain goals. Some of the behaviors that allow us to reach certain goals are learned—for example, learning how to study in order to get good grades.

2. d is the answer. Drive reduction theory suggests that imbalances create needs which create drives to restore balance. Going to a horror movie for enjoyment doesn't fit with this theory, because the behavior isn't coming from an imbalance. (p. 259)

a. Eating food is caused by a primary drive to ease hunger, according to drive reduction theory.

b. Earning money is caused by a secondary drive to have money, according to drive reduction theory.

c. Sleeping is caused by a primary drive to ease fatigue, according to drive reduction theory.

3. a is the answer. Arousal theory suggests that people want to stay at a preferred level of arousal. Jackson isn't satisfied with winning by a large margin, he'd rather the score be close, so that he will be at a higher level of arousal. (p. 260)

b. Drive reduction theory would suggest that as Jackson gets farther from a goal, he would be more motivated, but if Jackson is winning by a lot, he loses interest.

c. Incentive theory suggests that potential rewards are big motivators, but if Jackson is winning by a lot, he loses interest.

d. Performance theory isn't a theory of motivation discussed in your text.

4. b is the answer. The ventromedial nucleus is the stop-eating center. If it is damaged, no "stop eating" message will get through. (p. 262)

a. Damage to the lateral area would cause the people to stop eating.

c. Low glucose levels do cause increases in eating, but the eating would cause glucose levels to rise, curtailing eating.

d. Hunger pangs are one cue to eat, but they aren't strong enough to cause people to continue to eat when they cannot handle any more food.

5. *d* is the answer. People with bulimia nervosa binge and purge in an effort to control their weight. (pp. 265-266)
   a. Obesity is severe overweight.
   b. Weight obsession is not a type of eating disorder.
   c. Anorexia nervosa is characterized by self-starvation.

6. *c* is the answer. It is important that Julie take the job that will yield the most satisfaction, which she will find in jobs that provide opportunities for advancement and individual responsibility. She should also take the job with the fewest dissatisfying characteristics, such as low pay and a mediocre boss. (pp. 276–277)
   a. Company 1 has very few dissatisfying characteristics but no satisfying characteristics either.
   b. Company 2 offers a large amount of responsibility but several dissatisfying characteristics as well, such as low pay and a mediocre boss.
   d. Company 4 has very few dissatisfying characteristics but no satisfying characteristics. The job carries no responsibility and does not provide any chances for advancement.

7. *a* is the answer. Letting employees have control over the work environment generally improves employee satisfaction. (pp. 276–277)
   b, d. Extrinsic rewards, such as pay and vacation time, do not significantly increase satisfaction.
   c. Decreasing the workload would not be as effective as giving employees input and responsibility in their jobs.

8. *c* is the answer. Paula's need for belongingness and love (on Maslow's hierarchy) is not being fulfilled. (p. 278)
   a. We have physiological needs for things that are basic to survival, such as food and water.
   b. Safety needs refer to physical and emotional support from a primary caregiver.
   d. Our needs for esteem are met when we gain approval, admiration, and other types of positive evaluation from ourselves or others. Paula can give those to herself and does not necessarily need to have these needs fulfilled by others.

9. *d* is the answer. Multiple approach-avoidance conflicts occur when people have to choose between two or more alternatives, each of which has positive and negative aspects. (p. 279)
   a. Approach-approach conflicts occur when people have to choose between two alternatives with only desirable qualities.

   b. Avoidance-avoidance conflicts occur when people have to choose between two undesirable alternatives.
   c. An approach-avoidance conflict is one where the only possible activity has both positive and negative characteristics.

10. *c* is the answer. The pyramidal motor system controls voluntary movements, such as a posed smile. (p. 282)
    a. The extrapyramidal motor system controls involuntary emotional facial expressions such as smiling when something strikes you as funny.
    b, d. The basal ganglia, thalamus, and cerebellum do not differentially control voluntary versus involuntary emotional expressions.

11. *c* is the answer. The sympathetic nervous system was most activated by the near accident, because it is responsible for creating the fight or flight syndrome. (p. 282)
    a. The central nervous system oversees the activity of the autonomic and somatic nervous systems and their subsystems, but it was not most activated by the accident.
    b. The parasympathetic nervous system conserves energy and calms the person after an accident.
    d. The somatic system is in control of voluntary actions, not automatic ones.

12. *b* is the answer. According to the Schachter theory, our cognitive appraisals of situations can cause us to label identical physiological responses in several different ways. (pp. 286–288)
    a. According to the James theory, every emotion is associated with a unique physiological response.
    c. Darwin did not address the mechanism that labels emotions. He said that emotional expressions are inherited.
    d. Cannon thought the perception of and the experience of the emotion were simultaneous. He did not discuss cognitive appraisal.

13. *a* is the answer. The James theory of emotion states that we experience emotion based on our physiological responses. If this is true, every emotion should be associated with a unique pattern of physiological arousal. (pp. 284–285)
    b. According to the Cannon theory, the thalamus is the core of emotion. Peripheral responses do not determine which emotion we are feeling.
    c. According to Schachter's theory, the same pattern of physiological arousal can be attributed to different emotions based on our cognitive appraisal of the environment. Therefore, it is not necessary to have unique

patterns of physiological arousal for every emotion.

d. Darwin discussed the functions that emotion serves in survival.

14. *c* is the answer. Research has shown that, compared with people at rest, exercise-aroused people experience stronger feelings of attraction when they meet people of the opposite sex. When Lori and Carol get off the dance floor, they will transfer the excitation caused by dancing to the attractive men they see in the bar. (p. 287)

a, b, d. A clothing store, laundromat, and restaurant do not offer any activity that causes an increase in physiological arousal.

15. *c* is the answer. The facial feedback hypothesis is a variation on James's theory. It suggests that facial movements are information we interpret as part of our physiological response. According to James, we have a different set of facial expressions and bodily responses for each emotion. Some evidence shows that smiling will make a person feel happier. (p. 286)

a. This is an example in which Jill has used social referencing to adjust her behavior.

b. A compliment may be feedback that you look nice, but it is not part of the facial feedback hypothesis.

d. The facial feedback hypothesis proposes that feedback from our own faces informs us of our emotions. It does not deal with looking at other people's faces for evidence of emotion or lies.

Now turn to the quiz analysis table at the end of this chapter to find which areas you know well and which areas you need to work on. Circle the numbers in the table for items on Quiz 2 that you answered correctly.

For each question you answered correctly, circle its number. (Quiz 1 numbers are not shaded; Quiz 2 numbers are shaded.) Are there patterns in the types of questions or the topics you got wrong that could direct your further study? Did you improve from Quiz 1 to Quiz 2?

TOPIC	TYPE OF QUESTION		
	DEFINITION	COMPREHENSION	APPLICATION
Motivation			
Concepts			1
Theories	2		3, 4
			1, 2, 3
Hunger and eating	6		5
			4, 5
Sexual behavior			7
Achievement			8
			6, 7
Relations			9
			8
Conflicts			10
			9
Emotion			
Nature	11		
		10	11
Theories			12, 13, 14
		13	12, 14, 15
Communication			15

TOTAL CORRECT BY QUIZ:

QUIZ 1:	
QUIZ 2:	

Chapter 9

Human Development

LEARNING OBJECTIVES

1. Define developmental psychology. (p. 300)

2. Describe the history of the nature-nurture debate. Discuss the different views of development held by Gesell, Watson, and Piaget. Define maturation. (p. 300)

3. Describe how nature and nurture influence development to create similarities and differences among people. Explain how development is influenced by the *interaction* of genetic and environmental factors. (pp. 301-302)

4. Describe the process of prenatal development. Be sure to explain how a zygote is formed, and describe the changes that occur as the zygote becomes an embryo and then a fetus. (pp. 302–303)

5. Define and give examples of teratogen. Define critical period and name the stage associated with it. Describe the types of birth defects that can be caused by teratogens, including the pattern of defects known as fetal alcohol syndrome. (pp. 303–304)

6. Describe the capacities of a newborn's senses. Define reflex, and name three reflexes exhibited by newborns. Discuss how motor development is influenced by experimentation. (pp. 305–306)

7. Describe Piaget's theory of cognitive development. Define schemas, assimilation, and accommodation. (pp. 307–308)

8. Describe the development of mental abilities during the sensorimotor period. Define object permanence. (pp. 308–309)

9. Explain how research has led psychologists to modify Piaget's description of infants in the sensorimotor period. Discuss the experiments on object permanence and the role of experience in developing knowledge during infancy. (pp. 309–311)

10. Describe the changes in cognition that occur during the preoperational period. Discuss the ability to use symbols during this period. (pp. 311–312)

11. Define conservation. Describe the changes in cognition that occur during Piaget's stage of concrete operations. (pp. 312–313)

12. Discuss the criticisms of Piaget's theory of cognitive development, and discuss the information processing approach as an alternative to Piaget's theory. (pp. 313–314)

13. Discuss the possible explanations for infantile amnesia. (pp. 315–316)

14. Describe the impact of culture and early childhood experiences on cognitive development. (pp. 316–318)

15. Define temperament. Describe the different behaviors exhibited by easy, difficult, and slow-to-warm-up babies. (p. 319)

16. Define attachment and discuss how this type of relationship is formed between caregiver and infant. Describe Harlow's studies of motherless monkeys. (pp. 320–322)

17. Explain how the Strange Situation is used to study attachment. Describe how secure attachment patterns differ from avoidant, ambivalent, and disorganized attachment patterns. Discuss the question of whether day care damages the formation of a health mother-infant attachment. (pp. 322–324)

18. Compare and contrast the parenting styles of authoritarian, permissive, and authoritative parents. Describe the characteristics of children raised by each type of parent, and discuss the limitations of the research in this area. (pp. 325–326)

19. Describe the development of social relationships and social skills in children. Describe the development of gender roles. (pp. 326–328)

20. Define puberty, and discuss the physical and psychological changes and problems that occur during adolescence. Describe the relationship adolescents have with their parents and peers. (pp. 329–331)

21. Describe the development of both the personal and the ethnic identity. Define identity crisis. (pp. 331–332)

22. Describe the changes in cognition that occur during the <u>formal operational period</u>. (p. 332)

23. Describe the stages of moral reasoning suggested by Kohlberg. Define <u>preconventional</u>, <u>conventional</u>, and <u>postconventional</u> moral reasoning and give examples of statements that illustrate reasoning at each of these stages. Discuss the cultural and gender-related limitations of Kohlberg's stages. (pp. 333–335)

24. Describe the physical, cognitive, and social changes that occur during adulthood. (pp. 335-339)

25. Define <u>generativity</u>, <u>midlife transition</u>, and <u>terminal drop</u>. (p. 338, 339)

KEY TERMS

1. **Developmental psychology** is the area of specialization that documents the course and causes of people's social, emotional, moral, and intellectual development throughout the life span. (p. 300)

   Example: How do children learn to use language? Do infants respond to parents' emotional cues? Do cognitive changes occur during old age?

I. EXPLORING NATURE-NURTURE

2. **Maturation** refers to any development process (such as walking) that is guided by biological or genetic factors (nature). These processes occur in a fixed sequence and are usually unaffected by environmental conditions (nurture). (p. 300)

   Example: The development of secondary sexual characteristics occurs in a fixed sequence and is rarely affected by environmental conditions.

3. **Behavioral Genetics** is the study of how genes affect behavior. (p. 301)

   Example: Is intelligence an inherited characteristic? To what extent do genes determine temperament?

4. **Chromosomes** are made up of genes and carry an individual's genetic information. (p. 302)

   Example: Chromosomes carry the genetic information that determines one's sex. An XX pairing codes for a female and an XY for a male.

5. **Genes** are the genetic blueprint that govern the development of an individual. (p. 302)

6. Genes are built from **deoxyribonucleic acid (DNA)**, which provides the genetic code. (pp. 302-303)

II. BEGINNINGS

7. An **embryo** is that part of the zygote that will mature into an infant. (p. 303)

   Example: Towards the end of the second month of her pregnancy, Jenna has a sonogram in which she can see the baby's eyes, ears, nose and mouth. Jenna is seeing an embryo.

8. The embryo becomes a **fetus** in the third prenatal stage, which lasts from the third month of pregnancy until birth. (p. 303)

   Example: During the 8th stage of Jenna's pregnancy, Jenna's baby kicks and moves a lot. Jenna is being kicked by a fetus.

9. **Teratogens** are external substances that cause defects in the developing baby when introduced into the womb. (p. 303)

   Example: Alcohol drunk during pregnancy can be a teratogen.

10. **Critical period** refers to any time period during which some developmental process must occur; if it doesn't occur then, it never will. (p. 303)

    Example: If the heart, eyes, ears, hands, and feet do not appear during the embryonic period, they will not be formed at all.

11. **Fetal alcohol syndrome** occurs in infants born to mothers who consumed heavy—or sometimes even moderate—amounts of alcohol during pregnancy. The resulting defects include physical malformations of the face and mental retardation. (p. 304)

    Example: Margaret drank frequently during her pregnancy. After giving birth, her baby had facial malformations and showed signs of being mentally slow. Her baby has FAS.

12. **Reflexes** control the majority of movement in the first weeks and months of life. They are quick, unlearned responses to external stimuli. (pp. 305-306)

    Example: The rooting reflex causes an infant to turn its mouth toward any object that touches its cheek. The sucking reflex causes the newborn to suck on any object that touches its lips.

III. INFANCY AND CHILDHOOD: COGNITIVE DEVELOPMENT

13. A **schema** is a basic unit of knowledge that takes the form of a pattern of action, an image of an object, or a complex idea. (p. 308)

Example: Sucking on a pacifier is a schema consisting of a pattern of action.

14. **Assimilation** is the process of taking in information that adds to an existing schema. (p. 308)

Example: An infant who has learned to suck milk from a bottle will use the same sucking motion or schema when a pacifier is put in its mouth for the first time.

15. **Accommodation** is the process of taking in information that causes a person to modify an existing schema. (p. 308)

Example: Infants who have become very good at sucking milk from a bottle and are given a cup must learn new patterns of motor behavior (modify the old sucking schema) to get the liquid out of the cup and into their mouth. Watch small children just learning how to drink from a cup. They suck and slurp the liquid instead of pouring it into their mouth and swallowing.

16. The **sensorimotor period** is Piaget's first stage of cognitive development. The infant's mental activity is confined to sensory and motor functions such as looking and reaching. (pp. 308–310)

REMEMBER: Sensori means "sensory": vision, hearing, tasting, and so on. Motor means "movement": reaching, grasping, and pulling.

Example: During the sensorimotor period, when infant Jesse explores his world, he does so through sensory inputs (things he can see, hear, touch, etc.) and motor responses (manipulating objects, moving his hands, etc.).

17. **Object permanence** is acquired during the sensorimotor period. Because children form mental representations of objects and actions, they do not have to rely on sensory information to know that an object exists even when they cannot see or touch it. (p. 309)

Example: A child knows that a rattle exists when you put it behind your back, out of sight.

18. The **preoperational period** is Piaget's second stage of cognitive development, lasting from age two to age seven. Children learn to use symbols allowing them to talk, pretend, and draw. Thinking during this time is intuitive. (pp. 311–312)

Example: Elise likes to put on her big sister's dresses and makeup and pretend that she is going out shopping.

19. **Conservation** is the knowledge that a substance's number or amount does not change even when its shape or form does. This skill is first accomplished during the concrete operational stage. (p. 312)

Example: Ellen, who is babysitting for a nine-year-old and a four-year-old, pours each child a glass of lemonade. She gives the older child a tall skinny glass and the younger child a short fat glass. The four-year-old insists that the short fat glass does not contain as much lemonade as the tall skinny glass (that is, she does not understand the logic of complementarity), even after Ellen has poured the contents of the tall skinny glass into the short glass and back again (reversibility). The younger child, still in the preoperational period, cannot conserve.

20. **Concrete operations** is Piaget's third stage of cognitive development, occurring approximately between the ages of seven and eleven. During this stage, children can perform such operations as addition, subtraction, and conservation (reversibility, complementarity), and visual appearances no longer dominate thinking. (p. 313)

Example: A child in the concrete operational period is capable of thinking logically, and consequently is able to understand that lemonade poured from a tall, skinny glass into a short, fat glass is the same amount of liquid.

21. **Information processing** is a cognitive approach to studying cognitive development, concerning such matters as how information is taken in, how it is remembered or forgotten, and how it is used. This approach differs from Piaget's in that it focuses on the quantitative changes that take place in the child's mental abilities, not on the qualitative changes that occur at different stages. (p. 314)

Example: As Jane grows older, her school teachers are able to get her to focus on topics for longer and longer periods of time because her attention span has increased with age.

IV. INFANCY AND CHILDHOOD: SOCIAL AND EMOTIONAL DEVELOPMENT

22. **Temperament** is the style of emotional reactivity that an infant displays in response to the environment. It is the basic, natural disposition of an individual. (p. 319)

Example: When Sarah takes a bath, she squeals with delight, splashes in the water, and eagerly reaches for new toys. She has a very predictable schedule of eating and sleeping. Sarah is an easy baby. Franny, on the other hand, fusses all the time, cries very loudly whenever she encounters a new situation, person, or toy, and does not have a set schedule. Franny is a difficult baby.

23. **Attachment** is the close emotional relationship between an infant and his or her caregiver. For a <u>secure attachment</u> to develop, the caregiver must not only provide adequate, consistent care, but must also be loving, supportive, helpful, sensitive, and responsive. If the care is inadequate or the relationship is distant, the child may develop an <u>insecure attachment</u>. (pp. 320–322)

Example: Johnny has an anxious insecure attachment; he is upset when his mother leaves but ignores or avoids her when she returns after a brief separation. Carl's attachment is secure; he may or may not protest when his mother leaves, but he greets her enthusiastically when she returns.

24. **Socialization** is a process of teaching children society's rules and the skills they need. Examples of socialization patterns are authoritarian, permissive, and authoritative parenting. (p. 324)

Example: Jessica's parents rarely provide her direction. She gets to choose what she wants to do, when she wants to do it, and how. She never gets into trouble with them, even when she has misbehaved. Jessica's parents are using a permissive socialization style.

25. **Authoritarian parents** are firm, punitive, and unsympathetic. They demand children's obedience and value being authority figures. They do not encourage independence and seldom offer praise. (p. 325)

Example: Armand told his father he wanted to study hair design at the local beauty college. Rather than discuss the advantages and disadvantages of the choice with Armand, his father forbade him to apply to that college and ordered him to work over the summer mowing lawns.

26. **Permissive parents** give their children complete freedom, and their use of discipline is lax. (p. 325)

Example: Penny's parents often do not know where she is at night. She could stay overnight at a friend's house without needing to ask permission.

27. **Authoritative parents** reason with their children, are firm but understanding, and encourage give-and-take. As the children get older, the parents allow them increasing

responsibility. These parents set limits, but they also encourage independence. (p. 325)

Example: Kiersten's mother is affectionate and encourages her to come to her to talk about anything. They have an agreement about what behaviors are acceptable, and recently they compromised on a later curfew.

28. **Gender roles** are the general patterns of work, appearance, and behavior associated with being male or female. (pp. 327–329)

Example: In our society some occupations have traditionally been considered more appropriate for men, others more appropriate for women. Men have been encouraged to become doctors and women to become nurses; men have been encouraged to become police officers, and women have not.

V. ADOLESCENCE

29. **Puberty** is the condition of being able for the first time to reproduce. Its onset is characterized by menstruation in females and sperm production in males. (p. 329)

30. An **identity crisis** usually occurs during adolescence. By combining bits and pieces of self-knowledge learned in childhood, the individual must develop an integrated image of himself or herself as a unique person. (pp. 331–332)

Example: When Ray began college, he was rebellious and irresponsible at first. Eventually he settled down, chose a major, and became more conscientious again.

31. The **formal operational period** is Piaget's fourth stage of cognitive development; on average, it begins at age eleven. During this stage, children can think and reason about abstract concepts, generate hypotheses, and think logically. (p. 332)

Example: Children can think about abstract moral issues such as whether animals should be killed for fur or what the consequences of nuclear war might be.

32. **Preconventional moral reasoning**, according to Kohlberg's theory, is typical of children younger than nine years of age. Moral reasoning during this period is directed toward avoiding punishment and following rules to one's own advantage. (p. 333)

Example: Morgan doesn't take cookies from the jar when she isn't supposed to because she doesn't want to get grounded.

33. **Conventional moral reasoning**, according to Kohlberg's theory, is characterized by concern for other people due to social obligations such as caring for one's spouse and family. (p. 333)

> *Example:* Tristan doesn't take cookies from the jar when he isn't supposed to because it would disappoint his parents if he disobeyed them.

34. **Postconventional moral reasoning**, according to Kohlberg, is the highest level of moral reasoning; it is based upon personal standards or on universal principles of justice, equality, and respect for human life. (p. 333)

> *Example:* Underground resistance fighters during World War II disobeyed local and German laws in order to preserve the lives of fellow countrymen.

VI. ADULTHOOD

35. A crisis of **generativity** usually occurs during a person's thirties. People become concerned with producing something that they consider worthwhile. To resolve this crisis, people usually have children or decide to achieve an occupational goal. (p. 338)

> *Example:* David is undergoing a change in perspective. He has found a partner in life, and now he is concerned with having children.

36. A **midlife transition** often occurs during a person's forties, at which time the individual reevaluates the decisions he or she has made concerning goals and social relationships. (p. 338)

> *Example:* Lynne recently divorced and moved to a new state to become an occupational therapist.

37. **Terminal drop** is the decline in mental functioning that occurs in the months or years preceding death. (p. 339)

> *Example:* Ginny's grandfather has suddenly seemed to be less socially and intellectually sharp. He interrupts others and repeats himself without seeming aware of what he is doing. Six months later, Ginny's grandfather dies. Ginny's grandfather experienced a terminal drop in functioning prior to his death.

CONCEPTS AND EXERCISES

No. 1: Nature or Nurture

Completing this exercise should help you to achieve Learning Objectives 2 and 3.

Today, developmental psychologists think that nature (genetic factors) and nurture (environmental factors) interact to produce an individual's characteristics. Below is a list of situations. After each description, decide whether nature or nurture had more influence on the final characteristics.

1. Even though Pauline and Beth have spent just about the same amount of time lying in the sun, Pauline's tan is very dark and Beth's is a light brown. Pauline's ability to tan so darkly is probably a result of _____.

2. Piano majors Jane and Isabelle are very dedicated to practicing, and both work at it eight hours a day. Isabelle is very frustrated because her playing is not as musical as Jane's, despite her long hours at the piano. Jane's ability to play so musically is probably a result of _____.

3. Tom and Jim are identical twins. Their parents died in a car accident when they were nine weeks old. They had no other relatives, and separate adoptions were arranged. Tom's adoptive parents are language professors at the local university, and Jim's are advertising executives. At age twelve, Tom can speak three languages other than English; Jim is getting a D in English. The difference in their language abilities is probably due to _____.

4. Tony was slight of build in high school. When he entered college, he started working out. The first time he returned home for the summer, his mother was surprised to see his well-developed muscles. Tony's new physique is probably due to _____.

No. 2: The Toy Industry

Completing this exercise should help you to achieve Learning Objectives 7, 8, 10, 11, 12, and 22.

Bill has just landed a job with a large toy company. His first assignment is to develop a new line of toys designed for children in each of Piaget's stages of cognitive development. Match each of Bill's ideas (listed below) to the appropriate stage of cognitive development.

1. *A simple board game.* The winner is the first player to move a token completely around the board. The board itself is made of squares with pictures of animals, foods, family members (grandma, uncle, sister), and toys. Some of the squares have instructions to move ahead or fall back to the nearest square containing a picture of a certain animal, food, relative, or toy. For example, one square might instruct the player to move ahead to

the nearest picture of a horn; and another, to move back to the nearest picture of a cow. To start, players roll a die and move the appropriate number of squares. A player's turn ends if he or she lands on a square with a picture. If the player lands on a square with instructions, he or she must follow them. The game is designed so that the players practice counting and recognizing different classes of objects. _____

2. *A set of edible paints.* The paints come with a set of canvases that will not absorb paint. However, paint will adhere to the surface enough to remain in place. Each canvas contains an outline of a picture. The idea is for the child to paint a picture, then peel it off the board and eat it. _____

3. *A clown-face mobile painted in vibrant primary colors.* Each battery-operated clown face will, when pulled, emit a different melody or laugh, and the eyes in each face will light up. _____

4. *A board game called Planet Wars.* Each player receives a game piece in the shape of a planet. Some planets are more desirable than others, and a roll of the dice decides who gets which. Each planet comes with an army, several nearby star systems equipped with arsenals, an assortment of special weapons, and spy devices. The winner is the player who conquers the most planets. The players must generate hypotheses to help them form strategies for attack and must be able to logically anticipate the consequences of their own moves as well as those of their opponents. _____

CRITICAL THINKING

Sam and Martina are working on a kidnapping case. Curiously, the biological mother has no pictures of the child to give to the two detectives. She has described her child, however, as five years old, male, blond, blue-eyed, smiley, and very healthy. The child has been missing for over a week now. Sam and Martina feel sorry for the child; being kidnapped is a horrible ordeal. But since the mother is an alcoholic, they know that even if they find the boy, he won't come home to a very healthy situation.

Sam and Martina get a break. They receive a report from a homemaker, Ted, in a neighboring town. Ted says that a new child, Richie—five years old with blond hair and blue eyes—has suddenly appeared on the block and is living with a long-time neighbor of Ted's, whom he dislikes. The child doesn't seem to know his own name. Ted also mentions that he looks a little "funny" and appears to be mentally retarded. Ted knows that the neighbor is unable to have children and has wanted a child for quite some time. Also, as far as he knows, she doesn't have any relatives. In addition, she became

extremely flustered when Ted asked her about Richie's origins. So where had the little boy come from?

Sam decides that Richie is not the child they are looking for. Richie fits the physical description given by the mother whose child had been kidnapped, but she specifically said the boy was healthy. She also didn't mention anything odd about his looks. However, Martina is sure they have found the child.

Using the five critical thinking questions in your text, state Sam's original hypothesis and his evidence. Based on the clues in the story, what do you think Martina's alternative hypothesis is? What evidence does she have?

1. What is Sam's hypothesis upon hearing about the "new kid on the block"?

2. What evidence supports Sam's hypothesis?

3. What is Martina's alternative hypothesis?

4. What evidence supports Martina's alternative hypothesis?

5. What conclusions can Sam and Martina draw?

PERSONAL LEARNING ACTIVITIES

1. At which of Piaget's stages of cognitive development are you? What supports the classification you have given yourself? (Learning Objectives 7, 10, 11, and 22)

2. Describe the rules in your family when you were growing up and what happened when you broke a rule. Write whether you think your parent(s)/guardian(s) had an authoritarian, permissive, or authoritative parenting style and why. Mention which part of the descriptions in the text fit and which parts don't. (Learning Objective 18)

3. Watch an hour or so of children-oriented television, such as cartoons, and pay particular attention to the commercials. Take notes on what product is being sold, who is included (boys, girls, or both?), and their roles. For example, are both boys and girls shown flying toy fighter planes, or are the boys playing with planes and the girls looking on? Are the girls in the commercials giggling and brushing their doll's hair? Are boys giggling? Describe the implication of the commercial for gender roles. For example, the implication of both boys and girls washing dishes at a toy sink might be that both boys and girls help with cleaning. (Learning Objective 19)

4. Think back to a recent moral decision when you considered the reasons for and against doing something. List the reasons you gave at the time for

the choice you made. What sorts of reasons did you give? Were they related to how other people would react, to what was legal, or to whether you might get punished, for example? At what stage of moral reasoning would Kohlberg place you based on this decision? Can you think of other decisions that would place you at a different level? (Learning Objective 23)

5. Consider how you have aged over the last four years. How have your thoughts, feelings, and actions changed? Imagine yourself after another four years and describe your expectations about your lifestyle, relationships, ideas, emotional reactions, and behaviors. Does your description fit well with the text's description of the average person of that age? (Learning Objective 24 and 25)

WHAT SHOULD I WRITE ABOUT?

The study of human development offers numerous potential topics for term paper writers—the whole lifespan is fair game. If you like children, then you could write about child development. If you are more interested in adolescence or young adulthood (the typical college age student), then write about identity development. If you are an individual who is part of the "sandwich generation" who is caring for children of your own as well as aging parents, then you might write about the aging process. Everyone can find some topic to relate to in *Human Development*. Once you have identified that topic, try relating it to another topic in a different chapter of the text, similarly to how the *Linkages* section does.

Integrating two seemingly separate areas makes for an interesting paper. If you found prenatal development interesting, you might tie prenatal development and critical periods to what you learned about the nervous system structure and function in Chapter 2. What brain structures are affected by teratogens during the critical periods of prenatal development? How are they affected?

The topic possibilities become endless if you decide to integrate topics from two different chapters. You are limited only by your own creativity. If you found moral development intriguing in this chapter, then you might consider moving ahead and seeing how moral development might relate to cooperation within groups, a topic discussed in Chapter 14 on *Social Psychology*. Gender roles would also be related to *Social Psychology*, as most psychologists feel that gender has a strong social component.

Linking to topics outside of introductory psychology is viable as well. If you choose to write about Piaget's stages of development, you could integrate that topic with literature from Educational Psychology to describe why school curricula is organized as it is. Why should we focus on reading skills prior to math? Answers to this

question, and others, make for a good start to writing your term paper.

Some things to consider as you develop your term paper further include:

1. Think first about what interested you the most in this chapter. Finding a topic you care about will make the writing of the paper more like a pleasant learning experience than a chore.

2. Next, think about how that topic relates to others that you found interesting in the text, or even in other classes. You may even want to skim ahead to places you haven't read yet, just to make sure you aren't missing out on an interesting potential linkage of your own.

THE INTERNET

The Psychabilities web site that accompanies this text offers many resources relevant to this chapter. They include NetLab exercises, Thinking Critically and Evaluating Research exercises, ACE chapter quizzes, recommended web links, and articles on current events, books, and movies. Go to http://college.hmco.com, select Psychology, and then this textbook.

MULTIPLE-CHOICE QUESTIONS

SAMPLE QUIZ 1

1. A behaviorist believes that development is a result of
   a. maturational processes.
   b. natural growth guided by genetic factors.
   c. sexual impulses.
   d. the influence of external conditions.

2. Colleen is five years old. She is mentally retarded and her face is malformed. Her mother most likely
   a. took thalidomide during pregnancy.
   b. is a heroin addict.
   c. consumed alcohol during pregnancy.
   d. experienced severe stress during pregnancy.

3. The development of the cardiovascular and nervous systems and the organs begins during which stage of prenatal development?
   a. Germinal
   b. Embryonic
   c. Fertile
   d. Fetal

4. Object permanence is acquired during Piaget's _____ period of cognitive development.
   a. formal operations
   b. concrete operations

c. preoperational
d. sensorimotor

5. Gary's parents are constantly amazed at how their son has changed over the past year. Suddenly, he loves to study science, is a feminist, and wants to participate in an antinuclear power demonstration. Gary has moved into the _____ stage of cognitive development.
   a. sensorimotor
   b. preoperational
   c. concrete operations
   d. formal operations

6. The thinking of children who cannot yet conserve is dominated by
   a. auditory cues (hearing).
   b. visual cues.
   c. behavioral cues.
   d. verbal cues.

7. In assimilation,
   a. information is added to existing schemas.
   b. old schemas are modified.
   c. schemas don't change.
   d. none of the above hold true.

8. An authoritative parent is
   a. firm, punitive, and unsympathetic.
   b. very lax about discipline and gives the child complete freedom.
   c. firm but reasonable and explains why a child's behavior is incorrect.
   d. one who demands obedience to authority.

9. It is interesting to watch nine-month-old P.J. react to a new object. He holds onto his mother very tightly for several long moments and then, using the furniture to steady himself, walks toward the object and warily checks it out. P.J. has a temperament that is typical of
   a. easy babies.
   b. difficult babies.
   c. slow-to-warm-up babies.
   d. exploratory babies.

10. When two-year-old Michael's mother leaves the room for a minute, he cries and cannot be calmed. When she returns, however, he won't let his mother hold him; he fusses and squirms away. Michael's attachment to his mother is *most likely*
    a. insecure.
    b. secure.
    c. dependent.
    d. depressed.

11. Gloria, who is thirty years old, wants to have children, but feels she is just getting her career on track. Gloria is feeling a(n) _____ crisis, according to Erikson.
    a. intimacy
    b. integrity
    c. generativity
    d. autonomy

12. Tenita is an infant who is learning that she will be fed, clothed, and kept warm and dry. Tenita is most likely in Erikson's _____ stage of psychosocial development.
    a. intimacy versus isolation
    b. integrity versus despair
    c. generativity versus stagnation
    d. trust versus mistrust

13. During Kohlberg's second level of moral reasoning, children
    a. consider what they will gain by the moral decision.
    b. choose an action that will bring approval.
    c. make decisions from a human rights perspective.
    d. make decisions based on their personal standards.

14. Steve has grown five inches in the past year and gained twenty pounds. One moment he is depressed over the sudden appearance of acne on his face; a moment later he is elated as he runs out the door to play a game of football with his buddies. How old is he?
    a. Eight to ten years old
    b. Ten to twelve years old
    c. Twelve to fifteen years old
    d. Eighteen to twenty years old

15. Which of the following is characteristic of the thinking of an adult over the age of sixty-five?
    a. Information is registered at a slower pace.
    b. Mathematical ability increases.
    c. Reasoning capabilities increase due to years of practice.
    d. Verbal comprehension increases as a result of a larger vocabulary.

Total Correct (See answer key) _____

SAMPLE QUIZ 2

Use this quiz to reassess your learning after taking Quiz 1 and reviewing the chapter.

1. A developmental psychologist who takes the _____ approach would instruct a one-year-old's parents to let the child walk on its own and not try to rush the process.
   a. maturational
   b. behaviorist

   c. psychodynamic
   d. naturalistic

2. Karen, who is pregnant, drinks heavily and smokes almost two packs of cigarettes a day. Her doctor has told her that she must abstain from these activities at least during the _____ stage of her baby's prenatal development.
   a. germane
   b. embryonic
   c. fetal
   d. gestation

3. At Jackson's first birthday party, his parents, Susan and Lisa, showed all of their friends his grasping reflex. Susan and Lisa should
   a. be concerned that Jackson's brain is not developing normally.
   b. be concerned that Jackson's motor movements are not fluid.
   c. not be concerned because the grasping reflex lasts for the first 2 years.
   d. not be concerned because the grasping reflex is very useful.

4. Penny is going to decorate her newborn's room and wants the baby to enjoy looking all around it. Which of the following will meet her decorating needs?
   a. Wallpaper covered with very small blue flowers
   b. A mobile with very small butterflies for the far end of the room
   c. Curtains with large smiling clown faces for the window right next to the baby's bed
   d. A wall hanging of gray and white checked fabric

5. Ten-month-old Whitney grabs her aunt's car keys. Her aunt retrieves the keys and puts them in her pocket. Whitney then tries to get the keys out of her aunt's pocket. Whitney's behavior suggests that she has developed
   a. homeostasis.
   b. conservation.
   c. object permanence.
   d. visual adaptation.

6. Jeffrey learned to pick up bits of cereal and push his fingers and the cereal into his mouth. Jeffrey discovered, however, that this method did not work for yogurt and eventually learned that yogurt is eaten with a spoon. Jeffrey's modified behavior shows
   a. accommodation.
   b. assimilation.
   c. conservation.
   d. object permanence.

7. Claude enjoys pretending that he is baking cookies when he plays in sand. Claude made a ball of sand, flattened it, and exclaimed, "Wow, look how much bigger I made it!" According to Piaget, Claude is in the _____ stage of cognitive development.
   a. concrete operations
   b. formal operations
   c. preoperational
   d. sensorimotor

8. Recent studies indicate that many people have never developed beyond the stage of concrete operational thought. Which of the following statements lends support to this hypothesis?
   a. Many college students feel unprepared to select a career.
   b. Many day-to-day tasks require only concrete operational skill levels.
   c. Many adults are unable to solve problems requiring abstract reasoning skills.
   d. There is a wide variation in when people can solve conservation problems.

9. Research has found three main temperament patterns among infants. These patterns are called
   a. colicky, pleasant, and withdrawn.
   b. easy, difficult, and slow-to-warm-up.
   c. obnoxious, congenial, and good-fit.
   d. easy, medium, and hard.

10. Harry Harlow's study with monkeys indicated clearly that the monkeys spent time with the cloth monkey when they were motivated by the need for
   a. food and water.
   b. sex.
   c. affiliation.
   d. attachment.

11. When Aretha returns home after being at work all day, her nine-month-old son is excited to see her and smiles as he crawls toward her. Aretha's son *most likely* has a(n) _____ attachment.
   a. secure
   b. nonavoidant
   c. insecure
   d. bonding

12. Woody's parents gave him a strict curfew, never allowed him to visit with friends until homework was finished, and did not discuss their reasons for the rules. When Woody wrote his first play, they punished him for wasting his time when he should have been studying. Woody's parents have which parenting style, according to Baumrind?
   a. authoritarian
   b. authoritative
   c. insecure
   d. permissive

13. Since he graduated from college and began work in advertising, Jens has begun to feel lonely and abandoned. Most of his friends live out-of-state and those who live nearby are married, so even when he sees them he feels left out. Erikson would say that Jens is struggling with the crisis of
    a. identity versus role confusion.
    b. industry versus inferiority.
    c. integrity versus despair.
    d. intimacy versus isolation.

14. Ten-year-old Stanley saw his favorite candy bar at the checkout counter but did not have enough money to buy it. He contemplated putting the candy bar in his pocket but decided not to because he worried that stealing the candy bar would put him in jail. According to Kohlberg's stages of moral development, Stanley is *most likely* in the _____ stage.

    a. first
    b. second
    c. third
    d. sixth

15. Beretta is experiencing terminal drop. It is *most likely* that Beretta
    a. has just been born.
    b. is dying.
    c. is in early infancy.
    d. is in a midlife crisis.

Total Correct (See answer key) _____

ANSWERS TO CONCEPTS AND EXERCISES

No. 1: Nature or Nurture

1. *Nature*. Pauline tans more easily than Beth, despite their spending the same amount of time in the sun, because Pauline's inheritance predisposes her pigmentation to be more reactive to the sun. (pp. 300–302)

2. *Nature*. Jane plays well because she has a genetic inheritance that predisposes her to be musical. (pp. 300–302)

3. *Nurture*. Jim may not have been exposed to other languages in school or at home, but his poor performance in English indicates that he does not have a natural talent for languages. Tom's parents have provided a multilingual environment for him, and this factor, rather than a genetic predisposition,

is the likely reason why he can speak three languages. (pp. 300–302)

4. *Nurture*. Tony's genetic inheritance guided his physical development throughout high school. However, working out in the gym (an environmental factor, or nurture) was responsible for the changes in his muscles. (pp. 300–302)

No. 2: The Toy Industry

1. *Concrete operations*. During this stage of cognitive development, children learn how to do simple operations such as addition, subtraction, and conservation and to group objects into classes. (For example, cows, dogs, and rabbits are grouped as animals.) The board game encourages the child to practice counting and grouping objects into classes. (p. 313)

2. *Preoperational*. The ability to use symbols introduces the child to many new activities during this stage. Drawing involves creating a symbol of something in the real world. (pp. 311–312)

3. *Sensorimotor*. During this stage, an infant loves to look at large objects that move and that feature lots of contrast and complexity—especially smiling faces. The mobile is perfect for this age: it moves, it consists of faces, and its colors, lights, and sounds provide contrast. (pp. 308–310)

4. *Formal operations*. During this stage, adolescents learn to generate hypotheses and think logically about the outcome of events. To develop a strategy for the Planet Wars game, each player must create a plan (hypothesis) and think logically about the consequences of the plan's moves. (p. 332)

ANSWERS TO CRITICAL THINKING

1. Sam doesn't think they have solved the crime. His hypothesis is that Richie can't be the child they are looking for.

2. The evidence in support of Sam's hypothesis: Ted specifically said that Richie looked "funny" and appeared to be retarded, but the biological mother had described the child as very healthy.

3. Martina's alternative hypothesis: Richie is the little boy they are looking for.

4. The evidence in support of Martina's alternative hypothesis: The biological mother is an alcoholic and her son may have fetal alcohol syndrome. That would explain Ted's description of odd-looking facial features and mental retardation. She thinks it's possible that, due to guilt, the biological mother

didn't tell them about the fetal alcohol syndrome. Martina will want to collect additional evidence. She will want to know whether the mother was an alcoholic during her son's pregnancy and whether there are any medical records that discuss his health.

5. Martina thinks it may be reasonable at this point to conclude that they have the right child. (NOTE: Critical thinking is a constant process of hypothesizing, examining evidence, rehypothesizing, collecting more evidence, and so on. Martina may not be correct. Can you think of any other hypotheses that could explain these data?)

ANSWERS TO MULTIPLE-CHOICE QUESTIONS

Circle the question numbers you answered correctly.

Sample Quiz 1

1. *d* is the answer. A behaviorist believes that external conditions are responsible for the developmental process. For example, transferring to a better educational setting will alter the development of cognitive ability. (p. 300)
   a, b. A maturationalist believes that abilities unfold with age in a fixed sequence and are determined by nature—in short, that genetics controls development.
   c. A psychodynamic theorist believes that a child's natural sexual impulses and the parental reaction to those impulses guide development.

2. *c* is the answer. Mental retardation and facial malformations are symptoms of the fetal alcohol syndrome, which occurs in infants born to mothers who drink too much alcohol while pregnant. (p. 304)
   a, b, d. Drug use of any kind (whether recreational or medicinal) and stress levels can affect prenatal development. However, the combination of symptoms listed can be linked to one specific abuse: drinking alcohol.

3. *b* is the answer. Cardiovascular and nervous systems develop during the embryonic stage. A critical period exists: if certain systems and organs do not develop properly at this time, they never will. (p. 303)
   a. The germinal stage begins with fertilization and lasts for two weeks. The zygote divides rapidly, travels down the Fallopian tubes, and attaches to the uterine wall.
   c, d. There is no such thing as the fertile stage in prenatal development. You may be thinking of

the fetal stage. During this stage, systems integrate and the organs grow and begin to function more efficiently.

4. *d* is the answer. Object permanence is the ability to know that an object exists even when it is out of sight. Children acquire this ability during the sensorimotor period, the first stage of cognitive development. (p. 309)
   a. An adolescent acquires the ability to think hypothetically and to imagine logical consequences of events in the formal operational period.
   b. A child learns to perform simple operations—subtraction, addition, classification, seriation, and conservation—during the concrete operational period.
   c. A child acquires the ability to use symbols during the preoperational period.

5. *d* is the answer. Studying science involves thinking logically and being able to generate hypotheses. Being involved with feminist movements and nuclear demonstrations requires the ability to question social institutions and to think about the world as it might be or as it ought to be. (p. 332)
   a, b. Children in the sensorimotor or preoperational periods do not have the ability to question social institutions. They may have some knowledge of feminism or nuclear power plants, but they cannot think about or accurately imagine the consequences of nuclear war or the treatment of women as inferior.
   c. During the concrete operations period, children can think logically about objects they directly experience.

6. *b* is the answer. The ability to conserve involves realizing that a substance does not change in amount or number when its form changes. Thinking dominated by visual appearances makes conservation impossible. A child incapable of conserving would say that a tall skinny glass contains more liquid than a short fat glass, even when both glasses contain the same amount of liquid. (p. 312)
   a, c, d. Auditory, behavior, and verbal thinking are not typical during the preoperational period (the time during which conservation is not a typical skill).

7. *a* is the answer. When we assimilate information, we add information to an existing schema without changing it. (p. 308)
   b. In accommodation, old schemas are modified with new information.
   c. In assimilation, schemas may be added to, but are not significantly changed.

d. *a* is the answer, so one of the above is true.

8. *c* is the answer. Authoritative parents are firm but reasonable and provide explanations when a child's behavior is incorrect. They encourage the child to take responsibility and to be independent. (p. 325)
   a. Authoritarian parents are firm, punitive, and unsympathetic.
   b. Permissive parents are very lax about discipline and give their children complete freedom.
   d. Authoritarian parents demand obedience to authority figures.

9. *c* is the answer. P.J. initially appears shy and wary, but slowly warms up to exploring the new object (p. 319)
   a. An easy baby has predictable cycles of eating and sleeping, reacts cheerfully to a new situation, and seldom fusses.
   b. A difficult baby is irritable and irregular.
   d. Although some infants are more exploratory than others, there is no category or classification termed "exploratory."

10. *a* is the answer. Michael is exhibiting insecure attachment, because he squirms to get away when his mother returns after a separation. (p. 322)
    b. Securely attached children are happy to see their caregiver return after a separation and respond well to the caregiver's efforts at contact.
    c, d. Dependent and depressed are not examples of Baumrind's attachment styles.

11. *c* is the answer. The tension between career and children is a conflict between two types of generativity. People experiencing the generativity versus stagnation crisis often think about leaving their mark on the world. (p. 338)
    a. Erikson suggested that after the identity crisis, young adults seek intimacy. Secure love relationships are the focus, not children or career aspirations.
    b. Integrity versus despair is a crisis of old age in which people reflect on their lives. They may feel that their lives have been meaningful or they may feel despair at unaccomplished goals.
    d. Autonomy versus shame and doubt occurs at about age two when children try to control themselves and make decisions.

12. *d* is the answer. Infants learn whether the world is a predictable place during the trust versus mistrust crisis. If their needs are met, they will most likely resolve the crisis successfully. (p. 324)
    a. Intimacy versus isolation occurs in early adulthood.
    b. Integrity versus despair occurs in late adulthood.
    c. Generativity versus stagnation occurs in middle adulthood.

13. *b* is the answer. The second level of moral reasoning, the conventional level, is basically characterized by concern for others. Decisions are based on the potential for gaining the approval of others. (p. 333)
    b. Children in the preconventional level make moral decisions based on personal gain or loss.
    c. Adults in the postconventional level consider human rights or other universal ethical principles when making their moral decisions.
    d. Adolescents in the postconventional level make moral decisions based on their own personal standards.

14. *c* is the answer. Adolescence begins around age twelve in girls and between twelve and fourteen in boys. It can last up until the teenage years are complete. (p. 329)
    a, b, d. None of the other age groups corresponds to the beginning or middle of the adolescent period.

15. *a* is the answer. Studies show that the speed with which one processes information slows around the age of 65. (p. 336)
    b, c, d. Studies have shown that verbal comprehension, mathematical ability, and reasoning begin to decline after age sixty-seven.

Now turn to the quiz analysis table at the end of this chapter to find which areas you know well and which areas you need to work on. Circle the numbers in the table for items on Quiz 1 that you answered correctly.

ANSWERS TO MULTIPLE-CHOICE QUESTIONS

Circle the question numbers you answered correctly.

Sample Quiz 2

1. *a* is the answer. Gesell argued that the order of motor skill stages and the age at which they generally occur is set; therefore, someone with the same maturational viewpoint would suggest that parents cannot do much to alter this process. (p. 300)
   b. A behaviorist might suggest that rewards would encourage early walking behavior.

c. Psychodynamic theorists are not particularly interested in motor skills, but would rather know about toilet training, weaning, and other parenting choices that might affect the child adversely.

d. Naturalistic is not one of the approaches discussed in your text.

2. *b* is the answer. There is a critical period in the embryonic stage during which systems and organs must develop or they never will. Drugs such as nicotine and alcohol negatively affect this process. (p. 303)

a, d. There is no such thing as the "germane" stage (you may have been thinking of the germinal stage) or the gestation stage.

c. Alcohol and nicotine in the mother's system do affect development during the fetal stage, but not as severely as during the embryonic stage.

3. *a* is the answer. According to your text, reflexes should disappear as the infant's brain develops. If certain reflexes still exist after about four months of age, it may be a cause for worry. (pp. 305-306)

b. Infants are a little uncoordinated when learning to sit up, roll over, etc., but this isn't a cause for worry.

c, d. The grasping reflex should disappear after 3 or 4 months. While infants may find this reflex useful to have as an infant, they would probably find it frustrating to have an involuntary grasp at a point when they want to explore (which means picking up and letting go voluntarily). Of course, the larger issue is that reflexes remaining abnormally long usually indicate a serious problem in development.

4. *c* is the answer. Infants can see large objects featuring lots of contrast, contour, complexity, and movement. They enjoy looking at faces. The clown faces are large and smiling and may move with the breeze. (p. 305)

a. This wallpaper design may appeal to Penny, but her infant will not have the visual capability to see the small pattern.

b. A mobile is a good idea because the parts move, but the infant will be unable to see it in the far corner.

d. A wall hanging of brightly colored checks may provide enough contrast for the infant to see it. However, grey and white are not as contrasting as, say, blue and red.

5. *c* is the answer. Object permanence is the ability to know an object (or person!) exists when it is out of sight. Once object permanence develops, the child moves into the preoperational period of development, according to Piaget. (p. 309)

a. Homeostasis is achieved by regulating a function, such as body temperature. When we are too warm, our body achieves homeostasis by causing us to sweat.

b. Conservation is achieved, according to Piaget, when a child knows that the size or weight of an object remains the same even if the appearance changes.

d. Visual adaptation is not a term from your text.

6. *a* is the answer. In accommodation, new information changes a schema. (p. 308)

b. Assimilation is when new information is added to an unchanged schema.

c. Conservation is the ability to realize that the size, quantity, or mass of an object is the same although it looks different.

d. Children with object permanence know that an object exists even when it is hidden from view.

7. *c* is the answer. Children who cannot conserve amounts are not yet in the concrete operations stage. (p. 312)

a. Concrete operations requires the ability to conserve.

b. Formal operations requires the ability to think about abstract concepts.

d. Infants in the sensorimotor period explore the world through their senses. They do not have object permanence until the end of the sensorimotor period and cannot conserve amounts. Because Claude is pretending, however, we know that he has moved beyond the sensorimotor stage.

8. *c* is the answer. Concrete operational thought is characterized by the ability to use simple logic and mental manipulations, such as adding and subtracting. Only a person at the formal operations stage, according to Piaget, would be able to use logic concerning abstract ideas. (pp. 313, 332)

a. Feeling unprepared to choose a career is not directly related to being at Piaget's concrete operations stage.

b. The fact that many day-to-day tasks require only concrete operational skills doesn't necessarily mean that people don't have those skills.

d. People in the preoperations stage have difficulty solving conservation problems. Finding that there is variety in the age of achieving conservation doesn't show that adults haven't achieved beyond concrete operations.

9. *b* is the answer. Easy, difficult, and slow-to-warm-up are the terms used to describe temperament patterns in infants. (p. 319)

a, c, d. While these may have similar connotations, they are not the agreed-upon terms that psychologists use to communicate information about infant temperament.

10. *d* is the answer. Harlow's research showed that comfort and attachment were the reasons monkeys sought out the cloth mother. (pp. 320-321)
   a. Food was the reason to go to the wire mother.
   b, c. Sex and affiliation were not the subject of Harlow's work.

11. *a* is the answer. Secure attachment is characterized by the infant's happiness at the caregiver's return and positive response to the caregiver's efforts at contact. (p. 322)
   b. Nonavoidant is not an attachment style.
   c. Insecure infants avoid or ignore the caregiver upon her or his return and squirm to get away if she or he tries to make contact.
   d. Bonding is another word for attachment, not a type of attachment.

12. *a* is the answer. Authoritarian parents are strict and unyielding disciplinarians. (p. 325)
   b. Authoritative parents discuss rules and are more affectionate.
   c. Baumrind did not use the term insecure to describe parents.
   d. Permissive parents are less informed about their children's activities. They set few rules and rarely use discipline.

13. *d* is the answer. Jens is beginning to feel isolated, because he has not successfully resolved the crisis of intimacy versus isolation. (p. 337)

   a. Identity versus role confusion is a crisis Jens resolved when he went into advertising.
   b. Industry versus inferiority is a crisis experienced by children ages 6 through adolescence. They either feel curiosity or lose interest in schoolwork and other activities.
   c. Integrity versus despair is a crisis during which older people look back on their lives and decide if they accomplished what they wanted to.

14. *a* is the answer. In stage one of Kohlberg's theory obeying rules and avoiding punishment are the priorities. Since Stanley is thinking about jail as an outcome, he is in stage one. (p. 333)
   b. In stage two making a fair deal is the focus.
   c. The third stage brings an emphasis on meeting others' expectations.
   d. The sixth and highest stage of moral reasoning, according to Kohlberg, brings an emphasis on following universal principles, such as respect for life.

15. *b* is the answer. A few months or years before death, some people experience a sudden worsening of mental abilities. (p. 339)
   a, c, d. Terminal drop does not occur at birth or during infancy or midlife crises.

Now turn to the quiz analysis table at the end of this chapter to find which areas you know well and which areas you need to work on. Circle the numbers in the table for items on Quiz 2 that you answered correctly.

For each question you answered correctly, circle its number. (Quiz 1 numbers are not shaded; Quiz 2 numbers are shaded.) Are there patterns in the types of questions or the topics you got wrong that could direct your further study? Did you improve from Quiz 1 to Quiz 2?

TOPIC	TYPE OF QUESTION		
	DEFINITION	COMPREHENSION	APPLICATION
Exploring development		1	
			1
Beginnings		3	2
		3	2, 4
Infancy and Childhood			
Cognitive development	7	4, 6	5
	8	7	5, 6
Social and emotional development	8		9, 10, 12
	9	10	11, 12, 13
Adolescence		13	14
			14
Adulthood		15	11
			15

TOTAL CORRECT BY QUIZ:

QUIZ 1:
QUIZ 2:

Chapter 10

Health, Stress, and Coping

LEARNING OBJECTIVES

1. Define health psychology. List the objectives of health psychologists. (pp. 348–349)

2. Define stress, stressors, and stress reactions. Give examples of stressors. Be sure to include a catastrophic event, a life change or strain, a chronic stressor, and a daily hassle. (pp. 350–352)

3. Describe the Social Readjustment Rating Scale and the Life Experience Survey. Explain how each is used to measure stress. (p. 352)

4. Define general adaptation syndrome. Describe the alarm, resistance, and exhaustion stages of the model, and discuss the physiological changes that occur in each stage. Define diseases of adaptation. Discuss the major criticisms of Selye's model. (pp. 352–354)

5. Describe common emotional, cognitive, and behavioral stress responses. Explain how ruminative thinking, catastrophizing, mental sets, and functional fixedness are linked to stress. (pp. 354–356)

6. Define burnout and posttraumatic stress disorder. Describe the symptoms of each and discuss the conditions that can lead to both. (p. 356)

7. Explain why the appraisal of stressors, their predictability, and a feeling of control can reduce the impact of stressors. (pp. 357–359)

8. Discuss the role of coping resources and methods in combating stress. Give examples of problem-focused and emotion-focused coping strategies. Describe the effects of social support networks on the impact of stressful events. (pp. 359–361)

9. Describe disease-prone and disease-resistant personalities. Define dispositional optimism. Describe gender differences in stress responses. Discuss the quasi-experimental research on the relationship between personality and health. (pp. 361–363)

10. Define psychoneuroimmunology. Describe the components of the immune system. Discuss the relationship between stress and immune system functioning. (pp. 364–365)

11. Define cynical hostility and outline the evidence relating hostility to heart disease. (pp. 365–367)

12. Discuss the research examining the health-endangering behaviors described in your textbook. (pp. 367–368)

13. Define health promotion. Describe the four factors in Rosenstock's health-belief model. Discuss the role of other factors, including self-efficacy and intention, in altering behavioral health risks. (pp. 368–369)

14. Describe the five stages in changing behavioral health risks. (p. 369)

15. List the steps in a stress-coping program. Explain the importance of being able to recognize the difference between changeable and unchangeable stressors. (p. 370)

16. Describe cognitive coping strategies. Define cognitive restructuring. (p. 370)

17. Describe some emotional and behavioral coping strategies. (p. 371)

18. Describe physical coping strategies. Explain the possible problems of using drugs to alter stress or stress responses. Explain how progressive relaxation training can help people cope. (p. 371)

KEY TERMS

I. HEALTH PSYCHOLOGY

1. **Health psychology** is a field within psychology that does research to understand the psychological and behavior processes associated with achieving and maintaining health, treating illness, and preventing it. (p. 348)

Example: A psychologist studying how stress is related to illness is studying an issue within the field of health psychology.

II. UNDERSTANDING STRESS

2. **Stress** is the emotional and physiological process of adjusting to circumstances that disrupt, or threaten to disrupt, a person's physical or psychological functioning. (p. 350)

   Example: Marcus is five years old. He has just started day care and has been exposed to many childhood diseases. He is under stress because his body must adjust to fighting off these diseases.

3. **Stressors** are events and situations to which people must adjust. Almost any event or situation that causes change is a stressor. Other common factors that are considered stressors include trauma, conflict, and daily hassles. (p. 350)

   Example: Sharon has just been offered a new job. After graduation, she will move from a small town to a large city, have new responsibilities, and want to make new friends. Although these events are positive, they will involve big changes and therefore will be stressors.

4. **Stress reactions** are the physical, psychological, and behavioral responses people display when stressors appear. (p. 350)

   Example: Linda gets a rash (physical response) every time she has to study for an important exam. Marsha gets nervous (emotional response) in the middle of every exam. If Marsha cannot answer the first few questions immediately, she begins talking to herself (cognitive response), saying, "I am going to flunk this exam, which will make my grade point average go down. I will never get into law school. I'll probably have to work at minimum wage for the rest of my life. I'll hate it and probably get fired for my bad attitude. Face it, I am going to be a bag lady." When Jean started her new job, she was under a great deal of pressure. Her voice shook and she frowned more (behavioral responses).

5. The **general adaptation syndrome (GAS)** is Hans Selye's name for a series of physical reactions to stress. There are three stages: the alarm reaction, the resistance stage, and the exhaustion stage. (pp. 352-353)

   Example: To satisfy his intellectual curiosity, Bill is taking a full load of classes, teaching undergraduates, writing a book, and doing research for a professor in his department. At the beginning of the semester, Bill can feel his heart race as he hurries to make an appointment here or there on campus (alarm). During midterm exams, he is in a constant state of arousal but does not notice it. He is used to being busy all day (resistance). By the end of the semester, he has a constant cold, feels tired, and has high blood pressure (exhaustion). Bill's doctor tells him that he needs to take time to relax over term break. His body must have time to recuperate from trying to adjust to such an extraordinary level of stress.

6. **Diseases of adaptation** are illnesses promoted or caused by stressors. These can include colds and flu, arthritis, coronary disease, and high blood pressure. (p. 354)

   Example: Jenna is a single mother who is holding down two jobs and trying to take classes toward a bachelor's degree. She is under a lot of stress as she tries to juggle the responsibilities of motherhood, work, and school. After a while of trying manage these responsibilities, Jenna develops an ulcer. The ulcer was caused in part by the large number of stressors Jenna has encountered.

   REMEMBER: Diseases of adaptation are due to the body's efforts to adapt to stress.

7. **Burnout** occurs in some people as a response to a continual series of stressors. Burnout is characterized by an intensifying pattern of physical, psychological, and behavioral problems that are severe enough to interfere with normal day-to-day functioning. (p. 356)

   Example: After years as an emergency room doctor, Coralette seems detached from her friends. She is increasingly irritable, depressed, and impulsive. Although Coralette has always been reliable, she now often oversleeps and misses the beginning of her shift.

8. **Posttraumatic stress disorder** is a stress response to a traumatic experience characterized by anxiety, irritability, jumpiness, inability to concentrate or work productively, sexual dysfunction, emotional numbness, and difficulty getting along with others. (p. 356)

   Example: After witnessing the murder of a close friend, Charles has recurring nightmares and trouble sleeping. Charles is uncharacteristically rude, nervous, and distracted at work.

9. A **social support network** is a group of friends or other social contacts that can be relied upon to help during stressful situations. (p. 360)

   Example: Betty and Tess are sisters and best friends. Whenever they have a problem, they know they can count on each other or other family members to lend an ear or help in any way they can.

III. THE PHYSIOLOGY AND PSYCHOLOGY OF HEALTH AND ILLNESS

10. **Psychoneuroimmunology** is a field that studies the interaction between psychological and physiological processes that affect the body's ability to defend itself against disease. (p. 364)

Example: Rashaun studies how certain continuous stressors, such as poor working conditions, are related to infections like the flu, the common cold, and pneumonia. Rashaun is studying a topic related to psychneuroimmunology.

11. The **immune system** defends the body against invading substances and microorganisms. It contains special cells that attack and kill invaders, such as viruses, bacteria, and cancer cells. (p. 364)

Example: The stressful semester left Miguel's immune system compromised. Miguel contracted mononucleosis and had to postpone his final exams until after the semester break.

IV. PROMOTING HEALTHY BEHAVIOR

12. **Health promotion** is the process of learning healthy behavior patterns and eliminating behaviors that increase the risk of illness. (p. 368)

Example: Mariah smokes, gets only four hours of sleep per night, never exercises, and lives on burgers, fries, and ice cream. After living like this for over ten years, Mariah starts to get pneumonia on a regular basis. She decides to enroll in a smoking cessation program at the YWCA, joins a gym, and learns to cook healthy meals. Mariah and the people who are helping her learn these new behaviors are in a health promotion process.

13. **Cognitive restructuring** is a cognitive coping strategy. Changing or restructuring thoughts can help reduce either the stress or the stress reaction. (p. 370)

Example: Latifeh is a perfectionist. Whenever she has to give a presentation at work, she worries about every detail and every word she is going to say. This causes her to feel extremely anxious most of the time. Cognitive restructuring would entail changing her thoughts. Instead of expecting perfection at every presentation, she might say, "I am going to do the best that I can, and my best is usually more than satisfactory."

REMEMBER: Cognition means "thought." Restructuring means "altering a form." Cognitive restructuring is altering the form of thoughts in order to remove a stressor or reduce a stress reaction.

14. **Progressive relaxation training**, a physical coping strategy, teaches an individual to relax voluntary muscles. This leads to heart rate and blood pressure reduction and creates mental and emotional calmness. (p. 371)

Example: Joe is feeling stressed about the exam he is taking. To calm down, he clenches his fists for a few seconds, and then releases them. He focuses on the feeling of relaxation that results. He does this again for several other muscle groups, always focusing on the resulting relaxation after releasing the tensed muscles. After going through this process, Joe feels much calmer and proceeds with the exam.

CONCEPTS AND EXERCISES

No. 1: Recognizing Stressors

Completing this exercise should help you to achieve Learning Objectives 2, 3, and 7.

Following are several descriptions of people's daily lives. Underline all the stressors that you can find.

1. Michelle and Ned have been married for ten years and have two children. This morning, Michelle got a run in her nylons just as she was on her way out the door to take the children to school. She was going to go up and change but remembered that she had to come back to the house anyway to pick up the dog for his veterinary appointment. When Michelle did get back home, she started cleaning the house, only to find that the vacuum cleaner was broken. Sighing, she decided to scrub the bathrooms instead. By the time Ned came home, she had a headache from the children screaming, the dog whimpering, having to face dirty floors yet again, and struggling with dinner for the family.

2. Lee is trying to finish writing a grant proposal in the hopes of getting funding. The deadline for submitting the grant is in one week. Lee must also face a new crisis of some sort daily at work. His wife is starting to complain that he never spends time with her. Recently, he has started to have dizzy spells and can feel his heart pounding.

3. Jenny is five years old. Today is the first day of first grade. Jenny is horrified because she has to sit next to the neighborhood bully. He is always ramming his tricycle into hers or grabbing her swing on the playground and pushing it too high into the air. Jenny is spending the entire day imagining what he will do now that he sits next to her in class.

4. Jerry has just met his new roommate and cannot believe his bad luck. His roommate has told him that he goes to bed at 8:00 P.M., wants to study in the room every night until 7:45 P.M., must have complete quiet while he studies, and has some great posters of Bambi to hang on the walls. Jerry wants to do well in school; he was first in his high school class and wants to keep his ranking in college, but he is also worried about his social life.

No. 2: Recognizing Stress Reactions

Completing this exercise should help you to achieve Learning Objectives 4, 5, 6, and 18.

Following are several descriptions of stress reactions. Choose the name of the reaction from the list after the descriptions.

1. Boris's doctor has told him that he has an elevated level of corticosteroids. _____

2. Rosa's mother tells her that she constantly makes a mountain out of a molehill. _____

3. Lois, recently divorced, has been working three jobs for the past year to support her children. She is tired, irritable, and depressed. Her bosses are concerned because the quality of her work has gradually decreased. _____

4. Nancy knows that her husband is drinking too much. His behavior bothers her so much that she has begun taking Valium daily. _____

   ° Burnout
   ° Physical coping strategy
   ° Behavioral coping strategy
   ° Catastrophizing
   ° Resistance stage of GAS

CRITICAL THINKING

Sam and Martina are at the gym working out. Pete, an ex-cop who retired from the force when he won the lottery, still works out with them. Pete was telling them stories about the people in his new, very expensive neighborhood.

Pete says, "So this lady down the street, her name is Jenny, dies last week. A buddy of mine checked the pathologist's report; she had a massive heart attack. It's too bad. She was really nice. She was a high-priced lawyer, and her husband stayed home to take care of the kids. Now he can afford to hire a new live-in nanny for each day of the week. I hear she was loaded and had a huge insurance policy. She had such a lousy life, though. Her husband, Jeff, treated her badly, even when he knew she had a heart condition."

Sam asks, "What do you mean, really badly?"

"Well," Pete responds, "the team that cleans my house, Martha and Ed, also cleaned hers. Martha used to tell me all these stories about what Jeff used to do."

"Like what?" asks Martina.

"The usual stuff. He was having affairs. She knew because she would find women's things in the house. But Martha said he also did little things to drive her nuts all the time. For example, he would steal the papers out of her briefcase when he knew she had a big court case the next day. Martha said she heard him call her office one day, and pretending to be drunk, he made up stories about how she mistreated the kids. He would ruin her favorite clothes or 'forget' to pick up her clothes from the dry cleaners. He actually called her up once and told her that one of the kids had died in an accident and then told her he was kidding. Martha said it had been going on for two years. The guy's a sicko."

Sam says, "Yeah, if she had to die, it's too bad he didn't kill her. We could have at least put him in jail."

Martina speaks up and says, "Maybe he did kill her."

Using the five critical thinking questions in your text, the clues in the story, and what you have just learned about stress, answer the following.
1. What is Sam's hypothesis?
2. What evidence supports Sam's hypothesis?
3. What is Martina's alternative hypothesis?
4. What evidence supports Martina's hypothesis?
5. What conclusions are most reasonable? What additional evidence is needed to reach a conclusion?

PERSONAL LEARNING ACTIVITIES

1. Write down a list of the stressors you have experienced in the last week. Which was the most stressful for you? Next to each item write a label for the type of stressor—catastrophic event, life change or strain, chronic stressor, or daily hassle. (Learning Objective 2)

2. Recall the last time you experienced the alarm reaction stage of the general adaptation syndrome. What was the cause? How did your body respond? How did you manage to calm yourself? (Learning Objective 4)

3. Think of a stressful situation in which you might be likely to catastrophize. List positive, constructive comments you could make to yourself instead. (Learning Objectives 5 and 16)

4. Read through the list of stressors you wrote for Personal Learning Activity 1. How did you cope with the most stressful item on the list? Would your coping method be categorized as problem-focused or emotion-focused? (Learning Objective 8)

5. Describe some of your behaviors that are risks to, or good for, your health. For example, do you smoke or exercise regularly? Have you tried to change any of the health-related behaviors you listed? If so, at which of the five stages of readiness are you for each behavior? For example, if you recently began walking two miles a day, four days a week, you are in the action stage of readiness. If it's a behavior that you want to change, but you are at the contemplation stage, perhaps you could try making specific plans and take the first step toward change (preparation stage). (Learning Objectives 12, 13, and 14)

WHAT SHOULD I WRITE ABOUT?

Writing about topics related to *Health, Stress, and Coping* is a great opportunity to learn about something that has direct personal relevance. We all encounter stress, and we all have, or at least should have, an interest in our health and well-being. As you decide on a topic, make sure to pick something that you will enjoy learning about, and that you will be able to apply to your own life to improve your own health and coping skills.

Almost any topic in this chapter will fit that set of criteria. For example, if you or someone you love smokes, you might write a term paper on smoking cessation programs. You could either evaluate existing program's merits and shortcomings, or you could develop your own based on your research. This strategy could work for any unhealthy behavior—overeating, poor sleep habits, poor coping, and so on.

Another strategy might be to link the research on a health-related behavior and its outcomes to the insurance industry. For example, you might pick a controversial issue and write a "Pro/Con" paper on it in which you take a position. Some employers are now charging their employees who smoke extra for their insurance benefits on the grounds that smoking creates additional health-care costs. You could study the outcomes of smoking, the costs associated with those outcomes, and then evaluate if the positions that such employers and insurance companies are taking is a fair one. Again, this type of analysis could work with a variety of health related behaviors.

You may prefer, though, to focus on developing healthy behaviors rather than cessation of unhealthy ones. The "Pro/Con" paper is a term paper topic that will work well if you would prefer to focus on wellness, too. For example, you could write a paper that analyzes whether it is more appropriate to focus on treating illness or promoting health, including an analysis of which focus you feel is currently more dominant in society. The "Pro/Con" paper is a writing strategy that will well for nearly any topic, but is particularly suited to the study of health and well-being, as many of the issues in this chapter lend themselves to this two-sided focus. Does the smoking cessation program really work or not? Is it better to focus on health or well-being?

If you decide to write a "Pro/Con" paper, you want to make sure you can clearly identify the two sides you will be contrasting and evaluating in your paper. The whole point of a "Pro/Con" paper is to contrast two sides of an issue, and then end up supporting one or the other (the pro or the con). Here are some things to think about as you develop a "Pro/Con" paper:

1. What are the two sides of the issue? Are they clearly definable and distinct from each other?

2. What research supports each side of the issue? What research is critical of each side?

3. Which side appears to be the stronger position on the issue? Why? Can you relate your reasoning at all to what you have learned about research methodology? Can cause and effect truly be determined by the methodology used? Was an appropriate sample used? Use these kinds of questions to base your final stance in the paper on scientific reasoning.

THE INTERNET

The Psychabilities web site that accompanies this text offers many resources relevant to this chapter. They include NetLab exercises, Thinking Critically and Evaluating Research exercises, ACE chapter quizzes, recommended web links, and articles on current events, books, and movies. Go to http://college.hmco.com, select Psychology, and then this textbook.

MULTIPLE-CHOICE QUESTIONS

SAMPLE QUIZ 1

1. Which of the following is true of stress measurement?
   a. Stressors always involve major life events.
   b. Major stressors have a greater impact than several minor stressors.
   c. Sometimes consistent daily hassles cause severe stress reactions.
   d. Only a combination of major and minor stressors causes a severe stress reaction.

2. Which of the following would *not* be considered a stressor?
   a. Taking a three-week vacation
   b. Planning a wedding reception for five-hundred guests
   c. Being able to hear the neighbor's baby cry
   d. All of the above are stressors.

3. A group of people jumps into Lake Michigan's icy waters every January. The immediate rise in their heart rate is a sign that they have entered the _____ stage of the general adaptation syndrome.
   a. resistance
   b. exhaustion
   c. alarm reaction
   d. psychogenic diseuphoria

4. Which of the following has been said of Selye's general adaptation syndrome?
   a. It underemphasizes the biological processes involved in stress response.
   b. It adequately explains the contribution of psychological factors in reactions to stress.
   c. It overemphasizes the contribution of psychological factors in the determination of stress responses.
   d. It overemphasizes the biological processes involved in stress responses.

5. Mario has luckily survived an automobile crash. Afterward, he finds that his heart is beating rapidly; he feels angry for not avoiding the accident, and he is smoking cigarettes in an attempt to calm down. Rapid heart rate is a _____ stress response anger is a _____ stress response; and smoking cigarettes is a _____ stress response.
   a. behavioral; physical; psychological
   b. physical; psychological, behavioral
   c. physical; behavioral; psychological
   d. behavioral; psychological; physical

6. Overarousal can cause
   a. increased performance on nonpracticed tasks.
   b. thinking to become clear and less muddled.
   c. a reliance on mental sets.
   d. enhanced information processing.

7. Mario has been working two jobs for the past year and is taking a full load of classes. Mario is tired, irritable, and depressed. His bosses and teachers are concerned because the quality of his work has gradually decreased. Which of the following is Mario most likely experiencing?
   a. a behavioral stress response
   b. burnout
   c. a disease of adaptation
   d. posttraumatic stress disorder

8. Melissa and Randy both have mountains of work on their desks. Melissa rolls up her sleeves in eager anticipation. She knows the project in front of her will earn her a promotion. Randy cringes every time he walks into his office and surveys the mess. He can think only of how long it is going to take

him to finish. Which of them will experience the most stress?
   a. Melissa, because she is worried about getting promoted
   b. Randy, because he interprets the work as a stressor
   c. Melissa, because women are more prone to stress than men
   d. Randy and Melissa, because they both experience an equally large amount of stress

9. Badly managed problem-focused coping strategies include
   a. imagining a positive situation.
   b. trying to eliminate a stressor that can't be changed.
   c. accepting responsibility for the problem.
   d. both (a) and (c).

10. Cynical hostility is characterized by
    a. patience.
    b. low levels of aggression.
    c. distrust of others.
    d. very few emotional stress reactions.

11. According to your text, the most preventable risk factor for fatal illnesses in the United States is
    a. alcohol use.
    b. diet.
    c. smoking.
    d. unsafe sex.

12. Cognitive restructuring is a(n)
    a. emotional reaction to stress.
    b. attempt to change stress-producing thought patterns.
    c. plan to restructure the use of one's time.
    d. process of systematic relaxation.

13. An example of a person using a behavioral coping strategy is
    a. Bette, who exercises daily.
    b. Liang, who uses time management to ensure work is completed.
    c. Pollyanna, who says to herself, "Everything will be fine."
    d. Winston, who uses meditation to reduce his need for cigarettes.

14. Willy is taking sedatives in order to reduce his stress reactions. His family is trying to convince him to use another coping method. What might their reason be?
    a. Chemical coping methods provide only temporary relief from stress.
    b. Chemical coping methods can lead to addiction.

c. Chemical coping methods will not help Willy feel that he has control over the stressors in his life.

d. All of the above

15. Eduardo is learning a coping technique. His instructor has told him to alternate between tensing and relaxing his muscles. Which method is he learning?

a. Biofeedback training

b. A behavioral coping method

c. Progressive relaxation training

d. Stress reaction restructuring

Total Correct (See answer key) _____

SAMPLE QUIZ 2

Use this quiz to reassess your learning after taking Quiz 1 and reviewing the chapter.

1. Jane finds she's beginning to dislike her job because she hates the 45-minute commute in heavy, unpredictable traffic. Jane is experiencing stress from

a. conflict.

b. daily hassles.

c. cognitive dissonance.

d. burnout.

2. The Social Readjustment Rating Scale developed by Holmes and Rahe is designed to measure stress in terms of

a. the total number of unpleasant life events.

b. the amount of adjustment required by life changes.

c. negative readjustment units.

d. the degree of physical illness caused by life changes.

3. The fight-or-flight syndrome is part of the _____ stage of the GAS.

a. resistance

b. alarm

c. exhaustion

d. adaptation

4. Which of the following describes a person at the resistance stage of the general adaptation syndrome (GAS)?

a. Abel feels fine, but has a high level of corticosteroids.

b. Belle gets one head cold after another during an entire semester.

c. Elle's muscles are tense, her heart rate is increasing, and she is breathing hard.

d. Lee has an ulcer, but is treating it with prescription medicines.

5. Carrie is worried about her upcoming driver's license test. "If I fail this test, my friends will all laugh at me," she worries. "I just can't face my friends if I fail this, it would be the end for me." Carrie is illustrating the cognitive stress response called

a. sublimation.

b. reaction formation.

c. catastrophizing.

d. displacement.

6. Julie is feeling stress while completing a midterm exam. According to your text, which of the following would most likely reduce the amount of stress Julie is feeling?

a. The teacher said the test would be true-false questions, but it is essay format.

b. She thinks she is going to flunk the test.

c. She knew that the test would be hard.

d. She doesn't know anyone else in the class.

7. Manny, who was kidnapped and tortured by entertainment terrorists when he was a child, is now unable to concentrate or get along with others, and is often found huddled in a corner saying, "Why don't you go pick on someone your own size?" Manny is most likely suffering from

a. burnout.

b. posttraumatic stress disorder.

c. catastrophizing.

d. generalized anxiety disorder.

8. Whenever Rose feels the pressures of life crowding in on her she mentally focuses on positive thoughts and memories. Rose appears to be

a. situation-focused.

b. emotion-focused.

c. appraisal-focused.

d. problem-focused.

9. What is a social support network?

a. A group of people who volunteer to help those under stress

b. A set of government agencies that help those in need

c. A group of caregivers from the mental health community

d. A group of friends and social contacts that can offer help and support

10. The longitudinal quasi-experiment on the relationship between personality and health showed that participants who

a. were impulsive were more likely to die from accidents.

b. acted conscientiously were more likely to die of heart disease.

c. ate more healthily were more likely to get divorced.

d. stayed married were more likely to die young.

11. X, the immune system cell, has had quite the busy day. It has been speeding through the body's war zone eliminating virus and tumor cells. What kind of cell is X?
a. Natural killer
b. T-cell
c. Mitochondria
d. Antibody

12. Which of the following statements about alcohol abuse is *false*?
a. More than 1,000,000 alcohol-abuse-related deaths occur each year in the United States.
b. Alcohol abuse contributes to irreversible damage to brain tissue.
c. Alcohol does not seem to play a role in heart disease, stroke, cancer, or liver disease.
d. Alcohol abusers may experience disruption of reproductive functions.

13. Lenny has been smoking two packs of cigarettes a day for 15 years. Though his friends and family have been encouraging him to quit for years, Lenny hasn't really considered the ways in which smoking endangers his health and sees no reason to quit. In terms of being ready to quit smoking, Lenny can best be described as being at the stage of
a. contemplation.
b. maintenance.
c. precontemplation.
d. preparation.

14. A good stress-management program includes
a. systematic stress assessment.
b. goal setting.
c. effective plans for coping with stressors.
d. all of the above.

15. Doug is learning to help himself relax by tensing different muscle groups momentarily and then releasing them. Doug is learning
a. progressive relaxation training.
b. behavioral coping skills.
c. problem-focused coping skills.
d. emotion-focused coping skills.

ANSWERS TO CONCEPTS AND EXERCISES

No. 1: Recognizing Stressors
(pp. 350–352)

1. Got a run in her nylons, taking kids to school, picking up dog for his veterinary appointment, vacuum cleaner broken, children screaming, dog whimpering, dirty floors, struggling with dinner.

2. Deadline, new crisis, wife starting to complain.

3. First day of first grade, sit next to the neighborhood bully, ramming his tricycle into hers, grabbing her swing, pushing it too high.

4. New roommate, he goes to bed at 8 P.M., wants to study in the room every night until 7:45 P.M., must have complete quiet, has some great posters of Bambi.

No. 2: Recognizing Stress Reactions

1. *Resistance stage of GAS.* Elevated levels of corticosteroids are associated with the resistance stage of the GAS. During this stage a person may be unaware of the wear and tear their body is experiencing. (p. 353)

2. *Catastrophizing.* A person who makes a mountain out of a molehill is overemphasizing the negative consequences of an event. (p. 355)

3. *Burnout.* The stress caused by a divorce and working three jobs has led to burnout for Lois. Burnout causes people to become less reliable workers and to become withdrawn, depressed, or accident prone. (p. 356)

4. *Physical coping strategy.* Nancy is not making a logical response to her distress over her husband's use of a drug. Use of a drug is a physical coping strategy, but it can have extremely negative consequences. A person may become addicted to the drug and be unable to use other methods of coping. (p. 371)

ANSWERS TO CRITICAL THINKING

1. Sam's hypothesis is that Jenny died of a heart attack.

2. Sam is using the pathologist's report as evidence to support his hypothesis.

3. Martina hypothesizes that the husband, knowing his wife had a bad heart, behaved in ways that would expose her to very consistent and sometimes high levels of stress. Martina may think Jeff wants the insurance money all to himself.

4. Martina knows that ongoing little daily hassles can be just as stressful as major catastrophes. She also knows that consistent stress can lead to diseases of adaptation. The stress induced by Jenny's husband may have caused her health to deteriorate to the

point of her having a heart attack. (*NOTE:* Critical thinking is a constant process of hypothesizing, examining evidence, rehypothesizing, and collecting more evidence. Martina may not be correct.)

ANSWERS TO MULTIPLE-CHOICE QUESTIONS

Circle the question numbers you answered correctly.

Sample Quiz 1

1. *c* is the answer. Often minor daily hassles have a larger impact than one or two major stressors. (p. 352)
   a. Major life events, either positive or negative, are stressful, but small daily hassles are also stressful.
   b. Sometimes the cumulative effect of small but consistent stressors is larger than the effect of one or two major stressors.
   d. Even minor stressors alone can add up to major stress reactions.

2. *d* is the answer. Positive life events (marriage), any type of change (vacation), and consistent daily hassles (listening to a baby cry) are all stressors. (pp. 350-352)

3. *c* is the answer. When a stressor first hits, we enter the alarm reaction stage, according to Hans Selye. (pp. 352-354)
   a. The resistance stage occurs after we have been coping with a stressor for a while.
   b. Exhaustion occurs when our bodies are worn out from coping with a stressor for too long.
   d. Psychogenic diseuphoria is not one of the stages of the general adaptation syndrome.

4. *d* is the answer. (p. 354)
   a. Selye has been criticized for overemphasizing the role of biological factors in the determination of stress responses.
   b, c. People have commented that Selye did not focus on the role of psychological factors in the determination of stress responses.

5. *b* is the answer. Physical stress reactions are physiological responses such as increased breathing rate or nausea. Psychological reactions are emotional and cognitive responses such as feeling nervous or distracted. Actions such as talking too fast or hitting someone are behavioral stress reactions. (pp. 352–356)

a, c, d. See description of behavioral, physical, and psychological reactions above.

6. *c* is the answer. Overarousal can reduce creative problem solving, thereby creating a tendency to rely on mental sets and well-rehearsed behaviors. (p. 355)
   a. Overarousal decreases performance on nonpracticed tasks.
   b. Overarousal can cause thinking to become fuzzy.
   d. Overarousal can disrupt information processing.

7. *b* is the answer. Burnout is a response to chronic stress in which a person becomes more and more irritable, indifferent, and unreliable. (p. 356)
   a. Behavioral stress responses are changes in the way people look, act, or talk. Aggression, dropping out of school, and strained facial expressions are examples. Mario is experiencing burnout, which is a pattern of physical, psychological, and behavioral stress responses.
   c. A disease of adaptation is an illness that occurs in the exhaustion stage of the general adaptation syndrome.
   d. Posttraumatic stress disorder is also a combination of physical, psychological, and behavioral stress responses, but it happens after a catastrophic event.

8. *b* is the answer. The way that people interpret their stress affects the impact of their stressors. Randy is interpreting his work as a stressor instead of as an opportunity. Melissa is thinking of her work as a vehicle for furthering her career. (pp. 357–358)
   a. Melissa sees her workload in a positive way, so she will not experience as much stress.
   c. Women are no more prone to stress than men are.
   d. Randy will experience more stress than Melissa.

9. *b* is the answer. Trying to eliminate a stressor that can't be changed will probably produce even more stress than the original stressor. (p. 359)
   a. Imagining a positive situation is an emotion-focused coping skill.
   c. Accepting responsibility for the problem is an emotion-focused coping skill.
   d. *b* is the answer.

10. *c* is the answer. People who exhibit cynical hostility are suspicious, resentful, antagonistic, and distrustful of others. Cynical hostility is a risk factor in heart disease. (pp. 365-367)

a, b. People with cynical hostility are unlikely to be patient and nonaggressive.

d. People who exhibit cynical hostility are frequently angry.

11. *c* is the answer. Smoking is the most preventable risk factor for fatal illnesses. (p. 367)

   a, d. Alcohol abuse and unsafe sex can also lead to major health problems, but neither of these is the most preventable risk factor.

   b. Diet is important to health, but smoking, alcohol abuse, and unsafe sex are greater risks to health.

12. *b* is the answer. Cognitive restructuring involves substituting constructive thoughts for stressful, destructive thoughts. (p. 370)

   a. Emotional stress reactions include frustration, anger, and depression.

   c. Time management is important in reducing the stress caused by a tight schedule, but this coping method is behavioral, not cognitive.

   d. Progressive relaxation is the physiological coping method in which people are taught to completely relax their bodies.

13. *b* is the answer. Time management is an example of a behavioral coping strategy. (p. 371)

   a. Bette is engaging in a physical coping strategy.

   c. Pollyanna is engaging in a cognitive coping strategy.

   d. Winston is using a physical coping strategy.

14. *d* is the answer. Chemical methods of coping provide only temporary relief from stressors, they can be addictive, and they do not provide a sense of control over stressors. People attribute their enhanced sense of well-being to the drug instead of to their own behavior. (p. 371)

   a, b, c. All three of these are problems associated with chemical methods of coping.

15. *c* is the answer. Progressive relaxation training is a physiological coping method in which people learn to completely relax their muscles, thus reducing heart rate and blood pressure. To learn this technique, people are told to alternately tense and relax their muscles in order to better recognize the feelings of relaxation. (p. 371)

   a. Biofeedback training is also a physiological coping method. People are hooked up to machines that tell them about the physiological changes occurring in their bodies. Many people, once they recognize these changes, can learn to control them.

   b. Behavioral coping methods might involve taking a time-management course. Progressive relaxation training is a physiological coping method.

d. There is no such method as stress reaction restructuring.

Now turn to the quiz analysis table at the end of this chapter to find which areas you know well and which areas you need to work on. Circle the numbers in the table for items on Quiz 1 that you answered correctly.

ANSWERS TO MULTIPLE-CHOICE QUESTIONS

Circle the question numbers you answered correctly.

Sample Quiz 2

1. *b* is the answer. Daily hassles are the little things that may add up to big stress. For example, having to wait every day on a bus that is late, or losing the money you tucked in your pocket to buy an afternoon snack are daily hassles. (p. 352)

   a. Conflict generally refers to friction between people, but this is not one of the main stressors discussed in the text.

   c. Cognitive dissonance is a social psychology term that refers to feeling uncomfortable after noticing that your attitude doesn't match your actions.

   d. Burnout is a combination of physical, psychological, and behavioral reactions which eventually interferes with a person's ability to continue to work.

2. *b* is the answer. On the Social Readjustment Rating Scale (SRRS), people add up the scores for the life change events they have recently experienced. The events that require more adjustment receive the bigger scores. (p. 352)

   a, c. The SRRS doesn't just measure negative events; it also measures positive life changes.

   d. To find out the degree of physical illness *caused* by life changes we would need to do an experiment, not just administer the SRRS.

3. *b* is the answer. (p. 353)

   a. Resistance is the second stage of the general adaptation syndrome.

   c. Exhaustion is the third stage of the general adaptation syndrome.

   d. There is no such thing as the adaptation stage.

4. *a* is the answer. During the resistance stage of the GAS, the symptoms of the alarm reaction subside, but the body's energy is being drained and the immune system compromised. (p. 353)

   b, d. These are diseases of adaptation indicative of the exhaustion stage of the GAS.

c. Changes in heart rate, respiration, and muscle tension are part of the alarm reaction stage of the GAS.

5. c is the answer. Carrie is catastrophizing when she thinks of ever-worsening outcomes for her current stressful event. (p. 355)
a, b, d. These are defense mechanisms, which Freud believed were caused by our attempt to cope with unconscious conflicts.

6. c is the answer. If Julie knows the test will be hard, then she should be better able to deal with it. According to your text, stressors that are predictable have less impact than those that are unpredictable. (p. 358)
a. If Julie is surprised by the format of the test, she will most likely experience more stress.
b. If Julie believes she will fail the test, she may feel more stress.
d. If Julie doesn't know anyone in the class, she may receive less social support at the time of the test.

7. b is the answer. Posttraumatic stress disorder is a set of physical, psychological, and behavioral stress responses, most notably dreams or flashbacks concerning the traumatic event, irritability, and difficulty concentrating. (p. 356)
a. Burnout is not in reaction to an extremely traumatic event. Instead it results from the build up of chronic stress, such as that from a job for which a nearly impossible number of sales must be made each day.
c. Manny would be catastrophizing if he had a problem and was blowing it out of proportion.
d. Generalized anxiety disorder is a psychological disorder which causes a person to feel anxious for no identifiable reason.

8. b is the answer. An emotion-focused coping method tries to reduce intensity of the negative emotions resulting from a stressor. (p. 359)
a, c. Situation-focused and appraisal-focused are not coping methods discussed in your textbook.
d. Problem-focused coping methods try to change the event or problem causing the stress.

9. d is the answer. A social support network is a set of people who offer us help. (p. 360)
a. Your social support network may be your family, friends, and acquaintances. Volunteers also might provide some support, but generally our support comes from those closer to us.
b, c. People from government agencies or the mental health community could provide support, but generally our social support

network is made up of people who we know well.

10. a is the answer. People who were impulsive or low on conscientiousness were more likely to die from accidents or violence. (p. 362)
b, c, d. Those who were conscientious were more likely to stay married, eat healthily, and live longer.

11. a is the answer. A natural killer cell is a type of leukocyte that is especially good at antiviral and antitumor functions. (p. 364)
b. A T-cell is a type of leukocyte that matures in the thymus gland and that kills other cells.
c. Mitochondria are neurons' energy makers.
d. Antibodies are produced by B-cells to fight foreign toxins.

12. c is the answer. Alcohol *has* been linked to heart disease, stroke, cancer, liver disease, and more. (p. 367)
a, b, d. All these are true.

13. c is the answer. People in the first stage of readiness, precontemplation, don't perceive that they have a problem and aren't planning to change. (p. 369)
a. In the contemplation stage people are thinking about changing, because they know they have a problem.
b. In the maintenance stage people are keeping up their newly learned habits and behaviors.
d. The preparation stage requires that people have made specific plans to change.

14. d is the answer. An effective stress-management program includes a systematic stress assessment. You have to know what the problem is before you can solve it. Setting goals helps you decide whether to eliminate the stressor or attempt to reduce the impact of that stressor. Finally, an effective plan must be made in order to deal with the stressors you face. (p. 370)
a, b, c. All three of these are involved in an effective stress management program.

15. a is the answer. Tensing different muscle groups and then focusing on the resulting relaxation is progressive relaxation training. (p. 371)
b, c, d. Doug is learning a physical coping skill. None of the other responses has to do with changing one's physiological reaction to stress.

Now turn to the quiz analysis table at the end of this chapter to find which areas you know well and which areas you need to work on. Circle the numbers in the table for items on Quiz 2 that you answered correctly.

For each question you answered correctly, circle its number. (Quiz 1 numbers are not shaded; Quiz 2 numbers are shaded.) Are there patterns in the types of questions or the topics you got wrong that could direct your further study? Did you improve from Quiz 1 to Quiz 2?

TOPIC	TYPE OF QUESTION		
	DEFINITION	COMPREHENSION	APPLICATION
Understanding Stress			
Stressors		1	2
	2		
Stress Responses		4, 6	3, 5, 7
	3	1	4, 5, 7
Stress Mediators		9	8
	9	8, 10	6
Physiology and Psychology of Health and Illness			
Immune system			
		11	
Heart disease	10		
Risks		11	
	12		
Promoting healthy behavior	12		13, 14, 15
		14	13, 15

TOTAL CORRECT BY QUIZ:

QUIZ 1:	
QUIZ 2:	

Chapter 11

Personality

LEARNING OBJECTIVES

1. Define personality. (p. 377)

2. Describe the assumptions of Freud's psychodynamic approach to personality. (p. 378)

3. Define and describe the nature and function of the id, ego, and superego. Define the pleasure principle and reality principle. (pp. 378-379)

4. Define defense mechanism. Explain the purpose and give examples of defense mechanisms. (p. 379)

5. Name, define, and describe the psychosexual stages in Freud's theory of personality development. Compare and contrast the Oedipus and Electra complexes. (pp. 379–380)

6. Explain some of the variations on Freud's personality theory. Be sure to discuss the ideas of Jung and Horney. (pp. 380-381)

7. Define object relations and describe its role in contemporary psychodynamic theories of personality development. (p. 381)

8. Describe some applications and criticisms of the psychodynamic approach to personality. (p. 382)

9. Describe the three basic assumptions of the trait approach to personality. (p. 383)

10. Discuss Allport's trait theory and Eysenck's biological trait theory of personality. Define and describe the "big five" model. (pp. 383–386)

11. Discuss the debate of the role of heredity in personality development. Explain how twin and adoption studies are used to evaluate the degree to which personality is inherited. (pp. 387–388)

12. Describe some criticisms of the trait approach to personality. (pp. 388-389)

13. Describe the basic assumptions of the social-cognitive approach to personality. (p. 389)

14. Describe Rotter's expectancy theory, Bandura's reciprocal determinism and self-efficacy, and Mischel's person variables. (pp. 389–391)

15. Describe some applications and criticisms of the social-cognitive approach to personality. (pp. 391-392)

16. Describe the phenomenological approach to personality. (p. 392)

17. Describe Rogers' self theory and Maslow's humanistic psychology. Define self-actualization, self-concept, and conditions of worth. Explain the difference between a deficiency orientation and a growth orientation. (pp. 392–394)

18. Describe some applications and criticisms of the phenomenological approach. (p. 394)

19. Describe cultural differences in the concept of self. Explain how these differences influence the development of personality. (pp. 395–396)

20. Discuss the longitudinal studies of personality and their conclusions about the continuity of personality across the lifespan. (pp. 397–398)

21. Describe the three general methods of personality assessment. Discuss the difference between objective and projective tests and give examples of each. (pp. 398–401)

22. Describe some of the applications of personality tests. (p. 402)

KEY TERMS

1. **Personality** is the unique pattern of enduring psychological and behavioral characteristics by which each person can be compared and contrasted to others. (p. 377)

Example: When you say that your friend is smart, funny, and outgoing, you are describing behavioral (funny and outgoing) and psychological (smart) traits that are part of her personality.

REMEMBER: Those who study personality are interested in what makes each person unique.

I. THE PSYCHODYNAMIC APPROACH

2. The **psychodynamic approach** to personality, developed by Freud, emphasizes the role of unconscious mental processes in determining thoughts, feelings, and behavior. (p. 378)

Example: A psychologist taking the psychodynamic approach to personality would interpret a characteristic such as "funny" in light of potential unconscious fears or aggression. For example, he or she might say a funny person uses humor as a way of putting down people. It allows one to be "aggressive" in a socially acceptable way.

REMEMBER: Freud introduced the idea that psychological activity plays a major role in behavior, mental processes, and personality. Psych refers to "mental," and dynamic pertains to "energy, motion," and "forcefulness." Psychological factors have energy and play a forceful role in the determination of personality, behavior, and mental processes.

3. The **id**, one of the structures of personality, contains the basic instincts, desires, and impulses with which people are born. It operates on the pleasure principle. Eros is the instinct for pleasure and sex (life instincts). Thanatos is the death instinct, which can motivate aggressive and destructive behavior. The id seeks immediate gratification, regardless of society's rules or the rights and feelings of others. (p. 378)

Example: Freud might say that an infant cries whenever hungry, wet, bored, or frustrated because the infant's id wants instant fulfillment of every wish.

4. The **pleasure principle** is the operating principle by which the wants and desires of the id push people to do whatever feels good. (p. 378)

Example: A child screaming for a snack is operating on the pleasure principle.

REMEMBER: The id operates on the pleasure principle, guiding people to do whatever gives them pleasure.

5. The **ego** evolves from the id and attempts to satisfy the id's demands without breaking society's rules. The ego operates according to the reality principle. (p. 378)

Example: Suppose Thanatos (part of the id) creates a desire to cut people with knives. The ego would consider society's rules and laws about this type of activity, which say that cutting other people is wrong. But a person can become a surgeon and cut people on a daily basis. Being a physician who cuts people does not violate society's rules and may symbolically satisfy the id's demands.

6. The **reality principle** is the operating principle of the ego because the ego must find compromises between irrational id impulses and the demands of the real world. (p. 378)

Example: Naomi's id wants her to eat an entire plate of donuts, but the ego suggests a more moderate response, which may partially satisfy the id. Naomi decides to have one donut (or two).

7. The **superego** is formed from internalized values and dictates what people should do (the ego ideal) and what people should not do (the conscience). The superego can be thought of as operating on the morality principle. (p. 378)

Example: Suppose you are a small child in a candy store. Your id is "screaming" for candy. The conscience (part of the superego) is saying, "You know it is wrong to steal candy." The ego decides that the best way to handle this dilemma is for you to go home and ask your mother for your allowance. Then you can go back and buy the candy, satisfying both the id and the superego.

8. **Defense mechanisms** are unconscious psychological and behavioral tactics that help protect a person from anxiety by preventing conscious awareness of unacceptable id impulses and other unconscious material. (p. 379)

Example: Jansen has a new baby brother whom he dislikes for taking away his parents' attention. Jansen would be very upset about his intense dislike of his sibling if he were consciously aware of it; therefore, his ego employs a defense mechanism, reaction formation, to push the negative feelings into the unconscious. Now Jansen is overly attentive and affectionate with his brother.

9. The **psychosexual stages** of development are part of Freud's psychodynamic theory of personality. Each stage is distinguished by the part of the body from which a person derives dominant pleasure. The five stages are, in their respective order, oral, anal, phallic, latent, and genital. Failure to resolve the problems that occur during the oral, anal, or phallic stages can lead to fixation. (p. 379)

10. The **oral stage** occurs during the first year of life, when the child derives pleasure from the mouth. If a child is weaned too early or too late, problems that can lead to fixation may arise. (p. 380)

Example: Bill was weaned too early, thus depriving him of pleasure during the oral stage of personality development. As an adult, he talks quite a bit, is a heavy smoker, and loves to eat.

11. The **anal stage** occurs during the second year of life, when pleasure is derived from the anal area. If toilet training is too demanding or is begun too early or too late, problems that can lead to fixation may arise. (p. 380)

Example: Art was toilet trained at a very young age and is fixated at the anal stage. As an adult, he is very neat, orderly, and extremely organized.

12. The **phallic stage** occurs from three to five years of age, when pleasure is derived from the genital area. During this stage, boys experience the Oedipus complex and girls experience the Electra complex. A fixation at the phallic stage could lead to problems with authority or difficulties maintaining love relationships. (p. 380)

Example: Eve hasn't had a long-term romantic relationship, because she finds fault with each person she dates. Although Eve doesn't realize it, she wants people to match her unreasonably high expectations and becomes irritated when they don't.

13. The **Oedipus complex** is a constellation of impulses that occur during the phallic stage. A boy's id impulses involve sexual desire for the mother and a desire to eliminate the father, with whom the boy must compete for the mother's affection. However, the fear of retaliation causes boys to identify with their fathers and acquire male gender-role behaviors. (p. 380)

Example: Little Joey likes to do everything "just like Dad." Freud would argue that Joey's identification with his Father is a way to solve the Oedipal complex. Joey desires his mother sexually; but, fearing his father's wrath, identifies with his father instead.

14. The **Electra complex** occurs during the phallic stage when girls experience penis envy and transfer their love from their mothers to their fathers. To resolve this stage, girls identify with their mothers and acquire female gender-role behaviors. (p. 380)

Example: Little Erin likes to help her mother make dinner and clean house. She borrows her mother's make-up and likes to have her hair fixed just like her mom's. Freud would argue that Erin is identifying with her mother as a way to solve her Electra complex.

15. The **latency period** occurs after the phallic stage and lasts until puberty. Sexual impulses lie dormant during the latency period. (p. 380)

Example: Will is excited about playing soccer on his grade school team and works hard to do his homework well and on time.

16. The **genital stage** occurs from puberty onward. The genitals are once again the primary source of sexual pleasure. The satisfaction obtained during this stage is dependent upon the resolution of conflicts experienced in the earlier stages. (p. 380)

Example: Penny began college this year and has made many new friends. Although she is not sexually active, Penny believes that her current romantic relationship is secure enough that it may eventually lead to a sexual relationship.

II. THE TRAIT APPROACH

17. The **trait approach** views personality as a unique combination of dispositions or tendencies to think and behave in certain ways. The three basic assumptions of this approach are that dispositions are stable and consistent over time, that the tendency to think and behave in certain ways is consistent in diverse situations, and that each person has a unique combination of dispositions. (p. 383)

Example: When people say that they have a friend who is sociable, understanding, and generous, they are using the trait approach to describing personality.

18. The **big five** (or five-factor model) are the five factors that trait theorists believe best define the basic organization of personality. These factors are neuroticism, extraversion, openness, agreeableness, and conscientiousness. (pp. 385-386)

Example: Linda worries constantly about everything, is very talkative and outgoing, does not like to try new things, is somewhat argumentative, and always gets her work done on time. Linda is probably high on the big five traits of neuroticism, extraversion, and conscientiousness. She is probably low on the big five traits of agreeableness and openness.

REMEMBER: The first letters of the five traits spell the word "OCEAN."

III. THE SOCIAL-COGNITIVE APPROACH

19. The **social-cognitive approach** views personality as the array of behaviors that a person acquires through learning. Also important are the roles of learned thought patterns and the influence of social situations. (p. 389)

Example: Devorah explains that her friend has learned to be obnoxious at parties. Devorah believes they could shape her friend's behavior to be less obnoxious by rewarding her for more appropriate behavior.

20. **Self-efficacy**, a term used by Bandura, is the expectation of success in a given situation. These cognitive expectations may play a major role in determining behavior in that situation. (p. 390)

Example: Jessica has low self-efficacy in interviewing situations and expects to do poorly. She can never think of answers to questions or creative solutions to the problems posed by the interviewer. Sandra, in contrast, has high self-efficacy in interviewing situations. Because she expects to do well, she is confident and approachable. Interviewers enjoy talking with Sandra because she is enthusiastic and energetic. The interviewers' responses further enhance Sandra's self-efficacy.

IV. THE PHENOMENOLOGICAL APPROACH

21. The **phenomenological approach** (also called the humanistic approach) to personality focuses on the individual's unique perception, interpretation, and experience of reality. Phenomenological theorists assume that humans have an innate drive to grow and to fulfill their own unique potentials. (p. 392)

Example: Perry tells the jury that his client did not take her ill daughter, Sarah, to the hospital because she firmly believed that prayer would heal her and that taking Sarah to the hospital would show that she had no faith. In his summation, Perry argues that his client perceived that western medicine would not cure Sarah and might cause her death, because prayers from nonbelievers are not answered. Perry took a phenomenological approach to explain that his client's view of reality influenced her behavior.

22. **Self-actualization** is an innate tendency toward realizing one's potential. This concept is important in many phenomenological personality theories. If growth toward self-actualization is not impeded, a person will tend to be happy and comfortable. (p. 392)

Example: Adam wanted to be a nurse ever since kindergarten, when his younger sister was sick. In his nursing classes, Adam feels a sense of accomplishment and of motivation to learn more.

23. **Self-concept** is the way one thinks about oneself. Self-actualizing tendencies and others' evaluations influence one's self-concept. (p. 393)

Example: Lucy loves to bake in her play oven. Her whole family raves over how tasty her creations are, although Lucy's apple pie was a little chewy. Now Lucy thinks that she's a fine baker and a nice person for treating her family to new desserts every day.

24. **Conditions of worth** are the beliefs that a person's worth depends on displaying the "right" attitudes, behaviors, and values. These conditions are created whenever people, instead of their behaviors, are evaluated. (p. 393)

Example: Bruce sat on the desk folding all the papers into little squares, thinking that his mom would think it looked very neat. "No! Bad boy! Get down from there this instant!" yells Bruce's mom. Suddenly, he doesn't feel like his ideas are good ones. If this happens often enough, Bruce might come to believe that he is a bad person.

V. ASSESSING PERSONALITY

25. **Objective tests**, one type of personality test, are paper-and-pencil tests containing clear, specific questions, statements, or concepts to which a person writes responses. (p. 398)

Example: The multiple choice tests that you take in your classes are called objective tests because they can be graded objectively. Your score on an objective test can be compared mathematically with other students' scores.

REMEMBER: Objective tests are scored objectively. The scorer has a key that shows how to assign scores, rather than each scorer choosing a way of interpreting responses.

26. **Projective tests** are composed of unstructured stimuli that can be perceived and responded to in many ways. People who use these kinds of tests assume that responses will reflect aspects of personality. It is relatively difficult to transform these tests' responses into numerical scores. (p. 400)

Example: The TAT is a projective test that involves showing people pictures and asking them to tell a story about each picture. A psychologist then interprets their responses as meaningful indications about their personality.

CONCEPTS AND EXERCISES

No. 1: Explaining Behavior

Completing this exercise should help you to achieve Learning Objectives 2, 3, 5, 9, 10, 13, 16, and 17.

Jan's office is extremely neat and organized. His books are arranged alphabetically, and there is not a stray paper on the desk. His pencils, neatly arranged from shortest to longest, are so sharp that he could use them as weapons. Jan is a meticulous dresser. His clothes are never wrinkled, spotted, or torn. Match the following explanations of his behavior with the appropriate theorist or approach.

1. Jan has learned that being organized and well dressed will further his career. _____

2. Jan is fixated at the anal stage. _____

3. Being organized is one of the central traits of Jan's personality. _____

4. Jan has a personality in which he finds fulfillment in being neat and organized. _____

5. Jan may believe that he is worthwhile only if he displays neat and tidy behaviors. _____

   ° Rogers
   ° Social-cognitive
   ° Allport
   ° Adler
   ° Freud

No. 2: Treatment Goals

Completing this exercise should help you to achieve Learning Objectives 2, 9, 10, 12, 16, and 17.

Bobbie is extremely anxious and unhappy. Match the following goals with the appropriate approach to personality listed subsequently.

1. Bobbie should become aware of her unconscious conflicts and work to resolve them. _____

2. Bobbie should become aware of her real feelings and beliefs instead of trying to fulfill the conditions of worth that her parents and others impose on her. _____

3. Bobbie should learn to think positively and realize that she controls what happens to her. _____

4. Bobbie should take some tests to assess her personality traits. If the tests show she has a disorder, she should go through some form of treatment. She can take the tests again later to monitor her progress. _____

   ° Phenomenological
   ° Social-cognitive
   ° Psychodynamic
   ° Trait

CRITICAL THINKING

Sam and Martina are discussing the use of character witnesses in violent crime court cases. Sam believes that people's personalities are very stable across diverse situations. Therefore, character witnesses who can describe personality traits should give a good indication of whether a person is capable of doing a violent crime. Martina says that people can act very differently when provoked by a situation, so character witnesses may not know everything about how likely a person is to behave in a violent manner.

Using the five critical thinking questions in your text, the clues in the story, and what you have learned about personality, answer the following.

1. What is Sam's hypothesis?

2. What is Martina's alternative hypothesis?

3. In any given case, what kinds of evidence do you think Martina would collect to support her alternative hypothesis?

PERSONAL LEARNING ACTIVITIES

1. Pick a behavior that you engage in often. Describe that behavior using the psychodynamic, trait, social-cognitive, and phenomenological approaches. What are the differences in the conclusions of the four approaches? For example, procrastination could be explained as merely a personality characteristic or as an action rewarded in its early stages by the extra relaxation time it provides. (Learning Objectives 2, 9, 13, and 16)

2. Imagine a situation in which you have to decide whether or not to do something that is fun, but risky. What are the id, ego, and superego saying about the proposed behavior? Many people who want to lose weight may see candy and want to eat it, for instance. What are the id, ego, and superego saying about eating something that isn't nutritious? (Learning Objective 3)

3. Locate a news report that talks about the personality of someone in the story. What approach to personality is being taken in the story? Often when criminals, heroes, political candidates, and other people are discussed, people draw conclusions about why they acted as they did. Those conclusions may focus more on the influence of the situation, the person's family background, or the person's views. What does the report assume about the chances that the person will change? (Learning Objectives 2, 9, 13, and 16)

4. Describe your personality. How much do you think was inherited and how much was influenced by the environment? (Learning Objective 11)

5. Use magazine or newspaper photos, drawings, and advertisements to make your own projective test. Cut off any identifying information such as captions or product names and then present them to friends and have them tell a story about what is going on in the pictures. Do you see any differences in their responses? For example, does one friend consistently see conflict between people in the photos while another always tells a story with a happy ending? (Learning Objective 21)

WHAT SHOULD I WRITE ABOUT?

In the last chapter, we talked about how to write a position paper in which you take a stance on an issue and argue against other stances on that same issue. Although position papers are a great way to develop a paper, they are not the only strategy for writing term papers by any means. Some issues are more complex, and don't lend themselves to one side being completely true and the other completely false. *Personality* is a chapter full of such issues. If you find a topic you are interested in that doesn't seem to lend itself to a position, or "pro/con" paper, than you could try a different strategy.

Many excellent term papers analyze a topic from multiple angles. Given the four main approaches to personality discussed in your textbook, a term paper dealing with personality could easily have at least four angles. For example, you may be interested in personality development in children (called temperament by developmental psychologists). You could write a paper about how the four different approaches to personality would view personality development in infants. It is unlikely that only one approach to personality has the only "true" understanding of this process, and there is much to be learned by analyzing this issue from the perspective of the four different approaches. Almost any behavior of interest would lend itself to this type of analysis.

If you prefer not to focus on all four approaches, though, you could choose to study different theorists within one approach. For example, if you found the psychodynamic approach particularly interesting, you might study the variations that developed out of that approach, such as Adler, Jung, and Horney. Understanding how an approach develops and changes over time, and getting a handle on the socio-political context in which those changes take place, would be an excellent topic for a term paper.

As you develop your term paper on *Personality*, here are some questions to consider:

1. Is there a particular behavior you are interested in studying? If so, analyzing that behavior from the various perspectives can provide you some insight into the motivation behind that behavior. Doing so will not only give you a term paper topic, but will also help you learn about a behavior you are already interested in studying in the first place.

2. If not particular behavior comes to mind as a topic of interest, perhaps you would be better off studying different theorists within a single approach. You could research the different theorists' perspectives on personality, compare and contrast those views, and then point out the social and political forces that may have been involved in the new theorists ideas coming to the forefront.

THE INTERNET

The Psychabilities web site that accompanies this text offers many resources relevant to this chapter. They include NetLab exercises, Thinking Critically and Evaluating Research exercises, ACE chapter quizzes, recommended web links, and articles on current events, books, and movies. Go to http://college.hmco.com, select Psychology, and then this textbook.

MULTIPLE-CHOICE QUESTIONS

SAMPLE QUIZ 1

1. The study of personality is concerned mainly with
   a. abnormal behavior.
   b. the ways in which people are similar.
   c. the ways in which people are unique.
   d. social behaviors.

2. Maria is continually worrying about whether her actions are going to be socially acceptable. A Freudian psychologist *might* say her personality was being controlled by her
   a. ego.
   b. id.
   c. superego.
   d. defense mechanisms.

3. Larry is always talking on the phone, eating, drinking, smoking, or biting his fingernails. According to Freud, Larry is *probably* _____ fixated.
   a. orally
   b. phallically
   c. anally
   d. genitally

4. Which of the following is *not* a criticism of Freud's psychodynamic theory of personality?
   a. It is based on a sample of upper class Viennese people, most of who were women.
   b. The id, ego, and superego are such vague constructs that it is difficult to verify their existence and to measure them.
   c. It places too much emphasis on the observation and measurement of overt behaviors.
   d. Human beings are viewed as creatures driven mostly by the need to gratify instincts and unconscious desires.

5. Toni describes her best friend as intelligent, caring, extroverted, and lots of fun to be with. Which type of theorist would use the same type of description that Toni does?
   a. Trait
   b. Social-cognitive

c. Psychodynamic
d. Phenomenological

6. Which of the following is an example of a person exhibiting a secondary trait?
   a. Amy, who is obnoxious and opinionated only in seminar classes
   b. Arnold, whose entire life is devoted to ridding the world of thieves, murderers, and drug dealers
   c. Cathy, who usually sees the positive side of events
   d. Dave, who loves to help those less fortunate than himself

7. LaRhonda says that she once enjoyed driving fast and took a trip every weekend. Now, however, she says she would rather get together with friends, because all that driving was really a waste of money and harmful to the environment. A big five theorist would most likely describe LaRhonda's personality in terms of her
   a. level of the five psychic conflicts.
   b. perception of the benefits and costs of speeding, the value of friendship, and the positive and negative aspects of staying home.
   c. level of extraversion.
   d. level of psychoticism.

8. The belief that behavior can be situation-specific is a main argument *against* which approach to personality?
   a. Psychodynamic
   b. Social-cognitive
   c. Phenomenological
   d. Trait

9. Rotter's expectancy theory is part of the _____ approach to personality.
   a. trait
   b. phenomenological
   c. social-cognitive
   d. psychodynamic

10. Bart is a ten-year-old who is acting up in class, even when his teacher scolds him for his behavior. The teacher talks to the school psychologist, who suggests that Bart is rewarded by being the center of attention whenever he acts up. The school psychologist is probably using a(n) _____ approach to understand Bart's behavior.
    a. analytic
    b. social-cognitive
    c. big-five
    d. psychodynamic

11. Cloteal comes home from work and yells at her children, creating an atmosphere of fear for them.

This atmosphere affects the way the children think of their mother, which in turn affects the way they act toward her (for example, they are now withdrawn and quiet). This illustrates the concept of
   a. reciprocal determinism.
   b. psychic determinism.
   c. projection.
   d. reaction formation.

12. LaRhonda says that she once enjoyed driving fast and took a trip every weekend. Now, however, she says she would rather get together with friends, because all that driving was really a waste of money and harmful to the environment. A phenomenological theorist would describe LaRhonda's personality in terms of the
    a. change in her self-efficacy.
    b. change in her perceptions of driving.
    c. level of extraversion she is exhibiting.
    d. level of psychoticism she is exhibiting.

13. According to Carl Rogers, which of the following *best* illustrates a distorted self-experience?
    a. Voting for a candidate whose ideas you endorse
    b. Eating a lot of apples because you like them
    c. Watching *Beavis and Butthead* because your friends think it is cool
    d. Watching educational programs on public television.

14. A deficiency orientation occurs when people
    a. make do with less than perfect conditions.
    b. focus on things they do not have.
    c. attempt to fulfill their potentials.
    d. have a trait missing from their personality.

15. Mark has just looked through a series of pictures and described what he thinks are the stories underlying the scenes. Mark has just
    a. taken an objective test.
    b. taken the MMPI.
    c. taken a projective test.
    d. been interviewed.

Total Correct (See answer key) _____

SAMPLE QUIZ 2

Use this quiz to reassess your learning after taking Quiz 1 and reviewing the chapter.

Use the following conversation to answer questions 1 and 2.

Joe: I don't think we should hire him. I saw him in a barroom brawl a few months ago. Why hire someone who is going to be aggressive in any given situation?

Kim: His MMPI scores indicate that he isn't prone to violence.

Richard: His self-concept may not include violence.

Erika: Joe, how do you know that he's always going to be aggressive? Maybe the guy was just under stress at the time. Maybe he knows from past experience that a good fistfight relieves tension.

1. Which of the following approaches is *not* represented in the above conversation?
   a. Social-cognitive
   b. Psychodynamic
   c. Phenomenological
   d. Trait

2. Which two speakers agree with the trait approach to personality?
   a. Joe and Richard
   b. Erika and Kim
   c. Joe and Kim
   d. Richard and Erika

3. Miranda says, "I can't help the way I behave. I was born with these instincts, desires, and impulses and feel as though I must have immediate satisfaction." Joel says, "Well, at least I have some dignity and know how to control my behavior by doing the right things." Doug says, "You two are impossible! I'm the one who has to make compromises between your unreasoning demands for gratification and the constraints of the real world!" In this threesome, Miranda is the _____; Joel is the _____; and Doug is the _____.
   a. id; superego; ego
   b. superego; id; ego
   c. ego; superego; id
   d. id; ego; superego

4. Patty got really upset with her dog because it urinated all over her new carpet. She had an urge to hit her dog, but instead she punched her couch. The defense mechanism that Patty displayed is
   a. projection.
   b. displacement.
   c. reaction formation.
   d. rationalization.

5. Little Joey gets out of his bed and tries to get into his parents' bed so he can snuggle with Mommy. Yesterday he threw a tantrum because Mommy would not let him shower with her. He has also been acting fearful toward his father. According to psychodynamic theory, little Joey is going through the _____ stage.

a. oral
b. anal
c. phallic
d. genital

6. You describe your friend as outgoing, eccentric, generous, emotional, talkative, impulsive, and easygoing. Gordon Allport would say you have listed your friend's
   a. central traits.
   b. secondary traits.
   c. level of self-efficacy.
   d. level of externality.

7. Darrell agrees with the Big Five approach to personality; therefore, he is likely to be interested in a person's level of _____, but *not* in a person's level of _____.
   a. agreeableness; extraversion
   b. agreeableness; psychoticism
   c. neuroticism; conscientiousness
   d. neuroticism; openness

8. Which of the following is *not* a criticism of the trait theories of personality?
   a. They describe behavior better than they explain it.
   b. They create descriptions that may be too general.
   c. They ignore situational influences on behavior.
   d. They place too much emphasis on the unconscious.

9. Joe is an internal, according to Rotter's expectancy theory of personality. Therefore, you would expect Joe to
   a. ignore physical symptoms of illness.
   b. work on a factory assembly line.
   c. take a self-paced course at school.
   d. all of the above

10. When I think about Oregon, I talk about Oregon a lot. When I talk about Oregon, people around me start asking questions about Oregon. These relationships best illustrate
    a. observational learning.
    b. self-efficacy.
    c. self-actualization.
    d. reciprocal determinism.

11. Lontica is happily taping pages of her coloring book to the walls in her room when her father enters. "What are you—stupid?" her father bellows. "How many times have I told you that tape takes the paint off the walls and you should use your bulletin board?" Lontica's father may be creating a(n) _____, according to Rogers.

a. deficiency orientation
b. fixation
c. interdependent self-system
d. condition of worth

12. Grace tries not to stand out from the crowd. Not only does she describe herself in terms of her place in her family and work groups, but she also feels happiest when her interactions with her groups have gone well. Grace most likely
a. has an independent self-system.
b. has an interdependent self-system.
c. is an internal.
d. is an external.

13. Mrs. Fernandez is concerned that hiring practices in her firm are based too much on personality tests. She argues that many of the people hired are completely opposite from their personality profiles. The tests utilized *probably* have problems with
a. reliability.
b. validity.
c. contextual reliability standards.
d. standardization.

14. A projective test is usually
a. reliable.
b. valid.
c. easy to score.
d. none of the above.

15. Mimi wants to determine her client's level of depression using an objective test. Which of the following should be true of the measure?
a. The stimuli should be ambiguous.
b. The tester should interpret the numerical score based on norms.
c. The unstructured format will allow for reflection of an individual's level of depression.
d. All of the above.

Total Correct (See answer key) _____

ANSWERS TO CONCEPTS AND EXERCISES

No. 1: Explaining Behavior

1. *Social-cognitive*. A social-cognitive explanation would understand Jan's behavior by finding out what behaviors were rewarded in the past. (p. 389)

2. *Freud or Psychodynamic*. Freud believed that an unresolved crisis during the psychosexual development would lead to fixation. Adults who are fixated at the anal stage are extremely neat and tidy. (pp. 378-380)

3. *Allport*. Allport was a trait theorist. He believed that people have about seven central traits. (pp. 383-384)

4. *Adler*. Adler was a neoanalytic who believed that people adopt personalities in their quest to find fulfillment by attaining superiority. (p. 381)

5. *Rogers*. Rogers was a phenomenological theorist. He said that many people display behaviors because they believe these are the only ways in which to gain approval and thus positive self-evaluation. (pp. 392–394)

No. 2: Treatment Goals

1. *Psychodynamic*. Freud said that unconscious conflicts are the primary root of all mental disorders. In order to eliminate the anxiety these conflicts produce, patients should be made aware of them and work to resolve them. (p. 378)

2. *Phenomenological*. Rogers said that unhappy people are out of touch with their true feelings. They are probably behaving according to others' values instead of according to their own feelings and values. (pp. 392–394)

3. *Social-cognitive*. A social-cognitive approach suggests that Bobbie learn and practice more positive ways of thinking and behaving. (p. 389)

4. Trait. A trait theorist might suggest that Bobbie take objective tests, such as the MMPI, to describe her personality and identify any type of possible personality disorders. (p. 383)

ANSWERS TO CRITICAL THINKING

1. Sam hypothesizes that if someone doesn't usually exhibit tendencies toward violence, then he or she probably didn't commit a violent crime.

2. Martina knows that trait theories have been criticized because they tend to ignore situational influences on behavior. She would therefore hypothesize that someone who is generally not violent could be provoked into violence by a particular situation.

3. Martina would probably want to investigate both the person's general personality traits and aspects of the situation that could explain the onset of violent behavior.

ANSWERS TO MULTIPLE-CHOICE QUESTIONS

Circle the question numbers you answered correctly.

Sample Quiz 1

1. *c* is the answer. Personality researchers want to compare and contrast people by their unique psychological and behavioral characteristics. (p. 377)
   a. Psychologists in the clinical subfield study abnormal behavior and psychological disorders.
   b. Social psychologists and anthropologists are more interested in the ways in which people are similar than personality researchers are.
   d. Social behaviors are just one part of our personality and would also be studied by social psychologists.

2. *c* is the answer. The superego tells us what we should and shouldn't do, according to Freud. (p. 378)
   a. The ego is the mediator between the superego and the id.
   b. The id contains our basic instincts and impulses, many of which are socially unacceptable.
   d. Defense mechanisms are methods of keeping unpleasant knowledge from becoming conscious.

3. *a* is the answer. According to Freud, oral fixation is characterized by talking too much, overindulging in foods and beverages, and using "biting" sarcasm. (p. 380)
   b. Adults with phallic fixations would most likely have trouble dealing with authority, uncertain gender identity, and problems in romantic relationships.
   c. Adults with anal fixations would most likely be either stingy, overly clean and organized, and stubborn, or would be impulsive, sloppy, and disorganized.
   d. Behavior during the genital stage is the result of the previous stages; Freud wouldn't say people are fixated at the genital stage, since this is the stage in which adults are "meant" to be.

4. *c* is the answer. Freud did not place great emphasis on the measurement and observation of overt behaviors. He was more interested in dreams, free associations, and the underlying meanings of behaviors. (p. 382)
   a, b, d. All of these are criticisms of Freud's theory.

5. *a* is the answer. A trait theorist would describe a person in terms of such stable characteristics. (p. 383)

   b. A social-cognitive theorist would describe a person in terms of behaviors and thought patterns.
   c. A psychodynamic theorist would discuss the underlying unconscious conflicts that are responsible for a person's behavior.
   d. A phenomenological theorist would describe a person's perception of reality, values, and beliefs.

6. *a* is the answer. A secondary trait, according to Allport, is one that is specific to certain situations. (p. 384)
   b. Arnold has a trait that affects his whole life; this would not be a secondary trait, but a central trait.
   c, d. Cathy sounds like she is optimistic in most situations and Dave sounds like he is often helpful; therefore, these are not secondary traits.

7. *c* is the answer. A big five theorist believes in five basic traits: openness, conscientiousness, extraversion, agreeableness, and neuroticism. (pp. 385-386)
   a. A psychic conflict would interest the psychodynamic theorist, but none of them proposed five main conflicts.
   b. Perceptions are of interest to phenomenological theorists.
   d. Psychoticism is a trait, but not one of the big five. Psychoticism was proposed by Eysenck as one of three basic factors.

8. *d* is the answer. Trait theorists argue that behavior is a reflection of consistent and stable traits and that environmental or situational factors do not determine behavior. (pp. 388-389)
   a. Psychodynamic theorists have been criticized for adhering to Freud's emphasis on the unconscious and his use of patients' reports as a basis for psychosexual development theory. Freud was also accused of being sexist. But the belief in situation-specific behavior does not detract from the psychodynamic theory.
   b. Social-cognitive theorists have been accused of overemphasizing overt behavior and the environmental factors of reward and punishment and not attending enough to the individual's perceptions, feelings, and thoughts.
   c. Phenomenological concepts are difficult to measure, more descriptive than explanatory, and naive since they are so optimistic about the nature of men and women.

9. *c* is the answer. Rotter's expectancy theory is part of the social-cognitive approach. Rotter proposed that internals believe they control events and that

externals believe that others (fate, other people, luck, etc.) control events. (pp. 389–390)

a. Expectancies are not a trait or type, both of which are the foundations of the trait approach.

b. The phenomenological approach doesn't emphasize expectancies in the development of personality.

d. Psychodynamic theories do not emphasize expectancies; they tend to focus on unconscious mental processes.

10. *b* is the answer. The social-cognitive approach assumes that behavior is learned through classical and operant conditioning. In addition, learned thinking styles and social situations play a role in our personalities. Operant conditioning (see also Chapter 5) can explain Bart's behavior, because his disruptive behavior receives a reward. (p. 390)

a. Jung's neofreudian approach, known as analytic psychology, is concerned with the way we work out conflicts between impulses and societal restrictions, with our drives for growth, and our tendency towards introverted or extraverted personalities.

c. The big-five approach is an example of a trait approach. Our levels of openness, conscientiousness, extraversion, agreeableness, and neuroticism are the determinants of behavior, according to a big-five theorist.

d. The psychodynamic approach is concerned with unconscious conflicts and our psychosexual stage of development, not rewards.

11. *a* is the answer. Bandura's reciprocal determinism is a social-cognitive theory. An example of reciprocal determinism should follow the cyclical pattern of environment affecting behavior, which affects our thinking, which also affects behavior, which affects the environment, and on and on. (pp. 390-391)

b. Freud believed in psychic determinism, or the assumption that our personalities are caused by psychological, not biological or environmental conditions.

c. Projection is a Freudian defense mechanism in which we believe that our own unacceptable ideas or behaviors are someone else's. For example, Jenny is extremely attracted to Chris, but cannot admit to those feelings because Chris is married. Instead, Jenny claims that Chris is very attracted to her.

d. Reaction formation guides behavior in the direction opposite to that of the unwanted impulse. If Cloteal felt angry with her children and experienced reaction formation, she would lavish attention and love on them.

12. *b* is the answer. Phenomenological theorists focus on perceptions (p. 392)

a. Self-efficacy is a concept created by a social-cognitive theorist, Bandura.

c, d. These are traits, not perceptions.

13. *c* is the answer. According to Rogers, our self-concept may become distorted if our natural enjoyment of something is disapproved. If you only watch a TV program because your friends do, then Rogers would say you are setting yourself up for a distorted self-experience, such as, "I like TV shows with crass humor" or "Feeling uncomfortable is OK." (p. 392)

a, b, d. None of these has any stated contradiction between evaluation and behavior.

14. *b* is the answer. A deficiency orientation, according to Maslow, occurs when individuals focus on what they do not have instead of on what they do have. (p. 394)

a. If people focus on or derive satisfaction from what they have, they have a growth orientation.

c. Phenomenological theorists assume that we all attempt to fulfill our potentials.

d. A deficiency orientation is a phenomenological concept that is not related to traits.

15. *c* is the answer. Mark has just taken a projective test, most likely the Thematic Apperception Test. (p. 400)

a, b. An objective test is a paper-and-pencil test. Answers are written, not explained aloud, by the respondent. The MMPI is an objective test.

d. Interviews usually revolve around either structured or unstructured questions, not around ambiguous stimuli such as pictures and inkblots.

Now turn to the quiz analysis table at the end of this chapter to find which areas you know well and which areas you need to work on. Circle the numbers in the table for items on Quiz 1 that you answered correctly.

ANSWERS TO MULTIPLE-CHOICE QUESTIONS

Circle the question numbers you answered correctly.

Sample Quiz 2

1. *b* is the answer. Psychodynamic views of personality are not represented by anyone. (p. 378)

a. The social-cognitive approach is represented by Erika, because she refers to what "the guy" might have learned by experience.

c. The phenomenological approach is represented by Richard, because he refers to the self-concept.

d. The trait approach is represented by both Joe and Kim.

2. *c* is the answer. Joe assumes that the man in question will always be aggressive. Trait theorists assume that people have several traits that will be present in many different situations. Kim is talking about the MMPI, a personality test developed by trait theorists. (pp. 383)

a. Richard agrees with phenomenological theorists.

b. Erika agrees with social-cognitive theorists.

d. Richard agrees with phenomenological theorists, while Erika agrees with social-cognitive theorists.

3. *a* is the answer. Miranda is acting like the id, which contains our basic instincts and impulses. Joel sounds like the superego, which tells us what is right and wrong. Doug is acting like the ego, which mediates between the superego and the id, forming compromises. (p. 378)

b, c, d. None of these is in the correct order. See above.

4. *b* is the answer. Patty displaced her anger from her dog to her couch. (p. 379)

a. If Patty were using projection, she would have to unconsciously deny that she was upset and instead claim that someone else (a roommate, perhaps) is upset by the dog's behavior.

c. If Patty were exhibiting reaction formation, she would have to lavish love and affection on her dog, to keep from consciously recognizing that she wanted to hit her dog.

d. If Patty were rationalizing, she would come up with a logical explanation for whatever behavior she exhibited, whether it was hitting her dog or the couch. For example, "I was just checking to see if the couch pillows were dusty. I wasn't angry."

5. *c* is the answer. In Freud's phallic psychosexual stage, boys supposedly have sexual feelings for their mothers and a fear that their father will take revenge for these feelings. (p. 380)

a. Pleasure in the oral stage comes from the mouth.

b. Pleasure in the anal stage comes from bowel movements.

d. Pleasure in the genital stage comes from the genital area, as it did during the phallic stage; however, the sexual impulses are now presumably conscious and mature.

6. *a* is the answer. Most people can describe someone using about seven labels. Allport called these central traits. (pp. 383-384)

b. Allport also thought we had secondary traits, which are more tied to a situation. For example, a person who bluffs when playing cards might not bluff in other social situations.

c, d. Self-efficacy and expectancies (internal versus external) are social-cognitive concepts.

7. *b* is the answer. The big five approach believes that the basic personality dimensions are openness, conscientiousness, extraversion, agreeableness, and neuroticism, but not psychoticism. (pp. 385-386)

a, c, d. All of the traits listed are part of the big five.

8. *d* is the answer. Trait theories do not emphasize the unconscious as psychodynamic theories do. (pp. 388-389)

a. Traits are much better at describing than explaining behavior.

b. Many trait descriptions seem to fit a large number of people, thus reducing their value for describing a given person.

c. Trait descriptions do not explain situational influences on behavior. Trait theories imply stable behavior, driven by traits, in any situation.

9. *c* is the answer. Joe would be most likely to take a self-paced course because he would prefer being in control of his work pace. (pp. 389–390)

a, b. Joe would probably not ignore physical symptoms of illness or work very well on an assembly line. Externals would be more likely to exhibit these types of behavior.

d. *c* is the answer.

10. *d* is the answer. Thinking about Oregon caused talking about Oregon, which caused others to ask about Oregon, which indicates reciprocal determinism, according to Bandura. (pp. 390-391)

a. Observational learning is also a behavioral concept, but it only indicates a one-way effect of, for example, hearing about Oregon and remembering something about Oregon.

b. Self-efficacy is Bandura's term for a learned expectation of success.

c. Self-actualization is an inclination towards growth.

11. *d* is the answer. According to Rogers, when one person criticizes another, rather than only correcting the behavior, a condition of worth may be created. In a condition of worth, the criticized person believes that (s)he is not worthwhile because s(he) behaved in a disapproved of way. If

Lontica's father had tried to emphasize that the behavior was not correct, but that he still loved Lontica, she might not feel that her worth depended upon her behavior. (p. 393)

a. A deficiency orientation is another phenomenological concept, but it occurs when a person focuses on what is missing instead of on growth or satisfaction with current possessions.

b. A fixation will occur, according to Freud, if a person does not resolve conflicts at each stage of psychosexual development. Fixations are basically unrelated to parental reprimands.

c. Interdependent self-systems are more common in collectivist cultures, where one's place in groups is emphasized.

12. *b* is the answer. People with an interdependent self-system see themselves as a fraction of a whole. They tend not to be happy when singled out for attention, even if it is for personal achievement. (p. 396)

a. People with an independent self-system emphasize personal achievement rather than their place in a group.

c. This relates to Rotter's expectancy theory. Internals believe that they control events through their own efforts.

d. This is part of Rotter's expectancy theory. Externals believe that external forces control events.

13. *b* is the answer. If tests do not measure what they claim to measure, such as job skills, then their validity is questionable. (p. 398)

a. Reliability is repeatability of test results.

c. Contextual reliability standards is a made-up term.

d. Standardization is similarity of test administration. It is unknown whether the tests given in Mrs. Fernandez's firm are given in the same way each time they are given.

14. *d* is the answer. Projective tests involve presenting a subject with an unstructured and ambiguous stimulus. Personality is supposedly reflected in the subject's response. Because the tasks are unstructured, they tend to be relatively difficult to score, unreliable, and not as valid as objective tests. (p. 400)

a, b, c. All of these are true, which makes *d* the best answer.

15. *b* is the answer. A person's score on an objective test is more meaningful if it can be compared to the average person. If a person receives a 9, for example, on a test of depression, we don't know if that is cause for concern unless we know that a 5 is an average score. (p. 399)

a, c. Ambiguous stimuli and an unstructured format are part of a projective test.

d. Only *b* is the answer.

Now turn to the quiz analysis table at the end of this chapter to find which areas you know well and which areas you need to work on. Circle the numbers in the table for items on Quiz 2 that you answered correctly.

For each question you answered correctly, circle its number. (Quiz 1 numbers are not shaded; Quiz 2 numbers are shaded.) Are there patterns in the types of questions or the topics you got wrong that could direct your further study? Did you improve from Quiz 1 to Quiz 2?

TOPIC	TYPE OF QUESTION		
	DEFINITION	COMPREHENSION	APPLICATION
Psychodynamic	1	4	2, 3
			1, 3, 4, 5
Trait		8	5, 6, 7
		8	2, 6, 7
Social-Cognitive		9	10, 11
			9, 10
Phenomenological	14	13	12
			11
Culture			
			12
Assessing Personality			15
		14	13, 15

TOTAL CORRECT BY QUIZ:

QUIZ 1:
QUIZ 2:

Chapter 12

Psychological Disorders

LEARNING OBJECTIVES

1. Define psychopathology. Discuss the prevalence of mental disorder in the United States. (p. 409)

2. Describe the three criteria for abnormality, and discuss the limitations of each. Describe the practical approach and impaired functioning. (pp. 410–411)

3. Give examples of supernatural explanations of psychological disorders. Describe the biopsychosocial model of mental disorder. (pp. 411–412)

4. Describe and give an example illustrating the medical or neurobiological model of mental disorder. (pp. 412-413)

5. Describe the psychological model of mental disorder. Give examples to illustrate how psychodynamic, social-cognitive, and phenomenological theorists would explain mental disorder. (pp. 413-414)

6. Describe and give an example illustrating the sociocultural model of mental disorder. (p. 414)

7. Describe and give an example illustrating the diathesis-stress approach to mental disorder. (pp. 414-415)

8. Describe the contents of the Diagnostic and Statistical Manual of Mental Disorders (DSM-IV). List the five axes of the DSM-IV used in diagnosis. (p. 416)

9. Discuss the reliability and validity of diagnostic labels. Describe the problems associated with diagnosis. (pp. 416-420)

10. Define anxiety disorder. Specify which disorders are classified as anxiety disorders. (pp. 420–422)

11. Define phobia, and describe specific phobia, social phobia, and agoraphobia. (pp. 420-421)

12. Define and describe generalized anxiety disorder, panic disorder, and obsessive-compulsive disorder. Explain the difference between obsessions and compulsions. (pp. 421-422)

13. Discuss the biological and cognitive factors that may contribute to anxiety disorders. (pp. 422–423)

14. Discuss the learning principles that may be involved in the acquisition and maintenance of phobias. Discuss how humans are biologically prepared to learn certain phobias. (p. 423)

15. Define somatoform disorder. Describe conversion disorder, hypochondriasis, somatization disorder, and pain disorder. (p. 424)

16. Discuss the various theoretical explanations of how somatoform disorders develop. (p. 425)

17. Define dissociative disorder. Compare and contrast dissociative fugue and dissociative amnesia. Describe dissociative identity disorder. (pp. 425–426)

18. Discuss the various theoretical explanations of how dissociative disorders develop. (pp. 426)

19. Define mood disorders. Describe major depressive disorder, dysthymic disorder, bipolar disorder, mania, and cyclothymic disorder. (pp. 427–430)

20. Describe the relationship between depression and suicide. List the general guidelines for predicting suicide. (pp. 428-429)

21. Discuss the biological, psychological, and social factors that may contribute to the development of mood disorders. Describe how learned helplessness and attributional style may contribute to depression. (pp. 430–432)

22. Define schizophrenia. Describe the disorganized thought and language characteristic of schizophrenia. Give examples of neologisms, loose associations, and word salad. (p. 433)

23. Describe ideas of reference, thought broadcasting, thought blocking, thought withdrawal, thought insertions, and hallucinations. (pp. 433-434)

24. Compare and contrast paranoid, disorganized, catatonic, undifferentiated, and residual schizophrenia. List the percentage of the total schizophrenic population each type represents. (p. 435)

25. Describe the positive symptoms and negative symptoms of schizophrenia. (p. 434)

26. Discuss the biological, neurological, and psychological factors that may contribute to the development of schizophrenia. Describe the vulnerability theory of schizophrenia. (pp. 434–436)

27. Define personality disorder and describe personality disorders found in table 12.5 of your textbook. (p. 437)

28. Discuss the possible causes of antisocial personality disorder. Be sure to address the quasi-experimental research on the link between child abuse and antisocial personality disorder. (pp. 438-440)

29. Describe the differences between externalizing and internalizing disorders of childhood. Define conduct disorders, attention deficit hyperactivity disorder, separation anxiety disorder, and autistic disorder. (p. 440)

30. Define substance-related disorder, addiction, and alcoholism. (pp. 441–442)

31. Describe the problems associated with and the theoretical explanations for alcohol, heroin, and cocaine dependence. (pp. 442–443)

32. Discuss the laws designed to protect the rights of people with severe psychological disorders who are accused of a crime. (pp. 443-444)

KEY TERMS

1. **Psychopathology** involves patterns of thinking and behavior that are maladaptive, disruptive, or uncomfortable either for the person affected or for those with whom he or she associates. (p. 409)

REMEMBER: Psych refers to "mental" or "psychological," and pathos refers to "illness" or "sickness." Psychopathology means the study of mental illness or disorder.

I. DEFINING PSYCHOLOGICAL DISORDERS

2. **Impaired functioning** occurs when people cannot meet obligations appropriate to their social roles. (p. 411)

Example: Nora is too depressed to get out of bed and attend classes. Her friends are very worried because Nora hasn't felt like studying, eating, or even talking lately.

II. EXPLAINING PSYCHOLOGICAL DISORDERS

3. The **biopsychosocial model** explains the cause of psychological disorders in terms of a combination and interaction of biological, psychological, and sociocultural factors. (p. 412)

Example: Troy has been depressed lately. His psychologist sees the depression as due to a combination of improper neurotransmitter levels (biological factor), the experience of feeling guilty over his recent divorce (psychological factor), and the disapproval he endures from his family and friends for his failed marriage (sociocultural factors).

4. The **medical model**, also called the **neurobiological model**, attributes abnormal behavior to the presence of biochemical, genetic, or other physical problems. (pp. 412–413)

Example: Nora's doctor believes that her depression is caused by an imbalance of some neurotransmitter levels. Nora is taking an antidepressant to correct this physical problem.

5. The **psychological model** views abnormal behavior as caused by mental processes. (p. 413)

Example: The psychodynamic, cognitive-behavioral, and phenomenological approaches are examples of psychological models of abnormal behavior.

6. The **sociocultural model** of abnormal behavior looks for the influence of factors such as gender, social situations, cultural expectations, and historical eras on behavior. (p. 414)

Example: The greater tolerance for excessive drinking in men may make alcohol abuse more likely in men than in women.

7. The **diathesis-stress model** attributes abnormal behavior to more than one cause; the model recognizes the integration of a person's biological predisposition, environmental surroundings, and psychological factors in mental illness. (p. 415)

Example: Frank has a biological susceptibility to stress. Entering the combined medical and doctoral program put him under a lot of stress. He was very depressed by the end of his first semester. Jill tends to be less stress-sensitive and is handling the same program with much less trouble.

III. CLASSIFYING PSYCHOLOGICAL DISORDERS

IV. ANXIETY DISORDERS

8. **Anxiety disorders** are characterized by fear that causes a disruption in a person's life. Anxiety disorders include phobias, generalized anxiety disorders, panic disorder, obsessive-compulsive disorders, and posttraumatic stress disorder. (p. 420)

Example: Layla has been really worried lately, yet she can't pinpoint the cause of her anxiety. Her anxiety is starting to interfere with her ability to concentrate and do her job effectively. Layla has an anxiety disorder.

9. **Phobias** are strong, irrational fears of an object or situation that should not cause such a reaction. (p. 420)

Example: Specific phobias and social phobias are examples of particular types of phobias.

10. A **specific phobia** is a fear of something specific, such as heights, animals, or air travel. (p. 420)

Example: Claustrophobia is the fear of being in closed places.

11. A **social phobia** is a fear of being negatively evaluated by others or of doing something so impulsive or outrageous that public humiliation will result. (p. 421)

Example: Rosa is terrified of giving a speech to her class (social situation). She is afraid that she will be completely unable to speak and will embarrass herself by stammering until she blushes and has to run away.

12. **Agoraphobia** is the fear of being alone or away from the security of home. (p. 421)

Example: Eliza is afraid to leave her house. She cannot go shopping or out for an evening. She cannot hold a job or visit her friends and family. She cannot take her children to the doctor or drive them anywhere. Although she is less fearful when accompanied by her husband, she is still uncomfortable in any situation outside her home.

13. **Generalized anxiety disorder** involves relatively mild, but long-lasting, anxiety that is not focused on any object or situation. (p. 421)

Example: Leslie has had a feeling of vague apprehension for about six weeks and always feels as though something bad is going to happen to her. She cannot sleep and is constantly tired and irritable.

14. **Panic disorder** consists of attacks of extreme fear and panic that occur with no warning and no obvious cause. Symptoms include heart palpitations, chest pain or pressure, dizziness, sweating, and a feeling of faintness. (p. 421)

Example: Elise, a university professor, often experiences panic attacks. She can be in the middle of lecturing, driving her car, or browsing in a bookstore when she suddenly becomes terrified for no specific reason. She also experiences chest pain and dizziness during these episodes.

15. **Obsessive-compulsive disorder (OCD)** involves an obsession with particular thoughts or images, which motivates repetitive, uncontrollable behaviors. (p. 422)

Example: Jenn cannot enter a room and feel comfortable unless she touches all the walls first. If she cannot do this, she becomes very anxious and highly agitated.

V. SOMATOFORM DISORDERS

16. **Somatoform disorders** are characterized by the presence of physical symptoms of illness in the absence of a physical cause. They include conversion disorder, hypochondriasis, somatization disorder, and pain disorder. (p. 424)

REMEMBER: Soma means "body." Somatoform disorders are characterized by perceived body illnesses in the absence of an actual physical problem.

17. A **conversion disorder** is a condition in which a person reports being blind, deaf, paralyzed, insensitive to pain, or even pregnant, but is not. The imagined physical disabilities often help the person be removed from the stressful situation. (p. 424)

REMEMBER: Conversion means a "change from one state to another." Think of a person experiencing a changed physical state (blindness, deafness) but without physical explanation.

Example: Joanie is a volunteer nurse on a cancer ward. She calls the hospital and calmly tells them that she cannot come to work because she cannot move her legs. There is nothing physically wrong, but the problem allows her to avoid dealing with patients who are in great pain and near death.

18. **Hypochondriasis** is an unjustified concern that one has a serious illness. The hypochondriac makes frequent visits to doctors and will not be convinced that he or she is healthy. (p. 424)

Example: Jana is certain that she has cancer. When she has a cough, she thinks it is a symptom of lung cancer. When she has a stomachache, she thinks she has colon cancer. She constantly interprets vague symptoms as evidence of cancer, and then goes to the doctor to ask to be tested for the disease. Even when the doctor says she is cancer-free, Jana remains certain that she has the disease.

19. **Somatization disorder** is similar to hypochondriasis. People frequently go to the doctor with vague complaints about a multitude of physical problems rather than any specific disease. (p. 424)

Example: Leah visits the doctor once a month with some complaint. Usually her complaints are of a stomachache, headache, and trouble breathing. However, she can provide no specific details about what triggers these symptoms, and there is little physical evidence of them.

20. **Pain disorder** involves the experience of sometimes extreme pain in the absence of a physical cause. (p. 424)

Example: Kevin complains of constant back pain, but his doctor cannot find any physical explanation for the pain.

VI. DISSOCIATIVE DISORDERS

21. **Dissociative disorders** involve a sudden and usually temporary disruption in a person's memory, consciousness, or identity. (p. 425)

Example: Bill, lost in New York City, does not remember his name, home address, or workplace. He cannot remember anything that will give him a clue to his identity. Bill is suffering from a dissociative disorder.

REMEMBER: Dissociate means to "break a connection" or "disunite." Bill is disconnected from his past.

22. **Dissociative fugue** is a disorder in which a person experiences sudden memory loss, adopts a new identity, and moves to a new place. (p. 426)

Example: Allen has been experiencing a lot of stress at work and home lately. One day he seems to have disappeared without a trace. When the police finally find him, he is living in a large city 100 miles away from his home. He doesn't seem to know anything about his life as Allen; rather, he says he is Jorge, and has been an exotic dancer for years. Allen's new identity as Jorge is a dissociative fugue state.

23. **Dissociative amnesia** involves sudden loss of memory for personal information, but the person does not adopt a new identity and move to a new locale. (p. 426)

Example: Hope can't remember anything about herself. She can't tell you her name, her address, if she is married or not, or other important information.

24. **Dissociative identity disorder** (the least common dissociative disorder) is a condition in which a person reports having more than one identity, each of which speaks, acts, and writes in a very different way. (p. 426)

Example: Sometimes Rod acts like the football coach he is—he talks about football, studies film, and watches football games on TV. Other times, he says he wants to be called Sue. As Sue, he loves to cook gourmet meals and play croquet and have lawn parties. Rod has two distinct identities.

VII. MOOD DISORDERS

25. **Mood disorders** (also called affective disorders) are extreme changes in mood, lasting for extended periods of time, that are inconsistent with the happy or sad events in a person's life. (p. 427)

Example: Examples of mood disorders include major depressive disorder, dysthymic disorder, mania, and bipolar disorder.

26. **Major depressive disorder** is a mood disorder typified by feelings of sadness and hopelessness and an inability to enjoy oneself or take pleasure in anything. Simple tasks seem to require enormous effort, and concentration is impaired. (p. 427)

Example: Shelly is depressed. She sits on the couch and watches television without enjoying the shows. She lacks the energy to clean the house or to care for the children. She cries frequently for no apparent reason other than that she feels life is pointless.

27. **Delusions** are false beliefs. There are several types of delusions. (p. 427)

Example: Regina believes that she has been selected by the government to take over the moon once it is colonized. She anxiously checks the mail each day to see if her instructions have arrived from the president.

28. **Dysthymic disorder** is a form of mood disorder that is similar to depression but is less severe and lasts for a longer time. (p. 428)

Example: Jane has been feeling down for the past year. She can still function well in her job and at home, but she just hasn't been herself.

29. **Bipolar disorder** (manic-depression) is a form of mood disorder that involves extreme mood changes in which feelings of mania are followed by severe depression. (p. 429)

REMEMBER: Bi means "two," and polar means "extreme." A bipolar disorder is an affective disorder in which mood alternates between two opposite feelings: elation (mania) and extreme sadness (depression).

Example: Dan alternates between periods of wild, frenetic activity during which he is full of ideas and energy and periods of depression when he is so despondent he can barely get out of bed. Some of his ideas are of questionable wisdom, though, during the active periods, and during the depression he can't function well either.

30. **Mania** is an elated, very active emotional state. (p. 429)

Example: Lenny is a carpenter. While in a manic state, he decided to build a copy of the Empire State Building in his backyard. He called his office and quit his job, ordered supplies, and asked his neighbors to help him. When the people down the street tried to tell Lenny that he should check the city building codes before undertaking such an enormous task, he became belligerent. He stormed out of their house, accusing them of having no faith in the will, determination, and ability of American neighborhoods.

31. **Cyclothymic disorder** is a less severe form of bipolar disorder in which mood swings are not as extreme. (p. 430)

REMEMBER: A person's moods cycle between happiness and sadness in cyclothymic disorder.

Example: Julia's friends describe her as moody. Sometimes she is really vivacious and talkative. Other times she is really sad.

VIII. SCHIZOPHRENIA

32. **Schizophrenia** is characterized by several types of abnormal behaviors or disorders, including abnormalities in thinking, perception and attention, affect, motor behavior, personal identity, motivation, and day-to-day functioning. There are five types of schizophrenia: paranoid, disorganized, catatonic, undifferentiated, and residual. (pp. 433–436)

Example: Neologisms, an abnormality seen in schizophrenics' thinking, speaking, and writing, are words that have meaning only to the person speaking them. For example, the word teardom in "I hereby teardom your happiness" is a neologism. There is no such word.

33. **Hallucinations** are false perceptions that occur in schizophrenics. (p. 434)

Example: Many schizophrenics hear "voices" talking to them inside their heads. They may also report seeing things that don't really exist.

IX. PERSONALITY DISORDERS

34. **Personality disorders** are long-standing behavior patterns that create problems, usually for others, and are not as severe as mental disorders. (p. 437)

Example: Antisocial personality disorder is one type of personality disorder (see Key Term 35).

35. **Antisocial** personality disorder involves a long-term persistent pattern of impulsive, selfish, unscrupulous, even criminal behavior. People with antisocial personalities appear to have no morals and can be dangerous to the public because they very rarely experience deep feelings for anyone. Typically, they are smooth-talking, intelligent, charming liars who have no sense of responsibility. (p. 438)

Example: Andre, although quite charming, has been in trouble since his early teens. He has stolen cars, broken into people's homes, terrorized small children, and conned elderly people out of their social security checks. His parents and social workers have tried all sorts of remedies from punishment to counseling to no avail. Andre is now thirty and in prison for raping and murdering a teenage girl. The prison psychiatrist noted that Andre expresses no regret or remorse for his behavior.

X. A SAMPLING OF OTHER PSYCHOLOGICAL DISORDERS

36. **Substance-related disorders** are characterized by long-term drug use that causes physical or psychological harm to the user or others. (p. 441)

Example: Alcoholism is an example of a substance-related disorder (see Key Term 38).

37. **Addiction** is a physiological need for a substance. It is evident when a person needs more and more of a substance to achieve the desired effect. (pp. 441-442)

Example: Sheila is addicted to heroin. If she does not use heroin, she has all sorts of terrible withdrawal symptoms, including extreme nausea, chills, and fever. Her body physiologically requires heroin to ward off these symptoms.

38. **Alcoholism** is characterized by frequent and extreme consumption of alcoholic beverages. (p. 442)

Example: Nancy has been an alcoholic for twenty years. She began drinking socially when she moved to the suburbs. Eventually, she drank every day to the point of being drunk, and she finally lost her job. Her children have suffered because they do not have regular meals, cannot bring their friends home, and often hear their parents argue about their mother's drinking.

XI. MENTAL ILLNESS AND THE LAW

CONCEPTS AND EXERCISES

No. 1: Choosing a Jury

Completing this exercise should help you to achieve Learning Objective 2.

Connie, a fifty-year-old woman, has killed her husband. She has pleaded not guilty and will stand trial. The prosecution and the defense lawyer are now in the process of selecting jurors. Connie's lawyer will attempt to convince the jury that, although she has committed a crime, the long-standing physical and mental abuse that she and her children endured makes her behavior understandable. She should, therefore, receive a lesser sentence.

Connie's lawyer will want jurors with a particular approach to defining abnormality. Each juror will be presented with the following list of behaviors and asked if he or she thinks that the behaviors are abnormal and why.

- Getting drunk and singing at the top of your lungs
- Leading a hunger strike outside the White House
- Having a very high IQ
- Owning one hundred cats

If you were Connie's lawyer, which of the following two prospective jurors would you choose?

Prospective juror one: I think there are times when the situation calls for a little celebration. I remember when my first grandchild was born. I whooped it up a little myself. As for a hunger strike, well, I think that some people, because of the circumstances in their lives, have been mistreated in this society. Someone should protest for them.

I knew this fella who is powerful smart, and he is a bit strange, but heck, if we didn't have people who were a little bit different, the world would be an awful boring place.

'Bout them cats. Hmmm. I had an aunt who had more cats than she did hairs on her head. She loved those varmints as if they were kids. She wasn't any stranger than the other folk that I knew. She just didn't have anybody living at home anymore, and the cats gave her

something to care for and love. Everybody needs something to love.

Prospective juror two: The law strictly forbids drinking where I live, and based on that, I think people should not do it. Furthermore, if people want to change the system, they should do it through the proper channels. Holding a hunger strike is not the way to make a difference. People will only think you are a little weird if you sit on some steps and don't eat. I don't like very smart people. All the brainy people I knew in school were either uppity or nerds, not like everybody else. There are laws about the number of pets one is allowed to own, and I think that the law should be upheld at all times.

No. 2: Identifying Anxiety Disorders

Completing this exercise should help you to achieve Learning Objectives 10, 11, and 12.

Match the anxiety disorder from the list below to each description.

Aminda is terrified of talking in front of people. She even gets nervous in conversations in small groups of friends. She is certain that she will say something stupid and make a fool of herself. Aminda has a(n) _____.

Lindsey worries about germs all the time. She constantly frets that if she doesn't keep her house, clothing, and body clean enough, germs will take over and cause the spread of a dread disease. As a result of her constant worries, Lindsey cleans her house, clothes, and body incessantly. Immediately after washing her hands (or washing anything, for that matter), she feels a brief sense of relief. But the worry returns shortly, and she again feels the need to clean. Lindsey has _____.

Maury has been feeling really anxious lately, but he can't pinpoint exactly what he is worried about. Lately, he has been so worried in general that it has started to interfere with his work because he can't concentrate. Maury has _____.

Jean is in the middle of teaching her class, when she begins to experience a racing heart, chest pains, and difficulty breathing. Jean thinks she has a heart attack and is taken immediately to the emergency room. Upon being examined at the emergency room, though, Jean is told that she shows no evidence of a heart attack. She continues to experience more and more of these episodes in various situations. Jean has a(n) _____.

- social phobia
- panic disorder
- generalized anxiety disorder
- obsessive-compulsive disorder

CRITICAL THINKING

Sam and Martina are taking a break. Sam is reading the paper, and says to Martina, "Hey, listen to this story. There is a rise in the number of cases of multiple personality disorder here in town! In fact, according to this therapist, the number of cases is up at least 50%! I knew this town was getting stranger and stranger."

Martina listens carefully to Sam and replies, "It's not called multiple personality disorder anymore, Sam. Now the appropriate term is dissociative identity disorder. And let me see that article! Is the number of cases up only due to the diagnoses of that one therapist?"

Sam looks at the article and answers, "Yes, all the other therapists report a similar number of diagnoses as in past years. And in fact, those numbers remain pretty low. I guess this therapist is just specially trained to diagnose it better. He does specialize in hypnosis, which probably helps."

Martina muses, "I wouldn't be too sure about that, Sam. I bet there could be another explanation."

Using the five critical thinking questions in your text, the clues in the story, and what you have learned about psychological disorders, answer the following:

1. What is Sam's hypothesis?

2. What evidence supports Sam's hypothesis?

3. What is Martina's alternative hypothesis?

4. What evidence supports Martina's hypothesis? What other evidence might Martina need?

5. What conclusions are reasonable?

PERSONAL LEARNING ACTIVITIES

1. Write descriptions of behaviors you observed in the last month that you think are unusual. Evaluate them using each of the criteria (statistical infrequency, personal suffering, norm violation). Was one criterion more likely than the others to be labeled abnormal? According to the practical approach, are the behaviors abnormal? (Learning Objective 2)

2. Choose a disorder—perhaps the one you described in Personal Learning Activity 1—and describe what a psychodynamic, a social-cognitive, a biological, and a phenomenological theorist would believe caused the disorder. (Learning Objectives 4 and 5)

3. Consider the predictors of suicidal behavior. How could these predictors be used in a college dorm setting to insure that students at risk for suicide receive treatment before they take such desperate measures? How could you train Resident Hall Assistants to identify at-risk students and to get those students to the help they need? Find out what resources are available for at-risk students on your college campus, and design a plan for how to get assistance to at-risk students. (Learning Objective 20)

4. Go to the library and check out a casebook of psychological disorders. Find a case dealing with schizophrenia, and then try to identify examples of each of the following symptoms: any delusion (ideas of reference, thought broadcasting, etc.), any hallucination, neologisms, loose associations, word salad, and catatonia. (Learning Objectives 22, 23, 24, and 25)

5. Examine recent newspapers for reports on the use of the insanity defense. Of the reports on court cases generally, what percentage of cases can you identify that involve the insanity defense? Does this type of defense appear to get more press than the more standard court proceedings? Do you think that increased press coverage of cases involving mentally ill clients could create the perception that this defense allows people to "get away with murder?" (Learning Objective 32)

WHAT SHOULD I WRITE ABOUT?

Psychological Disorders is a chapter full of potentially fascinating term paper topics. Most students will not have difficulty identifying a topic of interest here. Any one of the sets of psychological disorders—anxiety, somatoform, dissociative, mood, personality, and substance-related disorders—would make a very interesting term paper topic. Most students, however, find it more difficult to shape the paper beyond identifying the initial, superficial topic. Yet, there are many strategies for doing this.

One strategy that helps to shape a topic further is to force yourself to go beyond the superficial in choosing your topic. Don't decide to write about "anxiety disorders." Determine what it is you want to write about anxiety disorders. Do you want to know more about the criteria for diagnosis? Do you want to study the sociocultural issues involved in diagnosing anxiety disorders? Or do you want to write a descriptive paper that contrasts the various types of anxiety disorders to each other? Determine what it is you want to learn about the superficial topic, and then make that more specific determination *your* term paper topic.

Once you've shaped your topic beyond the superficial, you can develop an outline that explores that topic from multiple perspectives, as we discussed doing in the previous chapter. After examining the research on your topic, spend some time determining what different perspectives exist. For example, what would a psychodynamic theorist say is the cause of a dissociative disorder? How does that perspective differ from the social-cognitive view understanding of those same disorders? Are there any other perspectives that should be considered? Once you have identified your perspectives that will help you to determine your outline. Probably you will have a main point for each one of the perspectives you identified in your research. It would be wise to then have an additional main point devoted to evaluating the validity of each of these perspectives, and then another devoted to making your conclusions explicit.

Once you've developed your outline, you are ready to write. Don't let yourself get frozen at writing the first line. The point of a first draft of any paper is to get *something* out there on the paper. Just write. You can make it sound better in the next review. Having the outline should facilitate writing the first draft, because you know specifically what you should be writing about. Stay focused on your outline, and get that information and analysis in your first draft. You can concentrate on improving what you write when you draw up your second draft of the paper. Very few excellent writers get their papers right the first time. What makes excellent writers excellent is their willingness to review their work and make changes to improve it. But you can't do that until you have something to work with, so go ahead and work on your first draft.

Here are questions to consider as you work:

1. Have you narrowed your topic enough, or is it still too superficial to be helpful to you?

2. What perspectives do you see in the literature you have reviewed for your paper? Which perspective seems most believable?

3. Have you developed an outline around those perspectives and the evaluation of them? Are you using that outline to develop your first draft?

THE INTERNET

The Psychabilities web site that accompanies this text offers many resources relevant to this chapter. They include NetLab exercises, Thinking Critically and Evaluating Research exercises, ACE chapter quizzes, recommended web links, and articles on current events, books, and movies. Go to http://college.hmco.com, select Psychology, and then this textbook.

MULTIPLE-CHOICE QUESTIONS

SAMPLE QUIZ 1

1. The impaired functioning criterion is most associated with which approach to defining abnormality?
   a. Statistical infrequency
   b. Psychopathological
   c. Norm violation
   d. Practical

2. Zelda is depressed. She is sitting in her cell after being condemned as a witch, according to the criteria set by the church. What model of abnormal behavior do her prosecutors believe in?
   a. Supernatural
   b. Medical
   c. Psychodynamic
   d. Phenomenological

3. The DSM-IV lists five axes for diagnosticians to use in evaluating people. Which of the following is *not* covered in one of the axes?
   a. Major psychological disorder description
   b. Physical condition
   c. Stress level
   d. Social status

4. Frank is so afraid of getting sick at the dinner table and being humiliated that he will not eat at a restaurant. Frank has
   a. a specific phobia.
   b. agoraphobia.
   c. a social phobia.
   d. an obsessive-compulsive disorder.

5. Karen always worries that she forgot to lock the door. In fact, she worries so much, that she often has to go back and check that she locked the door up to ten times before she leaves for the day. Worrying that she forgot to lock the door is a(n) _____, but repeatedly checking the door is a(n) _____.
   a. panic disorder; phobia
   b. phobia; panic disorder
   c. obsession; compulsion
   d. compulsion; obsession

6. "Massive repression of unwanted impulses or memories is responsible for dissociative disorders," is most likely a quote from a _____ theorist.
   a. social-cognitive
   b. phenomenological
   c. psychodynamic
   d. sociocultural

7. Nuwanda and a classmate are talking when Mary approaches and calls Nuwanda "Paul." Although Nuwanda explains that he's from Dallas, Mary convincingly argues that he is Paul, her next-door neighbor in Chicago for twenty years. Nuwanda's identification card confirms that his name is Paul, but he insists that he has no memory of living in Chicago or of being called Paul. Nuwanda/Paul most likely has
   a. dissociative amnesia.
   b. dissociative fugue.
   c. a conversion disorder.
   d. schizophrenia.

8. Philip displays bipolar disorder. Which statement would best describe him?
   a. He is sometimes very depressed and sometimes in a pleasant mood.
   b. He is alternately depressed and wildly elated.
   c. He has sudden onsets of depression that last for a few hours and then he feels fine.
   d. His disorder is a very common one.

9. Chris has been really down for the past couple of years. He just can't seem to shake the sadness that he constantly experiences. He is still fully functional at work, so it isn't as if this is really impairing his functioning seriously, but he is starting to wonder what is wrong. Chris probably has
   a. depression.
   b. dysthymic disorder.
   c. cyclothymic disorder.
   d. pain disorder.

10. Leslie has experienced a lot of pressure from her folks to become a concert violinist. She really just wants to be a normal kid. As the stress mounts, Leslie seems to develop paralysis from her wrist through her fingers, a condition known as glove anesthesia. Her parents are alarmed because this paralysis interferes with her violin career. But Leslie's doctors find no physiological explanation for the paralysis. Leslie has
    a. conversion disorder.
    b. hypochondriasis.
    c. somatization disorder.
    d. pain disorder.

11. Maggie's mother notices that Maggie has become much less concerned about her appearance and hygiene lately, but what concerns her even more is that Maggie seems to giggle inappropriately and has difficulty in communicating. When Maggie's mother asks her what is wrong, Maggie replies, "Nothing something bumpthing. I cannot say play day may lay." What disorder does Maggie most likely have?
    a. catatonic schizophrenia
    b. disorganized schizophrenia
    c. bipolar disorder
    d. dissociative identity disorder

12. While visiting a psychiatric ward, you overhear one of the patients deliver the following monologue: "Thereby the obfuscation incipient to redundant and undeniably factual parapsychosis is left in a state transcendental to the issue of man's inhumanity to buildings and federal income tax." This type of communication is called
    a. word salad.
    b. clang association.
    c. insertion
    d. attention association.

13. Andy is a charming, intelligent fellow. He often gets his roommates to loan him their cars, in spite of the fact that he rarely does anything in return for them. One night Andy wrecks his roommate's car. He doesn't even bother to apologize for it. Andy probably has _____ personality disorder.
    a. narcissistic
    b. antisocial
    c. obsessive-compulsive
    d. paranoid

14. Which of the following is a risk for substance abusers?
    a. AIDS
    b. Poor nutrition
    c. Suicide
    d. All of the above

15. Jimmie has been accused of murdering his young child. His lawyer claims that Jimmie is unable to understand the charges against him, and consequently can't even participate in his own defense. If Jimmie's lawyer is able to prove this, Jimmie will be declared
    a. not guilty by reason of insanity.
    b. guilty but mentally ill.
    c. mentally incompetent to stand trial.
    d. guilty.

Total Correct (See answer key) _____

SAMPLE QUIZ 2

Use this quiz to reassess your learning after taking Quiz 1 and reviewing the chapter.

1. According to the infrequency criterion, behavior would be considered abnormal if it
   a. caused discomfort.
   b. was uncommon.
   c. was bizarre but situationally appropriate.

d. impaired a person's ability to function.

2. Michael is reacting poorly to the news that his closest friend is dead. He is experiencing insomnia and sometimes believes he hears his friend's voice. After his condition worsens, Michael is diagnosed with schizophrenia. Ellyn maintains that Michael is having difficulties in coping because he inherited a predisposition towards schizophrenia, but she says it never would have appeared if he hadn't lost his closest friend. Ellyn is explaining Michael's abnormal behavior using the _____ model.
   a. diathesis-stress
   b. cognitive-behavioral
   c. supernatural
   d. phenomenological

3. Which of the following is no longer contained in the current DSM?
   a. Bipolar disorder
   b. Neurosis disorder
   c. Generalized anxiety disorder
   d. All are contained in the current DSM.

4. Because Shantha has recurring thoughts about losing her belongings, she is continually checking the location of knickknacks and making sure her doors are locked. Shantha's strange behavior is most likely
   a. an obsession.
   b. a compulsion.
   c. due to mania.
   d. due to a conversion disorder.

5. Tiffany is terrified of spiders. She is so terrified that when she sees one, she is unable to function effectively until someone has removed the spider from her presence. Tiffany has a(n)
   a. social phobia.
   b. agoraphobia.
   c. specific phobia.
   d. panic disorder.

6. Dr. Arenas, who has a psychodynamic orientation, is seeing a client with a conversion disorder. What will Dr. Arenas most likely say is the explanation for the patient's conversion disorder?
   a. The client has been reinforced for showing fear.
   b. The client's unconscious conflicts produced anxiety, which showed itself as a physical symptom.
   c. The client's repressed memories may have caused the amnesia.
   d. The client views the world as an unfriendly place.

7. The difference between dissociative fugue and dissociative amnesia is that

a. dissociative fugue involves the creation of a new identity and dissociative amnesia does not.
b. dissociative amnesia involves the creation of a new identity and dissociative fugue does not.
c. there is not difference between these two terms.
d. fugue involves the creation of multiple identities and amnesia does not.

8. Which of the following is NOT a characteristic one with dissociative identity disorder is likely to have?
   a. They are likely to have experienced severe abuse.
   b. They are likely to be skilled at self-hypnosis.
   c. They can escape trauma of abuse by creating new personalities.
   d. They are likely to have genius level IQ's.

9. Dysthymic disorder is to _____ as cyclothymic disorder is to _____.
   a. depression; mania
   b. depression; bipolar disorder
   c. mania; depression
   d. bipolar disorder; depression

10. Mercedes has just brought home a dog from the pound. She was told that the dog's previous owners kept it on a leash and beat it daily for no reason. Mercedes notices that when the neighborhood kids bother the dog, it does not even try to run away. Mercedes' dog most likely has
    a. generalized anxiety.
    b. learned helplessness.
    c. hypersensitive brainstem mechanisms.
    d. enlarged ventricles.

11. Javan is a schizophrenic. He says to his therapist, "You are by schlopfer." When Javan uses the term "schlopfer" he means "good friend." Which symptom of schizophrenia is Javan manifesting in his use of this term?
    a. word salad
    b. ideas of reference
    c. neologisms
    d. loose associations

12. Abraham is a catatonic schizophrenic. Which of the following symptoms is he most likely to exhibit?
    a. Alternation between bizarre poses and wild excitement
    b. Unorganized delusions, inappropriate giggling, and incoherent speech
    c. Delusions of grandeur and argumentativeness
    d. Strong fear of disease

13. What type of personality disorder would you expect to find among people in jail for fraud?
    a. Autistic
    b. Depressive
    c. Antisocial

d. Mood

14. Victor, a ten-year-old, tells a psychologist that he first came to the court system after setting a car on fire at age eight. In the numerous police contacts since then, he has been accused of theft, assault, and willful destruction of property. Victor most likely has
    a. autistic disorder.
    b. narcissistic personality disorder.
    c. conduct disorder.
    d. schizotypal personality disorder.

15. Which of the following are part of the McNaughton rule?
    a. Understanding what one is doing.
    b. Knowing what one did was wrong.
    c. Ability to resist the impulse to do wrong.
    d. Both A and B.

Total Correct (See answer key) _____

ANSWERS TO CONCEPTS AND EXERCISES

No. 1: Choosing a Jury

Connie's lawyer wants jurors who define abnormal behavior from the practical approach. He wants jurors who think that her behavior is understandable given the context or situation of her home life. Connie's lawyer should choose prospective juror 1. When evaluating the abnormality of each behavior listed, this person considers the context as well as the content of the behavior. Prospective juror 2 is very concerned about the frequency of behaviors (the statistical infrequency criterion) and the social rules about behaviors based on the legal system (the norm violation criterion). (pp. 410–411)

No. 2: Identifying Anxiety Disorders

° Aminda has a *social phobia*. She is very worried about public embarrassment, regardless of the specific situation. (p. 421)

° Lindsey has *obsessive-compulsive disorder*. Her constant worries about cleanliness and germs are obsessions (persistent thoughts), and her repeated cleaning behaviors are compulsions (repetitive action). (p. 422)

° Maury has *generalized anxiety disorder*. His worry is unfocused on a particular issue, unlike Aminda's phobia (anxiety focused on public embarrassment) and Lindsey's obsessive-compulsive disorder (anxiety focused on cleanliness). Because the reason for his anxiety can't be identified, we say his anxiety is general in nature; hence the name of his disorder. (p. 421)

° Jean has *panic disorder*. Her anxiety is very focused and takes on the form of physical symptoms like chest pain. Jean's mistaking her symptoms for a heart attack is very common among people experiencing panic disorder. (p. 421)

ANSWERS TO CRITICAL THINKING

1. Sam believes that the number of cases of dissociative identity disorder have actually increased.

2. The evidence is that, at least for one therapist, the number of cases diagnosed has increased by 50%.

3. Martina hypothesizes that the number of actual cases has not increased; rather, that this particular therapist who has seen an increase is overdiagnosing dissociative identity disorder.

4. The evidence is that only this therapist has seen an increase, while other therapists have not. Furthermore, the therapist who has seen an increase in the number of diagnoses also specializes in hypnosis. Because hypnosis creates a state of heightened suggestibility, this therapist may be able to elicit behavior consistent with dissociative identity disorder that might not otherwise appear. It would be helpful if Martina knew how the therapist used hypnosis in the diagnosis process.

5. Martina can't draw any conclusions until she obtains additional evidence about the way that this therapist is using hypnosis, and how this therapist goes about diagnosing his clients as having dissociative identity disorder.

ANSWERS TO MULTIPLE-CHOICE QUESTIONS

Circle the question numbers you answered correctly.

Sample Quiz 1

1. *d* is the answer. The impaired functioning criterion, part of the practical approach, asks whether a person can display the behavior in question and still meet the demands of everyday life. (p. 411)
   a, c. The impaired functioning criterion is not part of the statistical infrequency or norm violation criteria.
   b. Psychopathology, another word for mental illness, is not an approach to defining abnormality.

2. *a* is the answer. From the fifth to the fifteenth centuries, supernatural explanations of behavior disorders dominated. Religious leaders played a large role in deciding who was a witch or a heretic. (p. 411-412)
    b. The medical model says that abnormal behavior is caused by physical problems, not sorcery.
    c. The psychodynamic approach suggests that unconscious conflicts guide our behavior. A psychodynamic therapist would not classify someone as a witch.
    d. The phenomenological model suggests that we strive toward self-improvement.

3. *d* is the answer. (p. 416)
    a, b, c. The five axes comprise major disorder description, mental retardation or personality disorders, physical condition, stress level, and highest functioning level.

4. *c* is the answer. Never displaying a behavior in public, such as eating or writing, for fear of humiliation is called a social phobia. Frank is afraid that he will embarrass himself by getting sick in public, so he refuses to eat at restaurants. (p. 421)
    a. Specific phobias include fear of objects or situations, such as heights, dogs, or air travel, but do not include any social factors. In other words, people may have a fear of spiders and not feel worried that their fear will humiliate them.
    b. Agoraphobia is a fear of leaving one's home and, sometimes, of being alone.
    d. Obsessive-compulsive disorder is characterized by taking great pains to be organized, neat, clean, or particular about details or by recurring, unpleasant thoughts.

5. *c* is the answer. Persistent, worrisome thoughts are obsessions, and repetitious behavior that is driven by the thoughts refers to compulsions. (p. 422)
    a, b. Neither of the symptoms described reflects panic disorder or a phobia. A panic disorder refers to an intense wave of panic, including physical symptoms such as chest pain and dizziness. A phobia is an intense fear of some specific situation, but with no compulsive behavior accompanying it.
    d. This answer is backwards to the correct answer. See explanation for *c* above.

6. *c* is the answer. Dissociative disorders involve some degree of disruption in memory, consciousness, or personal identity. According to the psychodynamic model, psychological disorders are caused by unresolved unconscious psychological conflicts. When they threaten to become conscious and cause anxiety, the individual finds a way to keep them in the unconscious. To accomplish this, some people may forget not only unconscious material but also who they are or any of the personal bits of information that identify them. (pp. 425-426)
    a. A cognitive-behavioral theorist would say that an individual has been rewarded in some way for dissociating. Perhaps distressing anxiety is removed when the person forgets her or his identity or escapes into another personality.
    b. A phenomenological (or humanistic) theorist would say that an individual's multiple personalities actually represent the overt expression of dramatically conflicting perceptions of the world.
    d. A sociocultural theorist would look to society, the environment, and social roles for the cause of a disorder.

7. *b* is the answer. Paul has not only forgotten about his previous life, but he has moved to a new location and assumed a new identity as a student named Nuwanda. (p. 426)
    a. Dissociative amnesia is forgetting personally relevant information, but one does not move to a new location and create a new identity.
    c. Conversion disorders are a type of somatoform disorder in which people experience physical symptoms, like paralysis, that do not have a physical cause.
    d. Schizophrenia is characterized by more disordered thoughts and perceptions.

8. *b* is the answer. A bipolar disorder belongs to the family of affective disorders because it involves changes in mood and, consequently, behavior. (p. 429)
    a, c. A pleasant mood is normal, so there is only one symptom present in each answer: depression. Both mania and depression must be present before a bipolar disorder is suspected.
    d. Bipolar disorders are very rare (one out of a hundred) compared with depression (thirty out of a hundred).

9. *b* is the answer. Chris had dysthymia. This is a less intense sadness than major depression, but it tends to persist much longer than major depressive episodes. (p. 428)
    a. Depression is usually such an intense sadness that it interferes with ones functioning. Also, it usually would not last for as long as dysthymic disorder.
    c. Cyclothymic disorder refers to a less intense pattern of mood swings. One would alternate between happiness and sadness. Chris only experiences sadness.

d. Pain disorder is a somatoform disorder. It has nothing to do with abnormal experiences of mood.

10. *a* is the answer. Leslie has "converted" her psychological stress about being forced into a violin career to a physical symptom, glove anesthesia, that interferes with that career. (p. 424)
   b. Hypochondriasis involves a person developing an expertise in some dread disease, interpreting vague symptoms as symptoms of that disease, and constantly seeking medical treatment for those symptoms and that disease.
   c. Somatization disorder involves a person constantly seeking medical treatment for vague symptoms. It differs from hypochondriasis in that the person does not develop an expertise or focus on a particular disease.
   d. Pain disorder involves complaints of severe, constant pain. Leslie is not experiencing pain.

11. *b* is the answer. Disorganized schizophrenia is characterized by unrelated delusions and hallucinations, inappropriate laughter, and neglected personal hygiene. (p. 435)
   a. The most notable feature of catatonic schizophrenia is its disordered movement. A person may vary between wild excitement and total immobility.
   c. Bipolar disorder is a mood disorder in which a person varies from depression to mania.
   d. Dissociative identity disorder is a disorder in which a person has two or more personalities that speak, write, think, and act in different ways.

12. *a* is the answer. Schizophrenics typically have disorders of thought, both in content and form. Problems with form include word salad—that is, communication that is just a jumble of words. (p. 433)
   b. Clang associations are disorders of thought, but they usually involve words that rhyme or have double meanings.
   c. Schizophrenics complaining of thought insertions (a thought content disorder) believe that other people are placing thoughts in their heads.
   d. There is no such thing as attention association. (You are probably confusing two symptoms of schizophrenia: loose associations and disorders of attention.)

13. *b* is the answer. Andy, while charming and smart, displays no remorse for something that most "decent" people feel remorseful for. This is a characteristic of antisocial personality disorder. (p. 438)

a. Narcissistic personality disorder is in the same cluster as antisocial personality disorder, but has as its main symptom an exaggerated sense of self-importance.
c. Obsessive-compulsive personality disorder is in the anxious-fearful cluster of personality disorders, and emphasizes behavior similar to obsessive-compulsive disorder.
d. Paranoid personality disorder is in the odd-eccentric cluster, and emphasizes paranoia as a pervasive, personality trait.

14. *d* is the answer. Heroin and cocaine users are especially at risk for AIDS, but all substance abusers can suffer poor nutrition. Alcohol and other drugs are implicated in many suicides. (p. 443)

15. *c* is the answer. Jimmie will be declared mentally incompetent to stand trial. If he cannot participate in his own defense and understand the charges against him, he cannot even go to trial. (p. 444)
   a, b, d. If Jimmie cannot even go to trial, then none of these verdicts is possible. One must go to trial to achieve one of these verdicts.

Now turn to the quiz analysis table at the end of this chapter to find which areas you know well and which areas you need to work on. Circle the numbers in the table for items on Quiz 1 that you answered correctly.

ANSWERS TO MULTIPLE-CHOICE QUESTIONS

Circle the question numbers you answered correctly.

Sample Quiz 2

1. *b* is the answer. The statistical infrequency criterion says that a behavior is normal if many people in a given population display it, and abnormal if few people display the behavior. (p. 410)
   a. The practical approach considers the discomfort that a particular behavior causes as a factor for defining abnormality.
   c. Content and appropriateness are evaluated by the practical approach to defining abnormality.
   d. Meeting the demands of everyday life is part of the impaired functioning criterion, an important feature of the practical approach.

2. *a* is the answer. The diathesis-stress model suggests that some people inherit a tendency toward a disorder, but that it may not develop unless environmental stressors are severe. (p. 415)
   b. The cognitive-behavioral approach emphasizes learning.

c. The demonological or supernatural explanation of behavior is that it is caused by spirits or demons.

d. Perceptions are emphasized by phenomenological theorists.

3. *b* is the answer. Neither neurosis nor psychosis is contained in the DSM-IV because they are considered too vague to be of diagnostic use. (p. 416)

4. *b* is the answer. Compulsions are behaviors that the person thinks will keep harm from coming to him or herself, family, or friends. (p. 422)

a. An obsession is an unwanted, persistent thought, such as Shantha's about losing things.

c, d. Mania and conversion disorder do not cause unwanted, persistent thoughts and repetitive behaviors.

5. *c* is the answer. Tiffany has a specific phobia because she is afraid of a specific object—spiders. (p. 420)

a, b. Tiffany does not have social phobia or agoraphobia. A social phobia is fear of public embarrassment, and agoraphobia is a fear of not being able to be in a safe place. Both are more general than Tiffany's specific fear of spiders.

d. Tiffany does not have a panic disorder. It is difficult to determine what specific object or situation sets of a panic disorder. In this case, the feared object is known—spiders.

6. *b* is the answer. Conversion disorders are physical symptoms, like paralysis or blindness, without physical causes. A psychodynamic theorist would be likely to say that a person is translating an unacceptable unconscious desire or conflict into a symptom that excuses the person from the difficult situation. (p. 424)

a. The client may have been reinforced by getting out of an activity due to physical disability, but not for showing fear.

c. Repressed memories are a psychodynamic concept, but amnesia is not part of conversion disorder.

d. A phenomenological explanation would deal with such perceptions.

7. *a* is the answer. Dissociative fugue involves an individual creating a new identity to replace an old, forgotten one. Dissociative amnesia involves just forgetting important identifying information. (p. 426)

b, c, d. None of these describes the difference between these two disorders.

8. *d* is the answer. There is no evidence to suggest that individuals diagnosed with dissociative identity disorder have unusually high IQ's. (p. 426)

a, b, c. All of these tend to be true of patients with dissociative identity disorder.

9. *b* is the answer. Dysthymic disorder is a milder, but longer lasting version of depression. Cyclothymia is a milder, but longer lasting version of bipolar disorder. (p. 428)

a, c, d. None of these correctly identifies the relationship in this analogy.

10. *b* is the answer. Mercedes' dog has learned helplessness; it has learned or come to believe that its actions—barking and growling—will not control its environment by scaring the children away. (p. 431)

a. Generalized anxiety is worry and fear detached from any specific cause.

c. Hypersensitive brainstem mechanisms are associated with panic disorder in humans.

d. Enlarged ventricles are associated with schizophrenia in humans.

11. *c* is the answer. Javan is using a made up word as if it is a real word. Neologism literally means "new word," and that is exactly what Javan is doing. He is using a new word that is unfamiliar to anyone else. (p. 433)

a. Word salad involves jumbling a bunch of words together in no meaningful order. Javan's speech isn't jumbled, it just uses neologisms.

b. Ideas of reference refer to the belief that even common events are related to oneself somehow. Javan shows no evidence of this.

d. Loose associations are weak logical links between thoughts. We can't see enough of Javan's thought in this example to determine if he has loose associations or not.

12. *a* is the answer. Catatonic schizophrenia symptoms include movement extremes from immobility to wild flailing and a rejection of efforts to communicate. People with catatonic schizophrenia may show waxy flexibility, which allows them to be posed in any position. (p. 435)

b. These are more characteristic of a disorganized schizophrenic.

c. These are more characteristic of a paranoid schizophrenic.

d. Strong fear of disease is associated with hypochondriasis.

13. *c* is the answer. People in this category, also called psychopaths or sociopaths, display a long-term, persistent pattern of impulsive, selfish,

unscrupulous, and even criminal behavior. (pp. 437-438))

a. Autistic disorder is a psychological disorder of childhood. Those with autistic disorder have impaired language and social skills; therefore, they are unlikely to commit fraud.

b. Depression is a mood disorder, not a personality disorder, involving feelings of sadness and hopelessness and a loss of self-worth.

d. A mood disorder is not a personality disorder. Mood disorders, such as depression or mania, involve changes in emotions.

14. *c* is the answer. Conduct disorder falls under the externalizing category. Its primary features are aggressive, destructive, disobedient behaviors. (pp. 440-441)

a. Autistic disorder is neither an externalizing nor internalizing disorder. It is a severe condition usually diagnosed in the first 30 months of life and is characterized by ritualistic play, lack of attachment to caregivers, and lack of positive emotional expressions.

b. Narcissistic personality disorder is not a disorder of childhood and is identified when a person is egotistical, overly sensitive to criticism, and in need of attention.

d. Schizotypal personality disorder is similar to schizophrenia, but not as severe. People with this disorder may have odd beliefs, but they do not hallucinate.

15. *d* is the answer. Both understanding that what one was doing and knowing that it was wrong are known as the M'Naughton rule. (p. 444)

a, b. Both of these are part of the M'Naughton rule.

c. Being able to resist the impulse to do wrong is known as the irresistible impulse test.

Now turn to the quiz analysis table at the end of this chapter to find which areas you know well and which areas you need to work on. Circle the numbers in the table for items on Quiz 2 that you answered correctly.

For each question you answered correctly, circle its number. (Quiz 1 numbers are not shaded; Quiz 2 numbers are shaded.) Are there patterns in the types of questions or the topics you got wrong that could direct your further study? Did you improve from Quiz 1 to Quiz 2?

TOPIC	TYPE OF QUESTION		
	DEFINITION	COMPREHENSION	APPLICATION
Defining Psychological Disorders		1	
	1		
Explaining Disorders			2
			2
Classifying Disorders		3	
		3	
Anxiety Disorders			4, 5
			4, 5
Somatoform Disorders			10
			6
Dissociative Disorders		6	7
		7, 8	
Mood Disorders			8, 9
		9	10
Schizophrenia			11, 12
			11, 12
Personality Disorders			13
			13
Other Psychological Disorders		14	
			14
Mental Illness and the Law			15
	15		

TOTAL CORRECT BY QUIZ:

QUIZ 1:
QUIZ 2:

Chapter 13

Treatment of Psychological Disorders

LEARNING OBJECTIVES

1. Define psychotherapy. (p. 452)

2. Describe the common features of treatments. Compare and contrast psychiatrists, psychologists and other types of therapists. Describe the approach of an eclectic therapist. (pp. 452–453)

3. Describe the history, goals, and methods of psychoanalysis. Describe the differences between classical psychoanalysis and its modern variations. (pp. 453–455)

4. Describe the theoretical basis of the phenomenological approach to therapy. List the four assumptions on which phenomenological therapists operate. (pp. 455-456)

5. Describe client-centered therapy. Define and discuss the importance of unconditional positive regard, empathy, reflection, and congruence in this therapy. Compare and contrast client-centered therapy with Gestalt therapy. (pp. 456–458)

6. Define behavior therapy. Describe its basic features and the assumptions on which it is based. Explain the differences among behavior therapy, behavior modification, and cognitive-behavior therapy. (pp. 458–459)

7. Define systematic desensitization, modeling, assertiveness training, token economy, flooding, aversive conditioning, and the other behavioral methods of therapy. Give an example of each. Specify the type of learning (classical or operant

conditioning) each method is based on. (pp. 459-462)

8. Define cognitive-behavior therapy. Describe rational-emotive behavior therapy, cognitive restructuring, stress inoculation training, and Beck's cognitive therapy. (pp. 462–464)

9. Define and discuss the benefits of group, family, and couples therapy. (pp. 464–465)

10. Discuss the results of research that has attempted to evaluate the overall effectiveness of psychotherapy. Discuss the question of whether one approach to psychotherapy is better than the others. (pp. 466–468)

11. Discuss the controversy surrounding the use of empirically-supported therapies. List the questions that a potential client must consider before choosing a therapist and treatment approach. (pp. 468–471)

12. Discuss the importance of training psychotherapists to be sensitive to cultural factors in treatment. (pp. 471-472)

13. Describe the rules governing therapists and the rights held by clients in therapeutic relationships. (p. 472)

14. Describe the historical and present use of electroconvulsive therapy (ECT). (pp. 473–474)

15. Define neuroleptic (antipsychotic), antidepressant, lithium, and anxiolytic, and specify which is used for what type of psychological problem. Explain the side effects of these drugs. (pp. 474–476)

16. Discuss the research comparing the effectiveness of drugs with that of psychotherapy in the treatment of psychological disorders. Discuss the joint use of drugs and psychotherapy. (pp. 477-478)

17. Describe the ways that psychoactive drugs affect neurotransmitters and their receptors. Define reuptake. (p. 478)

18. Define community psychology. Describe the types of work involved in community psychologists' attempts to treat and prevent mental illness. (pp. 485, 478–480)

KEY TERMS

1. **Psychotherapy** is the treatment of psychological disorders using psychological methods, such as analyzing problems, talking about possible solutions, and encouraging more adaptive ways of thinking and acting. (p. 452)

Example: Psychoanalysis, client-centered therapy, Gestalt therapy, rational-emotive therapy, and cognitive-behavior therapy are all examples of psychotherapy.

I. BASIC FEATURES OF TREATMENT

2. **Psychiatrists** are medical doctors who specialize in the treatment of mental disorders. Psychiatrists usually use biological treatments and some psychotherapy. (p. 452)

Example: Jennifer has been feeling so anxious lately that it is really beginning to interfere with her work. She seeks help from a medical doctor who prescribes a drug to help reduce the anxiety, and who also talks with her about what might be causing the anxiety. Jennifer is seeking help from a psychiatrist.

3. **Psychologists** are people who practice some form of psychotherapy. Many have Ph.D.'s in clinical or counseling psychology and advanced specialty training. Currently, psychologists cannot by law prescribe medications to their clients. (p. 452)

Example: Jake has had an uncontrollable fear of spiders, and decides to seek help to overcome his fear. He seeks help from a therapist possessing a Ph.D. in clinical psychology who uses behavior therapy to help him overcome his fear. Jake is seeing a psychologist.

II. PSYCHODYNAMIC PSYCHOTHERAPY

4. **Psychoanalysis**, a method of psychotherapy, seeks to help clients gain insight by recognizing, understanding, and dealing with the unconscious thoughts and emotions presumed to cause their problems. Psychoanalysis also aims to help clients work through the many ways in which those unconscious causes appear in everyday behavior and social relationships. (p. 453)

Example: Jeff's therapist tells him to lay on a couch facing away from the therapist, and to share all of the thoughts that come to mind without editing out any of them at all. Jeff's therapist interprets Jeff's thoughts are representing an unresolved conflict with his father. Jeff's therapist is using psychoanalysis.

III. PHENOMENOLOGICAL PSYCHOTHERAPY

5. **Client-centered** (or **person-centered**) **therapy**, developed by Carl Rogers, assumes that a client has a drive toward self-actualization. This therapy is based on a relationship between client and therapist that is characterized by unconditional positive regard, empathy, and congruence. Wanting the client to learn to solve his

or her own problems, the therapist is nondirective and does not give advice. (p. 456)

Example: Nan is frustrated with her therapist because she never tells Nan how to solve her problems. Nan expresses this to the therapist, and the therapist reflects back to her, "You seem upset that I am not taking a more active role in determining your future. You sound a little scared about making changes to the way your life has been, which is completely understandable." Nan's is engaged in client-centered therapy.

6. **Unconditional positive regard** refers to an attitude of total acceptance and respect that a therapist must have toward a client to create a therapeutic environment. If a therapist does not express unconditional positive regard to the client, therapy will not enable the person to overcome his or her barriers to self-actualization. (p. 456)

Example: Mack admits to his therapist that he sometimes feels uncontrollable rage toward his boss. He wants to do violently awful things to him. Mack's therapist does not make Mack feel bad about these socially unacceptable feelings; rather, the therapist continues to show Mack respect as they explore together how these feelings may provide insight into the ways that Mack's job doesn't fulfill his need to self-actualize.

REMEMBER: The therapist communicates acceptance *without conditions;* even if the client admits to socially undesirable behaviors or views, the therapist is encouraging and respectful.

7. **Empathy**, an important feature of client-centered therapy, involves a therapist's trying to see the world as a client sees it. The therapist may show the client that understanding by not only listening attentively but also by reflecting what the client says. (p. 456)

Example: Yvonne came into therapy because she resented having to care for her younger sisters even though she knew that her mother was working three jobs. Yvonne's therapist must try to see the world from Yvonne's point of view and can accomplish this by understanding the constraints that Yvonne feels as a result of such tremendous responsibility.

8. **Reflection** is a method used in client-centered therapy. A therapist restates or paraphrases a client's responses in order to show that she or he is listening and to help the client be more in touch with feelings. (p. 456)

Example: Read the example for Key Term 7. The therapist might respond to Yvonne by saying, "You're tired of doing so much around the house with your sisters, which prevents you from going out and doing what you want. You're angry at your mom." The therapist has reflected what Yvonne has said, thus also demonstrating empathy.

9. **Congruence** (sometimes called genuineness) refers to a consistency in a therapist's feelings and behavior toward a client. The therapist's behavior toward the client must be a reflection of how he or she really feels; it cannot be an act. Ideally, the client will learn that openness and honesty can be the foundation of a human relationship. (p. 457)

Example: Read the examples for Key Terms 7 and 8. The therapist must genuinely feel empathy and unconditional positive regard for Yvonne. She cannot think to herself that Yvonne is spoiled and selfish. The therapist must actually accept Yvonne's feelings with unconditional positive regard for her worth as a person.

10. **Gestalt therapy** is a form of phenomenological treatment developed by Frederick Perls. A Gestalt therapist takes an active and directive role in helping a client become aware of denied feelings and impulses and learn how to discard foreign feelings, ideas, and values. Also, the therapist helps the client become more self-accepting. Methods used include dialogues with people, inanimate objects, and various body parts. (p. 457)

Example: When Renee describes how angry she became when her boss asked her to stay late, the therapist suggests they role-play the conversation between Renee and her boss. Renee finds that it really wasn't the request that made her the most angry; it was her perception that the boss assumed she had nothing better to do.

IV. BEHAVIOR THERAPY

11. **Behavior therapy** uses the principles of classical conditioning to change behavior by helping or teaching clients to act and think differently. Usually, an incorrectly learned association between a CS and a UCS is destroyed. (p. 459)

Example: Flooding and aversive conditioning are examples of behavior therapies. (See Table 13.6 on p. 476 of your text.)

12. **Behavior modification** uses the principles of operant conditioning to change behavior. (p. 459)

Example: Modeling is an example of behavior modification therapy. (See Table 13.6 on p. 476 of your text.)

13. **Systematic desensitization** is a therapy designed to reduce fears. First, the client is trained in progressive relaxation. Second, the client constructs an desensitization hierarchy. Then, the client and therapist together work their way through the hierarchy. When the client can maintain relaxation at while mentally focusing on one level of fear on the hierarchy, he or she can move to the next level. Although it initially may be stressful, the client will learn to maintain relaxation while thinking about the feared stimulus on that level. At that point, the client can continue moving through the hierarchy until he or she can maintain relaxation at all levels. (p. 459)

Example: Joe is afraid of snakes. First, his therapist trains him in how to relax his body and mind. Next, his therapist and he construct a list of things that scare him about snakes, ordering the list from least scary to most. The least scary is seeing a picture of the word snake; the most is actually holding a snake. Joe's therapist then helps him learn how to imagine himself in each scary situation on the list, starting with the least and progressing to the most, while maintaining the relaxed state.

14. **Modeling** is a behavior therapy that involves watching another perform a desired behavior. (p. 460)

Example: Priti is afraid of dogs. She watches her therapist pet various dogs, and then practices on a stuffed, toy dog at home. This process of seeing her therapist model the behavior she fears helps her overcome her fear of dogs.

15. **Assertiveness training** helps clients learn to express their feelings and stand up for their rights in situations in which they typically feel awkward and shy about doing so. (p. 460)

Example: Amber is very shy. She often gets pushed out of lines because she is too timid to assert herself. During an assertiveness training session with a group of shy people, Amber and the others take turns modeling more assertive behavior. Some people are assigned the role of "butting in line" in front of her, and Amber is to practice saying, "Excuse me, but I was here first." Amber is learning to stand up for herself.

16. **Positive reinforcement** is a behavior modification technique in which desirable behaviors are rewarded, so as to encourage their repetition. (p. 460)

Example: Mark is working with a hyperactive child. When the child completes a task without being distracted Mark rewards him with popcorn. After a while, the child has learned to work diligently on a task without being easily distracted.

17. A **token economy** is a system for reinforcing desirable behaviors with poker chips or other tokens that

can be exchanged later for desired rewards. A token economy is used primarily in institutional settings. (p. 460)

Example: Keisha is schizophrenic and is institutionalized. Her therapist gives her poker chips every time she brushes her teeth, takes a shower, and dresses herself appropriately. Keisha can then exchange these chips for TV privileges later in the day.

18. **Extinction** involves failing to reinforce an undesirable behavior, making the behavior less likely to occur in the future. (p. 460)

Example: Lizzie wants her children to learn not to interrupt adults while they are speaking. She notices that in the past, when her children have interrupted her, she has rewarded them by responding to their interruption. She decides to ignore her children when they interrupt her for non-emergencies, and respond to them only when they wait their turn. Her children quickly learn that if they want to be acknowledged, they need to politely wait their turn to speak.

19. **Flooding** is a fear-reduction treatment with extinction as its basis. It involves placing a client into the very situation they fear. When clients experience that situation and learn that no pain or injury will result, the fear subsides. (p. 461)

Example: Kirk is deathly afraid of heights. His therapist takes him to the top of the tallest building in the city and they walk around together. Although initially Kirk was terrified, he soon realizes nothing bad is going to happen and his fear subsides.

20. **Aversive conditioning** is a treatment geared towards reducing inappropriate or undesirable behaviors. It involves the client learning to associate the undesirable behavior with physical or psychological discomfort. (p. 461)

Example: Joel is an adolescent who has been getting involved in violent behavior. His parents are concerned and take him to a therapist who has Joel imagine violent behavior and then presented vivid descriptions of things Joel was afraid of. Joel learned to associated fear with violent behavior, reducing his desire to perform violent behavior. Joel experienced aversive conditioning.

21. **Punishment** is an operant conditioning technique that involves creating a negative consequence to an undesirable behavior, reducing the likelihood of repetition of the undesirable behavior. (p. 462)

Example: James is trying to teach his client to not react violently to criticism. He has tried many treatment methods, but none with success. Because his client's violent behavior has escalated to a negative level, he decides to punish his client for every violent statement or act that occurs in the context of therapy. He gives his client a mild electrical shock after each violent statement or act. James is using punishment.

22. **Cognitive-behavior therapy** attempts to pinpoint thought patterns that lead to depression, anger, or anxiety. Once these thoughts are recognized, they can be eliminated and replaced with more constructive thought patterns. (p. 462)

Example: Liza is depressed. Her therapist thinks that her depression is due to Liza's negative thought patterns. Liza often thinks, "I'm no good. No one would want to be friends with me. I don't have anyone to depend on because I have nothing to offer in a friendship." Liza's therapist works on helping Liza identify these negative thoughts, and on replacing them with more positive thoughts.

23. **Rational-emotive therapy** is a form of cognitive-behavior therapy developed by Albert Ellis. A client is taught to recognize self-defeating thought patterns and to replace them with more constructive thoughts. (p. 462)

Example: Brady is a personnel administrator. He feels uncomfortable because he is often faced with disciplinary decisions that result in angry employees. His therapist has pointed out that it is unrealistic to think that everyone will like him and be happy with his decisions all the time. Brady learns to treat people fairly and not to expect them to like all of his decisions.

24. **Cognitive therapy** consists of a type of cognitive restructuring in which a client sees that her or his depression is due in part to erroneous and illogical thought patterns. The therapist helps point out those thoughts that precede anxiety and depression and then works with the client to test the logic of those thoughts. (p. 463)

Example: Leslie is convinced that she will never be successful on her new job. As a result, she is very anxious. Her therapist helps her list the skills she will need on the new job. Then Leslie and the therapist recall past jobs where Leslie performed very well using just those skills. Leslie's therapist helps her see that her anxiety-producing thoughts about her performance are wrong.

V. GROUP, FAMILY, AND COUPLES THERAPY

25. **Group therapy** is psychotherapy conducted with groups of about five to ten people. The therapist can observe clients interacting with one another in real social situations; clients feel less alone when they realize that other people are struggling with similar problems; and clients can learn from one another. (p. 464)

Example: Misha is in a support group for teen mothers. The group members meet with a therapist once a week to discuss how things are going and to offer each other support.

26. **Family therapy** involves two or more individuals from the same family, one of whose problems make him or her the initially identified client, but the real client is the family. The goal of family therapy is to create harmony within the family by helping each member better understand the family's interactions and the problems they create. (p. 464)

Example: Robert has been hostile and depressed lately, but he is not attending therapy alone. Robert's parents and sometimes his siblings go to sessions with him. The therapist observes how the family members interact and tries to help them see how they affect each other.

27. **Couples therapy** is similar to family therapy; its focus is on communication between partners. (p. 465)

Example: Bart and Shannon are having marital difficulties. In therapy, Bart learns that when Shannon tells him about a problem she has at work, she just needs him to listen and be supportive rather than to try to "fix" the problem and coach her on how to deal with it. Shannon learns that when she criticizes Bart in an effort to help him, he feels that she doesn't think he is good enough for her. Both Bart and Shannon are learning how to improve their communication.

VI. EVALUATING PSYCHOTHERAPY

28. **Empirically-supported therapies** are therapies that have been validated by controlled research as effective for treating particular psychological disorders. (p. 469)

Example: Cognitive therapy has been identified as an empirically-supported therapy for treating depression. Other types of therapy have not been empirically supported by data showing the therapy works to improve the condition of the individual with depression.

VII. BIOLOGICAL TREATMENTS

29. **Electroconvulsive therapy (ECT)** involves passing electric current through the brain. Today, shock is applied to only one brain hemisphere, and patients are given a deep muscle relaxant prior to treatment to prevent injury. ECT is used to treat depression when other treatments have failed. (p. 473)

Example: Jess has experienced major depression. Her therapist is worried that Jess may attempt suicide, and all the therapies she has tried have failed. Jess' therapist decides to shock to part of Jess' brain after Jess has been anesthetized and given a muscle relaxant. Jess is receiving ECT.

30. **Neuroleptic (Antipsychotic)** drugs are used to treat severe psychopathology. These drugs are effective in reducing hallucinations, delusions, paranoid suspiciousness, and incoherence. Unfortunately, neuroleptics such as chlorpromazine and haloperidol can cause severe side effects such as tardive dyskinesia. (p. 474)

Example: Merina treats schizophrenics. She often finds that prescribing a Haldol can help reduce the hallucinations her patients experience.

31. **Antidepressants**, which increase levels of serotonin and norepinephrine, are useful in treating depression. This class of drugs includes monoamine oxidase inhibitors, tricyclic antidepressants, and fluoxetine. (p. 474)

Example: Prozac is an example of an antidepressent.

32. **Anxiolytics (tranquilizers)** are used to reduce anxiety, tension, and in some cases agoraphobia (Xanax). These drugs can be addictive and should not be combined with alcohol. (p. 475)

Example: Valium is an example of an anxiolytic.

VIII. COMMUNITY PSYCHOLOGY

33. **Community psychology** attempts to minimize or prevent psychological disorders. Community psychologists' efforts take two forms: attempts to eliminate causative factors of underlying psychological problems (such as poverty and inadequate or crowded housing) and early recognition of psychological problems and interventions designed to prevent problems from becoming worse. (pp. 478–480)

Example: Alyssa tries to find ways to reduce homelessness, and to get treatment to people who are homeless. She hopes that by decreasing homelessness, she will reduce the number of people who need psychological treatment in the first place, or at least reduce the severity of their problems.

CONCEPTS AND EXERCISES

No. 1: Identifying Specific Therapies

Completing this exercise should help you to achieve Learning Objective 2, 3, 4, 5, and 6.

Carly has been struggling with depression lately, and is trying to find a therapist that she is comfortable with She has had initial sessions with several therapists already. Identify the approach to therapy that each of the following therapists listed below takes.

- Dr. Daka says that to treat depression you have to help the client identify the negative thought pattern that lead to the experience of depression.

- Dr. Redmachre says that depression is a result of unconscious conflict. By bringing the conflict to consciousness in therapy, Dr. Redmachre believes it is likely to be resolved and consequently reduce the depression.

- Dr. Lightner says that if Carly wants to be in therapy, the two of them can explore what factors are blocking Carly from achieving all she can in life. Those factors are probably causing her depression. However, Dr. Lightner feels that it is not her place to offer Carly advice on what these factors are; rather, Carly can identify them herself given the appropriate support.

- Dr. Brown says that depression is a result of neurotransmitter imbalance, and a drug therapy will best help Carly.

  - Cognitive therapy
  - Gestalt therapy
  - Modeling
  - Client-centered therapy
  - Antidepressant therapy
  - Anxiolytic therapy
  - Psychoanalysis

No. 2: Differentiating Approaches to Therapy

Completing this exercise should help you to achieve Learning Objectives 3, 4,5, 8, 14, and 15.

Several psychotherapists have met at a convention to have dinner. Over coffee they argue about the various causes of abnormal behavior and mental processes. Decide what type of therapy each therapist probably practices.

Patricia: Clearly, thoughts in the unconscious drive behavior. If unconscious thoughts are revealed, the client can understand and possibly change the problematic behavior. You, on the other hand, Eliot, treat only the behavior and not the cause. _____

Eliot: What does it matter if I treat only the behavior? My goal is to create new behaviors that allow people to function in their environment. If they are functional, they will probably be successful and receive positive reinforcement, making them feel good about themselves. _____

Randa: She has a point, Eliot. If you would try to alter conscious thought patterns as I do, replacing problematic ones with functional ones, then many behaviors associated with those thoughts might change as well. _____

Ida: I think you are all a bit manipulative. We are therapists, but our clients have the ability to grow and change on their own. They just need to get in touch with their feelings. All we have to do is step back, accept them as people, and show them it's okay to accept themselves just as they are. _____

Lana: Pretty soon, you folks are going to be out of a job. When we understand how the brain works, we will be able to treat most psychological problems with drugs or corrective surgery. _____

CRITICAL THINKING

A concerned neighbor, Aida Schultz, calls the precinct with reports of an old man walking around the block. He appears to be slightly spastic and a bit dizzy and has odd dark spots on his arms and hands. She also says that the man keeps sticking his tongue out, whether there is someone in front of him or not. Other reports from this same neighborhood have been coming in regarding an old man who is scaring children. Sam and Martina go to check these reports out.

When they arrive at Aida Schultz's house, they ask where she last saw the man. She points down the block. Sam and Martina slowly cruise the street and then turn the corner.

"There he is!" cries Sam. "I bet he's the one who's been scaring all the kids around here. Let's go pick him up."

"Not so fast. There may be a reason for his symptoms," Martina remarks.

Using the five critical thinking questions in your text, the clues in the story, and what you have learned about psychotherapy, answer the following:

1. What is Sam's hypothesis?

2. What evidence supports Sam's hypothesis?

3. What is Martina's alternative hypothesis?

4. What evidence supports Martina's hypothesis? What other evidence might Martina need?

5. What conclusions are reasonable?

PERSONAL LEARNING ACTIVITIES

1. Free associate in writing for approximately fifteen minutes. Don't edit yourself, just write the thoughts that come to your mind. Then stop, and look back over what you read. How do you think a therapist practicing classic psychoanalysis would interpret what you wrote? Do you think free association is the only way to gain insight into people's problems? (Learning Objective 3)

2. Use reflection, a client-centered technique, in your next conversation with a friend. Was it difficult to summarize what your friend said? How did your friend react? (Learning Objective 5)

3. Think of a situation in which a cognitive-behavior technique could improve your reaction. Write the thing you usually say to yourself during the event and then write an alternative reaction. For example, if you tend to get nervous during exams, you could imagine what you usually say to yourself during testing situations and try to identify self-defeating thoughts. What would a rational-emotive therapist suggest that you say to yourself instead? You could write the alternatives to your usual thinking style in your notebook and look at it before your next test begins. (Learning Objective 8)

4. Interview two friends from different cultural background as to how they interpret the cause of a psychological disorder such as depression. Compare and contrast their explanations. If one cultural background is more individualist and one is more collectivist, do you see sharp differences in their explanations? How do you think that these differences might impact therapeutic success if the therapist and the client do not share the same understanding of the cause of a disorder? (Learning Objective 12)

5. Identify a local social service agency and interview a representative about the services they provide. How are the goals of the agency consistent with the goals of community psychology? Are there areas in which the agency's goals diverge from community psychology's goals? Are there gaps that you think a community psychologist could fill at the agency? (Learning Objective 18)

WHAT SHOULD I WRITE ABOUT?

In the previous chapter, we talked about writing about a single issue from multiple perspectives. Interpreting something from multiple viewpoints leads naturally to the question of which viewpoint has the most validity. Although many issues do not have a single viewpoint that has the market cornered on "truth," this question does bring up how important it is to evaluate the quality of information that you present in a term paper. You may find it interesting to write a term paper with the purpose of the paper being to evaluate the quality of existing information, with the ultimate goal being to forecast where future research needs to be focused. Evaluating the quality of information is at the heart of critical thinking.

You can use the five critical thinking questions discussed in each chapter of your textbook as a model of how to evaluate information. If your term paper's goal is to evaluate information, you must spend only part of your time writing about what existing research has found. A greater percentage of your writing in this type of paper should emphasize the credibility of those findings. You want to question if the conclusions were appropriate given the research methods used. You should ask yourself if the findings' generalizability is limited in any way. Aggressively question the basis of a finding using the five critical thinking questions, and then decide if the finding is believable or not.

Once you have evaluated a set of studies, you may find it useful to then back up and ask yourself about the quality of the position as a whole. Sometimes it is easy for young students of psychology to get bogged down in critiquing findings study by study, and they never really get to see the big picture. If you want to evaluate the quality of a position as a whole, you need to ask yourself if the problems or limitations that you identified in each study balance themselves out across the studies you reviewed. For example, is all the research you could find experimental in nature? If so, then even if the studies all agree in their findings, all the findings exist in the context of an experiment—a fairly artificial setting. The position would be stronger if the research was more balanced in methodology—some experiments, some naturalistic observations (field studies), and some surveys. If all studies agreed in their findings in spite of these vastly different methods, you would be able to have more confidence in the strength of that position. You will probably find it useful to review Chapter 1 if you write a paper about this, as much of the information in that chapter on research methods will be useful here.

Treatment of Psychological Disorders is a chapter that really lends itself to this type of term paper. Many topics in this chapter would be interesting to critique. Take any therapeutic method—cognitive therapy, flooding, client-centered therapy, drug treatments—and evaluate the effectiveness of that treatment on different psychological disorders. To do this, you have to be able to evaluate the quality of the evidence suggesting a treatment method is good or bad. Don't forget to use the five critical thinking questions as you do so:

1. What am I being asked to believe or accept?

2. Is there evidence available to support the claim?

3. Can that evidence be interpreted in another way?

4. What evidence would help to evaluate the alternatives?

5. What conclusions are most reasonable?

THE INTERNET

The Psychabilities web site that accompanies this text offers many resources relevant to this chapter. They include NetLab exercises, Thinking Critically and Evaluating Research exercises, ACE chapter quizzes, recommended web links, and articles on current events, books, and movies. Go to http://college.hmco.com, select Psychology, and then this textbook.

MULTIPLE-CHOICE QUESTIONS

SAMPLE QUIZ 1

1. The common features of any type of therapy include
   a. a client or patient.
   b. someone socially accepted as being able to help the client.
   c. a theoretical approach to understanding and treating the client's problems.
   d. all of the above.

2. As Dwayne prepares for an exam, he comments to his friend, Rerun, "This test is gonna be a seize." Rerun says, "A seize? Don't you mean 'a breeze?' " A _____ therapist would be most likely to think that Dwayne's comment indicates that he unknowingly fears freezing up during the exam and can't admit to it consciously.
   a. behavioral
   b. community
   c. phenomenological
   d. psychodynamic

3. Karma is a contemporary psychoanalyst. She tries to identify her clients' poor relationships during their formative years, and to provide a second chance within a therapeutic context for those relationships. She sees herself as the nurturing caregiver who will make up for support that was absent in infancy. Which contemporary psychoanalytic approach to therapy does Karma take?
   a. object relations
   b. supportive-expressive
   c. client-centered
   d. Gestalt

4. Phil is a psychotherapist who feels that it is very important that all his clients feel that he has high regard for them as people, no matter what issues come up in therapy. Which therapeutic orientation is most consistent with this perspective?
   a. short-term psychoanalysis
   b. client-centered therapy
   c. cognitive-behavioral therapy
   d. ECT therapy

5. Which of the following is not true of Gestalt therapy?
   a. It seeks to improve client self-awareness.
   b. It emphasizes unique, individual perceptions
   c. It emphasizes unconscious conflict.
   d. It uses dramatic methods like role-playing.

6. Which of the following statements is most consistent with behavior therapy's approach to the treatment of psychological disorders?
   a. People need the right context to self-actualize.
   b. Disorders should be treated medically.
   c. Psychological disorders are just learned behaviors.
   d. We need to identify the underlying cause of disordered behavior.

7. Lia is trying to help her client overcome her fear of dogs. She locks her client in a room full of friendly, harmless Chinese pugs. Although her client is initially terrified, she eventually calms down and realizes there is nothing to fear from most dogs. Lia is using a treatment technique known as
   a. systematic desensitization.
   b. in vivo desensitization.
   c. modeling.
   d. flooding.

8. Jane has been depressed for a while. Her therapist tells her that she experiences depression because Jane thinks the following types of thoughts all the time, "I can't do anything right. No one will ever think I am competent or worthwhile." Her therapist suggests that these thoughts are false beliefs that Jane has learned to think, and that their therapy should focus on replacing those thoughts with more positive, accurate thought processes. Jane's therapist is most likely using which treatment approach?
   a. Beck's cognitive therapy

b. Aversive conditioning
c. Neuroleptic therapy
d. Rational-emotive therapy

9. When Shau-Jin is angry at Wendy, he often says things like, "Why do you always criticize me?" and, "You're such a nag!" The therapy that would focus most on their communication pattern would be
a. couples therapy.
b. extinction.
c. rational emotive therapy (RET).
d. psychoanalysis.

10. An empirically supported therapy is one that
a. has data showing it is effective at treating all psychological disorders.
b. has data showing it is effective for particular psychological disorders.
c. has no data supporting it.
d. is culturally sensitive.

11. Julia is a psychotherapist. She has been experiencing a strong physical attraction to one of her clients lately. What can Julia ethically do about her attraction to her client?
a. Initiate a sexual relationship with him immediately.
b. Wait until the therapeutic relationship has ended and then ask him out.
c. Julia must wait at least two years before asking him out, to make sure the attraction is real.
d. Julia must wait for the therapeutic relationship to have been over for two years before asking him out, for her client's protection.

12. Which of the following psychological disorders is would be the best candidate for ECT?
a. schizophrenia
b. major depression
c. bipolar disorder
d. mania

13. Tico is talking incoherently and is experiencing so many hallucinations and delusions that her psychiatrist will most likely prescribe a(n)
a. antidepressant.
b. anxiolytic.
c. depressant.
d. neuroleptic.

14. Keisha believes that most psychological disorders can be effectively treated with drug therapies. Keisha prefers the _____ approach to treatment.
a. phenomenological
b. psychoanalytic
c. biological
d. cognitive-behavioral

15. Michel has spent the morning teaching preschool teachers the early signs of psychological problems, hoping that children can be helped before their problems become severe. What kind of psychologist is Michel?
a. Biological
b. Rational-emotive
c. Community
d. None of the above

Total Correct (See answer key) _____

SAMPLE QUIZ 2

Use this quiz to reassess your learning after taking Quiz 1 and reviewing the chapter.

1. Malinda is receiving treatment for depression, and as part of her treatment she is taking Prozac. To treat her in this manner, Malinda's therapist must be a(n)
a. psychologist.
b. psychiatrist.
c. licensed social worker.
d. licensed counselor.

2. Troy is talking to his therapist. His therapist tells him to share all of his thoughts with him. He tells Troy he must not edit himself as he speaks. Anything that comes to mind should be said out loud. Troy's therapist is using
a. free association.
b. flooding.
c. ECT.
d. client-centered therapy.

3. Brad's therapist is analyzing his dream to determine how it relates to his psychological problems. The therapist believes the dream will increase Brad's understanding of the cause of his problems. Brad's therapist most likely takes the _____ approach to treatment.
a. phenomenological
b. psychodynamic
c. biological
d. behavioral

4. Mac is a therapist who relies on his clients' natural drive toward growth. Marcia tells him that she thinks she's so ugly it is not worth it to exercise or try to dress nicely, and she asks him if he thinks she is ugly. Rather than interpreting Marcia's behavior, Mac discloses his honest reaction, saying, "Right now you think it is futile to try to improve your looks. Although I think you are attractive, what *you* think is much more important and it seems you are

discouraged." Mac is exhibiting _____, which is associated with _____ therapy.
a. analysis of transference; psychodynamic
b. congruence; client-centered
c. reflection; cognitive-behavioral
d. sympathy; phenomenological

5. LaVonne tells her therapist, "I feel like I'm never going to find my niche. I don't know what major to pick, what career to start, or even what my interests are. And no one I know really can help me find those answers." LaVonne's therapist replies, "You sound scared and alone. I'm sure that's very frightening." LaVonne's therapist is using which technique(s) associated with client-centered therapy?
a. reflection
b. empathy
c. congruence
d. both a and c

6. Which of the following describes flooding?
a. A client is gradually exposed to a feared stimulus.
b. A client is placed in a fearful situation and not allowed to escape.
c. A client learns not to let negative thoughts overwhelm or flood the mind.
d. A client receives a negative stimulus following an undesirable behavior.

7. Roberto has a dog phobia. He and his therapist go for a walk, and Roberto watches from across the street as his therapist approaches people who are walking their dogs. The therapist asks the owner if the dog is friendly, lets the dog sniff his hand, and gently pats the dog. The therapist is using _____ to help Roberto.
a. token economies
b. modeling
c. flooding
d. classical conditioning

8. Jane has gone to see a therapist because she is very depressed and dislikes herself. She doesn't get perfect grades and is not the most popular person on her dorm floor. What kind of therapy do you think would be best for Jane?
a. Antidepressant drugs
b. Rational-emotive therapy
c. Aversive conditioning
d. Token economy

9. Renee is talking to her clients. She says, "It seems that you are all part of the problems that Allison is experiencing. Although only Allison has a substance abuse problem, her sisters are so into being needed that they actually foster her

dependence so that Allison will need them. And as her parents, you indicate that you are disinterested in Allison, which makes her need to use drugs as a way of getting your attention." Renee is probably a
a. family therapist.
b. couples therapist.
c. group therapist.
d. client-centered therapist.

10. Which of the following is *not* a problem encountered in research on psychotherapy's effectiveness?
a. Statistically significant results may not be clinically significant.
b. The results of most studies were fabricated.
c. Research data that indicate that the success of psychotherapy have at times been ignored.
d. Therapists using different methods employ different measures of success.

11. Which of the following is NOT a reason for being culturally sensitive in the context of a therapeutic relationship?
a. Cultural sensitivity reduces miscommunications.
b. Cultural sensitivity facilitates trust.
c. Cultural sensitivity promotes empathy.
d. Cultural sensitivity lets you charge more.

12. Which of the following patients is the best candidate for ECT?
a. Rose, who has been taking antidepressants but has not shown any improvement.
b. Iris, who has schizophrenia.
c. Autumn, who is depressed and is responding well to psychotherapy.
d. Spring, who exhibits manic behavior.

13. Nina has been experiencing moods of extreme elation alternating with severe depression. What kind of drug will her doctor most likely prescribe?
a. Tricyclics
b. Phenothiazines
c. Monoamine oxidase inhibitors
d. Lithium

14. Martin has an anxiety disorder. Which type of drug should his doctor prescribe to him?
a. neuroleptics
b. antidepressants
c. anxiolytics
d. lithium

15. What do community psychologists do?
a. Treat psychological disorders once they have developed.
b. Treat and prevent psychological disorders by working for social change in communities.
c. Study psychological disorders, but offer no

treatments.

    d. Socialize within the community.

Total Correct (See answer key) _____

ANSWERS TO CONCEPTS AND EXERCISES

No. 1: Identifying Specific Therapies

Dr. Daka would offer Carly cognitive therapy. She would focus on negative thought patterns (cognitions) that lead to depression. (p. 462)

Dr. Redmacher would use psychoanalysis. She would try to identify how unconscious conflicts are affecting Carly's everyday life. (p. 453)

Dr. Lighter would provide client-centered therapy. Her focus would be on providing Carly unconditional positive regard in therapy so that Carly could identify and work through her problems better on her own, and then continue to self-actualize. (p. 456)

Dr. Brown would focus on antidepressant drug therapy. He would emphasize the biological roots of depression and treat those causes rather than offer a psychotherapy. (p. 474)

No. 2: Differentiating Approaches to Therapy

° *Psychoanalysis.* Patricia believes that unconscious mental processes cause behavior. Methods such as free association, dream analysis, transference, and analysis of everyday behaviors are designed to bring unconscious material into conscious awareness. (p. 453)

° *Behavior therapy.* Eliot's goal is to change behavior, not mental processes. Methods such as token economies, flooding, and aversive conditioning are designed to change behavior. (p. 459)

° *Cognitive-behavior therapy.* Randa believes that behavior can be changed by altering harmful conscious thought patterns. Cognitive restructuring and rational-emotive therapy are methods designed to alter thought patterns. (p. 462)

° *Phenomenological therapy.* Ida believes that her clients have a natural tendency toward growth and change. Clients simply need to get in touch with their feelings. Empathy, reflection, congruence, and unconditional positive regard help clients achieve this goal. (pp. 455–456)

° *Biological therapy.* Lana believes that altering the nervous system's chemical activity will change behavior. (pp. 473–476)

ANSWERS TO CRITICAL THINKING

1. Sam believes that this is the old man who has been scaring the neighborhood children.

2. The evidence is that the man matches the description called in by several neighbors.

3. Martina hypothesizes that the man may be suffering from tardive dyskinesia.

4. The evidence is that the old man appears to be dizzy and has odd pigmentation on his arms. He also exhibits tongue thrusting, which is also a common symptom of tardive dyskinesia. Martina may want to find where the man has been staying and ask those caring for him if he is taking neuroleptics.

5. Martina can't draw any conclusions until she obtains additional evidence.

ANSWERS TO MULTIPLE-CHOICE QUESTIONS

Circle the question numbers you answered correctly.

Sample Quiz 1

1. *d* is the answer. Therapies all involve a client, a therapist who is socially accepted as being able to help the client, and a theoretical approach (psychoanalytic, phenomenological, behavioral, biological) to understanding the client's problems and treating them. (pp. 452-453)

2. *d* is the answer. A psychodynamic therapist would be likely to find unconscious meaning in behaviors. (pp. 453-454)
   a. A behavioral therapist would focus on learning of behaviors, not unconscious meanings.
   b. A community psychologist works to prevent disorders.
   c. Phenomenological therapists are interested in a client's viewpoint, but would be unlikely to assume that Dwayne could not become aware of his fear.

3. *a* is the answer. Karma is trying to provide a therapeutic context for her clients to develop better relations with significant "objects" in their lives, in spite of the fact that early relations were not what they could have been. (p. 455)

b. Supportive-expressive therapy identifies core conflicts that appear across a variety of relations,
   not just early relationships.
c, d. Both client-centered and Gestalt therapies are phenomenological therapies, not contemporary psychoanalytic.

4. *b* is the answer. Phil emphasizes providing his clients with unconditional positive regard, which is a key element of client centered therapy. (p. 456)
   a. Short-term psychoanalysis would focus on using methods such as object relations therapy and supportive-expressive therapy.
   c. Cognitive-behavioral therapy emphasizes the client learning new thought and behavior patterns to replace old, maladaptive ones. Unconditional positive regard is not emphasized.
   d. ECT therapy is a biological treatment.

5. *c* is the answer. Psychoanalysis focuses on unconscious conflict, not Gestalt therapy. (pp. 457-458)
   a, b, d. All of these are true of Gestalt therapy.

6. *c* is the answer. Behavior therapy assumes that psychological disorders are just learned behaviors. New, more adaptive behaviors are learned in therapy to replace the old, maladaptive behavior. (p. 459)
   a. Self-actualization is emphasized in the phenomenological therapies.
   b. Treating psychological disorders medically is consistent with the biological approach to treatment.
   d. Identifying underlying causes of behavior is consistent with the psychodynamic approach to treatment.

7. *d* is the answer. Lia is flooding her client with the very stimulus she fears so that the client's association between fear and the dogs will ultimately be weakened. (p. 461)
   a, b. Systematic and in vivo desensitization both involve constructing a desensitization hierarchy and learning progressive relaxation. Neither of these techniques were used in this example.
   c. Modeling would involve Lia petting a dog in front her client so that the client could learn through observation that there was nothing to fear.

8. *d* is the answer. Rational-emotive behavior therapy focuses on identifying irrational beliefs and replacing them with more realistic, beneficial ones. (p. 462)

a. Beck's cognitive therapy focuses on teaching clients critical thinking skills so that they can better decide for themselves what beliefs are false versus true.
b. Aversive conditioning focuses on creating an aversive association between an inappropriate behavior and an unpleasant stimulus.
c. Neuroleptic therapy is a drug treatment.

9. *a* is the answer. Therapists often recommend couples therapy if communication with a partner seems to be a major problem. In couples therapy, people practice more constructive ways of getting ideas across. Rather than calling Wendy names or overgeneralizing, for example, Shau-Jin probably would be encouraged to say something about how he feels in the present situation. (p. 465)
   b. Extinction removes the reinforcers that usually follow a behavior. It is a behavior therapy that doesn't work on communication skills.
   c. Rational emotive therapy would concentrate on irrational ideas, not communication.
   d. Psychoanalysis would focus on unconscious conflicts rather than on communication.

10. *b* is the answer. Empirically supported therapies have been shown to be effective for particular problems, not for all psychological disorders. (p. 469)
    a, c, d. None of these is the correct definition of empirically supported therapy.

11. *d* is the answer. Because therapy is an intensely emotional experience, the therapeutic relationship must have been ended for at least two years before a romantic connection can be ethically initiated. (p. 472)
    a, b, c. All of these violate the *Ethical Principles of Psychologists and Code of Conduct*

12. *b* is the answer. Major depression that has not responded to drug and psychotherapies is the primary reason for using ECT today.
    a, c, d. None of these disorders are treated with ECT today.

13. *d* is the answer. Neuroleptics or antipsychotics reduce the intensity of psychotic symptoms such as Tico's. (p. 474)
    a. Antidepressants improve mood, but do not influence psychotic symptoms.
    b. Anxiolytics or tranquilizers reduce tension and anxiety.
    c. As discussed in Chapter 6, a depressant is a psychoactive drug that slows the activity of the central nervous system.

14. *c* is the answer. Drug therapies are a biological approach to treatment. (pp. 474-475)

a. The phenomenological approach emphasizes acceptance and self-actualization.

b. The psychoanalytic approach emphasizes uncovering unconscious conflicts.

d. The cognitive-behavioral approach emphasizes identifying inappropriate or maladaptive learned patterns of behavior and thought.

15. *c* is the answer. Community psychologists seek both to treat and to prevent psychological problems. Michel believes that if psychological problems are detected in their early stages, treatment will be shorter, less expensive, and possibly more effective. (p. 478)

a, b, d. Michel could believe in a psychoanalytic, phenomenological, biological, or behavioral approach to treating psychological problems. However, those who work to reduce stressors in the environment and in public domains such as schools are called community psychologists.

Now turn to the quiz analysis table at the end of this chapter to find which areas you know well and which areas you need to work on. Circle the numbers in the table for items on Quiz 1 that you answered correctly.

ANSWERS TO MULTIPLE-CHOICE QUESTIONS

Circle the question numbers you answered correctly.

Sample Quiz 2

1. *b* is the answer. To prescribe medication, a therapist must have a medical degree. The only treatment provider among these options to have a medical degree is a psychiatrist. (p. 452)

a, c, d. None of these providers can prescribe medication because none have a medical background.

2. *a* is the answer. Troy's therapist is asking him to free associate, which involves sharing all thoughts that come to mind in stream of consciousness fashion. (p. 454)

b. Flooding is a behavioral treatment method that involves exposing a client to a feared stimulus in a situation that does not permit escape.

c. ECT is a biological treatment method that involves delivering electrical shocks to the client's brain.

d. Client-centered therapy focuses on providing the client with unconditional positive regard.

3. *b* is the answer. Brad's therapist is using a classic psychoanalytic technique to gain insight into the unconscious. (p. 454)

a, c, d. Dream analysis is not used in any of these approaches.

4. *b* is the answer. Congruence between thoughts and actions is part of client-centered therapy. (p. 457)

a. Analysis of transference is a psychodynamic technique in which the client's reaction to the therapist is compared to conflicts with significant others in childhood.

c. Reflection is a client-centered therapy technique.

d. You may have been thinking of empathy, which is a client-centered technique.

5. *d* is the answer. Telling LaVonne that she sounds scared and alone is reflection, and acknowledging that this would be frightening is empathy. (p. 456)

a, b. Both of these are correct.

c. Congruence requires a therapist to act consistently with his or her own experience—it involves being genuine.

6. *b* is the answer. A client is exposed to the feared situation, object, or event and is not allowed to escape. Since the person cannot escape, he or she can come to realize that there is nothing to fear. (p. 461)

a. Gradual exposure to a feared stimulus takes place in systematic desensitization or participant modeling.

c. Cognitive restructuring can teach a client to replace destructive thoughts with more effective or constructive ones.

d. Presenting an unpleasant stimulus after an undesirable behavior is called punishment.

7. *b* is the answer. Modeling involves teaching a client desirable behaviors by demonstrating those behaviors and showing the client how to behave more calmly in feared situations. (p. 460)

a. Token economies involve receiving tokens for demonstrating desirable behaviors. The tokens can later be traded in for rewards or privileges. Roberto is not performing any behaviors; he is watching how his therapist behaves with dogs.

c. Flooding involves placing a client in a feared but harmless situation. Once deprived of his or her normally rewarding escape pattern, the client has no reason for continued anxiety. If Roberto and his therapist had shut themselves in a small room with a gentle, friendly dog, this would have been the answer.

d. Classical conditioning is a part of aversive conditioning and flooding. Modeling is based on operant conditioning.

8. *b* is the answer. Jane's ideas about having everyone like her and being a perfect student are probably at the root of her depression. Rational-emotive therapy will help her recognize and eliminate these unhealthy thoughts. (p. 462)

    a. Jane's depression might be alleviated by antidepressants, but it is obvious that her thought patterns about being liked and perfect will continue to cause her problems. Changing her thinking should alleviate her depression on a long-term basis.

    c. Aversive conditioning is used to decrease a specific behavior. Jane needs to change her thought patterns, not a specific behavior.

    d. Token economies are used to increase the occurrence of desired behaviors. Jane needs to change her thought patterns, not her overt behavior.

9. *a* is the answer. Renee is talking to a family, and interpreting one family member's psychological disorder as a reflection of problems in the entire family system. (p. 464)

    b. Couples therapy does not involve children and focuses on communication skills.

    c. Group therapy does not involve clients who are related to each other.

    d. Client-centered therapy is non-directive. Renee is being very directive in describing what she sees as the source of the problem.

10. *b* is the answer. Fabricated studies were not a problem mentioned in the text's discussion of the evaluative studies on psychotherapy. (pp. 466-467)

    a. Successful therapy means that a client perceives relief and is better able to function on a day-to-day basis. So, although tests may show improvement, demonstration of clinical significance is also important.

    c. Hans Eysenck, who conducted one of the first large-scale comparisons of psychotherapy effects, was accused of ignoring evidence that therapy did indeed help clients.

    d. A behavioral therapist would probably define the success of a client differently than a psychoanalyst would, making it difficult to compare the effectiveness of different types of therapy.

11. *d* is the answer. Cultural sensitivity does not allow a therapist to charge higher rates for his or her services. (pp. 471-472)

    a, b, c. All of these are reasons that therapists should be culturally sensitive.

12. *a* is the answer. Only depressed patients who have not responded well to other treatments are candidates for ECT therapy. (pp. 473-474)

    b, d. Schizophrenia and mania are not treated with ECT.

    c. If a patient is responding well to psychotherapy, there is no benefit to adding ECT to their treatment.

13. *d* is the answer. Lithium is used to treat bipolar disorders. (p. 475)

    a, c. Tricyclics and MAO inhibitors are used to treat depression.

    b. Phenothiazines are used to treat severe disorders such as schizophrenia.

14. *c* is the answer. Anxiolytics are used to treat anxiety disorders. (p. 475)

    a. Neuroleptics are used to reduce psychotic symptoms in schizophrenics.

    b. Antidepressants are used to treat depression.

    d. Lithium is used to treat bipolar disorder and mania.

15. *b* is the answer. Community psychologist both treat and work to prevent psychological disorders by working to change the social context in communities that facilitates the development of these disorders. (pp. 478-480)

    a, c. Community psychologists do not just treat or study psychological disorders, they also work to prevent them.

    d. Community psychologists do not simply socialize in the community.

Now turn to the quiz analysis table at the end of this chapter to find which areas you know well and which areas you need to work on. Circle the numbers in the table for items on Quiz 2 that you answered correctly.

For each question you answered correctly, circle its number. (Quiz 1 numbers are not shaded; Quiz 2 numbers are shaded.) Are there patterns in the types of questions or the topics you got wrong that could direct your further study? Did you improve from Quiz 1 to Quiz 2?

TOPIC	TYPE OF QUESTION		
	DEFINITION	**COMPREHENSION**	**APPLICATION**
Basic Features of Treatment		1	
			1
Psychodynamic Psychotherapy			2, 3
		3	2
Phenomenological Psychotherapy	5		4
			4, 5
Behavior Therapy		6	7, 8
		6	7, 8
Group, Family, Couples Therapy			9
			9
Evaluating Psychotherapy	10	11	
	11	10	
Biological Treatments		12	13
		14	12, 13
Community Psychology			14, 15
	15		

TOTAL CORRECT BY QUIZ:

QUIZ 1:
QUIZ 2:

Chapter 14

Social Psychology

LEARNING OBJECTIVES

1. Define <u>social psychology</u> and <u>social cognition</u>. Compare and contrast <u>self-concept</u> and <u>self-esteem</u>. (p. 487)

2. Discuss Festinger's theory of <u>social comparison</u>. Describe the role of <u>reference groups</u> in the process of self-evaluation, and give an example of downward social comparison. Define <u>relative deprivation</u>. (pp. 487–488)

3. Define <u>social identity</u> and discuss its influence on thought and behavior. (p. 488)

4. Define <u>social perception</u>. Describe the manner in which <u>schemas</u> influence first impressions. Explain why impressions change slowly. (pp. 488–490)

5. Define <u>self-fulfilling prophecies</u>. Discuss the relationship between self-fulfilling prophecies and impressions. (p. 490)

6. Define <u>attribution</u>. Discuss the importance of attributions, and give examples of internal and external attributions. (pp. 490–491)

7. Describe and give examples of the <u>fundamental attribution error</u>, ultimate attribution error, <u>actor-observer bias</u> and <u>self-serving bias</u>. Define unrealistic optimism. (pp. 491–492)

8. Define <u>attitude</u>. Describe the cognitive, affective, and behavioral components of attitudes and give an example of each. Discuss the factors that influence whether attitude-consistent behavior will occur. (pp. 493-494)

9. Discuss how attitudes are formed and changed. Include the mere exposure effect and the

of attitude change. (pp. 494–495)

10. Define and describe <u>cognitive dissonance theory</u>. (pp. 495–496)

11. Define and give examples of <u>stereotype</u>, <u>prejudice</u>, and <u>discrimination</u>. (pp. 496-497)

12. Compare and contrast the motivational, cognitive, and learning theories of prejudice and stereotyping. Describe the personality trait of authoritarianism. (pp. 497–498)

13. Describe the <u>contact hypothesis</u>. Discuss the specific conditions necessary for the contact hypothesis to hold true. (p. 499)

14. Describe the influences of the environment, similarity, and physical attractiveness on attraction. Define the <u>matching hypothesis</u>. (pp. 499–501)

15. Describe the most important components of an intimate relationship. Describe Sternberg's triangular theory of love. Compare and contrast romantic, companionate, and consummate love. Describe the factors that influence marital satisfaction. (pp. 501–502)

16. Define <u>norms</u> and describe their influence on social behavior. Define <u>deindividuation</u> and specify the factors increase its likelihood. (p. 503)

17. Define and give examples of <u>social facilitation</u> and <u>social impairment</u>. Describe the social factors that influence motivation and define <u>social loafing</u>. (pp. 504–505)

18. Compare and contrast <u>conformity</u> and <u>compliance</u>. Describe the role of norms in conformity and compliance. (pp. 505–506)

19. Describe the factors that lead to conformity. Explain the strategies for inducing compliance, including the foot-in-the-door technique, the door-in-the-face procedure, and the low-ball approach. (pp. 506-508)

20. Define <u>obedience</u>. Describe Milgram's study and his findings on obedience. Name and describe the factors that influence obedience. Discuss the ethical considerations in carrying out an experiment like Milgram's. (pp. 508–512)

21. Define <u>aggression</u>. Describe the genetic and biological influences on aggression. Discuss the roles of brain structures, hormones, and drugs in aggressive behavior. Describe the role of learning and cultural mechanisms in aggression. (pp. 512–514)

22. Define the <u>frustration-aggression hypothesis</u>. Describe the role of arousal and transferred excitation in aggression. Discuss the question of whether pornography causes aggression. Define

environmental psychology and describe the environmental influences on aggression. (pp. 514–518)

23. Define helping behavior and altruism. Describe how the arousal: cost-reward explains helping behavior. Describe the situational factors that influence helping behavior. Define bystander effect and diffusion of responsibility. (pp. 518–521)

24. Describe the empathy-altruism and evolutionary theories of helping. Discuss the study of helping behavior through a laboratory analogue experiment. Explain what conclusions are reasonable. (pp. 521-523)

25. Define cooperation, competition, and conflict. Give an example of a social dilemma. (p. 523-524)

26. Describe the personality characteristics of a good leader. Define the task-oriented and person-oriented leadership styles. Describe the types of situations that call for the use of each style. (p. 525)

27. Define groupthink. Specify the conditions that may increase its likelihood, and describe techniques that may reduce its likelihood. (pp. 525-526)

KEY TERMS

1. **Social psychology** focuses on the effects of the social world on the behavior and mental processes of individuals (p. 487)

   Example: Social psychologists are interested in studying the effects of different social contexts on whether or not a person is willing to help another in need.

2. **Social cognition** refers to the mental processes by which people perceive and react to others. (p. 487)

   Example: Self-concept is an example of social cognition. (see Key Term 3)

I. SOCIAL INFLUENCES ON THE SELF

3. Our **self-concept** is the set of beliefs we have about who we are and what we're like. (p. 487)

   Example: Mimi believes she is a responsible student, a caring friend, and a somewhat shy person.

4. **Self-esteem** consists of the evaluations we make about how worthy we are as human beings. (p. 487)

   Example: Although Joshua recently failed a thermodynamics quiz, he knows that he is smart and a good person.

5. The theory of **social comparison** states that in the absence of objective criteria, people compare themselves to others for the purpose of self-evaluation. (p. 487)

   Example: If you want to know how athletic you are, you might compare yourself to friends of the same sex.

6. **Reference groups** are the categories of people to which individuals see themselves belonging and to which they habitually compare themselves. (p. 487)

   Example: Jerome is an undergraduate student at a major university. He would probably consider his reference group to be other students; therefore, he would not compare his attractiveness or wardrobe to that of models he sees in magazines.

7. **Relative deprivation** occurs when a person's relative standing on any dimension is poor compared to that person's social reference group. (p. 488)

   Example: Rachel has just graduated with a Ph.D. in biology and taken a new job. At the university, she was considered one of the best students in her department. At her new job, she must start over and earn the respect of her superiors and peers. She experiences relative deprivation as she begins her new job.

8. **Social identity**, a part of our self-concept, is our belief about the groups to which we belong. (p. 488)

   Example: Karl says he is a German-American Lutheran farmer.

II. SOCIAL PERCEPTION

9. **Social perception** refers to the processes through which people interpret information about others. Social perception influences the conclusions that one makes about another person's personality style and why the person behaves in certain ways. (p. 488)

   Example: Ellen's roommate is really crabby lately. Ellen attributes her roommates crabbiness to the fact that her roommate was just dumped by her boyfriend.

10. **Schemas** are mental representations that affect what we pay attention to, what we remember, and how we judge the behavior of others. (p. 488)

   Example: Missy thinks that all Republicans are not trustworthy and that all Democrats are. This schema about political candidates influences how Missy perceives information about specific candidates in media campaigns.

11. A **self-fulfilling prophecy** is the process by which an impression of a person, object, or event elicits behavior that confirms the impression. (p. 490)

> *Example:* Jayne believed that she would never succeed in college. During her first semester, she found that she had to study much harder than she did in high school and decided it was a sign that she was stupid. Jayne quit studying, thinking that it was of no use, and flunked out of school.

12. **Attribution** is the process of explaining the causes of people's behavior, including one's own. Internal or external causes can account for behavior. (p. 490)

> *Example:* How would you respond to an inquiry about the causes of your grades? Would you say that you are smart and work hard (internal causes) or that you are lucky and consistently end up with easy professors (external causes)?

13. The **fundamental attribution error** is the tendency to attribute the behavior of others to internal factors. (p. 491)

> *Example:* Latanya's brother calls and tells her that he has just flunked an algebra exam. Before he can speak another word, Latanya is telling him that he is either lazy or stupid or both. She thinks that her brother's behavior, not situational factors, caused him to flunk his algebra test.

14. The **actor-observer bias** is the tendency to attribute one's own behavior to external factors, and others' behavior to internal factors, especially when the behavior is inappropriate or involves failure. (p. 491)

> *Example:* When John failed to stop at a stop sign, he attributed his behavior to the sun in his eyes and poor placement of the sign (external factors). When someone else runs a stop sign, however, John thinks they did so because of carelessness or lack of attention (internal factors).

15. The **self-serving bias** is the tendency to take credit for success, but to blame external causes for failure. (p. 492)

> *Example:* Jerry has noticed that whenever his company wins a big account with a new client, each person claims responsibility for the success. However, when a client decides to take its business elsewhere, everyone denies responsibility for the problems that precipitated the client's departure. People like to take credit for success, but do not like to take the blame for failure.

III. ATTITUDES

16. An **attitude** is the tendency to think, feel, or act positively or negatively toward objects in our environment. Therefore, it has cognitive, affective, and behavioral components. (p. 493)

> *Example:* Stephanie joins the marching band because she believes it challenges its members to become better musicians (cognitive component). She practices her clarinet nearly every day (behavioral component) and enjoys band practices and performances (affective component).

17. The **elaboration likelihood model** states that a message may change a person's attitude through a peripheral or central route. Taking a central route (such as critical thinking) to changing an attitude requires both the motivation and the ability to do so. (p. 494)

> *Example:* Matthew chose to purchase a generic medication after reading an informational pamphlet and discussing it with his doctor (central route). Jennifer chose to buy generic medicines after seeing a television commercial with a trustworthy, confident person describing their advantages (peripheral route).

18. The **cognitive dissonance theory** states that people prefer that their cognitions about themselves and the rest of the world be consistent with one another. When cognitions are inconsistent, or dissonant, people feel uneasy and are motivated to make them more consistent. (p. 495)

> *Example:* Jan is an advertising executive. She is working on a cigarette company's account, but she thinks that cigarettes should not be advertised to teenagers. Her attitudes and behavior are inconsistent. She will have to change her attitude about cigarette advertising or change jobs in order to reduce cognitive dissonance and the psychological tension it causes.

IV. PREJUDICE AND STEREOTYPES

19. **Stereotypes** are impressions or schemas of entire groups of people. Stereotypes operate on the false assumption that all members of a group share the same characteristics. This can lead to prejudice. (p. 496)

> *Example:* Vance is interviewing candidates for a position in his company. He has decided not to hire anyone with a Ph.D. He has been told by his peers that people with Ph.D.'s are flaky, absent-minded, and socially inept.

20. **Prejudice** is holding a preconceived positive or negative attitude about an individual based on her or his membership in a group of people. These attitudes have cognitive, affective, and behavioral components. (p. 496)

Example: Isa, an American, went to study in Russia for a year. She met a child on the street one day who asked her why Americans wanted to destroy the world with nuclear bombs. The child had never been exposed to Americans before but had prejudged them based on information from the press, her parents, and her peers.

21. **Discrimination** is the differential treatment of various groups that can be the behavioral component of prejudice. (p. 497)

Example: Gabrielle has brought her date, an artist, to meet her parents. She is very embarrassed because her father will not even speak to him. Later, she asks her father to explain his extremely rude behavior. He remarks that all artists are shiftless and no good and forbids her to see her friend again.

22. The **contact hypothesis** states that a person's prejudices and stereotypes about a group should be reduced with repeated friendly exposure (contact) to members of equal standing in that group. This provides an opportunity for prejudiced people to learn about members of the group as individuals. (p. 498)

Example: Anna grew up in the East. Her parents always told her that people who spoke with a southern accent were stupid and lazy. When Anna's company relocated her to Texas, she eventually came to enjoy interacting with other employees and found them to be competent at their jobs.

V. INTERPERSONAL ATTRACTION

23. The **matching hypothesis** states that a person is more likely to form committed relationships with others who are similar in physical attractiveness than with those who are notably more or less attractive. (p. 500)

Example: As you walk around your campus or neighborhood, look at the couples you see. They will often be about equal in attractiveness.

VI. SOCIAL INFLUENCE

24. **Norms** are learned, socially based rules that dictate correct and incorrect behavior for various situations. Norms vary with the culture, subculture, and situation. (p. 503)

Example: Many of your daily behaviors follow the social norms present in our culture. Sometimes it is easier to understand norms by thinking about what would happen if they were broken. Think, for instance, what would happen if you broke the social norm dictating that you may not go shopping wearing only your underwear.

25. **Deindividuation** occurs when people in a group temporarily lose their individuality and behave in ways that they would not otherwise. (p. 503)

Example: Molly is usually a very quiet individual. However, when in the crowd at a football game, she joined others in jeering and booing the officials.

26. **Social facilitation** occurs when the presence of other people improves performance. Usually, the presence of others increases arousal because it indicates to performers that they will be evaluated. (p. 504)

Example: Jon doesn't run as fast by himself as he does when in a race.

27. **Social impairment** occurs when the presence of other people hinders performance by increasing arousal. Usually, new, complex, or difficult tasks are most vulnerable to social impairment. (p. 504)

Example: Tony has practiced the song "Mad Man" on his bongo drums only a few times and is now playing it for his instructor. He is making even more mistakes than he did when he practiced by himself.

28. **Social loafing** occurs when an individual working in a group exerts less effort than when working alone because the group "hides" his or her individual performance. (p. 504)

Example: Helmut is a bright but lazy individual. In work groups at the office, he goes to all the meetings on his projects but exerts very little effort, knowing that nobody will really be able to measure his personal performance in the group.

29. **Conformity** occurs when people change their behavior or beliefs as a result of real or imagined unspoken group pressure. (p. 505)

Example: Jill wears a suit to the office because all her coworkers wear suits.

30. **Compliance** occurs when people adjust their behavior because of the directly expressed wishes of an individual or a group. (p. 505)

Example: Carlotta, Cecelia, and Carmen are sisters. Their mother tells them that if they want to go swimming, they must all clean their rooms. Carlotta and Cecelia hurry to straighten their rooms, but Carmen at first refuses to touch the mess in her bedroom. After Carlotta and Cecelia repeatedly ask Carmen to help, Carmen finally complies and cleans her room.

VII. OBEDIENCE

31. **Obedience** occurs when people comply with a demand, rather than a request, because they think they must or should do so. (p. 508)

Example: Carlotta's mother tells her that she must clean her room, and Carlotta obeys.

VIII. AGGRESSION

32. **Aggression** is an act intended to harm another person. (p. 512)

Example: Ned is playing in the sandbox at the playground when other children begin to insult him. He retaliates by throwing sand in their faces with the express purpose of hurting them.

33. The **frustration-aggression hypothesis** suggests that frustration produces a readiness to act aggressively but that aggression will occur only if there are cues in the environment that invite or are associated with an aggressive response. (p. 514)

Example: After attempting nine slam dunks of the basketball and missing them all, Kimberly notices a bully shoving her brother around the park. Although not usually violent, she reacts by punching the bully in the stomach.

34. **Environmental psychology** is the study of how people's behavior is affected by the environment in which they live. (p. 517)

Example: Heat, air pollution, noise, and overcrowding are environmental factors that contribute to aggression. Bill is a paramedic in Chicago. He hates the summer because the number of violent calls his ambulance receives increases dramatically as the temperature rises in June, July, and August.

IX. ALTRUISM AND HELPING BEHAVIOR

35. **Helping behavior** is any act that is intended to benefit another person. (p. 518)

Example: Sophie knows that one of her best friends is working extremely hard and has barely enough time to clean, cook, and do laundry. Sophie, an excellent cook, prepares three weeks' worth of dinners for her friend.

36. **Altruism** is a desire to help another person rather than benefit oneself. (p. 518)

Example: People who sacrifice their own lives in order to save others' are acting altruistically.

37. The **arousal: cost reward theory** explains that people help if they are distressed by someone's need and if the costs of not helping outweigh the costs of helping. (p. 519)

Example: Michael feels terrible when he sees that Mary's fall on the sidewalk has injured her and scattered her packages everywhere. He knows that he'll be late to work if he helps, but after a moment he decides that his guilt over not helping would be worse than having to explain his late arrival.

38. The **bystander effect** is the term for the following phenomenon: The chance that someone will help in an emergency tends to decrease as the number of people present increases. (p. 519)

Example: When Mary falls and injures herself in a crowd, most of the onlookers wait for someone else to do something. Each may be thinking that a person more qualified to help may be in the crowd. If Mary had fallen and injured herself with only one or two others present, those individuals would be very likely to assist her because they know no one else is there to help.

39. The **empathy-altruism theory** proposes that helping is often a result of empathy with the person in need of help. (p. 521)

Example: Sandeep knows what it feels like to be totally confused about a homework assignment, so he feels badly for his classmate Randy and stays after class to clarify the directions. Other students who don't feel empathy for Randy leave the two to work out the problem together.

40. **Cooperation** refers to any behavior that involves people working together to attain a shared goal. (p. 523)

Example: The people of a county might work together to get a health ordinance passed to protect the people of the county from adverse influences related to certain farming practices.

41. **Competition** refers to trying to attain a goal for oneself while simultaneously denying that goal to others. (p. 523)

Example: Two opponents running against each other for a single position in an election are competing against each other.

42. **Conflict** is experienced when a person or group believes that another person or group is interfering with the attainment of a desired goal. (p. 524)

Example: Jack wants to stay up late, but his roommate likes to go to bed early. They experience conflict because Jack and his roommate perceive each other to be interfering with their desired goals.

43. **Social dilemmas** are situations in which members of a group must choose between two options. One option is the most rational for each individual, but if everyone chooses it then everyone will be worse off than if they had chosen the other option. (p. 524)

Example: Most people enjoy public television programs. However, these programs depend on viewer donations to stay on the air. It is individually most rational to watch the shows for free and let others donate to keep the programs on air. However, if everyone thinks and acts like this, then public television programs will not have enough money to stay on air and we will all be worse off than if we had donated something to them.

X. GROUP PROCESSES

44. **Task-oriented leaders** are those who provide close supervision, discourage group discussion, and give many directives. (p. 525)

Example: Rebecca knows that to get the construction estimate out by noon, she'll need to give each worker a job. As they work on their separate contributions, she'll track their progress to ensure that each can accomplish her or his part. Rebecca doesn't think it's necessary to get the workers' opinions, especially since there is not much time.

45. **Person-oriented leaders** are those who provide loose supervision, ask for group members' ideas and opinions, and demonstrate concern for subordinates' feelings. (p. 525)

Example: Each time his group has a new project, Lorcan first asks group members to contribute ideas without censoring them. Eventually the group works together to choose the best ideas and Lorcan tries to ensure that everyone is in agreement.

46. **Groupthink** is the deterioration, over time, of a small, closely knit group's ability to evaluate realistically the available options and the decisions it makes. (p. 525)

Example: The union leaders discussing the latest contract proposal tend to ignore any suggestion that it is fair. The head of the union does not believe they should accept any contract that gives them a cut in pay. The small group discussing it is unaware that some union members are willing to make that sacrifice; therefore, they keep rejecting the company's offers.

CONCEPTS AND EXERCISES

Completing this exercise should help you to achieve Learning Objectives 12, 13, 14, and 15.

For each of the descriptions, decide which theory or concept best fits the situation.

1. Karen is an office clerk. When students come to help for the summer, she is extremely rude and orders them around. However, when her boss tells her what to do, Karen is extremely obedient and efficient. _____

2. Carlos and Sanya are not very sexually aroused by one another, but both believe strongly that they will remain married for many years to come. Carlos and Sanya discuss their hopes and dreams as well as daily events. _____

3. Lucy and Ricky have a fiery relationship and feel that they can share much with each other, but they aren't sure how long their relationship will last.

    _____

4. When Dino's parents saw people who appeared to be from a different racial or ethnic group, they looked at each other and then watched the people as long as they were in the neighborhood. Dino noticed their behavior and now feels suspicious of anyone who appears different from him.

    _____

    ° Motivational theory of prejudice
    ° Learning theory of prejudice
    ° Cognitive theory of prejudice
    ° Contact hypothesis
    ° Matching hypothesis
    ° Romantic love
    ° Companionate love
    ° Consummate love

No. 2: Sales Training

Completing this exercise should help you to achieve Learning Objectives 16, 18 and 19.

George fits the stereotype of a particularly sleazy used car salesman, but he sells new cars. He trains his new staff by telling them about some of the successful strategies he has used in the past. Use the list below to name the strategies that George is describing.

1. "Nobody wants to spend money on cars these days, especially not on the extras, what with the recession and all. So you gotta get 'em warmed up to the idea a little at a time. First, get them to buy the inexpensive extras, like power locks. Then you can move up to the medium-priced gadgets, like a better-than-average stereo. When they agree to buy the car and all the gadgets you've sold so far, go for the big, expensive ones, like a sunroof." _____

2. "Guys come in here all the time lookin' for a car that basically does the same thing, ya know. I mean he has to drive to work, the wife goes to the grocery store, and he takes the kids to baseball practice. Ninety percent of the guys coming in here will tell ya the same thing. But we got a problem. We have to sell a variety of cars. Sometimes it's easy 'cause this guy likes the red one and that guy likes the blue one. But if you have to move inventory, get a guy to agree to buy a moderately priced car. Get him all excited about how great that car is, how good he is going to look in it, and on and on. Then tell him, oops! you forgot; it isn't available anymore. Then show him one that is even more expensive. I guarantee you, nine times outta ten, he's gonna buy it." _____

3. "So you got a customer who is worried about spending too much money. So show him all the really expensive cars that are definitely out of his price range. When he starts to get a little fussy, tell him he's right; you shouldn't have been trying to sell him an expensive car. Then start showing him the price range he can afford. After seein' all those big price tickets on the fancy cars, the one he buys will seem small in comparison. You'll probably even be able to get an extra thousand or so outta him for the car." _____

- ° Low-ball
- ° Foot-in-the-door
- ° Door-in-the-face
- ° Reciprocity norm

CRITICAL THINKING

Sam and Martina are trying to discover the motive for a murder. When questioned, the killer, a forty-year-old man named Brian Canton, said he just felt like killing the victim even though he didn't know him. Sam decides that Brian has an antisocial personality and leaves the interrogation room. Martina is not so sure and continues to talk to Brian.

Later, Sam is incredibly frustrated. "Look, Martina, the guy is admitting to a classic symptom of antisocial personality. He just *felt like it*. He hasn't shown any signs of remorse. This is an easy one. We finally have a break here."

Martina snaps, "If you had stayed in the room for a little while longer, you would have picked up some information that would have led you to an alternative hypothesis."

"Oh yeah? Like what?" asks Sam.

Martina replies, "He kept telling me how much he hated killing that guy. And he kept wanting to know if anything bad would happen to his family. Doesn't sound like an antisocial personality to me. Besides, do you know how rare antisocial personalities are? The guy would have a criminal record a mile long." Martina thinks for a minute. "I've got it. That guy was a paid assassin. I'll be right back. I need to ask some more questions. Sam, you go take care of the paperwork on this one. We'll meet later."

That afternoon Sam and Martina get together again. Sam sighs and says, "Okay, I know you've got it figured out. Let's hear the answers to those questions you always use."

Using the five critical thinking questions in your text, the clues in the story, and what you have learned about cognitive dissonance, answer the following.

1. What is Sam's hypothesis?
2. What evidence supports Sam's hypothesis?
3. What is Martina's alternative hypothesis?
4. What additional evidence supports Martina's hypothesis?
5. What conclusions are reasonable?

PERSONAL LEARNING ACTIVITIES

1. Answer the following questions. Are you attractive? Are you extremely intelligent? Do you dress well? Are you well educated? The individuals or groups of people to whom you compare yourself when answering these questions are your reference groups. Who made up your reference groups? Were the groups different for each question? Think about where you will be in ten years. How might your reference groups change? In what situations could you experience relative deprivation? (Learning Objective 2)

2. Sit in a public place for about ten minutes and write notes on the behavior of people you observe. Later in the day look over your descriptions for evidence of characteristics you attributed to the people. For example, did you write only comments such as, "Saw a person wearing a backpack walk by with his head tilted down. When he turned the corner, he bumped into another person." Or did you make assumptions about motives, occupations, and personalities? The same situation, for instance, might have been described as follows: "Watched a depressed and frustrated student carelessly crash into another person." Identify instances where you may have been influenced by the fundamental attribution error or prejudices. To do so, you could get a friend to observe the same situation with you and see how your notes compare. (Learning Objectives 7 and 11)

3. Describe the norms you follow during a usual day. Do you stand facing forward in an elevator, walk on the right side of sidewalks, and talk quietly in a library? (Learning Objective 16)

4. Violate a norm as an experiment. (Don't do anything dangerous or illegal, of course!) Perhaps you could stand at a door and open it for each approaching person or make a paper hat and walk around in public wearing it. It would also violate a norm if you sat right next to someone when there were many empty seats on a bus. How did other people react to you? How did it make you feel? Based on your experience, outline some of the reasons people generally follow norms. (Learning Objective 1 and 16)

5. Try to get someone to comply with a request by using the foot-in-the-door, door-in-the-face, or low-ball technique. For example, you might see if someone is more likely to photocopy notes for you, help you pick up litter, or carry your backpack if you try one of the above methods rather than just asking. (Learning Objective 18 and 19)

WHAT SHOULD I WRITE ABOUT?

As you study the final chapter in this text on *Social Psychology*, you have the opportunity to put all the other topics you have studied this semester into the social context in which they occur. It is a chance to reflect back on the other topics you have studied, and think about how they integrate into the present topic. It is also an opportunity to reflect back on the writing strategies you have used this semester. Thinking about what you have done, what worked, and what didn't is a valuable exercise because it will make you a better writer in the long run.

As you started the semester, the topics in this particular column emphasized simply selecting a topic. As you became a more advanced student of psychology, the focus of this column shifted to emphasize how to develop that topic. And as you progressed even further through the textbook, the emphasis grew to be more on writing strategies and developing the term paper itself. Reflect on what you did in each of these stages. What strategy was particularly useful for you in selecting a superficial topic? What strategy didn't? In what ways were you successful in developing that topic further? And when it came to writing the paper, what strategies and situations facilitated you getting that done?

As *Social Psychology* emphasizes the role of the context in determining behavior, you have an opportunity now to identify how the context influenced your own writing efforts. Think about what situations you worked best in. Do you function really well early in the morning? Or are you a night owl? Be honest with yourself. When do you produce the best quality work—not just what habits (good or bad) do you currently prefer? Where do you work well? Is the library a good spot, or do you get distracted there? Do you prefer some "background noise" as you work, or do you need it to be absolutely quiet? Again, look at the quality of writing you do in those situations, not just what you "like" to do. Liking a situation, and performing well in that situation, although often related, are conceptually distinct. You need to separate those issues to really evaluate which context is best for you as a writer.

As you begin to identify the situational factors that influence your writing, you are on your way to being a really fine writer. Many students believe that people are either a good or bad writers—writing skills don't really change. But nothing could be further from the truth. Although writing is a skill that some students take to more naturally than others, the *real* difference is in the time, thought, and effort that good writers put in. It takes all three of these components to facilitate writing a good term paper. If you put in a lot of time, without trying while you are doing so, or without thinking about the topic, you probably won't produce a great paper. Likewise, thinking a lot about a paper without spending the time on the actual writing is an equally poor strategy. To be a great writer, it takes time, thought, and effort. And part of the thinking side of writing a term paper should eventually involve identifying the context in which you work best. What better time to do that than when you are studying the effects of a context on human behavior?

Here are some questions to guide you as you analyze what strategies and situations are effective for you:

1. What strategies worked for you in selecting an initial topic? Think about the topics that were easy for you to select. What about that selection process was useful?

2. How were you able to develop that topic further? Did your strategies work? What about your strategies could be improved?

3. In what situation did you find it easiest to think clearly and produce high quality papers? Compare papers that you performed your best on to papers you felt you could have done better on. What was different about the settings in which you worked on those papers?

THE INTERNET

The Psychabilities web site that accompanies this text offers many resources relevant to this chapter. They include NetLab exercises, Thinking Critically and Evaluating Research exercises, ACE chapter quizzes, recommended web links, and articles on current events, books, and movies. Go to http://college.hmco.com, select Psychology, and then this textbook.

MULTIPLE-CHOICE QUESTIONS

SAMPLE QUIZ 1

1. Cindy is preparing to switch from her public school to an exclusive private school for gifted students. Because Cindy won't be the smartest student any more, she will be more likely to experience _____ at the private school than at the public school.
   a. cognitive dissonance
   b. the fundamental attribution error
   c. relative deprivation
   d. self-fulfilling prophecies

2. When Lance introduced himself to Nathan, he mentioned that he worked as a cashier in a supermarket. Nathan remembered all of Lance's comments about food and car repairs and remembered none of his comments about English poets and politics. Nathan's perception was most likely biased by
   a. discrimination.
   b. a schema.
   c. social comparison.
   d. the actor-observer bias.

3. Janelle met Jake at a party. At the party, Jake was drunk, loud, and obnoxious. Janelle decides he is a total jerk. Later that week, Janelle runs into Jake at the coffeehouse where Jake is pleasant and mild-mannered. After meeting Jake at the coffeehouse, Janelle will think that Jake is
   a. a total jerk still.
   b. pleasant and mild-mannered.
   c. a little bit of a jerk, but mostly all right.

   d. she won't know what to think of Jake.
   e.

4. Felicia's first novel has sold over 1 million copies, but Felicia thinks it is due to luck. She thinks other best-selling novels are written by talented writers; therefore, she is demonstrating the
   a. fundamental attribution error.
   b. actor-observer bias.
   c. self-perception theory.
   d. self-serving bias.

5. Erik always says that looks are not important to him when he asks a woman out; however, recently he did not invite either of two women he liked to a dance because he didn't think they were attractive. When his friend points out the difference between what Erik said was important and what was really influencing him, Erik most likely experienced
   a. the actor-observer bias.
   b. cognitive dissonance.
   c. deindividuation.
   d. the mere exposure bias.

6. Casisi complies with the requests of teachers, elder relatives, and his boss. However, when a younger sibling or an acquaintance makes a request, he doesn't feel obligated to fulfill it. Casisi likes the security of feeling part of a group, so he'll sometimes taunt or harass people who aren't members of his ethnic group. Casisi's behavior is best explained by the _____ theory of prejudice.
   a. motivational
   b. cognitive
   c. contact
   d. learning

7. Susan has just moved into a new dormitory. She will most likely become good friends with the women
   a. on the floor above hers.
   b. in the dorm next door.
   c. in the room next door.
   d. at the other end of the hall.

8. With whom would you be most likely to fall in love at first sight?
   a. Your tour guide in the Mojave Desert in August
   b. The person who fills your gas tank when you are in a hurry
   c. The person you bump into on the quad on a beautiful spring day
   d. There is an equal probability that you would fall in love with any of the above.

9. Stacey's auto racing time has not improved in days. Although she knows the course well, she is no

longer improving. To increase her speed Stacey should
a. have someone race against her.
b. eject her staff and race the course without anyone recording times.
c. combat deindividuation.
d. reduce the bystander effect.

10. In the foot-in-the-door technique,
a. larger and larger requests are made.
b. a straightforward request is made.
c. a very large request is made, followed by a smaller one.
d. the original commitment is devalued, and a request is made for more.

11. According to Milgrim's research, a new member of a street gang would be *most likely* to defy the gang leader's request to rob a store owner if
a. the gang leader was standing next to the new member.
b. other gang members had robbed stores in the past.
c. the gang leader had a gun.
d. other gang members had already refused the same request.

12. Which is not true of the relationship between pornography and aggression?
a. Portrayals of violence affect attitudes toward aggression.
b. Men are more aggressive toward women but not toward men after viewing aggressive pornography.
c. Some rapists become aroused after viewing aggressive pornography.
d. All of the above are true.

13. Brian is aggravated because he needs to discuss a group project with his classmate Kevin, who keeps ignoring him. When Brian suggests a meeting time, Kevin tells him that a meeting is impossible. Brian then pushes Kevin against a wall and rips up his appointment book. Brian's behavior best fits the _____ of aggression.
a. biological theory
b. deindividuation theory
c. frustration-aggression hypothesis
d. social dilemma hypothesis

14. Diffusion of responsibility occurs when
a. many people are present when someone needs help.
b. groups try to make decisions.
c. a leader divides work equally among his or her staff.
d. people do not take responsibility for aggressive acts.

15. Mary, the president of the student council, wants to reduce the likelihood of groupthink. In order to be successful, she should most likely
a. isolate the group from other student groups.
b. forcefully explain her position before allowing others to contribute ideas.
c. suggest that everyone contribute suggestions anonymously.
d. use task-oriented leadership.

Total Correct (See answer key) _____

SAMPLE QUIZ 2

Use this quiz to reassess your learning after taking Quiz 1 and reviewing the chapter.

1. Our social identity is our
a. desire to be like our peers.
b. desire to be like our idols.
c. belief about our self-worth.
d. belief about the groups to which we belong.

2. According to the fundamental attribution error, we
a. always attribute our behavior to internal causes.
b. always make an internal attribution for our successes.
c. usually attribute others' behavior to external causes.
d. usually attribute others' behavior to internal causes.

3. While talking about her daughter Nicole, Clarissa says, "I have taught Nicole to be considerate, thoughtful, and moral, but Nicole's father is responsible for her inability to manage her money." This is an illustration of
a. the fundamental attribution error.
b. the self-serving bias.
c. the actor-observer bias.
d. relative deprivation.

4. When Mark sees a television commercial that shows a couple meeting and falling in love, he immediately phones the number they list to sign up for the dating service. Mark most likely used _____ to change his attitude.
a. a central route
b. a peripheral route
c. "cognitive busyness"
d. "cognitive dissonance"

5. Margie wants to reduce children's prejudices; therefore, she decides to run an after-school program in her grade school to bring together students of different backgrounds for games, study sessions, and snacks. Based on the description of successful intergroup contact given in the text,

which of the following would bring Margie the most success?

a. Allow the children to choose sides for a game of basketball.

b. Have the different ethnic groups describe their families' customs.

c. Design a project that will require all the children to cooperate in order to succeed.

d. Point out the errors of the high-status children.

6. Claudia and Kathy are good friends. Claudia likes Elizabeth, but Kathy does not. This difference in their attitudes creates problems when they try to plan social gatherings. Claudia and Kathy's relationship is

a. balanced.

b. imbalanced.

c. dissonant.

d. distinctive.

7. At the football game, Bob felt swept up in the excitement and rushed onto the field with the rest of the fans. If Bob had thought things through, he would not have helped the mob push over the goal posts, but he experienced

a. deindividuation.

b. diffusion of responsibility.

c. social facilitation.

d. compliance.

8. Perry is traveling in France. As he walks into his hotel, he notices everyone handing ten francs to the doorman. Perry also hands the doorman ten francs. This is an example of

a. conformity.

b. compliance.

c. obedience.

d. social facilitation.

9. Ethan has just joined a new group of friends. They want to break windows at the back of the school building for fun. Ethan protests, but the group keeps saying, "Aw, why not come with us? Are you a chicken?" He finally decides to go along with the group; therefore, Ethan has

a. conformed.

b. complied.

c. obeyed.

d. competed.

10. Naomi has decided to do an experiment on obedience. She has asked confederates to stop people on the sidewalk and order them to put money in an empty parking meter close by. Which confederate will produce the highest obedience rate?

a. An old man dressed in tattered clothes

b. A man dressed in tennis shorts and carrying a racket

c. A man dressed in a white air force uniform

d. A young man dressed in jeans and a t-shirt

11. Donna is angry at her two sons, because she found them in their room having a laser fight way past their bedtime. They were using their toothbrushes as laser guns. She decides not to let them watch any more violent cartoons. Donna's decision is in agreement with which approach to aggression?

a. Biological

b. Learning

c. Frustration-aggression hypothesis

d. Instinct

12. Agatha is moving to a big city to begin her career. She wants to find a very safe apartment to live in. Which of the following should she choose?

a. An area near the airport because her job requires her to travel quite a bit

b. An area that has zoning laws restricting the number of occupants per building

c. A high-rise apartment building

d. An area near the plant where she works, despite the smell

13. Patty has just broken her leg. In which situation will she receive the most help?

a. On the university commons during a rally

b. In the auditorium where new students are signing up for classes

c. On her way home for a shower in her baggy, ripped sweats

d. If she screams that she needs help

14. The shelter for homeless people has a large number of volunteers who were once homeless. When such volunteers are asked why they contribute so much to the shelter, they often say it's because they know what it feels like to be without a home. Their explanation fits best with the _____ theory of helping.

a. arousal: cost-reward

b. empathy-altruism

c. environmental

d. evolutionary

15. Karen is the coordinator of all the psychology teachers. She asks for opinions and suggestions from all the teachers regarding any task the group must accomplish. What style of leadership is she using?

a. Tit-for-tat

b. Person-oriented

c. Task-oriented

d. Autocratic

Total Correct (See answer key) _____

ANSWERS TO CONCEPTS AND EXERCISES

No. 1: Prejudice and Love

1. *Motivational theory of prejudice.* Karen orders around people she sees as having lower status, but obeys people she sees as having higher status; therefore, she may have an authoritarian personality. An authoritarian personality motivates people to identify with their in-group and dislike other groups. (p. 497)

2. *Companionate love.* Carlos and Sanya are low on passion and high on commitment and intimacy, according to Sternberg's theory. (p. 502)

3. *Romantic love.* Lucy and Ricky have a high level of passion and intimacy, but a low level of commitment. (p. 502)

4. *Learning theory of prejudice.* Dino learned discriminatory behaviors from his parents through observational learning. Although Dino may have had very little contact with the ethnic group, he now has suspicions about anyone from the group. (p. 498)

No. 2: Sales Training

1. *Foot-in-the-door.* Once George gets a customer to buy the less expensive options, the customer has let George get his foot in the door and may be more easily convinced that more expensive options are worthwhile. (p. 507)

2. *Low-ball.* After a customer has agreed to buy a car, the customer is unlikely to back out of the deal completely when told that the car is unavailable. George used low-ball to gain compliance by getting the person to agree to buy one car, preventing the purchase, and then getting the customer to buy a more expensive car. (p. 508)

3. *Door-in-the-face.* A customer who was shown many unaffordable, expensive cars may be relieved when George finally shows the affordably priced cars. After continually saying "no" to the expensive cars (like slamming the door in George's face), the customer may feel that buying a less expensive car is a compromise. (p. 508)

ANSWERS TO CRITICAL THINKING

1. Sam hypothesizes that Brian has an antisocial personality.

2. The evidence is Brian's remark that he just felt like killing the guy.

3. Martina hypothesizes, based on cognitive dissonance theory, that Brian got paid to do the killing but didn't really want to do it.

4. Martina probably wants to find out if Brian or any member of his family needed money.

5. What conclusions are most reasonable? If Brian answered yes, Martina could conclude that Brian was a paid assassin. But she probably shouldn't form a conclusion just yet. What else could Martina ask Brian that would support her hypothesis?

ANSWERS TO MULTIPLE-CHOICE QUESTIONS

Circle the question numbers you answered correctly.

Sample Quiz 1

1. *c* is the answer. Going from being one of the best to being average can make a person feel sad for the loss of status, although an objective measure would show that Cindy is as smart as she ever was. (p. 488)
   a. Cognitive dissonance is experienced when attitudes or attitudes and behaviors are not in line with one another.
   b. The fundamental attribution error is the tendency to believe that others' behaviors are caused by their personal characteristics rather than by the environment.
   d. Self-fulfilling prophecies occur when we allow our expectations to influence our actions, which, in turn, influence those around us into behaving as we expected.

2. *b* is the answer. When Nathan thought about Lance's job, it most likely activated a schema for cashiers or supermarket workers that didn't include interests in poetry and politics. (p. 488)
   a. Discrimination is the behavioral component of a prejudicial attitude, but it does not bias memory.
   c. Social comparison is the process by which we compare ourselves to others. Nathan may have been comparing himself to Lance, but it was not an influence on his memory.
   d. The actor-observer bias relates to internal versus external attributions, not memory for personal information.

3. *a* is the answer. First impressions tend to have powerful, lasting effects. (p. 490)
   b, c. The information that Jake is pleasant and mild-mannered will be interpreted through

Janelle's schema that Jake is a jerk. She will probably see him as phony, rather than genuinely nice.

d. Janelle will know what to think about Jake. She will see him as a jerk.

4. b is the answer. The actor-observer bias occurs when we attribute our own behavior to external factors, such as luck, and others' behavior to internal factors, such as talent. (p. 491)

a. According to the fundamental attribution error, we attribute other people's behavior to internal factors—in this case, creativity. Felicia is attributing her own behavior to an external cause, luck.

c. Self-perception involves determining one's own attitudes. The question asks why Felicia attributes the success of her book to luck, not what her attitudes are.

d. The self-serving bias predicts that Felicia will take personal credit for her success.

5. b is the answer. When our behavior doesn't match our beliefs (cognitive component), we feel uncomfortable and motivated to change either the attitude or the behavior. (p. 495)

a. The actor-observer bias has to do with attributing behavior to external versus internal causes; it doesn't deal with disagreement between components of an attitude.

c. Deindividuation is the feeling of losing oneself in a crowd.

d. The mere exposure effect occurs when people who see each other often are more likely to become friends.

6. a is the answer. Motivation theory suggests that people with authoritarian personalities view the world as a strict social hierarchy. These people know whom they have to obey and from whom they can demand discipline. They often stereotype people of lower status. (p. 497)

b. Cognitive theorists emphasize that the cognitive shortcuts we use to make sense of our social world can contribute to stereotypes.

c. The contact hypothesis states that prejudice will decrease as contact between groups increases.

d. Learning theory proposes that we learn stereotypes and prejudices by watching others and by being reinforced when we express prejudice.

7. c is the answer. Research has shown that next-door neighbors are more likely to become good friends than are people who live at opposite ends of the hall or farther away. (p. 499)

a, b, d. People tend to like those with whom they have the most contact. Susan will probably have more contact with the women living next door.

8. c is the answer. You are much more likely to be attracted to people if you meet them in a comfortable setting. (p. 500)

a. You would be hot and sticky, not comfortable, on a tour of the Mojave Desert in August.

b. If you were in a hurry, you would not have sufficient contact with a gas station attendant.

d. You would be more attracted to the person you met in comfortable physical surroundings.

9. a is the answer. When a task is well-rehearsed, people often perform better with others present. If Stacey knows the course well, then having someone race her may be the motivation she needs to push herself to drive her best. (p. 504)

b. A well-rehearsed activity is not usually harmed by the presence of others; therefore, such social impairment shouldn't be a factor for Stacey.

c. Deindividuation is feeling "swept up" by the mood of a crowd.

d. The bystander effect is related to diffusion of responsibility, which is the hesitance of people to help when others are around. Each person puts the responsibility of helping on the other bystanders.

10. a is the answer. (pp. 507–508)

b. Asking for something is a request, not a technique for inducing compliance.

c. The door-in-the-face technique involves making a large request, having it denied, and then making a smaller request.

d. The low-ball technique occurs when a person claims the original commitment won't work and asks for more.

11. d is the answer. When even one person disobeys an order, it makes it easier for others to also disobey. (p. 510)

a, b, c. Any of these would make it harder to defy the gang leader's order.

12. d is the answer. Portrayals of violence do alter attitudes toward violence, arouse some rapists, and cause an increase in men's aggression toward women but not toward other men. (pp. 515–517)

a, b, c. All of these are true.

13. c is the answer. Brian was frustrated by Kevin's lack of cooperation and, therefore, was more likely to behave aggressively toward Kevin. (p. 514)

a. Biological theories of aggression would cite high testosterone levels or damage to certain brain areas as the cause of aggression. Brian's physiological state is not described.

b. Deindividuation is the sense that one won't be held responsible for actions committed while in a crowd of people. Brian is not in a crowd; he could easily be identified as the person who assaulted Kevin. There is no such thing as deindividuation theory.

d. A social dilemma involves making a decision about an action that will take some investment of time, effort, or money versus an action that is easier but more harmful to the society as a whole. Social dilemmas are situations, not hypotheses.

14. *a* is the answer. When many people are present, diffusion of responsibility occurs, and helping behavior is reduced. (p. 519)

b. Diffusion of responsibility is not related to group decision making. (You may be thinking of groupthink, the inability of a small, closely knit group to evaluate realistically the decisions it makes.)

c. Diffusion of responsibility is related to helping behavior, not to leadership styles.

d. Diffusion of responsibility is related to helping behavior, not to aggression.

15. *c* is the answer. When people hear others all pushing for the same idea, they are more hesitant to disagree. If suggestions were made anonymously, perhaps more ideas would be proposed. (p. 526)

a, b. Group isolation and leaders who take a firm stand contribute to groupthink.

d. Task-oriented leadership would mean that Mary would give instructions rather than consult the group, but it would not improve the choices made, nor would it make groupthink unlikely. Mary might still feel she had the support of the group for the ideas she was directing them to carry out.

Now turn to the quiz analysis table at the end of this chapter to find which areas you know well and which areas you need to work on. Circle the numbers in the table for items on Quiz 1 that you answered correctly.

ANSWERS TO MULTIPLE-CHOICE QUESTIONS

Circle the question numbers you answered correctly.

Sample Quiz 2

1. *d* is the answer. Our social identity is our belief about our membership in groups. (p. 488)

a, b. We may want to be like our peers or idols, but *d* is the best answer.

c. Self-esteem is our belief about our self-worth.

2. *d* is the answer. According to the fundamental attribution error, we usually attribute others' behavior to internal causes. (p. 491)

a. According to the fundamental attribution error, we attribute others' behavior to internal causes.

b. According to the self-serving bias, we attribute our successes to internal causes.

c. According to the fundamental attribution error, we usually attribute others' behavior to internal, not external, causes.

3. *b* is the answer. According to the self-serving bias, we take credit for success but blame external causes for failure. Nicole's mother is taking credit for Nicole's good habits and qualities but not for her bad ones. (p. 492)

a. According to the fundamental attribution error, Nicole's mother should attribute Nicole's behavior to Nicole's internal characteristics. Instead, she believes that the causes of Nicole's behavior are her and her husband's style of raising their daughter (characteristics that are external to Nicole).

c. The actor-observer bias is the tendency to attribute our own behavior to an external cause. Nicole's mother is making attributions about Nicole's behavior, not her own.

d. People experience relative deprivation when they compare themselves to others who have a higher standard of living.

4. *b* is the answer. Mark is not thinking critically about the dating service. He is using appearances (happy couples) to make his decision. (p. 494)

a. A central route would be one that considers the content of the message to be more important than the communicator.

c. Cognitive "busyness" occurs when we are involved in thinking about something other than the decision to be made. It makes a peripheral route to decision-making more likely. Mark is not described as being busy thinking about something else.

d. Cognitive dissonance occurs when thoughts, behaviors, and attitudes are inconsistent with one another.

5. *c* is the answer. Cooperation is an important factor in determining the success of contact in reducing prejudice. Activities like the jigsaw technique often help reduce prejudice. (pp. 498)

a, d. A sports competition or the singling out of a few individuals will probably not reduce prejudices, and in fact, may worsen them.

b. A presentation of information may help students understand each other, but won't be as effective as having the students cooperate.

6. *b* is the answer. A relationship is imbalanced if friends disagree on their evaluation of a third person. (p. 500)
   a. In a balanced relationship, friends agree on their evaluation of a third person.
   c. Perhaps you were thinking of cognitive dissonance. It deals with disagreement in one person's attitudes, behaviors, and feelings.
   d. Relationships are not rated on distinctiveness; behaviors are. In addition, we don't know if Claudia and Karen's behavior is distinctive without having information about their behavior toward many other people.

7. *a* is the answer. Much of mob behavior can be explained by the loss of personal identity that comes with getting caught up in the group mentality. (p. 503)
   b. Diffusion of responsibility is the spreading around of responsibility for helping when many people see someone in need.
   c. Social facilitation occurs when our performance benefits from the presence of other people. Bob is just going along with the mob, not improving a personal performance.
   d. Bob is not complying with a request, he is conforming to the riotous behavior of others.

8. *a* is the answer. Perry, as a result of unspoken pressure, is conforming. (p. 505)
   b. If someone had suggested that he give the doorman ten francs, this would have been the correct alternative.
   c. If someone in authority had demanded that he give the doorman ten francs, this would have been the correct alternative.
   d. Social facilitation occurs when an activity goes better while others are present. This doesn't relate to Perry's situation.

9. *b* is the answer. Ethan is changing his behavior in response to expressed (spoken) social influence. (p. 505)
   a. Conformity occurs when people change their behavior in response to real or imagined unspoken peer pressure.
   c. Ethan's friends are not authority figures who demanded that he go along with them; they just applied social pressure.
   d. Ethan was not in competition with his friends; they were asking him to go with them.

10. *c* is the answer. The uniform will communicate a prestigious and authoritative presence. Obedience increases as the prestige and authority of the person giving the orders increase. (p. 510)
    a, b, d. None of these types of clothing communicates prestige or authority.

11. *b* is the answer. According to the learning approach, we can learn aggression by watching others' aggressive behavior. The boys may have learned their aggressive behavior from watching violent cartoons. (p. 514)
    a. According to the biological viewpoint, aggression is caused by physical factors, not by learning.
    c. According to the frustration-aggression hypothesis, aggression is displayed if a person is frustrated and there are aggressive cues in the environment.
    d. Instinct theory proposes that aggression is natural, not learned.

12. *b* is the answer. As crowding increases, so does aggression. Living in an area where zoning laws limit crowding would be safer than living in any of the other alternatives. (pp. 517-518)
    a. Living near the airport will increase the noise in Agatha's neighborhood. Unwanted noise has been associated with increases in aggression.
    c. People who live in high-rise buildings are more likely to act aggressively.
    d. Air pollution raises levels of aggression.

13. *d* is the answer. Patty's screams communicate that she does in fact need help. Research has demonstrated that when people clearly understand that a person is in need of aid, the incidence of helping behavior increases. (p. 519)
    a. A rally is usually well attended. When many people are present, diffusion of responsibility occurs, and helping behavior is less likely.
    b. People who are unfamiliar with their surroundings are usually less likely to help. New students are probably unfamiliar with their surroundings.
    c. An attractive, well-dressed person is much more likely to be helped. Patty probably doesn't look too attractive in her baggy, ripped sweats.

14. *b* is the answer. According to the empathy-altruism theory of helping behavior, if people know what the person in need feels like, they will be more likely to help. (p. 521)
    a. The arousal: cost-reward theory doesn't focus on empathy for the person in need; it focuses on the upset of the helper. If the person is upset enough by the other person's plight, he or she is likely to evaluate the price of helping.
    c. There isn't an environmental theory of helping behavior, although population density and noise do influence helping.
    d. The evolutionary theory states that we are more likely to help relatives. Evolutionary theorists do not take empathy or arousal into account.

15. *b* is the answer. The person-oriented style is characterized by asking group members for their opinions. (p. 525)
    a. The tit-for-tat method is a competitive strategy, not a leadership style.
    c. A task-oriented style is characterized by giving directives without input from the group.

    d. There is no such thing as an autocratic style of leadership.

Now turn to the quiz analysis table at the end of this chapter to find which areas you know well and which areas you need to work on. Circle the numbers in the table for items on Quiz 2 that you answered correctly.

For each question you answered correctly, circle its number. (Quiz 1 numbers are not shaded; Quiz 2 numbers are shaded.) Are there patterns in the types of questions or the topics you got wrong that could direct your further study? Did you improve from Quiz 1 to Quiz 2?

TOPIC	TYPE OF QUESTION		
	DEFINITION	COMPREHENSION	APPLICATION
Social Influences on the Self			1
	1		
Social Perception			2, 3, 4
	2		3
Attitudes			5
			4
Prejudice and Stereotypes		6	
			5
Interpersonal Attraction			7, 8
		6	
Social Influence	10		9
			7, 8, 9
Obedience			11
			10
Aggression		12	13
			11, 12
Altruism and Helping Behavior	14		
			13, 14
Group Processes			15
			15

TOTAL CORRECT BY QUIZ:

QUIZ 1:	
QUIZ 2:	

Appendix

Statistics in Psychological Research

LEARNING OBJECTIVES

1. Describe the differences between descriptive and inferential statistics. (p. A-1)

2. Define null hypothesis. (p. A-1)

3. Describe a frequency histogram, and explain why it is used. (pp. A-1-A-2)

4. Name the four basic categories of descriptive statistics. Define central tendency, and describe the three measures of central tendency. Explain how to calculate the mean, median, and mode for a given data set. (p. A-2)

5. Define variability, and describe the two measures of it. (pp. A-2-A-3)

6. Discuss the features of a normal distribution. (pp. A-3-A-4)

7. Define percentile score and standard score, and explain how to use each one. (p. A-4)

8. Define t test. Specify the formula for calculating a t value as well as the procedures for interpreting it. (pp. A-4-A-5)

9. Define analysis of variance, and explain when this statistic is used. (p. A-5)

KEY TERMS

1. The **null-hypothesis** asserts that the independent variable manipulated by the experimenter has no effect on the dependent variable measured by the experimenter. (p. A-1)

Example: Dr. Smith is doing an experiment to see if a new teaching method helps improve student learning. In one section, he uses the new method, and in a second section he uses the old method. The null hypothesis is that there will be no difference in the learning between the two sections.

2. A **frequency histogram** is a graphic display of data in the form of bars that tell how often different data values occur. (p. A-1)

REMEMBER: Frequency means "how often." This graph tells you how often various scores occurred.

3. **Normal distribution** describes a data set in which the scores fall symmetrically around the mean; it is represented by a bell-shaped curve. The scores are scattered so that half are above the mean and half below. The mean, median, and mode are always equal in a normal distribution. (p. A-3)

REMEMBER: If you are having problems understanding what a normal distribution is, be sure to do the exercise "A Statistical Report Card."

4. A **percentile score** indicates the percentage of people or observations that fall below a given score in a normal distribution. (p. A-3)

Example: If your psychology exam score is at the 95th percentile, you know that you did better than 95 percent of the people who took the test. It does not mean that you answered 95 percent of the questions correctly.

5. **Standard scores** express the value of a score by indicating its distance in standard deviations from the mean. (p. A-4)

Example: A standard score of +1.5 means that the score is 1.5 standard deviations above the mean of the distribution.

6. The *t* test is one inferential statistical method used to analyze data. The outcome of this test indicates whether the differences found between two means are the result of chance factors or changes in the dependent variable produced by the independent variable. (p. A-4)

Example: Liesel conducts an experiment to see if using mneumonics improves memory. She has one group study a list of words organized mneumonically, and another group just studies a list of words with no menumonic organization. She then compares how well the two groups perform on a memory test. The statistical tool used to compare the mean scores of the two experimental groups is the test.

CONCEPTS AND EXERCISES

Statistics and the Consumer

Completing this exercise should help you to achieve Learning Objectives 4 and 5.

Richard has just won the lottery and has hired you to help him spend his money. He has given you a stack of statistical documentation on the qualities of all the brand-name items he wants to buy. Because Richard knows nothing about statistics, you must choose the best brand for the money.

1. Richard wants a sports car and cares only about its maximum speed. Your information says that the mean maximum speed of car A is 180 mph; the standard deviation for all the speed trials is 32 mph. The mean maximum speed of car B is 173 mph, with a standard deviation of 5 mph. Which car should Richard buy? _____

2. Richard is overweight and wants to get in shape. Clients at the Body Beautiful Fitness Center have achieved a mean loss of 35 pounds with a standard deviation of 20 pounds. Clients at the Bare Bones Fitness Center have achieved a mean loss of 25 pounds with a standard deviation of 4 pounds. At which center can Richard be more sure of losing 20–25 pounds? _____

CRITICAL THINKING

Sam and Martina are investigating allegations that a local landlord has used lead-based paint in his apartment complex. Two of the eight children who live in the complex with their parents have been diagnosed with ADHD, have experienced hearing problems, and have complained of headaches. All of these symptoms can be signs of lead poisoning in children, and the parents of those two children have accused the landlord of using lead-based paint.

As part of their investigation, Sam and Martina order tests of the levels of lead the children in this complex have absorbed, and then compare them to the levels absorbed by eight children in a neighboring complex that is known to be lead-free. When the results of the tests come back, Sam exclaims, "Ah-ha! I knew that landlord was guilty as soon as I interviewed him! He couldn't even look me in the eye, and now these test results show just what I expected. The children in his building have higher mean levels of lead absorption compared to the children in the other building. Let's go arrest him!"

"Not so fast, rookie," Martina chuckles. "Let me see those results." Sam hands them over to Martina and as she reviews the results, she shakes her head in dismay over Sam's impulsive conclusion. He really should have paid better attention in his statistics class in school. Martina looks not only at the mean levels of lead absorption, but examines the standard deviations of those two groups as well. "Sam," Martina says, "I think you'd better check this out before you arrest the landlord for lead poisoning. We may have a different villain than you are thinking." Martina shows Sam that the standard deviation for the group living in the accused landlord's building is much larger than that of the clean building. "I think we had better start questioning the parents of the two children who are showing the symptoms."

Using the five critical thinking questions in your text, state Sam's original hypothesis and his evidence. Based on the clues in the story, what do you think Martina's alternative hypothesis is?

1. What is Sam's hypothesis?

2. What evidence does he have?

3. What is Martina's probable alternative hypothesis?

4. What is the evidence that supports her hypothesis? What else would you want to know if you were Martina?

5. What conclusion can be drawn?

PERSONAL LEARNING ACTIVITY

Take a survey and compute measures of central tendency on your data. For example, you could find out at what age people first got a job, drove a car, or had a date. You might find that the modal age for a first date is higher than the mean or median age. (Learning Objective 4)

THE INTERNET

The Psychabilities web site that accompanies this text offers many resources relevant to this chapter. They include NetLab exercises, Thinking Critically and Evaluating Research exercises, ACE chapter quizzes, recommended web links, and articles on current events, books, and movies. Go to http://college.hmco.com, select Psychology, and then this textbook.

MULTIPLE-CHOICE QUESTIONS

SAMPLE QUIZ 1

1. If a visual presentation of data is required, you would use a
   a. frequency histogram.
   b. normal distribution.

c. measure of central tendency.
d. measure of variability.

Donald is a high school football coach. He has kept track of the number of touchdowns his players have made during every game. Using the data that he has collected, answer the next three questions.
Data: 1, 2, 3, 3, 8, 10, 7, 6, 5

2. What is the mode?
   a. 3
   b. 4
   c. 5
   d. 6

3. What is the median?
   a. 3
   b. 4
   c. 5
   d. 6

4. What is the mean?
   a. 3
   b. 4
   c. 5
   d. 6

5. Which of the following data sets would best fit the definition of a normal distribution?
   a. 1, 1, 2, 4, 6, 7, 8, 23
   b. 1, 6, 6, 12, 100, 100, 200
   c. 1, 2, 3, 4, 5, 5, 5, 6, 7, 8, 9
   d. 2, 4, 6, 8, 10, 10, 11

6. Researchers use _____ statistical methods to make conclusions about their data.
   a. descriptive
   b. significant
   c. inferential
   d. standard

Total Correct (See answer key) _____

SAMPLE QUIZ 2

Use this quiz to reassess your learning after taking quiz 1 and reviewing the appendix.

1. To best illustrate the differences in the weekly sales figures for each type of fat-free cookie, the "Cookie Man" should show
   a. the median overall cookie sales.
   b. a histogram indicating the weekly sales of each variety of cookies.
   c. the range of weekly sales figures for each cookie type.
   d. the standard deviation for each cookie type.

2. N is equal to the number of
   a. participants in an experiment.
   b. observations in a data set.
   c. independent variables in an experiment.
   d. dependent variables in a data set.

3. You have decided to buy a certain kind of car because you heard that it gets great gas mileage. According to a consumer magazine, the mean gas mileage obtained during testing was 30, the median was 26, and the mode was 25. If you purchase this kind of car, the gas mileage you are likely to get will most likely
   a. be more than 30 miles per gallon.
   b. vary from 20 to 40 miles per gallon.
   c. be less than 30 miles per gallon.
   d. be 28 miles per gallon.

4. Maxine found that she scored at the 93rd percentile on her calculus exam. This means that
   a. she got 93 percent of the problems correct.
   b. seven other people in the class scored higher than Maxine.
   c. she scored higher than 93 percent of the calculus class on the test.
   d. she did 93 problems correctly.

When Vitus asked his psychology and rhetoric classmates to rate his personality on a scale from 1 (irritating) to 10 (extremely pleasant), he received the following data:

Psychology class:　1　9　4　6　3　3　9
Rhetoric class:　　8　7　7　8　8　9　9

5. What are the mean and median ratings of his psychology class?
   a. 3, 6
   b. 5, 4
   c. 5, 6
   d. 6, 5

6. Which of the following statements best describes the above sets of ratings?
   a. The rhetoric class has extremely high variability.
   b. The rhetoric class has more variability than the psychology class.
   c. The psychology class has more variability than the rhetoric class.
   d. The psychology class has extremely high variability.

Total Correct (See answer key) _____

ANSWERS TO CONCEPTS AND EXERCISES

Statistics and the Consumer

1. *B.* Richard wants to buy a car that is consistently fast. Car A has a higher mean speed than car B over all the time trials. However, the standard deviation is very large. This indicates that car A is fast but not consistently fast, and that there was much variation in the data from the time trials. Car B's speed is 7 miles per hour slower than car A's, but the variation is low. Therefore, Richard should buy car B since he can depend on it to be more consistently fast. (pp. A-2–A-3)

2. *Bare Bones.* If Richard wants to be sure to lose weight, he should go to the Bare Bones Fitness Center. Even though the mean weight loss there is lower by 10 pounds, the variability is low, which means that most people who have gone there have lost close to 25 pounds. The Body Beautiful Fitness Center has a higher mean weight loss but also a higher variability, which means that some people have lost a lot of weight there, while others have lost very little. (pp. A-2–A-3)

ANSWERS TO CRITICAL THINKING

1. Sam believes that the accused landlord has been using lead-based paint, and is responsible for the symptoms of lead-poisoning two of the children now show.

2. The mean level of lead absorption of children living in the accused landlord's building is higher than the mean level of the children living in the lead-free building.

3. Martina thinks that the parents of the children who have symptoms of lead poisoning may be at fault.

4. Martina knows that you can't assume that the difference between the means of two groups is statistically significant without examining the standard deviations of the two groups. Martina sees that the standard deviation of the group living in the accused landlord's building is much larger than that of the group living in the lead-free building. This suggests that the difference between the two means may be influenced more by a couple of extreme cases than a true statistically significant difference. Martina and Sam should probably find out if those extreme cases are the children who are showing symptoms of lead-poisoning, and then question the parents of those children to find out if they could be responsible for any lead hazards their children have encountered.

5. If the answer to Martina's continued investigation turns out the way she thinks it will, she will need to determine if the parents purposefully poisoned the children or if it was an accident. *NOTE:* Critical thinking is a constant process of hypothesizing, examining evidence, rehypothesizing, collecting more evidence, and so on. Martina may not be correct. Can you think of any other hypothesis that could explain the symptoms the children are showing?

ANSWERS TO MULTIPLE-CHOICE QUESTIONS

Circle the question numbers you answered correctly.

Sample Quiz 1

1. *a* is the answer. (p. A-1)
   b. A normal distribution describes a certain type of data set. It is not used to present data.
   c. A measure of central tendency is a numerical, not visual, description of data.
   d. A measure of variability is a numerical, not visual, description of data.

2. *a* is the answer. The mode is the most frequently occurring score, which is 3. (p. A-2)
   b, d. Neither 4 nor 6 is any type of measure of central tendency for this data set.
   c. 5 is the median and the mean for this data set, but not the mode.

3. *c* is the answer. To find the median, rearrange the scores from lowest to highest and then find the score that splits the data in half. The data from lowest to highest: 1, 2, 3, 3, 5, 6, 7, 8, 10. There are nine scores, so the fifth score will split the set such that half the scores (four) are below it and half (four) are above it. The value of the fifth score is 5. (p. A-2)

4. *c* is the answer. The mean is 5. It is calculated by adding all the scores and then dividing by the number of scores. The sum of all the scores is 45, which, divided by 9 (the total number of scores), is 5. (p. A-2)
   a. 3 is the mode for this data set, not the mean.
   b, d. Neither 4 nor 6 is any type of measure of central tendency for this data set.

5. *c* is the answer. The mean, median, and mode are equal in a normal distribution. (p. A-3)
   a, b, d. None of these data sets has a mean, a median, and a mode that are all equal.

6. *c* is the answer. Inferential statistics are the mathematical procedures psychologists use to draw conclusions from data and make inferences about what they mean. (p. A-4)
   a. Descriptive statistics only summarize and present data.
   b. There is no such thing as a "significant statistical" method. Researchers use inferential statistics to conclude from data that experimental results are statistically significant.
   d. There is no such thing as a standard statistic.

Now turn to the quiz analysis table at the end of this appendix to find which areas you know well and which areas you need to work on. Circle the numbers in the table for items on Quiz 1 that you answered correctly.

ANSWERS TO MULTIPLE-CHOICE QUESTIONS

Circle the question numbers you answered correctly.

Sample Quiz 2

1. *b* is the answer. A frequency histogram would show visually how the weekly sales figures differed. (p. A-1)
   a. The median overall cookie sales would be one number indicating how sales generally have gone.
   c. The range of sales figures would show how large the variation in cookie sales had been each week, but would not be a good illustration of how many cookies were sold each week. After all, if 10,000 boxes of Cookie One were sold one week, and the next week it was 20,000, that would be a range of 10,000. If we compared the weekly sales of Cookie Two— 50,000 and 60,000 (a range of 10,000)—we would see no difference in the figures for cookie types one and two.
   d. Like the range, the standard deviation describes variability rather than general sales figures.

2. *b* is the answer. Observations or scores are numerical representations of the measurement of the dependent variable. The total number of observations is called *N*. (p. A-2)
   a. If each subject gives two responses or answers in an experiment, then the total number of observations, *N*, will be equal to twice the size of the sample. Therefore, counting the number of subjects will not always give the value of *N*.

c, d. The number of independent or dependent variables will not tell you how many observations a data set has.

3. *c* is the answer. Since the mode and median are both below 30, you should suspect that the mean has been artificially inflated by a few extreme, unrepresentative scores. Therefore, the gas mileage will probably be lower than 30 miles per gallon. (p. A-2)
   a, b, d. The mean has been inflated by a few extreme unrepresentative scores. The car's mileage will be lower than 30 miles per gallon. However, you cannot predict on the basis of the data given just how much lower it will be, nor can you predict what the range of performance will be.

4. *c* is the answer. A percentile score indicates the percentage of people or observations that fall below a given score in a normal distribution. Therefore, 93 percent of Maxine's calculus class received scores that were lower than hers. (p. A-3)
   a. A percentile does not show how many problems Maxine answered correctly. It does show how well Maxine did relative to the other people in her class.
   b. How many people did better or worse than Maxine cannot be calculated unless the number of people in her class is known.
   d. The percentile is not related to the number of problems on the test.

5. *b* is the answer. The mean is calculated by adding the scores and dividing by the number of observations. Thirty-five divided by 7 is 5. To find the median, you must put the scores in order (1, 3, 3, 4, 6, 9, 9) and choose the middle one (4). (p. A-3)
   a, c, d. None of these correctly identifies the mean and the median of the psychology class.

6. *c* is the answer. Even without calculating a standard deviation, one can see that the ratings of the rhetoric class are all within one point of the mean, which is 8. The rhetoric class has a range of 2, and the psychology class has a range of 8. (pp. A-2-A-3)
   a, d. Neither class has extremely high variability.
   b. The ratings of Vitus's psychology classmates vary more than those of his rhetoric classmates.

Now go to the quiz analysis table below to find which areas you know well and which areas you need to work on. Circle the numbers in the table for items on Quiz 2 that you answered correctly.

For each question you answered correctly, circle its number. (Quiz 1 numbers are not shaded; Quiz 2 numbers are shaded.) Are there patterns in the types of questions or the topics you got wrong that could direct your further study? Did you improve from Quiz 1 to Quiz 2?

TOPIC	TYPE OF QUESTION		
	DEFINITION	COMPREHENSION	APPLICATION
Describing Data			
Frequency histogram	1		
			1
Descriptive statistics			2, 3, 4, 5
	2		3, 4, 5, 6
Inferential Statistics	6		

TOTAL CORRECT BY QUIZ:

QUIZ 1:
QUIZ 2: